SKYSTONE AND SILVER

The Collector's Book of Southwest Indian Jewelry

Carl Rosnek and Joseph Stacey

PRENTICE-HALL, INC., ENGLEWOOD CLIFFS, N.J.

SKYSTONE AND SILVER:
The Collector's Book of Southwest Indian Jewelry
by Carl Rosnek and Joseph Stacey

Printed in the United States of America

Prentice-Hall International, Inc., London
Prentice-Hall of Australia, Pty. Ltd., Sydney
Prentice-Hall of Canada, Ltd., Toronto
Prentice-Hall of India Private Ltd., New Delhi
Prentice-Hall of Japan, Inc., Tokyo
Prentice-Hall of Southeast Asia Pte. Ltd., Singapore

10 9 8 7 6 5 4 3 2 1

Library of Congress Cataloging in Publication Data

Rosnek, Carl
Skystone and silver.

Includes index.
1. Indians of North America—Southwest, New—Costume and adornment. 2. Jewelry—Southwest, New. 3. Jewelry—Collectors and collecting. I. Stacey, Joseph, joint author. II. Title.
E78.S7R67 739.27'0979 76-29060
ISBN 0-13-812834-0

Production Editor: Dorothy Lachmann
Book Design by Linda Huber
Art Direction by Hal Siegel

Acknowledgments

It is not fair to name names of those who have contributed to this book without naming every name—but this is an intention which time and circumstance have conspired to defeat. Acknowledging the help of a great many whose names do not appear in these pages, may we at least earnestly thank Helen Pinion Wells, Marjel DeLauer, Dwight Myers, Clara Lee Tanner, and also the "cameo contributors":

Tobe A. Turpen, Jr., Katie Noe, Paul Hulderman, Joe Tanner, Jim Godber, Don and Nita Hoel, Al Packard, Phil Woodard, Robert Nadler, Bob Ward, John and Patricia Woodard, Robert Ashton, Charles Loloma, Anita Da, Phil Navaysa, Preston Monongye, Kenneth Begay, Larry Golsh, Johnny and Marlene Rosetta, Michael McCleve, Veronica Orr, Laura Gilpin, Sallie Wagner, Dr. Bertha Dutton, Barton and Margaret Wright, David L. Neumann, Betty T. Toulouse, Maggie Wilson, Jerry Jacka, Dr. Patrick T. Houlihan, H. Thomas Cain, "Banker M," and Harmer Johnson.

Retrospect and Outlook

From the very special vantage point of this writer, this may be the last and most important book on the subject of Indian jewelry. In text and illustrations it is an up-to-date encyclopedic presentation of the development and inherent interest of one of the most fascinating chapters in the history of personal adornment.

My first conscious confrontation with Indian jewelry was in the early 1950s, when we accompanied a small group of Kansas City advertising and merchandising executives on a Saturday excursion to Lawrence, Kansas. We were attracted to a display of Indian jewelry in a little shop off the main thoroughfare. The owner, Pat Reed, had been a law enforcement officer on the reservations, and had an "inside track to the best silversmiths and traders." We purchased an inexpensive ring from Mr. Reed in appreciation for his interesting stories about the Indians and their way of life. On our way back to Kansas City we all commented on the appeal of Indian crafts, but we more or less arrived at the same question: as a merchandising idea and a fashion item—what do you do with it?

We moved to Arizona in the mid-fifties and noticed that the well-dressed Westerner wore Indian-inspired belt buckles and bola ties, women wore squaw dresses to show off turquoise and silver necklaces. The first new friends we made were Katy Lavers and "Doc" Herron. Katy operated the Teepee Indian store in Casa Grande and Doc was one the best known Indian traders in the Southwest. Through Doc we met Fred Wilson, Dick Mullen, Fred Schafer, and others involved in acquiring fine Indian artifacts, as well as Western Americana, for wealthy Eastern and Midwest collectors. They seemed little interested in "off the street" shoppers and individual transactions. The worth of fine Indian jewelry, even in those days, was difficult to evaluate. A necklace would be weighed in the hand and after an exchange of offers and counter-offers a price finally agreed upon. A fine piece would go from trader to trader, "keystoned," or doubled in price, from hand to hand. We soon learned how the traders controlled the traffic of Indian jewelry to and from the reservation. The fine pieces not in the possession of the Indians were immediately "high graded" out of circulation for a trader's personal collection or were traded to other collectors waiting to pay premium prices for one-of-a-kind specimens. The run-of-the-mill jewelry was usually sold to the curio and souvenir outlets. In many cases such as with Fred Harvey and C. G. Wallace, Indian craftsmen worked from the trader's ideas, designs, and materials.

As Southwest Indian jewelry became oriented more and more to tourists, the craft gradually lost any chance it might have had to evolve into a pure native art, often hindered by the combination of Indians with little business sense and traders with little sense of refined taste. The Indian jewelry business was languishing when the first sign of the coming surge of interest appeared. The influential *Wall Street Journal*, in an article concerning the unavoidable inflation, suggested that among hedges against a high percentage of loss turquoise and silver Indian jewelry offered one of the best possibilities. Rumor, legend, or fact, the whisper became a roar, echoed, and re-echoed from East to West and back.

In spring of 1972, Ollie McNamara, Fashion Design Coordinator for Saks Fifth Avenue, Phoenix, used some borrowed Indian jewelry to accessorize a fashion show. The visual impact caused customers to clamor for this spectacular jewelry. This was quickly picked up by Ollie's husband, Gerry McNamara, General Manager of the store. Noted in the trade for his astute interpretation of signs and trends, Mr. McNamara, accompanied by a group of knowledgeable traders, left immediately for the Navajo, Zuni, and Santo Domingo reservations, with side trips to the inter-tribal ceremonials at Gallup. Saks opened the fall season of 1972 with an attractive collection of authentic Indian jewelry, specially selected for their discerning clientele. Thus started a trend which quickly changed attitudes, theories, and logic related to the appreciation and merchandising of Indian jewelry.

In the *New York Post*, November 15, 1972, Fashion Editor Eugenia Sheppard reported: "It looks as if the American Indians are ready to take back Manhattan. . . . The furor for anything native Indian, from bead headbands, to jewelry, to fringed leather jackets, first broke out in the college crowd a couple of years ago. As with most fashions, by the next season the excitement seemed to be dying down, but all the time it was actually running underground. Now it is breaking out again in a much more significant way for a much more serious, sophisticated and expensive audience."

Then in *Newsweek*, April 2, 1973, an article headed "Tribal Chic": "With the plight of the American Indian high on the list of latest liberal causes, it was only a matter of time until Indian artifacts became the latest word in fashion. Almost overnight, the heavy, silver and turquoise jewelry of the Southwest tribes . . . has become a national fad . . . ."

These were but two of the early signs preceding the surge into the big money market. My own strange and curious mind picked up perhaps one of the more significant signs in the syndrome while reading an essay titled "Civilization and Its Discontents" by Sigmund Freud:

"The enjoyment of beauty produces a particular, mildly intoxicating kind of sensation. There is no very evident use in beauty itself. The necessity of it for cultural purposes is not apparent. And yet civilization somehow could not do without it. The science of aesthetics investigates the conditions in which things are regarded as beautiful. Psychoanalysis attributes its derivation from the realms of sexual sensation. Beauty and attraction are first of all qualities of a sexual object."

Beauty and sexual attraction are but the two prime reasons we wear jewelry. Other important factors in our relationships with jewelry are: our life styles, the mode and patterns of our clothing, and the prevailing interpretation of symbols, mores, and customs. With all of these, jewelry must relate harmoniously.

The urge to adorn dates back beyond prehistory. There was never a time when it could be said that there is not a woman who does not desire jewelry as a means of enhancing her beauty. In today's "civilized" societies of liberated women and men, both sexes have learned to make the most out of whatever it is in jewelry that intensifies an erotic aura; Indian jewelry can be worn by men and women, right on target with the emerging unisex trend. And that's the way it was when all the signs and elements came together to cause a tidal wave in the great sea of skystone and silver.

Back in the reservation country the natives were beginning to feel some tremors. Don Hoel began opening vaults of high quality authentic Indian jewelry; Bill McGee's Indian Den, Tanners, and the Jewel Box seemed to be making the right moves, and then came the big shake that put the surge into the wave—the January 1974 *Arizona Highways* magazine with 28 pages of life-size full-color reproductions of Indian jewelry. Single copies of the record breaking edition sold for as much as $50. I had personally selected every piece illustrated and took full responsibility for what might have been nothing more than a glorious jewelry catalog. After four reprints it was decided to take advantage of the energy crisis to promote Indian arts and crafts in place of tourism. The six editions of the "Collector Series" included three jewelry issues; August 1974 featured the masterpieces of the C. G. Wallace collection, March 1975 was devoted to old pawn jewelry. The Indian thing was now the in-thing for rich and poor alike.

The now famous January 1974 *Arizona Highways* awakened every Indian silversmith, made publishers out of photographers, and turned every storekeeper and filling station operator who had an old display case and a piece of red or blue velvet into an Indian trader. Now in 1974, prices ranged from $29 to $6000 for a single piece and sets up to $25,000. Throughout the Southwest, schools "for making your own Indian Jewelry" attracted more non-Indians than Indians. In 1974–1975, there was more so-called Indian jewelry manufactured, bought, and sold than in 100 years before. In those two short years turquoise treaters became millionaires, and enough machine-made beads, oriental heishi, rolled wire braid, and die stamped leaves were made to fill a good part of the Grand Canyon.

The tidal wave crested during 1974–1975. The waves still come and go with the tides, but the beaches are clean once again. What do the signs point to for Indian jewelry in the future, as an art form, as an investment, as a business? What about the real Indian jewelry, the one-of-a-kind high fashion fine art specimens? When the wave of high prices crashed the shores of an eager-to-buy market, heirlooms came out of musty trunks, collections came out of safe deposit boxes and family vaults as adornments for those willing to pay top prices for great pieces. Inflated prices added thousands to tax deductions for museum benefactors. The famous C. G. Wallace collection brought more than one million dollars at auction after he had gifted the Heard Museum with five hundred prime specimens which might have sold for at least another half million.

The very fine handmade pieces will always be valued highly as art, as investment, and they will become more and more difficult to acquire. Handmade Indian jewelry does not mean the same thing today as it did fifty years ago. Today's handmade jewelry is not always better or more valuable than the better pieces made from machine-made components. A good machine-made silver bead is often heavier and better finished than handmade beads by unskilled workers. Generally speaking, the Indian jewelry now being turned out at Zuni and Gallup is more ornate and more refined in finished detail, but the one thing too often still sadly lacking is simple basic good taste. The most intricately wrought pieces are marvelous demonstrations of skill. A needlepoint necklace or a fine piece of channel work represents hours and hours of meticulous craftsmanship. They make spectacular pieces in a museum display or in a dealer's showcase where they bring oh's and ah's for the character of the materials and the degree of excellence of the craft, yet as an accessory to a Stavropoulis ball gown, that is something else again.

Today there are many non-Indian and part-Indian artists and craftsmen who have been denied recognition and a place in the market. They have been unfairly discriminated against by the trader who claims he will carry nothing that is not Indian made, which in reality is often an out for not wanting to pay for quality work.

As long as the finished product is excellent in concept, design, and execution, as long as it shows quality and compatibility of materials—and does not pretend to be something it is not—it should matter little that it was made by a full-blooded Indian American, a one-eighth Indian American, or a 100 percent non-Indian American.

As for the Indian silversmith and his work, Preston Monongye sums it up best, "Now we find there is a new art emerging from the old, ...the Indian silversmith can no longer be stereotyped, he has branched out into many avenues of jewelrymaking and he has done a very fine artistic job of this."

Among contemporary Southwest jewelers who are Indians, there are several whose work has met with international recognition. Foremost is undoubtedly Charles Loloma, Hopi. For sheer craftsmanship, his jewelry is unsurpassed and he is without peer in understanding basic design. The work of Charles Loloma represents a standard of beauty and good taste comparable to that of the finest jewelsmiths, regardless of ethnic origin or culture. Charles Loloma is the most creative American jewelry designer today. The world is beating a path to the Loloma workshop in the Hopi mesas; the millionaire collector from Indianapolis, the fashion-wise Dallas socialite and the fine jewelry buyer from a distinguished department store are happy and eager to pay the price for a Loloma ring or whatever else is available. Loloma knows what the product of genius is worth. He needs no agent and has no exclusive dealer representation. Dealers pay full retail price, then keystone, and are content to upgrade their display cases until just the right buyer comes along. Preston Monongye, Hopi/Mission Indian, is another innovative artisan who is individualistic in his execution, a master lapidarian, an outstanding artist in many media.

In the marketplace, department stores have all but phased out their Indian jewelry stocks. Six out of seven Navajo tribal art and craft outlets have suspended retail sales activities. Prestigious specialty shops in the Southwest continue to merchandise "high fashion" Indian jewelry, and Saks' discerning buyers still seek out fine authentic pieces. Otherwise the Indian jewelry business has settled into the same channels as before "the great wave". It will take generations to change the status of Zuni and Gallup as the source centers for fine Indian jewelry. And the same dependable established traders will be doing business for those who appreciate the best in old and contemporary Indian jewelry. Although there is little hand work done these days, the master craftsman has not sacrificed his sense of quality. There are enough Indian jewelsmiths working to supply the demand of a high priced market. True, it is not the same as the old Indian jewelry, it is more elaborate, more precise, more flamboyant, but the basic esthetic appeal of gold, silver, turquoise, and coral are there awaiting the patina of time.

The fundamental primitive beauty and the stunning esthetic value of turquoise and silver will always be identified with the best image of Indianism in the Southwest. The jewelry of the Indian silversmith of the past will be an expression of beauty identified with a culture inevitably being lost in the mist of history. The masterpieces of the period from 1870 to 1970 should be removed from the marketplace and preserved as unreplaceable treasures of art.

The old classic pieces are beyond dollars and cents appraisal, they are precious and priceless and their true value must be measured as archeological testimony to the talents of a wonderful race of people who beat the odds and did things not indigenous to their needs and character. The real wonder and mystique of Indian jewelry is that the Indian was able to achieve as much as he did under the most adverse handicaps, very unlike the artists and artisans of the Old World, who lived and worked in an atmosphere of pampered elegance for patrons who appreciated and encouraged the development of the fine arts. It is ironical that the person called the Cellini of the Southwest was a Sicilian-born goldsmith named Frank Patania, who, forced to leave New York for reasons of health, went west to Santa Fe and Tucson where he taught Indian silversmiths. He in turn learned from the Indians. He was the first and unquestionably the greatest non-Indian creator of turquoise and silver jewelry in the Southwest. Who knows what might have happened if Frank Patania had been in Zuni during the time of C. G. Wallace.

We like to think that in the world of art there is nothing absolutely new, and on the other hand nothing totally dies. It is all a process of evolution, and one day a new and singular native American jewelry will be born of a concept inspired by a two-thousand-year-old American Indian art form.

Joseph Stacey
Arizona

CONTENTS

The following is a key to the abbreviations used for frequently-cited collections and artifact sources in the photograph captions.

MAI, HF .... Museum of the American Indian, Heye Foundation
FHFAC, HM............. Fred Harvey Fine Arts Collection, Heard Museum
HMC .... Heard Museum Collection
MRMM .... Millicent A. Rogers Memorial Museum
PC .... Private Collection
PCs .... Private Collections
DNHC.................. Don and Nita Hoel Collection
AG..................... Ashton Gallery
HC..................... The Harmsen Collection
RT .... Rare Things
BTC.................... The Bear Track Collection
JFPGW .... Jim Fowler's Period Gallery West
BC .... Le Boutelierre Collection
ED .... Bea and Gene Gordon, The Eagle Dancer
GRIACC .... Gila River Indian Arts and Crafts Center

Preface

This book is about the metal and gemstone jewelry originated by the Indians of the United States Southwest. Much has been written on this subject, especially in recent years when this superb craft has reached levels of popularity that would stun into speechlessness the Indian smiths who first created it.

We are hardly wordless now, however. Scholars, dealers, traders, professional writers, Indians, and many others have written about Indian jewelry. Only two things seem certain: the last word on it will never be written, and no two writers will ever agree on everything.

Why this book, then? It is not meant to be scholarly. There have been a few—a very, very few—worthwhile scholarly works on the subject; the same is true of so-called popular works.

When I was young I held a schoolboy's hero worship for Indians which even years of formal education about them failed to diminish. I grew up among them, I have broken bread with them in their homes, danced at their social dances with them, worked in carrot fields and potato sheds with them—hard work with long hours and little pay. I still respect and admire them greatly, and I have learned one thing about them, through all these associations, that no class or book could ever teach me: though they are Indians and hold to their racial and tribal origins with proud tenacity, they are, above all, human—they know fear and courage, hunger and fullness, laughter and tears. They came close to annihilation, but they have endured and multiplied. They are preeminently The People.

And they are wondrously creative. From earliest times everything they made to ensure their survival has not only been functional but borne the esthetic credentials of those who even when materially poor were spiritually rich. Their basketry, their pottery, and their textiles are proof of this.

And there is their jewelry.

Turquoise, for Indians of the Southwest, is a legendary stone; it represents the sky, and the sky is eternal, the home of the sun which gives life to everything, the repository of rain which ensures growth and fruition. (In their heyday on the Great Plains, Sioux war leaders admonished their followers when going into battle: "Be brave. This is a good day to die; only the sky endures forever.") In the Southwest turquoise was the Sky Stone; to look upon it in the morning was to bring success for the rest of the day; it brought good health and happiness; it represented the heroes and the deeds and the settings of the creation myths. It was a gift from the gods—and a gift to the gods. Representations of sacred animals, which the Pueblo Indians kept in their ceremonial chambers and fed with cornmeal and pollen, were carved from turquoise and other stones. Adaptations of them are made today by Zuni and other Indian lapidaries, to be worn as necklaces. Turquoise, as well as other stones, is set in silver, much of it in the style developed by the early craftsmen but some of it breathtakingly modern, the work of mature and sophisticated artists.

Gold, copper, brass, and other metals have been used by Indian smiths, but silver is most characteristic; although they learned the art of silversmithing from Europeans in the nineteenth century, by developing their own styles and forms they have made it, somehow, wholly Indian in nature, especially when combined with turquoise.

I have not thought it proper to write on the subject of this jewelry without saying something about the Indians themselves and about the Europeans who influenced—directly or indirectly—this craft. Neither do I think it fitting to ignore the traders and the dealers in Indian jewelry; without them, for better or for worse, the world would be largely unaware of this art—and much the poorer for it. Included are cameo quotes from curators, traders, dealers, smiths and others who devote their lives in one way or another to Indian jewelry.

I take complete responsibility for any errors in the narrative text. They are mine alone, for I have said what I wish to say and largely in the manner I wish to say it. But it is comforting to know that the pictures in this book really need no text. They say all that needs to be said.

Carl E. Rosnek
New Mexico

PART ONE

1

SETTING THE STAGE

Nothing today is more characteristic of the Indians of our United States Southwest than the silver and turquoise jewelry made by them and which is in such demand. Many attribute this superb art form only to the Navajos of Arizona and New Mexico, and there is little dispute that it was they who developed this craft; but the neighboring Pueblo Indians, and in particular the Zunis, have a tradition of lapidary and ornament-making skills which goes far back into prehistoric times. The Navajos, on the other hand, did not begin making their silver jewelry until the middle of the last century, if that early; it was their good fortune, as well as their good sense, to be in the right place at the right time and to draw together the traditions and skills of many cultures, European as well as Indian, and to fuse them into something that was distinctively Navajo, distinctively Indian.

Much has been written, or rewritten, about the Navajos and silversmithing, but there still are only a few primary sources, and these have been cited again and again. Washington Matthews, Arthur Woodward, and John Adair come quickly to mind. Adair, who wrote in the 1940s, quotes Woodward, who wrote in the 1930s; neither agrees fully with Matthews, who wrote in the 1880s, and Matthews' conclusions as to the origins of Navajo silversmithing are not considered as reliable as those of the other two.

Because this book is for the collector and the potential collector, we shall be drawing on these sources, too, while adding a little more. We want, for instance, to set the art of silversmithing by the Southwestern Indians in its historical background, since nothing happens entirely without cause or stimulus. We shall describe how Indian jewelry was made in the beginning, as well as today, not only for its intrinsic interest, but because such knowledge is vital in learning to tell the genuine article from the fake; unfortunately, this is imperative now, for popularity and value have brought forth the faker and the fraud. It is no wonder, then, that the average buyer is often confused and hesitant.

It is here that this book will enter a new dimension, for instead of repeating what others have said about silver and turquoise jewelry, we shall go to the people who make it, sell it, and treasure it—those who dedicate their lives to producing, and encouraging the enjoyment of, genuine Indian jewelry. We shall examine jewelry from the practical point of view, with the object of giving the collector more insight and helping him to decide what is genuine and what is spurious, what is ethical and what is not. And if words cannot tell it, then the pictures in this book will leave little doubt.

First it will be useful to define certain terms and concepts which will be used throughout this book. The *Southwest*, for example, refers here basically to Arizona and New Mexico plus parts of neighboring states (California, Nevada, Utah, Colorado, Texas, and the Mexican states of Sonora and Chihuahua).

We should remember that all of this area

formerly belonged to the Republic of Mexico, and before that to Spain—and before that it was at least nominally linked at one time or another to native Indian empires, the capitals of which were in central Mexico. For these empires, perhaps mercantile in nature, the Southwest was a trading market and source of raw material and slaves, and possibly also an area for missionary efforts like those of Christian Spaniards in later times. Sovereignty over Mexico ultimately devolved upon the Aztec Empire, which was broken only by the Spanish conquest under Cortes. It is no accident that the Spanish were eventually to occupy almost exactly the same area—from California to Kansas and from New Mexico south—that once was dominated by the great Mexican civilizations: With the destruction of the Aztec Empire a vacuum had been created; the Spanish simply refilled it.

In this respect it must be remembered that the present international boundary between Mexico and the United States has existed only since 1853—and that all sorts of renegades and outlaws ignored the boundary with considerable success for nearly forty years after that.

Another definition: arbitrarily, we say that the historic era in our Southwest began with the Coronado expedition in 1540, although the Spanish did not settle there until 1598; and then the colonists were unaware of much that was going on, even under their own noses.

Thus, prehistoric times ended in 1540; they began with the coming of the first *Homo sapiens* to the New World 15,000 to 20,000 years ago, or even earlier.

Pueblos refers to the Indians whom the Spanish first encountered in northern Arizona and New Mexico in 1540. They lived in stone- and adobe-walled villages as distinguished from the brush structures and skin-tented villages of the nomadic Indians, and the wattle-and-daub houses of the sedentary native peoples in southern Arizona and northern Sonora. Although the Spanish word for any permanent village is *pueblo*, in the Southwest it has become associated with the Indians who live in adobe or stone houses in New Mexico and Arizona or their ancestors.

The *Apaches* and *Navajos* are two Southwestern Indian tribes whose members speak mutually intelligible dialects of the great Athapascan language group. The evidence is that the two tribes once were one, a rather loose-knit association of primitive hunting bands who came into the Southwest at about the same time as the Spanish—but this point is still hotly debated. At any rate, there is no mention of the Navajos in Spanish records until the year 1626, when a chronicler referred to them as the *Apaches de Navaju*. The Navajos maintained much closer contact with the Pueblo Indians than did their Apache kinsmen, and adopted many of the Pueblo religious and secular customs. They later appropriated many of the Spanish, Mexican, and Anglo-American cultural traits, including the art of silversmithing, which was already known to the Indians of Central Mexico, and the setting of turquoise (also known in Central Mexico), which was mined and often shaped, ground, and polished by the prehistoric Indians of the American Southwest. When this occurred, several wheels had turned full circle.

2

PREHISTORIC INDIANS AND THEIR JEWELRY

In defining some of the terms of this book we have launched ourselves in it, for it truly begins with the first peoples who came to the Western Hemisphere at least 15,000 years ago. We presume, because of his arrival in the New World relatively late in the evolutionary time scale, that the first American was *Homo sapiens*, or modern man. Beyond that the presumption becomes even ruder; we do not known what he looked like, for we have found none of his skeletal remains. It may be that he was of a generalized Mongoloid (yellow) racial type, but there is other evidence to indicate that he may have been of the proto-Caucasoid (white) strain that still is found dotted around the shores of the Pacific Ocean, as seen in the Aborigines of Australia and the Ainu of Japan.

In any event, these first men in the United States Southwest were hunters, who killed such game as mammoth, a now-extinct form of bison, the giant sloth, camel, and a kind of horse. While basically hunters, these people also gathered the seeds, roots, and berries of plants which grew wild around them, and gradually their diet shifted to a preponderance of plant over animal food. This did not happen overnight, nor did it happen at the same time in every area of the Southwest. Perhaps this came about because the extinction of their customary game (which resulted from a change in the glacial climate to a warmer one) made it necessary to rely on the increasingly more abundant plant food; it may be that these people found subsistence easier through gathering plants rather than hunting unpredictable game; it may be that certain new ideas and techniques were filtering north into our Southwest from more advanced areas in Mexico and Central America. In any event, archeological findings indicate that projectile points (spearheads in this case) of these early peoples eventually gave way to grinding stones and other stone implements, which shows that the hunters were adapting their living patterns to the seasonal nature of the wild plants. Storage pits dating from these times indicate that these people were putting something by for the off seasons, perhaps even saving and sowing their own wild plant seeds, and thus domesticating them. The major change came about 5,000 years ago, with the introduction from its homeland in Mexico or Central America of a primitive variety of corn, a plant domesticated from certain wild grasses. The later addition of squash and beans gave a protein-balanced diet—especially when supplemented with wild game—that was nutritionally complete. Other aspects of these peoples' lives were changing, too.

The first dwellings were probably either simple brush shelters or natural caves and rock overhangs, perhaps with their open sides partly blocked off with piled stones; we assume this because traces of these peoples' fires, their stone tools, grinding stones, and projectile points, and sometimes seeds and the bones of their prey, have been found in such places. For hunting, these people armed themselves with large spears, which they thrust or jabbed into their quarry, or

with smaller dart-sized missiles, which they probably launched with spear throwers or *atlatls*—flat pieces of wood a foot or so in length with a socket to receive the butt of a lance or dart. By using this mechanical extension of his arm, a hunter or warrior could throw his weapon much farther and with greater force than he could throw it unaided. Bows and arrows did not appear in this area until after the coming of the Christian era.

The earliest hunters and gatherers demonstrated, in their artifacts which have survived the millennia, two traits characteristic of their descendants even to modern silversmiths and makers of beads: pride of workmanship and a sense of proportion and design. These traits are best exemplified in the spear and dart points which the early peoples shaped by hand for use in the hunt, and perhaps in war as well. These projectile points are by no means crude and clumsy; they were shaped superbly by craftsmen who had a complete grasp of the physical qualities and potentialities of the stone they were working, along with a premeditated image of what each point would look like, in that it would conform in size and shape to all the other points characteristic of this group of objects. The result is a deadly instrument whose craftsmanship is equaled only by its utilitarian beauty; it is, in short, a work of art.

As Charles DiPeso, director of the Amerind Foundation, writes:

> The ancient killing tool designs—such as the Sandia, Folsom and Clovis Fluted projectiles, generally categorized as chipped stone—associated with these early frontiersmen are in truth frozen bits of art which attest to the capabilities of these folk in producing extraordinarily complicated tools with both dexterity and artistry. These craftsmen had an intimate knowledge of stone. Their folk art included the skillful chipping and specific shaping of these lethal artifacts which they manufactured to their group's specific design mode. [*El Palacio*, Vol. 82, No. 1, 1976, p. 3]

Care in crafting and the innate ability to decorate the most utilitarian objects with good taste and skill continued to manifest itself among the Indians of the Southwest as the centuries passed—in pottery, in textiles, in architecture, and in personal and religious adornment as well as in weaponry and other tools and trappings of the chase.

Beginning several centuries before the birth of Christ and continuing past the opening of Christian times, a number of significant events occurred in the Southwest, particularly in the desert regions of southern Arizona. Here a group of people was taking the basic traits of the hunters and gatherers and combining them with permanent houses, pottery, agricultural irrigation, bows and arrows, and other characteristics. These prehistoric people would be designated by archeologists as the *Hohokam,* who were very likely the ancestors of our present-day Pima and Papago Indians. Their dwellings were semisubterranean pit houses; that is, the floors were excavated below ground level and the sloping sides and flat roofs were supported by interior posts and beams upon which rested a layer of poles topped with clay. It was in these first Hohokam levels, dating two centuries before Christ, that fragments of turquoise were found, marking the initial recorded appearance of this gemstone in the Southwest.

David Snow, in tracing the use of turquoise in prehistoric America, (*Turquoise*, Museum of New Mexico Press, 1973) has cited other archeologists to place the first known uses of turquoise artifacts at 900-200 B.C. in the South American Andes and of turquoise mosaics at 700-650 B.C. in the Valley of Mexico. It is very likely that specific dates will change with further excavation and interpretation, but the relative time frame should remain generally intact.

Before we focus on turquoise and its appearance in the prehistoric Southwest, let us complete our brief description of the peoples of that time and place, for this has a bearing on the history of jewelrymaking there.

While the Hohokam retained the pit house form of dwelling throughout their 2,000-year span, to the north, in the higher elevations of Arizona, southern Utah and Colorado, and northern New Mexico, the prehistoric peoples remained in their caves and rock overhangs a bit longer. Since the latter were masters at weaving the fibers of native plants into baskets and sandals, they were given the name *Basketmakers.* Eventually they began to build pit houses within their rock shelters, and later brought them out into the open. However, they soon built surface dwellings in rows, like modern apartment houses, so that the wall of each house was common to the house adjoining it. Later, and again like our modern apartment houses, these dwellings would become two, three, four, and even five stories in height, and instead of being built in rows some were built in squares around a central plaza—an obvious defensive measure. These ancient communities were similar to such modern Indian villages as Taos, or to Old Oraibi or Zuni. The prehistoric

View of a cliff dwelling ("Cliff Palace") at Mesa Verde, Colorado, one of the most spectacular Anasazi ruins.
(Michal Heron)

Prehistoric Hohokam pendants of shell and stone from central Arizona. *(Jerry Jacka)*

successors to the Basketmakers are termed *Anasazi* by archeologists, and these people retained one form of semisubterranean room: the *kiva,* or underground ceremonial chamber. Because our modern Pueblo Indians still have such structures we know that they were used by the men (and to some extent the women) of various clans to perform the secret parts of their religious ceremonies, and also as a place to weave the cotton they grew into sashes and kilts, which were used locally or traded extensively. Here, too, were carved the clan fetishes of turquoise, shell, or wood, whose adaptations as necklaces are highly prized by collectors today.

The Hohokam do not seem to have had special rooms for their religious ceremonies, but unlike the Anasazi they built step pyramids of earth faced with adobe clay which were small-scale imitations of the great stone temple mounds of central Mexico, such as Monte Alban and Teotihuacan. The Hohokam also made various forms of jewelry; they inlaid flakes of turquoise mosaic on backings of shell, wood, and bone. The shell was traded from the Gulf of California or the Pacific coast of southern California; the Hohokam painted designs on or carved whole shell, or made bracelets of cut circles of shell; they also etched shell with the acid juices of the saguaro cactus. These desert people made slate palettes for mixing body paints, and these were carved much as they were in central Mexico. Again, the Hohokam built sunken ball courts of earth which were modeled after the great stone courts of Mexico and Yucatan.

Other objects found among the Hohokam which show a close and continued relation with the Mexican civilizations are half-moon-shaped obsidian flakes, whose use is not known; mirrors made of iron pyrite; macaw feathers which must have been traded from Mexico, and copper bells (very much resembling our sleighbells) which were common in Mexico. Tests have shown, however, that these bells were cast in southern Arizona or nothern Sonora, of copper ore indigenous to the area. Despite this, no evidence ever has been recorded that the Hohokam or Anasazi cast or worked gold or silver.

As noted, the Anasazi and their descendants, the Pueblo Indians, ultimately built their houses above ground; the Hohokam apparently never did. However, about the middle of the fourteenth century A.D., the pit house villages of the Hohokam began to be clustered around adobe-walled compounds which contained multistoried structures, again of adobe, of apparent religious significance and whose orientation along lines commensurate with an extensive knowledge of astronomy is unmistakable. Other buildings within these compounds appear to have been the apartments or official chambers of personages of considerable consequence; still other areas might have housed garrison troops or served as caravanserais for merchant trains. At first it was believed that the compounds represented the presence among the Hohokam of refugee Anasazi groups, called the Salado, fleeing from intruding Apache and Navajo raiders; however, present evidence indicates that the Athapascans did not appear in the Southwest until two centuries later. One current postulation is that these compounds were the work of representatives of the great commercial empires in the Valley of Mexico and that they functioned much like the extraterritorial enclaves of the foreign powers in Manchu and later China.

The obvious defensive features of many Southwestern communities in late prehistoric times may reveal the presence of Mexican slave raiders, booty gatherers, or traders, aided by their local allies. As Outposts of Empire, the Pueblos and other Indians of the prehistoric Southwest could well have been warring among themselves, instigated by rival Mexican cultures or mercantile organizations. Viewed from this perspective—which is by no means accepted by all archeologists today—the traditional picture of peaceloving Pueblos and sedentary desert dwellers diminishes considerably.

However the overall picture is interpreted—and it will always shift in light of new archeological discoveries and fresher perspectives—there is considerable evidence that the prehistoric cultures of our United States Southwest were in continuous contact with the great civilizations of Mexico and that they received a number of socioreligious beliefs and traits from there, as well as material objects. In return, an equally impressive commercial array went south, including slaves, woven cotton, turkeys, levies of warriors, perhaps, and certainly great amounts of worked and unworked turquoise.

As we have noted, fragments of turquoise were recorded from pre-Christian levels in the Hohokam village of Snaketown in southern Arizona. Other findings of turquoise are reported from ruins dating from the beginning of the Christian era to the tenth century A.D., but Snow writes that the number of turquoise pieces recovered from the time period is small. Beginning in the tenth century (A.D. 900) the output of turquoise in the Southwest shows a significant

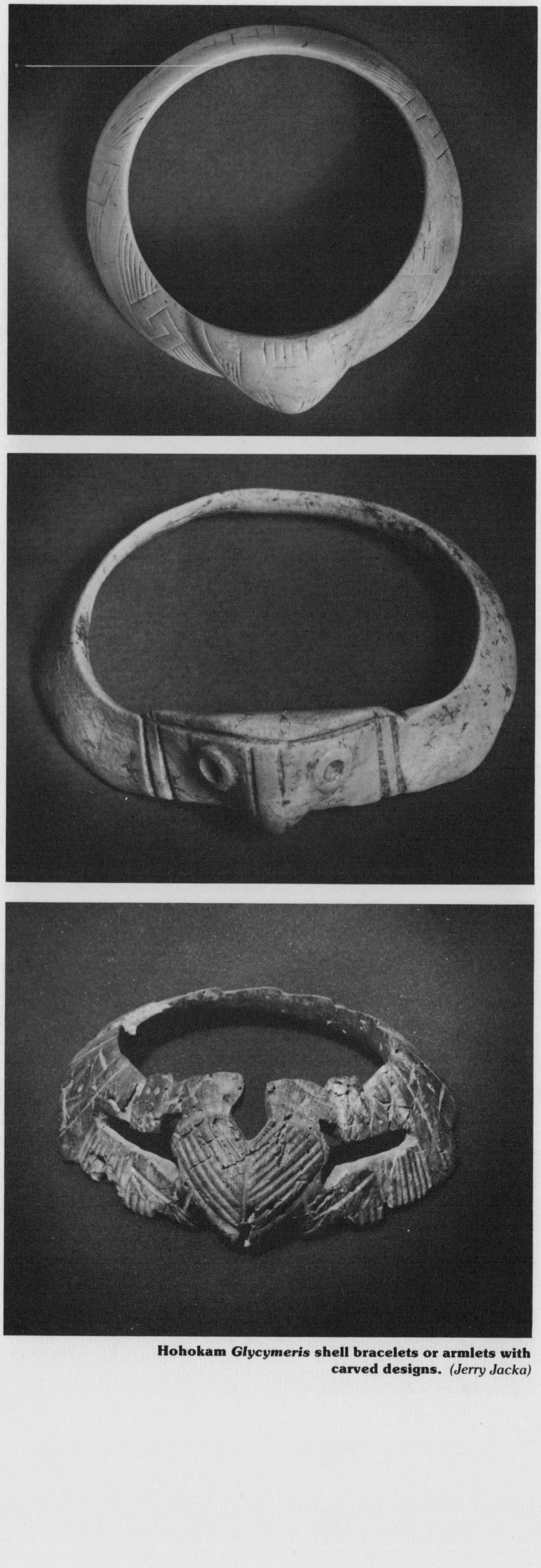

Hohokam *Glycymeris* shell bracelets or armlets with carved designs. *(Jerry Jacka)*

increase, and this date corresponds to the period of increased demand for this stone in central Mexico. It also equates roughly with the beginnings of gold- and silversmithing in that area. We know from Cortes and other chroniclers of his era that turquoise was highly prized by the Mexican Aztecs and their predecessors; in fact, they considered it more valuable than silver or gold. Their name for it was *chalchihuitl* (chahl-chee-WEE-tul), which now has a score of variant spellings. It is interesting to note that the present-day Spanish-Americans of northern New Mexico, descendants of the original Spanish colonists from New Spain, commonly refer to turquoise as *charchihuite* rather than by the Castilian Spanish word *turquesa*. Nor is it at all certain that the Aztec (Nahuatl) word *chalchihuitl* referred to turquoise; Northrop (1975) and others believe it was applied to jadeite from Mexico and Guatemala. It could have meant either stone, no matter how unlikely that seems, since the Spanish conquistadores and colonists do not appear to have differentiated between them.

Whatever they called it, Mexican craftsmen were using increasing amounts of turquoise beginning in the tenth century, and they were still using it when the Spaniards arrived in 1519. Evidence indicates that the Indians of the Southwest were using greater quantities of the stone locally, too, as well as exporting it, for it appears much more commonly in the ruins dating from the tenth century onward. Its beauty, in varying shades from green to robin's-egg and sky blue, made it highly prized everywhere. Modern Indians have called it the *Sky Stone,* and magical properties often were attributed to it. For instance, it is said that if a sweetheart were unfaithful, the turquoise he or she wore would lose its color. Since low-grade turquoise has a tendency to fade, this saying may have proved disastrous to a number of otherwise innocent romances. Another legend has it that if a person looks upon turquoise on awakening in the morning his day will be a good one. Turquoise is often used by the Navajos in healing ceremonies, for it is believed to possess excellent curative powers; the stone is placed against the afflicted part of the patient's body. In fact, turquoise is a "happy " stone, a good and benign gem in all of its aspects and usages; there is no sinister aura to it at all. To wear the Sky Stone is to insure good luck, good health, and happiness.

Prehistoric shamans or magicians made extensive use of the Sky Stone; one twelfth-century burial at Ridge Ruin, Arizona, contained the skeleton of a man laid to rest with a turquoise-encrusted basket plus 180 beads, 4 pendants, 2 plugs, and more than 800 pieces of mosaic inlays. There also were 423 projectile points, 3,600 gray stone beads, many wooden objects, and beads and pendants of bone, shell, calcite and lignite. (This was reported on by its excavator, archeologist John C. McGregor, in an article in the *Proceedings of the American Philosophical Society* in 1943.) Snow comments on this and on a similar burial at Hawikuh, New Mexico—a Zuni village which we shall encounter again—which contained far fewer turquoises and other riches, saying that both burials probably were of members of religious or ceremonial society, interred with their paraphernalia. Pueblo Bonito, in New Mexico's spectacular Chaco Canyon, yielded more than 65,000 pieces of worked and unworked turquoise; this Great Pueblo Period ruin dates from the thirteenth century, and—quoting Snow in *Turquoise,* —suggests by its yield that "turquoise must be ranked as a major prehistoric commodity, and the mining, manufacturing and commercial activities connected with it indicate an economic pattern of some magnitude."

Magnitude is the proper word to use in speaking of the turquoise industry in the great Mexican civilizations and in what is now the United States Southwest. In fact, one cannot speak of the one area without referring to the other. While acknowledging the uncertainty over which stone was called *chalchihuitl* by the ancient Mexicans, we can still be certain that turquoise was valued greatly by them and that it was traded south to them in large quantities. In fact, the evidence is that there were few or no natural deposits of turquoise anywhere near the great population centers of Mexico in prehistoric times. But gold and silver were present in abundance in Mexico. Aside from numerous archeological discoveries, we know from such eyewitnesses as Hernan Cortes, Bernal Diaz del Castillo, and, later, Sahagun and many others that these artisans had by the sixteenth century achieved a level of sophistication that excited the wonder and the greed not only of the conquistadores but of all Europe. We know also that objects of gold and silver were set with the feathers of the quetzal bird (these feathers also being considered of greater value than the precious metals) and with a number of stones, including not only turquoise but jade and jadeite, jet, garnet, rough emeralds, and even pearls. In fact, the whole panorama of the manufacture of what we today would call precious jewelry poses so many intriguing questions about the sources and contacts of early Mexican civilizations that it must be considered a key factor in any definitive interpretation, but little has been done in this area. It is easy to beat raw gold into pleasing objects of adornment; it is time-consuming but not difficult to shape, grind, polish, and even pierce gemstones such as turquoise by hand. It is entirely another matter to master metallurgy to the point that ores can be smelted, the metal extracted and then be remelted and drawn, cast, or beaten into exquisite articles of jewlery, set with stones in such a manner that their beauty matches that of articles made by the great artisans of Renaissance Europe and Asia.

Likewise, copper sometimes appears naturally in metallic—or native metal—form, and we know that pre-Columbian Indians all over North America utilized native copper wherever it was found. But again, it is something else entirely to take copper ore in its most common form, smelt the metal from the rock, and recast it into usable objects. Yet that was done by prehistoric Indians, not only in central Mexico but in the United States Southwest. We have found the smelters of the Hohokam, we know that they cast copper bells by the lost-wax method, and we know that the metal came from local ores, for this has been proved by laboratory analyses.

But no objects of gold or silver have been reported from prehistoric ruins in the Southwest, although the evidence of centuries-long trade and other contacts between them and the metalworking areas of Mexico is incontrovertible. Logically, this would imply that the Indians of the Southwest had no interest in these metals, or else their trade was proscribed by the Mexican oligarchs, or both. (We do know that gold and silver were reserved for the use of the aristocracy and the priesthood in central Mexico.)

The first Europeans to contact the Indians of the Southwest discovered that the natives were well aware of the existence of natural deposits of such ores and that they placed no particular value on them. The Indians quickly learned to keep all such knowledge to themselves, for to reveal the whereabouts of such deposits was to ensure the destruction of tribal hunting grounds and the enslavement or extinction of one's people.

The situation concerning turquoise was the reverse: it was much loved by the Indians, but the Europeans were largely indifferent to it; only the hard crystalline gemstones such as emeralds, rubies, diamonds, and sapphires had appreciable value to them, and there were none of these to be found in the Southwest. David Neumann has said that turquoise has had a cyclical appeal in European-derived civilizations (*Turquoise,* 1973), its latest popularity being directly associated with the great upsurge in interest in the silver and turquoise jewelry of our Southwestern Indians. While the use of silver has, in a sense, been reintroduced to the Indians of the Southwest only in comparatively recent times, turquoise has served for centuries as an object of adornment, with at least a collateral religious significance, and certainly as a standard of commercial exchange not unlike that of gold in our own civilization. That was true in prehistoric times, and it remained so even after the coming of the European. It is true today, especially since the white man has developed a serious appreciation of its esthetic qualities.

We know that prehistoric turquoise mines existed in New Mexico, Arizona, California, Colorado, and Nevada and that they were extensively worked by the Indians over the centuries, as proved by the presence at these sites of datable pieces of broken pottery. Since the prehistoric Indians had no iron tools, the methods of extraction of the turquoise from its matrix in the host rock were crude and laborious; yet what is most impressive is the enormous quantities of tailings or rock debris left by these primitive miners at the better sites.

Perhaps the most extensive prehistoric mining operations were carried on at a place called Mount Chalchihuitl near the town of Los Cerrillos, south of Santa Fe, New Mexico. (The area still produces highgrade commercial stones, known as Cerrillos turquoise.) The main pit of the prehistoric mine at Mount Chalchihuitl is as deep as 130 feet on its upper side, 200 feet wide at the rim, and nearly 100 feet across at the bottom. The tailings from these excavations covered 2.5 acres, representing approximately 100,000 tons of rock. The turquoise was loosened from its native rock matrix by means of picks or hammers pecked from hard basaltic stone and hafted in hardwood handles held in place in special grooves by rawhide lashings; the lashings were affixed when the hide was wet and when dry it shrank to hold the wood to the stone so securely that an ax or hammer could be used to fell trees as well as to break rock.

As the mine deepened, access to the working levels was gained by means of a so-called chicken ladder—a tree trunk sloped down to the bottom of the pit and notched for toeholds. The turquoise was freed in chunks from the seams or veins in which it usually occurs and hoisted to the surface in baskets. Here the miners further chipped away the host rock by means of hand-held hammerstones. Once the gemstone was free of useless host rock and light enough to carry, it was taken to the villages, which might be a considerable distance away.

It is unclear whether certain villages or areas specialized in the processing of turquoise and its manufacture into finished articles of jewelry. It is unknown whether certain individuals within a village concentrated entirely upon the manufacture of turquoise objects, and whether certain villages "owned" the turquoise mines.

What is clear is that long before the Spanish arrived the Southwestern Indians were manufacturing some types of turquoise jewelry very much like those seen today; only the methods were cruder. In village workshops the rough turquoise was freed of its matrix, shaped, ground, and polished. If beads or pendants were to be pierced, tiny quartz drill points were set in the end of a bow-rotated drill. The stones were polished with fine sand abrasives and by rubbing them with soft leather. A bead necklace could take weeks to finish, but the end result was a handsome piece of jewelry. If the stone was to be mounted it was affixd by pine pitch or animal glue to shell, bone, or wood.

Metal, of course, was lacking in the prehistoric Southwest, but along with the beads mentioned above, Indians were utilizing mosaic inlay techniques, they were shaping and drilling pendants, and they were making heishi necklaces from shell traded in from the Pacific coast; again, only the methods were cruder and more painstaking than they are today.

The Santo Domingo Indians of New Mexico say they were working with shell long before the arrival of the Spaniards, and the Zunis were highly proficient lapidaries in pre-Spanish times; archeological evidence supports this.

Fetishes were in wide use among prehistoric Indians; sometimes these were merely stones or other natural objects whose shapes suggested those of animals or men, but the Indians learned to grind or carve stone into more lifelike and realistic forms. These fetishes were kept in kivas, or in the custody of clan leaders, as they are now. Fetish necklaces sold in many Indian goods shops today are adaptations of these prehistoric objects, and fetishes themselves are often seen in these same stores. Sometimes they are of turquoise, sometimes inlaid with other stones such as jet; other modern fetishes might be animal forms of basalt or other stones with turquoise inlays representing eyes or hearts. In ancient times—as well as today—fetishes played important secret roles in ceremonies held in kivas. Turquoise stones were sealed in niches in the wall of kivas or buried under the floors; they also were placed as sacrifices in shrines about the countryside, and were set in the doorways of prehistoric houses—their benificent magical properties helping to ward off bad luck or ill health from those who dwelt within. We do not know precisely what rituals may have accompanied the use of turquoise or fetishes in prehistoric times, and in the late twentieth-century Pueblo Indians are likely to be more guarded in discussing such matters. But the common occurrence of turquoise and other native gemstones indicates an importance for them that transcends mere prettiness.

The first Spanish rumors of the fabled Seven Cities of Cibola mention not only streets paved of gold but precious stones set in the houses, and by inference at least, an abundance of jewelry. We know now that the only stones of any worth were turquoise, but the minds of those sixteenth-century Spaniards had little difficulty in equating this alleged magnificence with the scenes which greeted Cortes on his arrival in Mexico.

It is ironic that the prehistoric Indian lapidaries, working with the modest but magical Sky Stone, unwittingly served to attract the first European tourists to our Southwest—and that the lure still lives.

3
SPANISH-MEXICAN INFLUENCES

It is reasonable to assume that the Spanish colonists would have introduced significant technological improvements in jewelrymaking to the Indians and taught them the art of working silver, but such was not the case. Two centuries were to elapse after the Spanish conquest before silversmiths were common in the area, and by that time they were citizens of Mexico.

But only twenty years after Cortes conquered Montezuma's capital of Tenochtitlán and paralyzed the great Indian civilizations of central Mexico, the Europeans of New Spain mounted their first expedition into what was to become, almost exactly three centuries later, the Southwestern United States.

That expedition was led by Francisco Vasquez de Coronado. Coronado's expedition was prompted by the reports of four Spaniards, including the Moorish slave Estevan, who had been shipwrecked in 1528 on the Texas coast of the Gulf of Mexico and enslaved by the Indians living there. The four eventually escaped their captors and after years of harrowing adventures made their way back to their countrymen, encountering them north of Culiacan in 1536. During their wanderings the four men had heard countless stories of the fabled Seven Cities of Cibola, which lay to the north of their own route, but which by all accounts rivaled the cities of the Valley of Mexico in golden riches and in the quality of their civilization.

The viceroy of New Spain was captivated by these rumors, but before mounting a major expedition to the area he sent a Franciscan friar, Marcos de Niza, northward in 1539 with a small party guided by the Moor Estevan. The group left from Culiacan and, presumably following the established Indian trade routes through what is now Arizona, eventually reached the vicinity of the Zuni pueblos in extreme western New Mexico (there was more than one Zuni pueblo at that time). Estevan, with an escort party, reached the Zuni village of Hawikuh ahead of Fray Marcos—there is some reason to suspect that the friar never got anywhere near the villages—where they found no gold and little finery of any kind except turquoise and woven cotton blankets. Apparently Estevan antagonized the Zunis by his greed for the turquoise and his attitude toward their women. He and most of his party were slain; the friar and his party retreated to Mexico. Once returned to the Spanish capital, however, Fray Marcos made even more extravagant claims of wealth for these northern villages, and Coronado was authorized to lead an expedition in force into the area, where he arrived in 1540. He spent two years in what is now Arizona and New Mexico, during which he, or members of his expedition, looked upon the Grand Canyon, the Hopi villages, and the Indian pueblos at Acoma and along the Rio Grande as far north as Taos and eastward to Pecos Pueblo, on the fringe of the Great Plains. Coronado even made a wild foray into present-day Kansas, but he found no gold or riches of any spectacular kind and in 1542 returned to Mexico in failure. During the next fifty years several other expeditions made their way into Arizona and New Mexico; many of the explorers and priests met death in one fashion or another, and none could establish a permanent foothold in the area until 1598. In that year a large group of colonists under Don Juan de Onate founded a settlement at the present pueblo of San Juan, which they later abandoned in favor of a new provincial capital, Santa Fe. The Spaniards long since had given up thoughts of finding great wealth here; they were interested now in settling the land and in converting the Indians to Christianity—a project in which the natives cooperated with a notable lack of enthusiasm and in which the Spaniards (and later the Anglo-Americans) were never fully successful.

Coronado's expedition had included armorers to maintain the metal equippage of its soldiers, and the first settlers brought blacksmiths with them as vital members of a colony established so far from regular sources of supply and refurbishment. The Spaniards also were aware of deposits of minerals—iron, lead, silver, copper and gold—and they had a habit of referring to the natural deposits as mines, implying that they were worked at one time or another, but in fact few of them were seriously exploited, for in the years since Coronado's expedition Apaches and Navajos had penetrated the entire area, the Comanches were raiding from the plains, and the Pueblo Indians were growing increasingly hostile toward their arrogant Spanish masters. In 1680 the Pueblos rose against the Spanish, massacred many of them, and drove the remainder from their fortified capital of Santa Fe. The Spanish retreated as far south as present-day Ciudad Juarez—then known as El Paso del Norte—and it was not until twelve years later that they were able to return and reestablish their authority over the Rio Grande pueblos. They never returned permanently to the Hopi villages, and the Apaches and Navajos remained as elusive as ever, sometimes trading with the Pueblo Indians and the Spanish, sometimes raiding them for sheep and horses and for women and children to capture as slaves. (Although slavery was officially outlawed by the Spanish Crown and Church, it was practiced openly in these borderlands throughout Spanish and Mexican times and even into the era of U.S. hegemony.) When mounted on captured Spanish horses, the hostile Indians were even more deadly; they completely choked off the western trade routes from the Santa Cruz and San Pedro rivers north of the Gila River. The eastern line of communication, through Chihuahua to El Paso del Norte and northward to Santa Fe, could be traveled safely only by large caravans with armed escorts, so pervasive had the Apache attacks become.

Thus, the poverty-stricken colonies in northern New Mexico were not looked upon by the colonial authorities in Mexico City as areas of great potential commercial exploitation; they were thought of as buffer zones protecting the more settled areas of New Spain against hostile Indians and—with luck—as sources of raw materials. Further, during the later years of their dominion in northern New Mexico, the Spanish grew increasingly fearful of encroachment by the French from the Louisiana Territory, by the Russians along the Pacific coast, and later by the Americans, whose fur trappers sought to trade their catches in Taos and Santa Fe and whose merchants in the Missouri Territory envisioned, correctly, that there were fortunes to be made in trading with the Spanish colonies in New Mexico, so isolated from their own countrymen far to the south.

Under such conditions, for more than two centuries metalworking in northern New Mexico remained largely a utilitarian trade practiced by blacksmiths; it never became the means for production in quantity of luxury goods, which instead were brought in by the settlers as family heirlooms or else imported at great cost from Chihuahua and farther south. In fact, as E. Boyd observed (*Popular Arts of Spanish New Mexico*, Museum of New Mexico Press, 1974), the failure to find and develop sources of gold and silver in the area in Spanish times "did not have as much effect upon the lives of the settlers as the lack of iron which restricted their activities and their possessions to a pattern experienced by European peasants of the Dark Ages. Contemporary wills, in their itemization of household articles, vividly point up the values set upon iron or steel objects and also wooden ones which required metal tools to make them."

Since even iron had to be imported from the south, and only then in scanty amounts, articles made from it were much prized. It was reworked when its original usefulness had passed, and substitutes were sought for it, such as locks made of wood; basic tools which deteriorated or broke under prolonged use were reshaped from the original metal, Boyd says, growing smaller with each reworking.

Mission records show that priests were allotted a precise number of nails, axes, hoes, and locks, and when these ran out or were broken,

Though the Apaches did not develop a silverworking tradition, they often wore conchas and other ornaments of German silver, silver, copper, and brass acquired by trade or raid from other tribes. The men in this photograph are San Carlos Apaches. *(Museum of New Mexico, Ben Wittick)*

alternate materials had to be found. Metal was scarce and highly valued in this frontier province.

This is not to say that the Spanish colonists were entirely lacking in objects of silver; even Onate's first settlers included individuals of wealth who declared on the omnipresent official forms of the royal bureaucracy various items like silver tableware, jewelry, armor, and riding gear. The religious brought with them the vessels necessary to administering the sacraments, which by church law had to be made of silver and gold (although stories of great wealth amassed by priests and buried in or around their missions apparently are pure hokum). New waves of settlers brought new articles of precious metals, and merchants imported more from central Mexico, where it was being worked with increasing artistry by *plateros* (silversmiths) licensed under royal decree. Indeed, silver table service was a status symbol among the earliest colonists and remained so even after American occupation of the area.

But there were no specialized plateros, and when silver objects broke or wore through they were mended—usually with noticeable crudity—by the blacksmiths in the employ of the wealthier colonists. There is evidence, according to Leona D. Boylan, author of *Spanish Colonial Silver* (Museum of New Mexico Press, 1975), that local blacksmiths manufactured silver objects—using imported vessels as models—from bullion brought north from Chihuahua. The results are described as crude and massive.

The scarcity of silver and the lack of silversmiths on the northern frontier is demonstrated in a report written in 1776 by Fray Francisco Atanasio Dominguez, who had been sent from Mexico to make a full survey of the economic and spiritual conditions of the provincial missions. Dominguez mentions that in that year the parishioners of Taos had joined with their priest in assembling 18 ounces of silver belonging to the Church and private individuals there. This modest quantity was carefully weighed in the presence of witnesses and sent to Chihuahua, where a silversmith was to fashion a ciborium and cruets from it. Chihuahua was hundreds of miles to the south beyond deserts frequented by hostile Indians; certainly this scant horde of silver would not have been sent there had competent plateros been present in the Taos-Santa Fe area.

It was not until early in the nineteenth century that true silversmiths worked in northern New Mexico; the first of these were scarcely masters of their trade. A silver peace medal, inset with a Spanish coin dated 1797, was found in Nebraska in recent years; it is believed that it was given to Indians living there in 1806 by a Spanish officer who had been sent from Santa Fe in that year with a strong military force to counteract the influence of Zebulon Montgomery Pike's American expedition of 1805-7. The Spaniards traveled as far north as Nebraska, where, as Pike noted, they handed out "flags, medals, etc." to the Pawnees. The workmanship of the medal is far from superior, and it probably was made in Santa Fe at the time the Spaniards outfitted their expedition.

By this time the Spanish hold on Mexico was faltering and authorities in Mexico City were greatly disturbed by American penetration of their northern provinces in the wake of the United States' purchase of the Louisiana Territory from Napoleon Bonaparte. The Spanish government refused to allow Americans to enter its provinces, hoping to deter the growing demand for trade between New Mexico and the United States.

In 1821 the Mexicans overthrew Spanish rule. Trade with the Americans was encouraged, the Santa Fe Trail was opened from Missouri, and Manifest Destiny decreed that it was only a matter of time until New Mexico became a part of the United States. This became fact in 1846 when General Stephen Watts Kearny and his Army of the West occupied Santa Fe. But in the generation of Mexican rule plateros from the south entered the area in significant numbers, thus creating the conditions which would lead to the birth of silversmithing among the Navajos and other Indians of the new United States Southwest.

The art of silversmithing prospered more in New Mexico during the twenty-five years of Mexican rule than it had in the more than two centuries under the Spanish. There are at least two reasons for this, the first being that under the Mexicans the Spanish bureaucracy fell apart; the royal fifth—a 20 percent tax levied on all gold and silver objects manufactured in the colonies—was a thing of the past. Such taxes and prohibitions as were imposed by the bewildering succession of governments in Mexico City were honored as much in the breach as in their observance. The central government of Mexico was to remain weak and bankrupt, by and large, for more than a century, and although the early laws prohibited the export of silver and gold, silver was in fact flowing northward from Chihuahua in great quantities, to be smuggled into the United States over the Santa Fe Trail.

The trail itself, and the commerce it created, was the second lure which must have drawn silversmiths north from Chihuahua. It was opened in 1821, and instant profits were realized by the Anglo traders and the merchants of Santa Fe. New Mexico was, by any standards, a poor province, but it must not be thought that all New Mexicans lacked cash and disposable commodities. There was a solid class of *ricos*—wealthy landholders, merchants, and government officials—whose grace, if not their style, impressed even the dour Yankee traders. The Americans were shocked at seeing women smoke cheroots and by their unconcealed love of gambling, fandangos, and other amusements. The newcomers also noted that the Spanish women bedecked themselves heavily with jewelry of silver and gold, probably locally made. Manuel Armijo, the last Mexican governor of New Mexico, is reputed to have owned a solid silver bathtub, but its origins are not known.

The monetary benefits and new merchandise of the trail trade helped convert northern New Mexico from its essential barter economy to one of cash, and while at first the Santa Fe Trail ended in the remote capital, later trail merchants stopped there only long enough to declare their cargoes to the local customs officials, then proceeded directly to Chihuahua where they disposed of their wares for silver and other items. In 1829 a trail from Santa Fe to California was opened, and within ten years thousands of sheep were being driven annually to the mission villages along the Pacific coast, principally Los Angeles.

The class of ricos in northern New Mexico widened and prospered, infused with the new blood of Anglo-American traders who established homes there and often married local women. Although provincial coffers remained chronically empty due to the impotence and impermanence of the governments in Mexico City, many of the local citizens did very well for themselves, legally or otherwise. There was now a need for skilled silversmiths, and the means to pay them, and the records indicate that they were there.

Military rosters during the period from 1828 to 1842 list three recruits who described their civilian occupations as plateros. We know that a blacksmith's forge was built at the pueblo of Zuni during this period or shortly thereafter, although it must have been operated by Europeans, for the Zuni apparently had little knowledge of smithing until taught by Navajo smiths in the 1870s; but an engraving of the forge was executed by a member of an American expedition which visited the pueblo in 1852. As mentioned, American travelers were continually impressed by the opulence of the table services used by the wealthier New Mexicans. At least some of this silver service was of a heavy style that Boylan has described as Northern Provincial, meaning it was created in northern New Mexico.

In addition to the town-dwelling smiths, artisans settled in outposts of likely security or made their way about the region; as itinerant smiths they traded with the Spanish villagers or made their way into Indian country, bartering bridle gear and silver buttons and other jewelry for horses or sheep. The weight and sheen of silver made it very prestigious among the Indians. It is possible that because of their special skills plateros enjoyed some sort of protected status among the usually hostile Navajos, who raided or traded as they saw fit with the New Mexicans. Numerous pictures and descriptions of the Navajos in the period between 1828 and 1846 when the United States occupied New Mexico, prove beyond doubt that many of the Indians wore Mexican-style split-legged trousers adorned with silver buttons (a custom which continued into the twentieth century); their shirts, worn outside the trousers, were held in place by leather belts studded with *concha* (Spanish for "*shell*") discs of brass or silver. The conchas (now often corrupted to *conchos*) could have been obtained from the Plains Indians, but it is most likely they were acquired from Mexican plateros. The Navajos also are shown wearing necklaces of (presumably) hollow beads, sometimes with cruciform pendants, and they bedecked themselves with bracelets of twisted brass or silver wire. But all of these ornaments were easily obtainable by then from the plateros, and there is no solid evidence to indicate that Navajos were making their own jewelry before the American occupation of the territory in 1846. Others have observed that merely watching a Mexican silversmith would not be enough to enable a Navajo to master the art; what was needed were at least a few simple tools and a period of tutelage under a practicing smith. Most authorities feel that the Navajos lacked these until the early 1850s, but the question remains: if the Indians could trade horses and other livestock and goods for finished silver products from the Mexican plateros with whom they were in contact, why could they not purchase their own schooling and materials?

4

THE MANY-BRACELETS PEOPLE

When the United States occupied New Mexico in 1846, the military authorities, among other things, promised the new citizens that they would be protected from the constant raiding by hostile Indians, including the Navajos. The United States Army's first efforts to make its word good in this respect were far from successful. It was one thing to hurl curses at the hostiles, but it was another matter to catch and punish them; after all, the Spanish had known this for centuries.

When first mentioned in Spanish documents in the early 1600s, the Navajos ("Apaches de Navaju") were described as living only a few leagues up the Chama River from the New Mexico settlement of Abiquiu. They lived north and west of there, too, for this corresponds with the Navajos' own legends of *Dinetah*, the homeland, the land of The People. Like many "primitive" peoples, the Navajos considered themselves preeminent among all other humans; thus they called themselves *Dineh*, The People. As their language proves, they were closely related to the tribes we now call Apache, and the early Spanish reference to them bears that out. When they first arrived in Dinetah is not certain, but archeological evidence does not support their presence there earlier than the sixteenth century; it is possible that they entered the area at about the same time that the Spanish did. It is likely that they were being pushed there from the east due to pressure from the Comanches, for the Jicarilla Apaches were at that time still to the east of the Navajos; the Lipan Apaches were being driven south across the plains of Texas and ultimately would be shoved beyond the Rio Grande into Mexico. The Gila Apaches were south of the Navajos, and we know that the two groups, perhaps in the customary behavior of close kin, were fighting with each other as often as they were at peace.

The Navajos maintained friendly relations with some of the Pueblo Indians in the Rio Grande area and warred with others, but their alliances and enmities would shift with changing circumstances. This became equally true when the Spaniards colonized the area, for periods of peace alternated with times of hostility. To complicate matters more, the Navajos lived in loose bands or territorial groups, and one band might be trading with the Spanish and the Pueblo Indians while another group was commiting depredations in other areas. From 1600 until the middle of the nineteenth century the Navajos were driven southward by the Utes to the north of them and westward by the Spanish and Mexicans settled along or near the Rio Grande.

The Spanish described the Navajos as farmers, and so they were, but not to the extent of the neighboring Pueblo Indians, from whom the Navajos must have learned that art. It is more likely that they planted crops such as corn in the springtime and left the plants to the vagaries of the weather while they raided or hunted, returning to harvest them in the fall.

The earliest known dwellings of the Navajos were the three-forked-stick *hogans*. These were

Navajo man wearing Isleta cross and other necklaces, and a First Phase concha belt with "open center slot" or "diamond slot" center openings for the belt to pass through. Published as Plate XX in Washington Matthews' "Navajo Silversmiths," ***Second Annual Report to the Bureau of American Ethnology,*** **1881.** *(Smithsonian Institution)*

constructed by linking the tops of three central poles across a shallow depression dug in the ground; the spaces were then filled by smaller poles and covered with earth. A short entryway extended from the dwelling, always facing east. To defend themselves from the Utes, the Navajos during one phase built houses and towers of stone, much like those of the Pueblo Indians, and after the Pueblo Revolt of 1680 was put down by the Spanish, the Navajos were joined in these communities by Pueblo Indians fearful of reprisals by the returning conquistadores.

The Navajos learned much, and adopted much, from the Pueblos, just as they were to do from the Spanish and the Americans. Many of the traits which differentiate the Navajos from their Apache cousins were picked up during their long association with the descendants of the prehistoric Anasazi (a Navajo word meaning "Ancient Ones").

And the contact was close: after the Pueblo Revolt against the Spanish in 1680 and the reconquest of 1692, many Pueblo Indians fled to the Navajo country and lived among them for years. In the eighteenth century long periods of drought forced many Hopis to leave their mesa-top villages in Arizona and live among the Navajos to the east. These prolonged and intimate relationships between the two cultures could not help but change the genetic and cultural makeup of each society, and it was the less sophisticated Navajo lifeways which underwent the most obvious transformations.

But differences remained, for Navajos had been pragmatists from their first appearance in the Southwest; they had taken what they wished from the cultures they encountered, and in every instance turned these new traits into things which were distinctively Navajo.

Perhaps one of the greatest differences between the Navajos and their Pueblo neighbors was that the Pueblos remained in one village throughout the year, with a relatively complex social structure relating the individual to his clan, his moiety (related group of clans) if it existed, and the village as a whole, with definite officers—often hereditary—to make such decisions as were necessary for the commonweal of the village and to see that all abided by these decisions. Even here, however, social ostracism, rather than forcible punishment, was usually enough to bring any recalcitrant individual back into line, for a village might well have existed on the same site for decades, or even centuries, and obligatory relationships were firmly established by usage and tradition.

The Navajos, on the other hand, dwelt in scattered clusters of hogans—each home well separated from the others—which represented extended-family groupings. In addition, the Navajos, being sheep herders, migrated twice yearly, from summer to winter pasturage and back. (The Navajos are not, as Kluckhohn points out in *The Navaho*, true nomads, but they are mobile within fixed and sometimes extensive territorial limits.) The prereservation Navajos had recognized leaders, but these usually achieved their preeminence by reason of personal wisdom, bravery, wealth, generosity, and kindness to less fortunate tribesmen and knowledge of ceremonial and religious lore. Leadership might tend to remain within certain families, but there was no guarantee that this would be so, and in any event an individual was free to disregard his leader's counsel or to transfer his allegiance elsewhere. The failure of Europeans of all nationalities to comprehend this fact of Navajo life (and it was true of Apaches and of the Indians of the Great Plains as well) led to more misunderstandings and warfare than any other single factor in the history of relationships between the two peoples. Both the Spanish and Anglo-Americans considered an agreement or treaty between themselves and the leader of one band of Navajos to be binding upon the whole tribe, when in fact the Navajo captain could not guarantee that everyone in his own group would abide by the terms of the pact. When the whites could not find a suitable Indian leader to sign a treaty they would appoint one—to the great amusement, and often the contempt, of his fellow tribesmen.

The Navajos had clans—groups related to a legendary common ancestor—whose members were forbidden to intermarry, and some of these clans are equated with those which exist among the Pueblo Indians. There is one Navajo clan, however, which claims its descent from a group of Athapascan-speaking people who lived along the Pacific coast and traveled eastward until they rejoined their own people. Descent in all clans was traced through the mother, not the father, and when a couple married they went to live with the bride's family. Despite this, the husband was forbidden to look upon his mother-in-law, although he was free to marry his first wife's sisters, or unrelated women, if he could support them.

Since some Apache groups appear to lack clans, it is assumed that the Navajos acquired theirs from their Pueblo neighbors, and it is certain that much of their religious organization was adopted from the Pueblos, including the masked dancers and great parts of certain ceremonies or "sings," which lasted over a period of days and nights (much of the public part of Navajo ceremonials takes place after dark—the reverse of usual Pueblo ritual). The musical and other sounds of a Navajo ceremony such as the Enemy Way or Squaw Dance, as it is commonly referred to by whites, are beyond description: a massed chorus grouped near a pyre of burning logs shouts a wild eerie chant into the cool night air, pungent with the smell of burning juniper or pinyon wood, while the dancers—in this case dressed in everyday attire—circle the fire. In the privacy of a hogan or brush shelter the singer or medicine man is conducting certain prescribed rituals over a "patient," but—in the Enemy Way—the guests have come from miles around "to have a good time" and they must be fed by the patient or his family, in addition to paying the singer for his medicoreligious services. When the guests run into the hundreds this can come close to bankrupting a family, at least temporarily. Squaw Dances are so called because the dancing consists of mixed unmarried couples circling the great fire, each couple wrapped in one blanket, sometimes slipping out—to the taunts and catcalls of spectators—into the darkness beyond the firelight. But the proper name for these ceremonies, Enemy Way, denotes their real nature, for they are performed to rid the patient of contamination suffered from contact with outsiders, as in warfare or involuntary association with strangers. After World Wars I and II and the Korean and Southeast Asian conflicts Navajos who had been in the armed services felt it necessary to have this sing performed for them upon their return to Navajoland; in the old days, such rites were held for men returning from a raid against the Utes or Spaniards or Anglo-Americans. Enemy Way dances take place only in the summertime; in the winter, the great *Yei* (Holy People) ceremonies are held, some of them lasting as long as thirteen days. While outsiders are tolerated at Enemy Way dances, their presence is discouraged at the *Yeibichei* rites lest the outsiders somehow subvert the positive power of the ritual. How long the Navajos have had these ceremonies is open to question; Kluckhohn mentions the "tantalizing" reference in a 1713 Spanish document to "the great dances of the Navajos." (A Spanish document of 1795 states that Navajo captains, or chiefs, were heavily adorned with silver jewelry, but again, that is the extent of the reference. It is possible that the silver came as gifts of the Spanish.) But the character of Navajo rituals and the religious ideologies expressed by them indicate a heavy borrowing from the Pueblo people in the not-too-distant past. Navajo singers or medicine men learned the long and complicated rituals and chants beginning as youngsters under the tutelage of practicing shamans. If taught by a relative, usually no fee was involved other than helping the teacher with various household chores or assisting at sings and ceremonies, but if the profession was learned from a nonrelative a fee of sheep or other goods was required. A dedicated spectator could memorize the words of a ritual chant as well as the physical movements—sandpainting, sprinkling of pollen, use of the mouth, hands, and religious accoutrements—but such a practice was called "stealing" the ceremony, and one who acquired his skills in such a manner was subject to severe pressures from properly established professionals, including the claim that his ministrations might well result in even harsher misfortunes for the already-ill patient who was unwise enough to employ the singer of stolen rituals. (In exactly the same manner, Navajo silversmiths did not like to be watched by nonsmiths while they worked, being fearful that the observer would "steal" their art.)

Again, relating to religion and its unsanctioned usages, Pueblos and Navajos share a fear of witchcraft and sorcery that is incomprehensible to those who do not know them well. This fear pervades nearly every facet of their lives and is the key to explaining much that is otherwise "irrational" or inexplicable in their behavior. The Spanish colonists of northern New Mexico also lived in great fear of witches and sorcerers, who abounded among them until the mid-twentieth century. In all three cultures, misfortune of any sort—the failure of bread to rise, the death of a sheep, a flaw in the casting of silver—all of these things would be blamed by Navajo, Pueblo, or Spaniard not on natural causes but upon a spell cast by a malevolent practitioner of the black arts who either held a personal grudge against his or her victim or was employed by someone who did.

Navajo legends describe The People before and just after their arrival in Dinetah as being incredibly poor and cold and hungry, clad in rags and bark and eating wild seeds and berries, always half-starved. It was in this dim period that the culture heroes of the Navajos began to acquire —as gifts of the gods—the various material and ritual items which turned them into a thriving people: corn, beans, peaches, and squash to grow and eat; the hogan to dwell in; and chants and ceremonies to ensure individual and tribal good fortune. Moreover, at the time the Navajos and other Indian groups were being curbed by the United States government, the horse, the sheep, and other early European cultural items were in the process of mythification as gifts of the Indian gods. But the earliest gifts of their Pueblo neighbors had long since become an integral part of Navajo life and the original debts transferred to the gods that had evolved from long contact.

By the late eighteenth and early nineteenth centuries the Navajos were a much different people than those who inhabited the original Dinetah. They had been moving west and south, as noted, under pressure from Utes and Spaniards, but by now the Navajos had a well-developed tribal structure and—most important of all—they had the horse. It is no wonder that this animal was regarded as a gift from the gods, for it liberated the Navajos and other Indians from strict dependence upon their immediate environment, enabling them to hunt game and to go on raiding and trading expeditions over vast territories, hitherto undreamed of. We know that in the late eighteenth century the Navajos were raiding the Pawnees in what is now Nebraska; by the mid-nineteenth century the Blackfeet of northern Montana were thoroughly familiar with the Navajos and other Indians of the Southwest; the Blackfeet called the Navajos the Sheep Eaters or the Many-Bracelets People, which brings us to the time of Atsidi Sani and the beginnings of silversmithing.

5

THE BEGINNINGS OF INDIAN SILVERSMITHING

It is altogether unlikely that we shall ever know for certain who the first Navajo silversmith was or when he first practiced his art, but Navajo lore, backed by some historical documentation, has it that the first such man was Atsidi Sani (Navajo for *"Old Smith")*, and that he learned smithing sometime between 1853 and 1870. But there is other evidence, as we shall see, that a number of Navajo smiths were working in silver before 1864—and in the end all we can do is to paraphrase Voltaire and say that if Atsidi Sani had not existed it would be necessary to invent him. However, there is no doubt about Atsidi Sani: he was flesh and blood, he worked iron and later silver, and—at least partly because of this—he became a great man among his people. He was an actual person, historically verified, and he has become a legend that would be hard to destroy, for he also is a symbol, an archetype, and if from a distance of more than a century we find it difficult to separate fact from conjecture, it does not really make much difference, for Atsidi Sani is the grandfather of all Navajo smiths; he is to the Navajos as Odysseus was to Homer; he is the spirit become flesh.

There has been controversy whether Atsidi Sani learned to work silver at the time he learned to work with iron, and when he first had the opportunity to do so. Historical evidence indicates he was exposed to the blacksmith's art no later than 1853.

In that year, seven years after New Mexico (which at that time also included what is now Arizona) became a territory of the United States, the federal government sent a retired Army captain, Henry L. Dodge, into the heart of Navajo country to act as their agent. Dodge understood Indians and got along well with them; he established an agency at Pass Washington, not far from present-day Fort Defiance, in the fall of 1853, and on November 16 of that year he wrote to the *Santa Fe Weekly Gazette*:

> I have with me George Carter who is their blacksmith, a man of sterling worth and every inch a soldier—a Mexican silversmith, an assistant, Juan Anea, my interpreter, and two Mexican servants. (In Woodward, pp. 18-19)

This totally ambiguous paragraph established only that there was an Anglo blacksmith (*"their* blacksmith," as Dodge put it) and a Mexican silversmith in the Navajo country in 1853—but we know that there was a forge at Zuni in that year, too. However, we also know that Atsidi Sani lived in the Pass Washington area and that in 1858, under the name of Herrero, he was "elected" head chief of the Navajos in the Fort Defiance area. (Unfortunately, Henry Dodge was killed by Apaches in the fall of 1856, and the Navajos became hostile again until they were put down by a military campaign against them in the fall of 1858, just before Herrero was named head chief.) Chee Dodge, an Indian who was to become a noted leader of the Navajos in his own right and who knew Atsidi Sani well, told Arthur Woodward that the Old Smith went to the forges at Pass

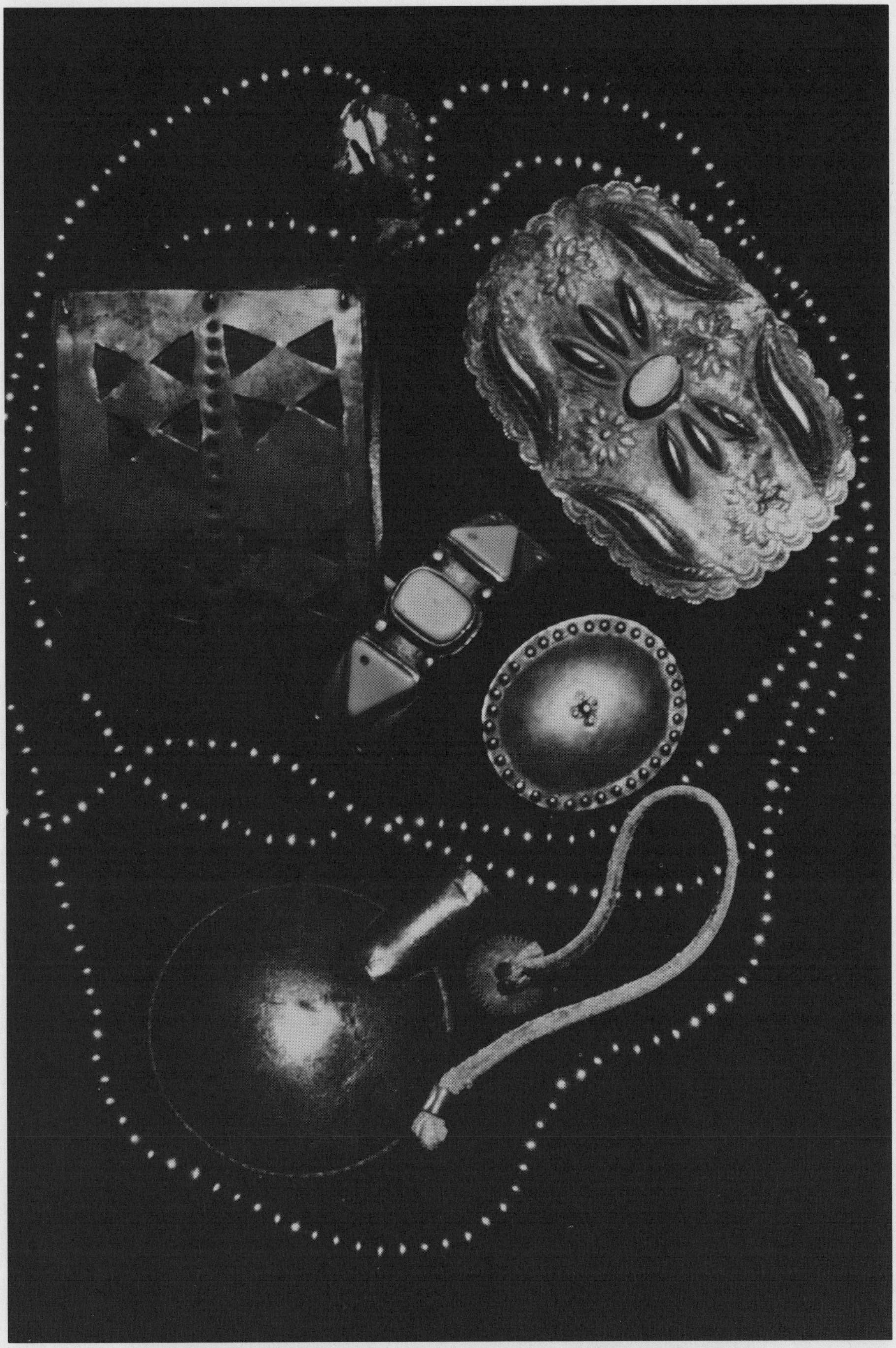

A selection of very early worked metal pieces. The long strand is brass beads traded to the Sioux by the French; all the other pieces are Navajo-made brass items. Note cutout design of the ketoh at upper left, and the fact that the metal is wired to the leather. At upper right is a belt buckle; the bracelet in the center is set with Hubbell glass trade beads. *(RT, Richard Polson)*

Washington and "looked on and learned some things."

Atsidi Sani's "paper name" of Herrero is of some interest, since in Spanish *herrero* specifically means a man who works in iron; a smith in general is a *forjador*, a goldsmith is an *orfebre*, and a silversmith a *platero*. Chee Dodge and other contemporary Navajos are generally agreed that Atsidi Sani worked with iron in the early 1850s but did not learn how to work in silver until after 1868. But in saying that Atsidi Sani was the first Navajo to work in silver—and only after 1868—they are contradicting evidence which has come to light in recent years.

A 1975 catalog of the Navajo Arts and Crafts Enterprise (successor to the old Navajo Arts and Crafts Guild) has this to say about the origins of Navajo silversmithing:

> In the late 1850's and early 1860's it became the custom of Mexican silversmiths from the Rio Grande valley to roam throughout the Navajo country producing copper, brass and silver jewelry and other artifacts in exchange for horses. It was from these itinerant silversmiths that the Navajo first learned their metal art. Silver beads were among the first things pioneer Navajo silversmiths made, by beating them from old Mexican silver coins.
>
> Atsidi Sani (old Smith) was the first known Navajo silversmith. He worked first with iron and later started working with silver.

We also know from E. Boyd *(op. cit.)* that for some decades before 1850 Mexican smiths had been operating on the periphery of Navajo country, perhaps even traveling among the Indians making bridles for horses as well as buttons and other adornments. Certainly these plateros possessed no greatly sophisticated facilities for smithing; whatever they had could have been bought, taken by force, or copied by the Navajos. There is no reason why simpler and cruder forms of jewelry could not have been made by the Navajos before the Long Walk to Fort Sumner in 1864, and there is direct evidence that they were.

Fort Sumner is the watershed of recent Navajo history. It is the momentous event which has shaped the thinking of all Navajos since then. It is also the crucial date in the history of Navajo silversmithing, for it has long been assumed that the Indians could not have worked silver before then. It has been further assumed that while Atsidi Sani worked iron before the Long Walk, he did not know how to work silver until after the Fort Sumner episode, when he learned it from a friendly Mexican smith who lived around Mount Taylor, near present-day Grants, New Mexico, and that he subsequently taught the art to four of his sons, while he himself continued to work mainly with iron. It was the sons, the legends have it, who spread the knowledge of silversmithing among other Navajos.

Another version of the origins of Navajo silversmithing is that certain men learned the art from the post blacksmith at Fort Sumner, or from Mexican plateros around the fort.

Regardless of historical fact there is little doubt that in the Navajo mind the creation of silver jewelry as an art form is associated with the great surge of liberation from their desperately unhappy years as prisoners of war at Fort Sumner, New Mexico.

The Fort Sumner experiment was conceived by General James H. Carleton, who commanded the Union armies in New Mexico Territory after Confederate forces had been driven out in 1862. In those Civil War years, with troops drained off for the great campaigns in the East, Indian depredations had increased alarmingly; but with the ouster of the Confederates from New Mexico, Carleton saw Fort Sumner, not as a concentration camp, but as a place where hostile Indians could be gathered, taught the white man's ways, and educated as useful members of modern society. Fort Sumner was built on the Pecos River in eastern New Mexico; the land around it was flat, treeless, and alkaline; despite this Carleton thought it a suitable place to teach the Indians farming. In 1863, Carleton sent his troops into the field against the Mescalero Apaches, with orders shoot to kill any man who resisted and to bring all captives in to Fort Sumner. By the summer of that year about 400 Mescaleros had been gathered there, and Carleton turned his attention next to the Navajos. Colonel Christopher ("Kit") Carson, victor over the Mescaleros, moved his soldiers into the Fort Defiance-Canyon de Chelly area of northeastern Arizona. Carson, a resident of Taos, New Mexico, and already renowned as a plainsman, trapper, and Indian fighter, began the systematic destruction of Navajo flocks, crops, and orchards, starving the Indians into submission during the winter of 1863-64. Although hundreds of Navajos escaped by fleeing to the wildest areas of northeastern Arizona, by the spring of 1864 around 8,000 Navajos had surrendered and been sent on the Long Walk of more than 300 miles from Arizona to Fort Sumner. Only children and cripples were allowed by their soldier escorts to ride in wagons, and scores of Navajos, weakened by hunger and exposure, died along the way. Once there, conditions were little better. Promised food was

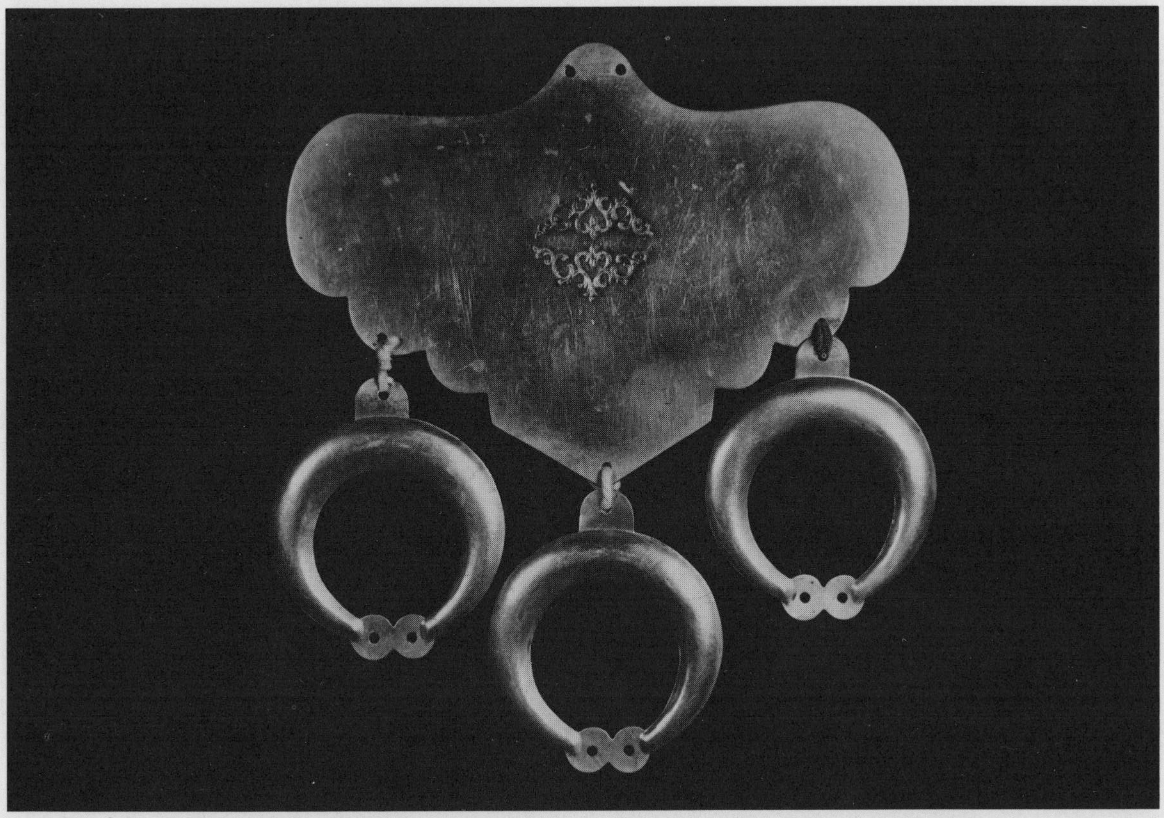

Breast ornament of German silver, Kiowa, Oklahoma. Note the similarity of the three circular pendants to the Spanish naja form. *(MAI, HF)*

not delivered, there was no wood for fires or dwellings, crops were planted but destroyed by bad weather or insects. The Navajos could not get along with their Mescalero kinsmen, and they were raided by the still-unsubdued Comanches from the nearby plains. In all, about 3,000 Navajos died at Fort Sumner. Finally recognizing its failure, the federal government in June 1868 signed a treaty with the Navajos there, allowing them to return to their homeland. The Long Walk was over, but, as among the displaced persons of Europe after World War II, the horror and hopelessness of those days has never been forgotten.

It seems reasonable to expect that the state of silversmithing among the Navajos during those Fort Sumner days would be well known, but unfortunately, little was said about it by those whites who were their warders in captivity. Photographs of Navajos taken at Fort Sumner show very little jewelry being worn, but this in itself is negative evidence and proves nothing. Of more interest, but again tantalizing, are the comments of Major Henry Davis Wallen, who was commandant at Fort Sumner when the Navajos were first being brought there early in 1864. In April of that year Wallen wrote a report to his superiors in Santa Fe in which he described the appearance and habits of his Navajo captives. Considering the prejudices of his time, Wallen was quite objective toward the Indians and not unsympathetic; he praised their intelligence and their ability to learn and improvise: "Some of them," he wrote, "are quite clever as silversmiths." Unfortunately, this is all he had to say about silversmithing, but since he wrote this early in 1864, before all of the Indians had reached Fort Sumner, his comments would substantiate the claim that the Navajos already knew how to work silver before their captivity. *(Fort Sumner,* Museum of New Mexico Press, 1974.)

Norman Feder has conclusively demonstrated the existence of an extensive metalworking tradition among the Plains Indians, beginning as early as the first decade of the nineteenth century (See *American Indian Tradition,* Vol. 8, nos. 2 and 3, 1962). Beginning with hair plates, pectorals, and crosses, all of which were wrought—that is, hammered by hand—from coins, brass kettles, and pots and silver sheet, the Plains Indians were able with a few crude tools to create a large body of metal ornaments. The crescent-shaped pendant, which Navajos call a *naja,* is a common motif among the southern Plains Indians. Feder says that these Indians—he does not mention Navajos—obtained design elements such as these from

Spanish sources, but he also cites the influence of the large trading centers along the Missouri River, where manufactured metal jewelry or unworked metal was available to the Plains Indian smiths. The metalworking traditions came into full flower, Feder says, around 1830, when the American Fur Company and the Hudson's Bay Company were vying for the Indian trade in the upper Plains area. It was at this time that Mexican plateros in the Rio Grande area were becoming common and feeding their own products into the Indian trade, both east and west of the Rio Grande valley.

Ruxton (1849), in describing the Spanish women of Taos, New Mexico, says that "massive crosses of the precious metals, wrought from the gold and silver of their own placeras, hang pendant on their breasts." (Quoted in Feder.)

The Comanches, who had intercourse with the Spanish of northern New Mexico from earliest times, wore many ornaments of metal, including German silver in later years and before that, true silver. (German silver is an alloy of copper, zinc and nickel in a 3:1:1 ratio; it contains no silver.) Feder says the Kiowas obtained German silver in 1866, according to their own calendars or Winter Counts, and quotes another source (Mooney, 1898) as saying that in the "old days these ornaments were made for them, of genuine silver, by Mexican silversmiths near the present Silver City, New Mexico." Mooney was quite likely referring to the Spanish community of Santa Rita del Cobre in southwestern New Mexico, not far from Silver City.

Arthur Woodward (1950) gives a date for the appearance of German silver among the Plains Indians in the 1830s, but Feder says the earliest available date he has for this is 1863-65. He says that an unverified report gives the first manufacturing date of German silver in the United States as 1863, by the J. Wharton Company of Philadelphia, and further, that after that time sheet metal in the form of German silver was available to the Plains Indians from traders throughout the area.

Feder also clearly demonstrates that sheet metal, whether silver, German silver, brass, coins, or pots and pans, can be hand-wrought with an absolute minimum of tools, and he makes it plain that this was the case during the early part of the nineteenth century and continuing until around 1880, when the art largely died out among the Plains Indians (although it is still continued to some extent today, using the same small repertoire of basic tools).

What does this mean in relation to Navajo silversmithing? It means that from the early nineteenth century the Navajos could, and in all likelihood did, make their own wrought pieces of metal ornament, either from brass, copper, or even of silver obtained from Mexican plateros. We know that in 1853 a forge was in existence at the pueblo of Zuni and also at Pass Washington, where the Navajos could easily observe and learn the techniques of casting silver, either into ingots or predesigned molds (sandcasts); they had ample opportunity to watch the post blacksmith at Fort Sumner, and, after their release from captivity in 1868, at Fort Wingate, not to mention the

German silver bracelets with incised decorations, Osage, Oklahoma. *(MAI, HF)*

Silver arm bands of the type issued as gifts to the (Eastern tribes) Indians by the U.S. government, 1792-1796.
(MAI, HF)

Mexican plateros who plied their trade in that area during the post-Sumner period.

It is logical, although not fully supported by documented dates, to postulate that the Navajos made wrought silver objects long before their Fort Sumner period (based upon some references, as early as the 1820s) but that cast silver, or silver worked with the aid of a forge, awaited a time of exposure to blacksmiths and a less warlike and more stable era when crude forges could be constructed by copying European models. Such necessities for casting and annealing also depended upon leisure time, for the first smiths did not practice their trade full time (in fact, this was largely true, particularly on the Navajo Reservation, as late as the 1930s); for reasons of survival, smiths were involved in the daily chores of tending livestock, shearing sheep in season, providing food and shelter, and in ritual or ceremonial matters—all the responsibilities of eking out a living in a harsh environment.

There are other references in old letters, reports, newspaper articles, and the like which indicate that the Navajos were working silver prior to 1864, but before we cite them let us examine the technology of silverworking, for if we know how silver was worked in those days we should be able to set the limits of what Navajo smiths could or could not make with crude tools, forges, fluxes, solders, bellows, and dies—or if, indeed, they had the capability of making or obtaining these vital aids in working silver.

Workable silver was available to the Navajos by mid-nineteenth century in the form of American silver dollars and smaller coins, or later, Mexican pesos. Drawn silver wire for filigree work apparently was present in northern New Mexico from Mexican times until well into the twentieth century, according to E. Boyd (op. cit.). It could be cut and shaped cold into bracelet form, depending upon its gauge. Buttons could be hammered cold by first making a rounded or conical mold in wood—or scrap iron if the proper tools were available—and hammering the coin until it fit the mold. A punch could pierce the hole or holes necessary for affixing the button with a leather thong. The original design on the coin could be hammered out before it was shaped, and the button could be worn plain, or simple new designs could be filed or engraved with the point of an awl; again, no heat would be necessary. To affix a silver or copper eye to the reverse side of a button would require both solder and high heat, not always available to the pre-Sumner Navajo. The problems of high heat and iron tools were the principal ones that beset early Navajo silversmiths. Silver coins could be pounded or hammered cold only so much; after a certain point cold silver cracks when it is hammered. Again, a coin can be melted down in a crucible, poured into a flat cast, and then hammered under heat into the desired shape, for say, a bracelet, but to melt silver in the early days required a bellows and forge. These were items that the Navajos could—and later did—make easily from materials always ready to hand; whether they did so before the Long Walk is not documented. What the Navajos could not obtain easily would be such items as hammers, pieces of scrap iron large enough to serve as anvils, tongs, and files. These would have to be gotten from Europeans, and while there is no reason they could not have been obtained from Mexican plateros before Fort Sumner, again there is no documentation that they did. It seems to be generally agreed that the Navajos did not use dies (for stamping silver), solder, and probably flux for lowering the melting point of the metal until the 1880s; turquoise, of course, was not set in silver before then. In addition to minimal iron tools, a forge, and a bellows, what the early Navajos also needed was the leisure in which to work metal; while this might have been available in the 1840s, it was not easy to come by during the period from 1852 onward, when the Indians were either being harassed by military expeditions of the U.S. Army or, in their turn, raiding the Mexican and American settlements along the Rio Grande.

But John P. Wilson, a historian-archeologist writing in the booklet *Fort Sumner,* cites some notes written in 1869 by one Edward Palmer, evidently a commentary on two bracelets acquired by that otherwise unidentified individual:

> These are used for the wrists by the Navajoes of New Mex. One is a broad, thick, heavy brass ring, deeply marked, while the other is silver. This tribe does not wear much brass around the wrists and silver ones now are very rarely [*sic*]. Formerly they were made by the Navajoes out of Mexican coin and were much used, but of late the tribe has had many wars and ornamentations has [*sic*] been impossible for want of means. (P. 18)

Palmer, of course, was writing in the year after the Navajos returned from Fort Sumner, and it is possible that silversmiths were resuming their old trade—or that they were just learning it from Mexican plateros around Fort Wingate (near present-day Gallup, New Mexico), where the Navajos first stayed on their return from Fort Sumner.

It was at Fort Wingate that Washington Matthews encountered the Navajos and made studies of them, including one on silversmithing. Matthews was a surgeon with the U.S. Army, and already had published anthropological material on the Hidatsa Indians of the Dakotas when he was assigned to duty at Fort Wingate. His description of Navajo silversmithing was published by the Bureau of American Ethnology in its 1880-81 annual report, and as John Adair has noted, is the only known contemporary document on silversmithing that we have. When Matthews wrote, the tribe had been back from Fort Sumner for ten years, and the homecoming had not been easy. The Indians at first had no flocks of sheep, these having been destroyed by Carson; there was no seed for crops and later there were disputes over grazing lands and homesites. Only gradually did the situation ease, being helped along in large part by the emergence of the Indian traders, individuals who were licensed by the federal government to establish trading posts in Indian country to trade with the Navajos for foodstuffs, clothing, and other necessities. It has been fashionable in recent years to speak disparagingly of the Indian trader, and while a few of them no doubt merit harsh words it is equally true that many of them—such as the Wetherills and the Hubbells and other great trading families—were not only the salvation of the Indians but staunch friends in the constant battle against government neglect and broken promises and corruption; in addition, it was the traders who encouraged the arts of silversmithing and rug weaving, ultimately finding markets for these products which by now have exceeded anyone's wildest dreams. If the traders' prices were high, so were the costs of freighting in merchandise; the life was a lonely one, and often traders and their families were isolated by bad weather for weeks or months at a time; many tried but could not take it. From this point on, we shall encounter the trader often, for he was banker, translator, adviser, and ombudsman to the Indians and even today plays a role in their economic life. By the late 1870s the trader already was shaping the role he was to play increasingly in later years, for Washington Matthews writes of the improvements the Navajos had made in their silversmithing in the past fifteen years with the comment, "Doubtless the tools obtained from American and Mexican traders have influenced their art. Old white residents of the Navajo country tell me that the art has improved greatly within their recollection... and they attribute this change largely to the recent introduction of fine files and emery paper."

Other tools purchased from the traders included hammers, pliers, tongs, scissors, and sometimes punches and cold chisels, although Matthews says the Indians usually made their own punches and chisels. In fact, the Navajo was capable of improvising any of his tools, and he could also obtain flux and solder from minerals found on the reservation.

Matthews said the Navajos originally used hard stones as anvils, and even in his time these still were in some use. Mostly, however, the Indians were using scrap iron, such as an old

An early Navajo silversmith posed outside of his summer shelter. *(Museum of New Mexico, Ben Wittick)*

wedge or the kingbolt of a wagon. The wedge was steadied by being driven into the ground; the kingbolt was pounded into a log.

Forges were made of adobe and stone. A round passageway was constructed at one end, into which the nozzle of the bellows could be inserted. The bellows was made of goatskin, a tube about 10 inches in diameter and 12 inches long, tied at one end to the nozzle and nailed at the other to a circular disk of wood in which was the valve. Two or more hoops of wood were placed in the goatskin to keep it distended, and the tube was constricted between them with buckskin thongs. The disk end of the bellows had two handles, one for pumping and the other to hold the assembly off the ground—which was usually the floor of the smith's hogan. A deepened fire pit in the forge held the crucible when it was placed into the coals. The crucible could be made of local clay by the smith, but this did not hold up well, as a rule, and rather than buy one from the trader the Navajos preferred to use bits of prehistoric pottery which they could pick up from ancient pueblo ruins near their homes (such ruins are everywhere in Navajo country). These shards served well as crucibles, which, when made by the smith, were rounded on the bottom and triangular at the top and about 2 inches in each dimension. Ingot molds were made of local volcanic stone into which a form approximating the shape of the desired object was carved with a knife, the stone being very soft.

The silver ingots of those days were either U.S. coins or Mexican pesos. Around 1890 the U.S. government began clamping down on the practice of melting down its coins for use in jewelry, or of defacing them (with solder and loops) to be worn as buttons or ornaments on clothing. This ban was not enforced overnight, and the practice of using coins as buttons continued at least into the 1940s, if not later. However, as the nineteenth century drew to a close, traders stocked Mexican pesos for the smiths; the pesos were obtained in large quantities from banks in El Paso and continued to be used until 1930 or somewhat earlier, according to some historians and authorities, when the Mexican government forbade export of its pesos for this use. Searching for new sources, traders arranged with U.S. smelters to produce a 1-ounce silver slug, square in shape and of the fineness of coin silver, which was readily adopted by Indian silversmiths. In 1938, with the creation of the Arts and Crafts Board by the U.S. government (its purposes were improving the status of silversmiths and finding new markets for their products), the use of sterling silver was encouraged, and today most silver used in Indian jewelry is sterling in fineness.

Pure silver is 1.000 fine, meaning that there are no impurities or alloys in the metal; it has a melting point of 1,761°F. Sterling silver is 0.925 fine; alloys which harden it slightly account for the remaining 0.075 percent of the composition of this metal, which has a melting point of 1,640°F. Coin silver has a purity of 0.900, and its melting point is 1,615°F. Alloys and fluxes (chemical additives) lower the melting point of pure silver. Alloys make silver less malleable; thus a purer silver is commonly used for making bezels and other intricate work. When heated, silver (like other metals) assumes colors which are indicative of its temperature at the time; a medium dark red color appears when the metal is between 900 and 1,280°F; silver turns bright red between 1,280 and 1,590°F and cherry red between 1,600 and 1,750°F.

When cold silver is worked extensively it becomes strain-hardened and cracks; if it is too hot—a cherry red—it is at or near its melting point, and if struck too hard will fly apart. To be easily worked silver must be annealed—heated to between 900 and 1,200°F, dark to bright red in color. (Our source for these statistics is *Creative Gold- and Silversmithing* by Choate and De May.) There are tricks to every trade and exceptions to every rule; a skilled smith can do many things which the book says he can't, and this should be borne in mind constantly not only regarding technical figures but dates as well.

American coins used by Navajo smiths before

Navajo buttons made from pesos, pre-1910. Fluting was done by filing. *(FHFAC, HM, Al Abrams)*

the 1890s contained 0.100 alloy and were harder to work; Mexican coins were purer in silver and had a better luster, but they were softer and did not wear as well as U.S. coinage of the period. Old timers say they can spot the difference in luster given off by old Navajo silver, determining whether U.S. or Mexican coins were used, and thus giving some idea of age. Others, equally knowledgeable, doubt this; at best, it is a very risky criterion.

Using the early coins and the equipment described above, the Navajo method of making an object of silver would be as follows:

The coin was placed in the crucible, which was put into the charcoal fire in the forge, fanned hotter by the bellows. Flux was added to lower the melting point. When the metal became molten the crucible was taken from the fire with tongs and the metal quickly poured into the ingot mold, which was greased with animal fat to prevent the silver from sticking to the stone. When the metal had hardened and cooled somewhat it was turned out of the mold and hammered into the desired shape, being annealed in the fire as often as necessary to maintain the proper heat. Hammer and pliers applied to the object on the anvil gave it whatever bends or joints were necessary, and these joints or seams were soldered together by being filled with scraps of silver, borax, and saliva, then fused with a blowpipe (usually handmade by the smith from brass wire), which was blown through flame supplied by a braid of rags soaked in mutton or other grease. Once the solder had cooled it was smoothed by rubbing it on sandstone, then with sand or ashes—wet or dry—then with a file bought from the trader, and finally with emery paper. When the metal came from the forge it was blackened and burned in color, and at a point prior to its final polishing it was blanched in a mineral substance found on the reservation, a hydrous sulphate of alumina called almogen. (Acid is used today.)

In Matthews's day there were no turquoise sets, nor were there dies in any quantity for designs, and such decoration as the silver received was rendered (before final polishing) with a file, a cold chisel, a punch, or engraved with the point of a metal awl.

Casting first came into use about 1875; the earliest examples of casting in the collections of the Laboratory of Anthropology and the School of American Research in Santa Fe date from about that time.

Sandcasts—a distinctively Navajo and often strikingly beautiful method of shaping silver—were and still are made as described above, except that the stone mold is carved with the complete design chosen for the finished piece. Another flat but uncarved piece of stone is fitted to match the carved piece exactly. On the carved piece a channel is cut to take the molten silver to the design, and tiny channels are cut from the edge of the design to the outside of the stone; these allow the air to escape when the silver is poured into the cast. While the silver is melting in the crucible, the stones of the cast—bound together tightly—are heating beside the forge, since they would crack if the molten silver were poured into them while they were cold. When the silver is liquid it is quickly removed from the fire and

The progression of a cast silver "butterfly" from first out of the mold, at right, to finished piece. A file is used to remove the spare silver, then rough edges are polished away on a buffing wheel. *(Museum of New Mexico, Sallie Wagner)*

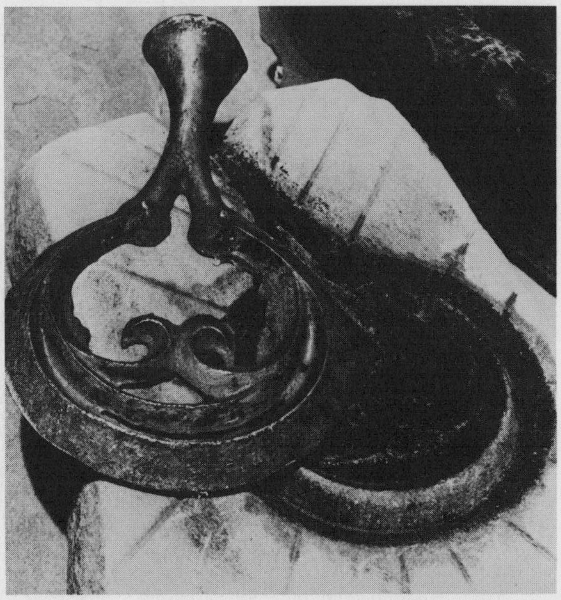

The silver cast of a naja as it is removed from the stone mold. The large spur of silver at the top (which shows how the molten silver was poured into the mold) will be removed and the cast filed, blanched, and polished to its final form. *(HMC, Al Abrams)*

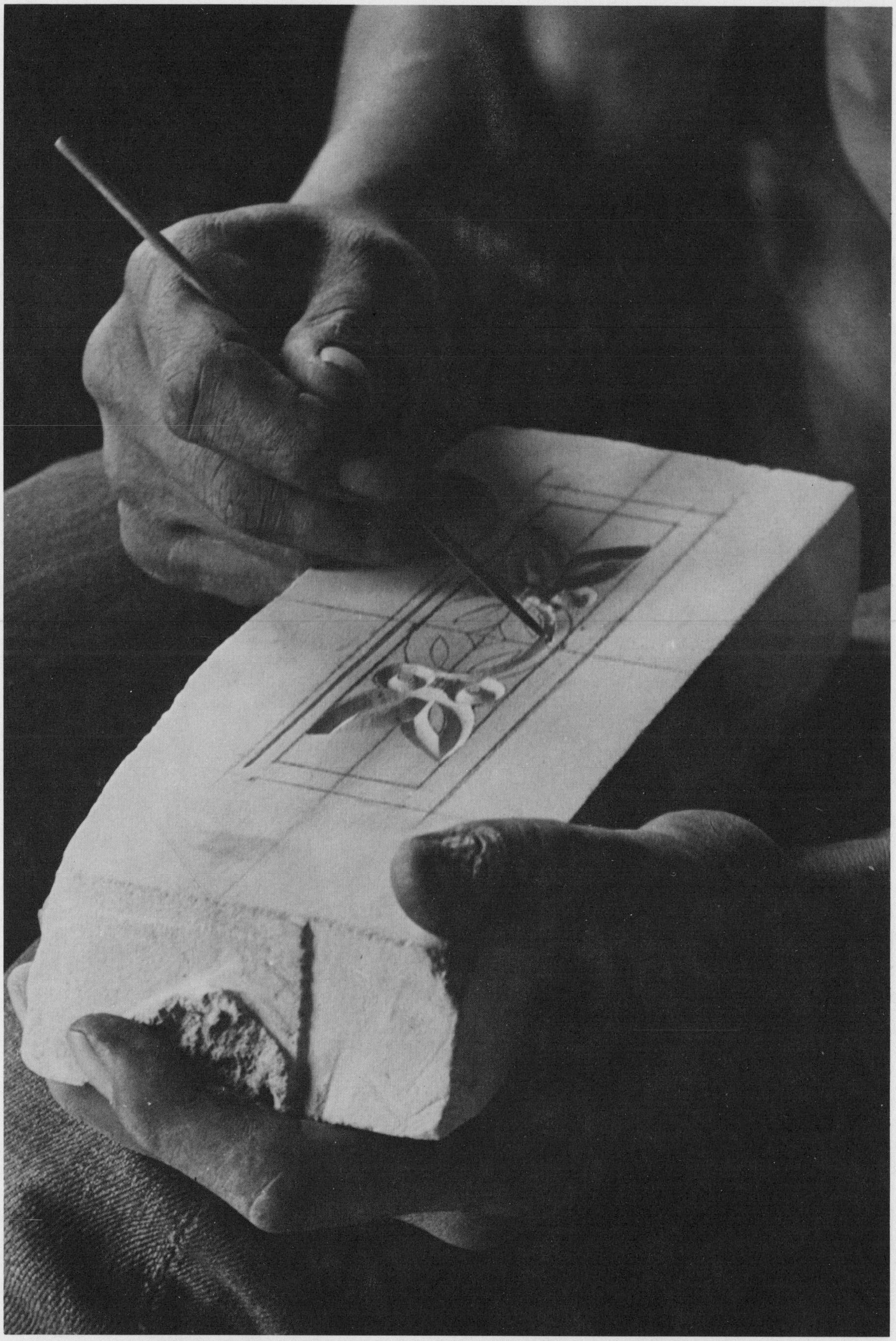

Carving a mold for a sandcast bracelet. The earliest designs were freehand; with the advent of measuring tools (rulers and calipers) designs became more exact in shape and layout. *(Laura Gilpin)*

poured into the mold; this must be done smoothly and without delay or the silver will harden before it fills the mold. After a few minutes the bands are removed. If the cast is perfect—by no means is this always the case—the silver is removed, blanched, filed, and polished. If the cast is not perfect, it is remelted and poured again.

It should be added that these creations are called sandcasts because they are supposedly cast in sandstone, a sedimentary rock whose deep red color is often seen on the Navajo reservation. However, the stone most often used for sandcasts is actually a volcanic tuff of pumice found locally; much softer and easier to carve than sandstone and not as subject to cracking.

By Matthews's time the Navajos were making all of their now-traditional items of silver jewelry, but turquoise sets were just coming into use; they did not become common until the late 1880s or early 1890s, and Matthews does not mention them in his 1880-81 report. He does mention plain silver conchas, mounted on leather for use as belts; rings and bracelets, either cast flat or wrought round; hollow silver beads, used in necklaces which also used both single-and double-bar crosses

Navajo leather pouch with buttons and decorations of coin silver. Buttons such as these, made in a simple dome mold, are among the earliest styles made. *(AG, Al Abrams)*

interspersed with the beads or used as pendants to the necklaces (he does not mention the squash-blossom or pomegranate beads); buttons and rosettes; bridle ornaments, powder chargers, and tobacco canteens (sometimes erroneously called powder canteens). Matthews's contemporaries, such as Lieutenant John G. Bourke, mention additional items such as silver loop earrings, headstalls for horses and saddle ornaments; silver buttons or small conchas used to decorate pouches and baldrics, and smaller ones for the seams of trousers and shirts; the *ketoh* or bowguard; bracelets triangular in cross-section; and mother-in-law bells—small silver bells whose tinkle would warn a man of the approach of his mother-in-law and enable him to leave without casting eyes upon her, a serious breach of Navajo etiquette.

We shall examine the state and peculiarities of jewelrymaking among the Navajos at this point in time more fully, but first let us note the spread of silversmithing to the Pueblos and other tribes.

At the pueblo of Zuni, as we have seen, metalworking was a relatively old art, for the Zunis were making articles of copper and brass perhaps as early as the 1840s. We know that a forge existed there as early as 1852, and one Zuni reputedly was a good ironworker who practiced his trade at about this time. But the art of silversmithing apparently was introduced to Zuni only in 1872 by a Navajo named Atsidi Chon ("Ugly Smith").

Atsidi Chon had a Zuni friend, Lanyade, with whom he stayed for a year around 1872, and to whom he taught the art of silversmithing. In his classic *Navajo and Pueblo Silversmiths* Adair quotes Lanyade as saying that Atsidi Chon made things of silver that the Zunis had never had before his arrival. These included bridles and concha belts, bowguards, and silver crosses copied from the copper ones the Zunis made. Atsidi Chon also had crude dies of scrap iron, and he taught Lanyade how to make his own dies. In return for teaching him how to work silver, Lanyade paid Atsidi Chon one good horse.

In the beginning, Zuni silverwork was like that of the Navajos from whom they learned or copied. (We shall note that later on both Navajo and Zuni jewelry became lighter and less massive, but for different reasons.)

It was the Zuni Lanyade who first taught the Hopis how to work in silver, in 1898, when Lanyade lived with a Hopi acquaintance named Sikyatala in the village of Sichomovi on the First Mesa. (Lanyade apparently was visiting many of the pueblos in Arizona and New Mexico, supplying the new demand for silverwork that had grown among Southwestern Indians with its introduction by the Navajos.) Again at Hopi, as at Zuni, silverwork at first was done in the style of the Navajos, and remained imitative for forty years or more, when the Museum of Northern Arizona at Flagstaff, in an effort to develop a distinctively Hopi style of silverwork, instituted a program toward this end in 1938. This style was known as *overlay*, and we shall examine it more closely later.

Indians of Acoma Pueblo may have been among the first to work silver, perhaps—according to Adair—as early as 1870. But like the Rio Grande pueblos—with the exception of Santo Domingo—Acoma failed to establish or maintain a strong tradition of silversmithing. Although individual smiths from Taos to Isleta have made names for themselves over the decades as artisans, only at Santo Domingo has there been a wide interest in the craft. Even here, until very recent times, the interest evolved around the Santo Domingans' traditional role as makers of shell beads and as traders; they are entrepreneurs par excellence and have been so for decades. The first Santo Domingan to learn silversmithing learned the art from a white man in Santa Fe in 1893.

A Hopi girl c. 1900 wearing turquoise mosaic earrings usually worn by the unmarried, and a coin silver necklace, in addition to older nonsilver pieces. *(Museum of New Mexico, Carl N. Werntz)*

Turquoise was first set in silver by the Indians of the Southwest during the 1880s. At first it was nothing more than a decoration for the silver made by the Navajos, and the Sky Stone was used as well as garnets (which are common in the Southwest) to set off the metalwork of the Navajo smiths. Indian smiths of other tribes at the beginnings of stonework, too, were content to do no more than accept their lead.

We have sketched the spread of silverwork among the various tribes of the Southwest, but before we follow the trends which were to develop in silversmithing, especially with the use of turquoise sets, let us take stock of the craft as it appeared around 1880 among the Navajos.

Two important developments which had occurred among the Navajos by this decade were the use of solder and the use of dies.

Solder gave the smith dimensions of decoration that had not been available to him before. Filigree work could be attached to bracelets and other forms of jewelry; bezels could be made which would make it possible to set the silver with turquoise and other stones; the two hemispheres of the hollow silver bead could be joined; round and triangular shaped strips of silver could be put together into a pleasantly varied bracelet form—and so could a number of narrow strips of silver be separated slightly from one another along the top of the wrist, then bent to join by means of a soldered transverse strip at the opening. (Navajos and other Southwestern Indians do not usually make full-round bracelets, although they were worn in the area in prehistoric times, made of shell.) Soldering was crude at first, and for flux the Indians used minerals found on the reservation; but later they obtained from traders commercial solder and improved factory-made tools which would ultimately enable them to do delicate clusterwork, needlepoint, and channelwork. In the beginning the smiths made their own blowpipes by hammering pieces of brass wire flat on their anvils, bending them into a tube, and bending the tube and constricting it slightly at the flame end. Grease-soaked rags or small bits of charcoal supplied the flame.

Dies for silverwork may have developed from stamps used for putting designs on leather; these, as Boyd has noted, were used by Spanish leatherworkers and tinsmiths who used tin cans transported to northern New Mexico over the Santa Fe Trail to make candle sconces, mirror frames, simple chandeliers, small boxes, and a variety of other items which were lacking in the homes of the less-affluent settlers. Both Navajos and Zunis used stamped tin sheets as ornaments on bowguards before silver came into use. Until traders offered commercial dies for sale, the Indians made them from broken nails, bolts, or other pieces of scrap metal. The first dies were narrow cold chisels, which could make only a short straight line, or punches, which when tapped lightly would make a circular depression. When tapped hard, of course, the punch made a round hole in the metal, either for decoration or through which a thong could be passed. Male and female die sets also were made. These were used in shaping buttons and conchas. The female die contained the reverse of the pattern that would appear on the silver: Depressions in the female die would be raised areas on a concha or button, and vice versa. The silver was placed against the female die and the male die was struck—from the reverse side—smartly into the female die. Traders later obtained commercially made dies, sometimes with designs supplied by the traders and which had no meaning for the smiths but which were presumed by other whites to be of Indian origin. The results, as Indian jewelry dealer Neumann has written, were sometimes "idiotic" (*Turquoise*, 1973). This has led, however, to a minibody of literature devoted to telling tourists and others the "meaning" of designs stamped on Indian silver. The truth is that, with few exceptions, there is no meaning to the designs; they are meant to embellish, not tell a cabalistic story.

While some dies may bear a whole design element, most of them contain smaller units which, while they can stand alone, can also be combined with other die designs in an infinite variety.

The first dies contained only the simplest geometric elements: straight lines, arcs, circles, and the like. They were stamped rather sparingly on the silver, for from the beginning the Indian generally had better taste than the tourist for whom the traders created die patterns in later years. In some instances the traders made up their "Indian" designs from whole cloth; in other instances they were inspired—if that is the word—by designs on prehistoric Indian pottery, or elements from Navajo sandpaintings, and sometimes by motifs from Plains or Eastern Indians. Thus, even if an Indian-derived design *did* have a meaning for the Indian originally, it was not likely to be that which appears on cards still obtainable in some tourist shops. But all of this remained in the future for the early smiths, who in any event lacked the sophisticated die-making tools necessary for complex (and often cluttered) patterns. And just as many of the better smiths do today, the early smiths made their own dies; they had to, for in the beginning there was no outside source. (It also is true that the first commercial dies were those made for stamping leather.)

Early stamped and repousséed silver ketoh, showing the elaborate designs possible with just a few simple stamps. C. 1890s. *(FHFAC, HM, Al Abrams)*

The Indians make their dies by heating the end of a bolt or piece of scrap metal until the temper is drawn, then filing or hammering the design into the face; once the desired lines are implanted, the die is heated to above redhot and the working end plunged into water and the heat allowed to draw down into it from the shank until a cherry red color is reached, whereupon it is quenched. This creates the male die. The female is made by heating the end of a blank until it is red

"Pedro and Anselina," a young Navajo couple c. 1880s. Note the mixture of old nonsilver and silver jewelry. The use of beads hung from pins died out when Navajo women stopped wearing the old-style "squaw dress." *(Museum of New Mexico, Ben Wittick)*

hot, then striking it with a male die until it has reached the required depth.

Photographs of Navajos taken during the 1880s show them already heavily decorated with silver jewelry, both cast and wrought. There are concha belts, both with the diamond-shaped aperture for stringing on leather and with soldered loops, and either cast and wrought buckles (the earliest belts had no buckles and were tied on with leather thongs); there are hollow-bead necklaces with pendant najas; there are loop earrings and finger rings; there are bowguards, cast and wrought; there are silver buttons for clothing and larger ones for leather baldrics. Some of the Navajos are wearing more than one necklace, and many men are wearing two concha belts, a custom that was to persist for some time as an unequivocal form of conspicuous consumption. Turquoise is either very scarce or totally lacking in most photographs, but solder and dies obviously are in use.

Concha belts are said by some to have come to the Navajos by way of the southern Plains Indian tribes. As we have seen, these tribes produced excellent silversmiths. The Plains Indians wore long strings of conchas—in their hair—and they were usually made of German silver. The original conchas of the Plains Indian, and among the early Navajos, were thin, round, and lightweight. The edges of the Plains Indian conchas almost never were scalloped, as the earliest specimens of Navajo conchas were. The Mexicans also used conchas, which were both scalloped around the edges and heavily decorated with complicated designs. It is maintained that the Navajos got the idea for the concha from the Plains Indians but later adapted the Spanish-Mexican form of decoration for them—which seems a very complicated theory, considering the Navajos could have learned everything they needed to learn from the Spaniards and Mexicans.

The earliest Navajo conchas extant are of silver, with scalloped edges, elemental stamping, and sometimes crude engraving, as with an awl. In the center of the concha, an oval or diamond-shaped aperture is cut, with a band of metal remaining through which a leather belt can be passed. The Navajos favored the diamond-shaped center section so much that they continued to stamp this design on their conchas in later years, even though a belt loop was soldered on the inside of the concha. When dies became common the surface of the conchas would often be heavily stamped, although even today many collectors still favor the almost-undecorated plaques with the diamond slot cut in the center. (After the use of turquoise became common, it was employed with telling effect to set off a concha, with a large central stone being favored most often, but with a variety of other types of sets.) Although the Spanish word for the silver plaque is *concha* (shell), Anglo usage has corrupted this to *concho*, and this is much more commonly heard nowadays.

Silver earrings of the 1880s consisted of large hoops, sometimes plain with a round silver bead or even a squash-blossom bead dangling from the low point of the loop. Sometimes, too, an undecorated silver pendant, triangular in shape, was worn in the pierced ears of men, with the broad end lowermost. Later, the silver gave way to turquoise pendants of the same shape.

The squash-blossom bead, most authorities agree, was copied from Mexican smiths, who modeled theirs on the shape of the pomegranate. The term *squash-blossom* was probably coined by an Anglo trader. The petallike additions which turn a round bead into a squash-blossom can be three, four, or even five in number. Navajo silver necklaces of this period consist of hollow round beads, sometimes regularly interspersed with squash-blossoms or one- or two-barred flat silver crosses, usually not further decorated. Sometimes, however, these crosses would include an appendage at the bottom representing the Sacred Heart of Jesus motif so dear to the Spaniard or Mexican. Often a necklace would contain nothing but the round, hollow beads. These were made by cusping a flat disc of silver into a hemispheric mold or female die and afterward grinding the flat edge on sandstone until it matched its mate. The hemispheres were punched with holes and strung in coupled pairs on a piece of wire, with finer wire being wound around to ensure a tight fit of the seams, which were then filled with scraps of silver, borax, and saliva and soldered with a blowtorch. Afterward, the seams were filed and polished smooth.

Early in their history, Navajo bead necklaces were set off with a horseshoe-shaped device known as a *naja* (or *nazhi* or *najahe*), with the open end at the bottom. Although sometimes wrought, the naja was more often cast; it could be decorated with filed lines or later stamped with dies. The naja apparently came to the Navajos via the Spanish-Mexican route, from Old World sources as ancient as the Romans and Moors; they were traditionally worn as amulets to ward off the Evil Eye. Although the ends of the naja could be plain or terminate in small circles, the early Navajo pieces sometimes ended in the

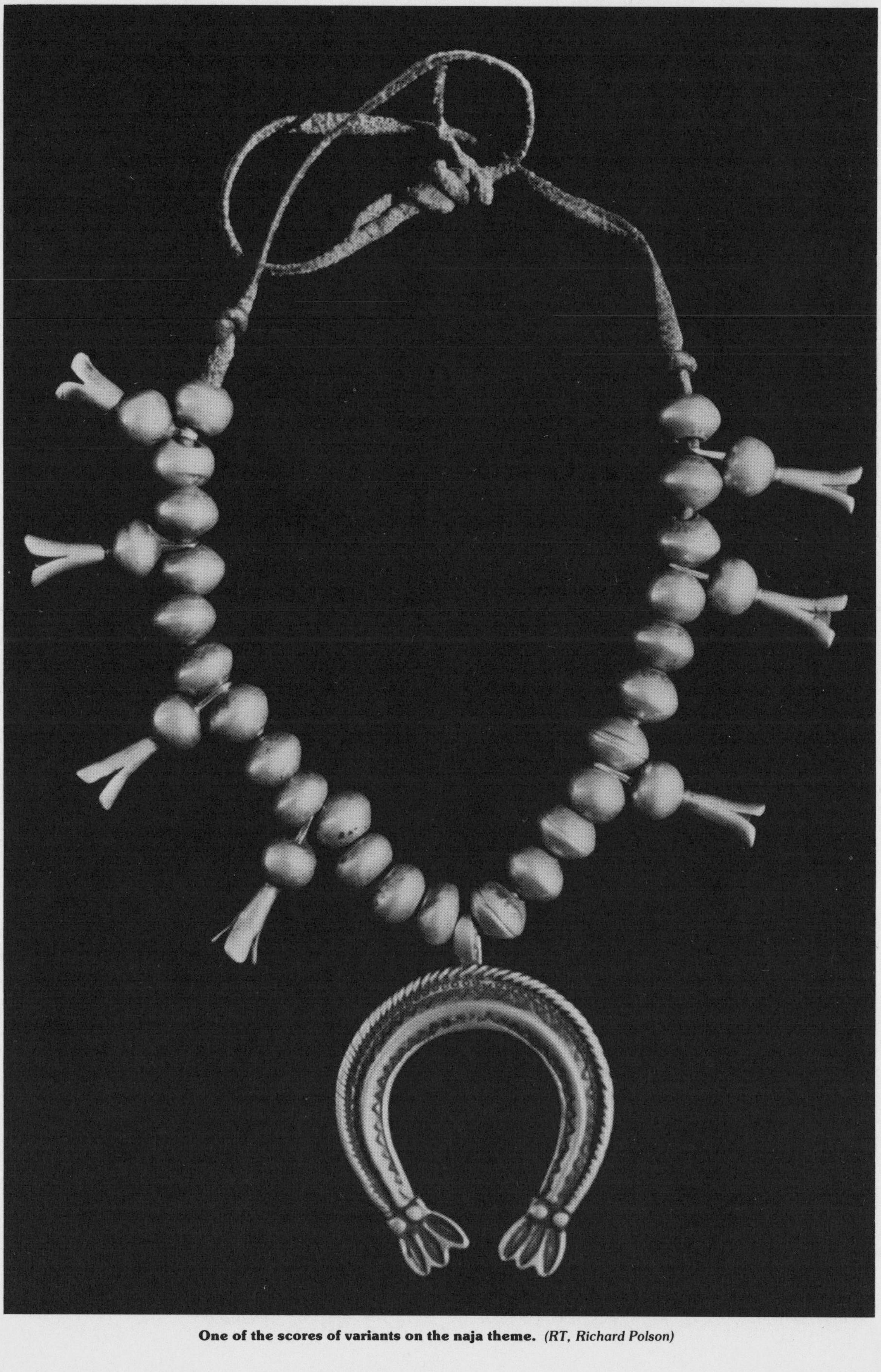

One of the scores of variants on the naja theme. *(RT, Richard Polson)*

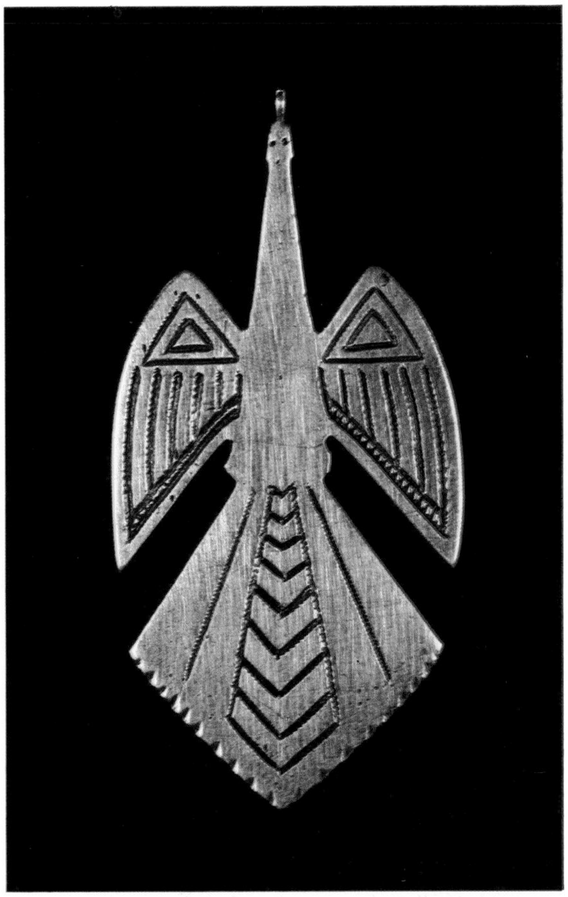

German silver ornament in the shape of a peyote bird. Kiowa, c. 1890s. The design was cut and stamped by a Plains Indian smith. *(MAI, HF, Carmelo Guadagno)*

Wide copper cuff bracelets made of hammered copper with grooves filed in. Shawnee, 1800s. *(MAI, Carmelo Guadagno)*

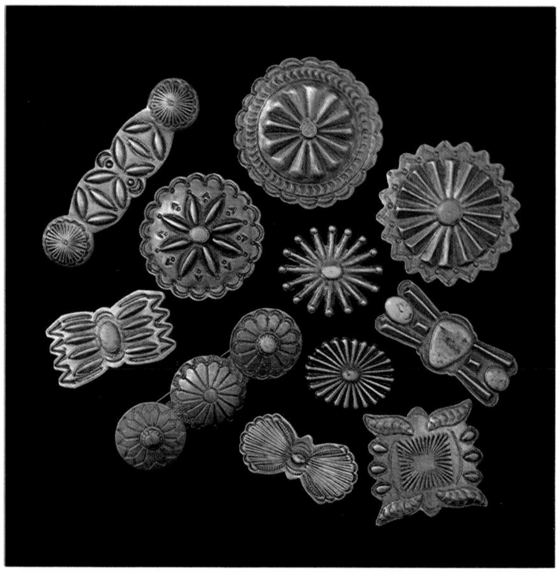

A selection of buttons and dress pins in styles popular from 1900 to 1940. *(RT, Richard Polson)*

Navajo coin silver buttons and a blouse ornament, all made before 1900. *(FHFAC, HM, Al Abrams)*

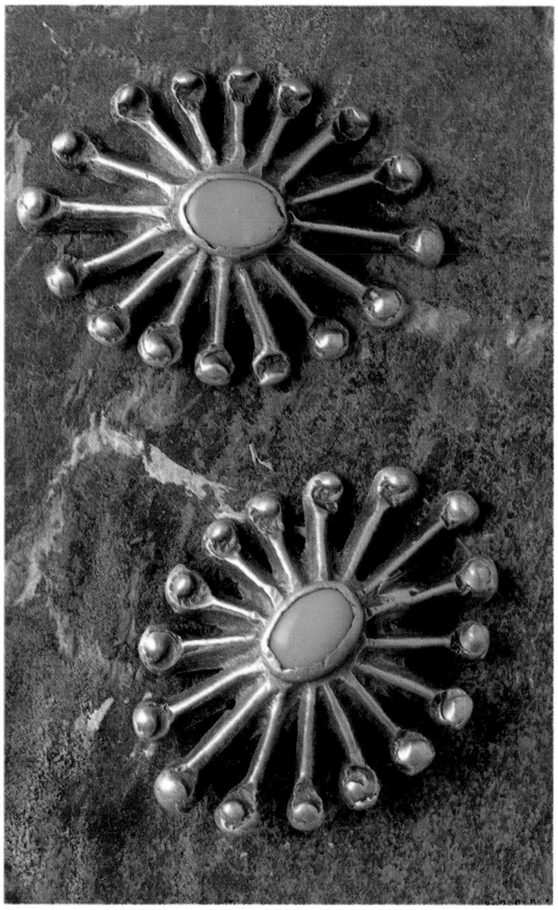

Two pre-1900 cast buttons in the sunburst style. The bezels are an early style which was bent over the stone to hold it on. *(FHFAC, HM, Al Abrams)*

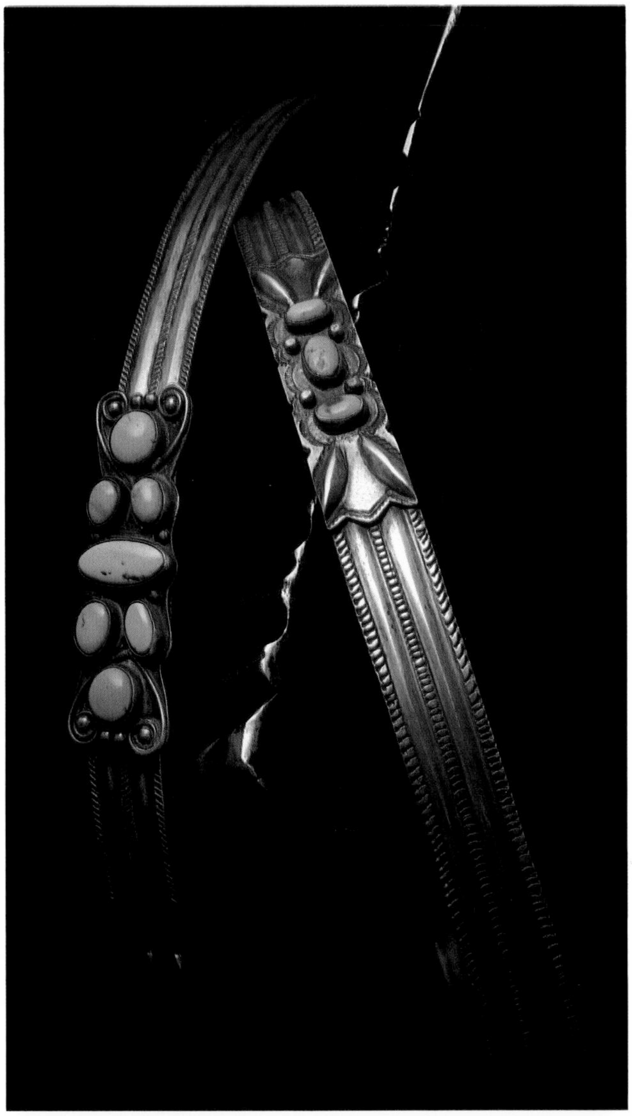

Left: **Silver hatbands were used in the early 1900s to replace the grosgrain ribbons on the black stetson hats popular on the reservation. They were also used in the 1920s as belts for women with small waists. The anvil these are resting on has grooves for swedging.** *(FHFAC, HM, Al Abrams)*
Below: **Navajo ear bobs set in handmade serrated silver bezels, c. 1900s.** *(FHFAC, HM, Al Abrams)*

Above: **Navajo woman's earrings with stamped decorations, c. early 1900s.** *(FHFAC, HM, Al Abrams)*
Left: **Navajo sandcast ketoh. The heart and corn plant motifs shown here were first used in the 1890s.** *(MRMM, Al Abrams)*

Single strand of handmade coin silver hollow beads. Navajo, 1870s. Note the "punched out" effect of the holes, characteristic of early handmade silver beads. *(FHFAC, HM, Al Abrams)*

Left: **Early coin silver bracelet showing leather stamp decorations. The variation in the color of the stones is an example of how turquoise can change color with time and wearing.** *(PC, Al Abrams)*

Below left: **Coin silver bracelet set with varying-sized hand-cut and hand-polished turquoise mounted in high bezels. Navajo, c. 1910.** *(PC, Al Abrams)*

Navajo row bracelet which shows a combination of all handmade elements. The stones were hand cut and polished and set in individually made bezels on a hammered silver band. The edges of the band were filed down and a hand-drawn square silver wire with a filed-in twisted rope pattern was soldered on. The silver drops were also individually made. C. 1910. *(HFAC, HM, Al Abrams)*

◄Navajo row bracelet with hand-cut stones, c. 1920s. The arrow stamp on this bracelet and the one below are examples of Anglo-created "Indian" designs. *(HMC, Al Abrams)*

◄Two Navajo bracelets. The combination of swedged triangular bars and interior flat bars or twisted wire was popular from the 1920s through the 1940s. *(FHFAC, HM, Al Abrams)*

◄The serrated-edge bezels in this Navajo bracelet were among the early devices used to mount stones on silver. This one dates about 1910. Note the reverse of the repoussé design on the inside of the bracelet. *(PC, Al Abrams)*

◄Early Navajo bracelet, c. 1890. The turquoise in this bracelet is probably as thick as it looks. Later pieces usually have backing to raise the stone to the height desired by the smith. *(MRMM, Al Abrams)*

The three bracelets on this page show the difference in the Navajo and Zuni concept of a row of stones. The bracelet on top is a typical Navajo row bracelet from the 1920s; the two bracelets on the bottom are both Zuni from the 1930s. *(FHFAC, HM, Al Abrams)*

A contemporary cluster bracelet set with matched, irregularly shaped turquoise stones set in scalloped-edge bezels. The bracelet was made by Mark Chee, a Navajo smith noted for his old-style designs and heavy silverwork. *(Pueblo One Indian Arts Gallery, John Miller, Ted Hill Photography)*

Top left: **This simple Navajo bracelet shows how a silversmith many times would take a pleasing stone and set it to show off the stone, not the silverwork. The gradations in the color of the stone are typical of turquoise from the Blue Gem mine. C. 1935.** *(PC, Al Abrams)*
Lower left: **Many 1930s Navajo sandcast silver bracelets such as this one are of more complex design than those made more recently. This style was sold both plain and set with turquoise. The corn plant motif used here was frequently used in that period and is a common one today.** *(FHFAC, HM, Al Abrams)*
Top right: **A more ornate Navajo row bracelet than is usually found. Note the additions of silver balls, twisted wire, and shaped wire and loop sections. This bracelet was made in the 1930s.** *(AG, Al Abrams)*
Lower right: **Zuni style man's cluster bracelet. The workmanship and slightly irregularly shaped stones date this to the 1920s.** *(AG, Al Abrams)*

Left: **A fine example of how delicate Zuni channelwork can be. Even though the design of this bracelet is excellent, and workmanship superior, the silversmith had to fill in several small gaps between the silver and turquoise.** *(HMC, Al Abrams)*
Right: **Navajo row bracelet on twisted wire set with Bisbee turquoise, c. 1940s.** *(PC, Al Abrams)*
Bottom: **These three bracelets made by the late Fred Peshlikai are all set with fine spiderweb turquoise stones and show the variations in design of which a fine silversmith is capable.**
(Rick Tanner's Collection of Old Pawn, Markow Photo)

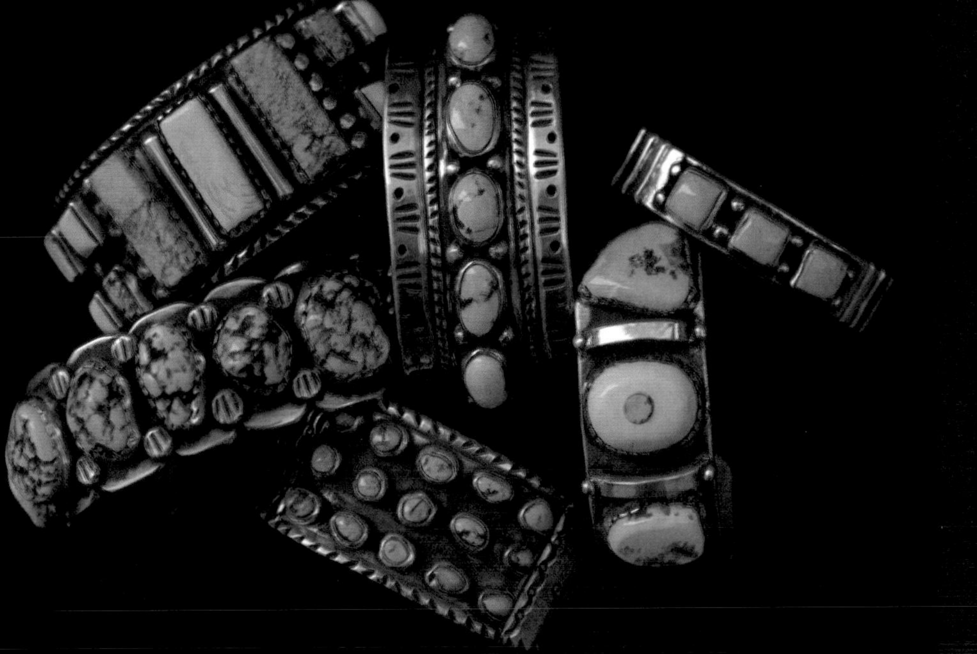

Contemporary Anglo-made Indian style bracelets of turquoise, ivory, and silver, made by George Stumpff. With modern tools available, the crudeness of these pieces is probably an attempt to reproduce details of earlier Indian-made bracelets. *(RT, Richard Polson)*

Two contemporary Zuni bracelets. The upper one, in "petit point," was made by Edith Tsibethsaye. The maker of the bottom one, in needlepoint, is unknown. Both are set with Lone Mountain turquoise. The individual stones in the bottom bracelet are somewhat wider than those found in earlier traditional needlepoint pieces. Stones for modern needlepoint are usually cut specifically for the purpose (rather than being waste slivers used when the style originated). *(Tanner's Indian Art Collection, Jerry Jacka)*

Right: **This heishi bracelet in turquoise and coral by Charles Loloma is one of the many new nontraditional styles created by this Hopi artist.** *(PC, K.J. McCullough)*

Below: **Contemporary set by Navajo Lee Yazzie. The grooving of the silver is a contemporary rendition of old-style filed decoration.** *(PC, John Miller, Ted Hill Photography)*

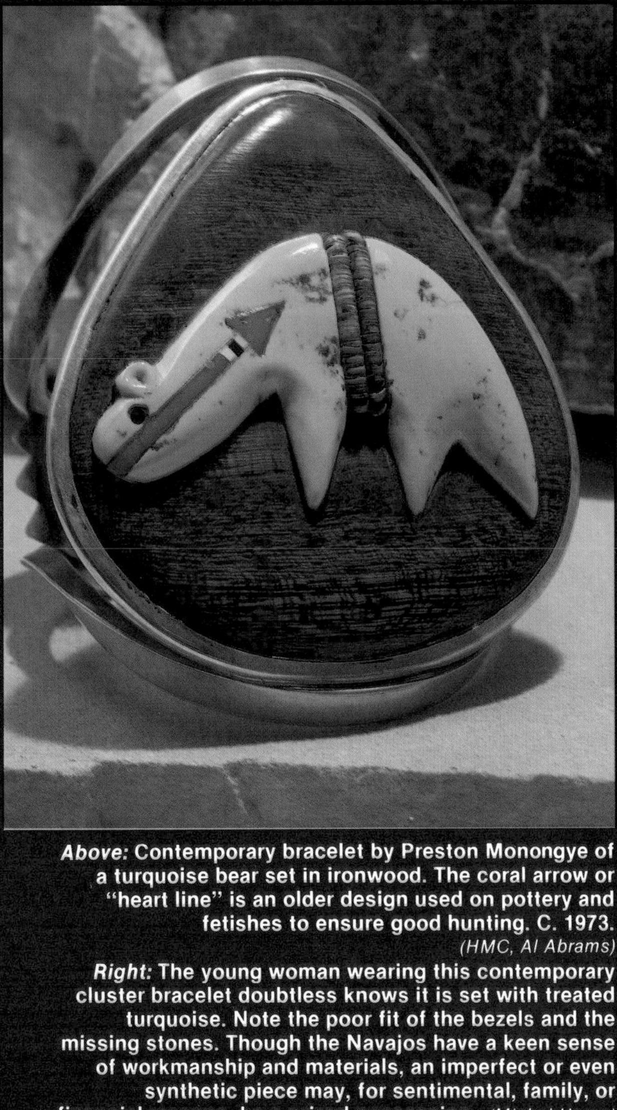

Above: **Contemporary bracelet by Preston Monongye of a turquoise bear set in ironwood. The coral arrow or "heart line" is an older design used on pottery and fetishes to ensure good hunting. C. 1973.** *(HMC, Al Abrams)*

Right: **The young woman wearing this contemporary cluster bracelet doubtless knows it is set with treated turquoise. Note the poor fit of the bezels and the missing stones. Though the Navajos have a keen sense of workmanship and materials, an imperfect or even synthetic piece may, for sentimental, family, or financial reasons, be a prized possession.** *(Michal Heron)*

Two Navajo concha belts shown against a typical microcosm of Monument Valley, Arizona. Many people feel the mystic appeal of Indian jewelry is strongest in its native setting. *(Keams Canyon Arts and Crafts, Jerry Jacka)*

Top: **Third Phase coin silver belt buckle made about 1930. The shape, simple turquoise sets, and repoussé design are very typical of that time period.** *(RT, Richard Polson)*
Bottom: **Concha from the belt buckle above. This is one of the more ornate (and most common) of the Navajo belt styles.** *(RT, Richard Polson)*

Second Phase Navajo coin silver concha belt made in the 1870s or 1880s. Many of the scratches on the silver surface are the result of long wear. Decorations are filed, cut, punched, and stamped. *(AG, Al Abrams)*

shape of human hands, the design being part of the cast. Navajos also used the cross described above as the lower ornament of a bead necklace, but this design was more often favored by the early Pueblo smiths who were, nominally at least, Roman Catholics. It was the Pueblos, too, who favored the Sacred Heart embellishment.

The *ketoh* (also called *gato*) or bowguard was a distinctively Navajo piece of jewelry, which was derived from a once-utilitarian source that stayed on as a form of pure decoration, its original purpose far outlived. As any archer knows, the repeated snap or twang of the released bowstring can cut a bowman's wrist to shreds; the earliest protection for hunters and warriors was a plain wide leather band strapped to the wrist of the hand that held the bow. When metals came to the Navajo, a sheet of brass or tin—often plain or sparely decorated with punch and cold chisel—was affixed to the leather. Later, silver was used, both wrought and cast, and heavily stamped. Long after the bow gave way to musket and rifle this superb form of decoration was retained; it was much prized by Pueblo Indians as well, who used it in their own dances and ceremonials, as well as for other dress-up occasions. This form of jewelry is distinctively masculine in size and form, and it is strange that the ketoh is not worn more by whites, but it is rarely sought by them except for collections.

The first Navajo silver bracelets were nothing but round or triangular bars of silver bought from the trader (who often carried spools of it in varying gauges) and cut and bent to fit the wrist. (The Navajos had earlier done this with copper and brass wire.) Sometimes the silver was filed or cut with chisels to make rude decorations; sometimes two or three strands of the lighter gauges were twisted together to form one thick strand. Early smiths also cast silver into flat bands, then wrought them into wide bracelets which could be stamped with dies. Bracelets also were "sandcast," much as they are today, although the early designs tend to be distinctive in their simplicity and less highly decorated, other than for the simple clean lines of the cast. Bracelets have always been the most common, and most favored, form of Navajo jewelry, and today they are the most commonly purchased items in the dealer's showcases. Perhaps this is because they are obviously larger than rings but can still be seen by their wearer, whereas the decorative and esthetic effects of necklaces, earrings, buttons, and brooches must often be taken on trust by the proud owner.

The earliest Navajo rings were nothing more than bands of metal welded in circular shape to fit the fingers. Sometimes the bands were bifurcated on their tops, or even divided into three, four, or five prongs, as they often are today. Designs could be cut on these prongs, before turquoise came to be set there. Rings also were cast.

Buttons, as described earlier, were made by cusping a silver disc into a rounded female die; sometimes the mold was conical, rather than hemispherical, in shape. The first buttons had two holes in the apex, through which a leather thong or piece of thread was passed to attach the button to clothing. Buttons with only one hole have been reported; a knotted thong was passed through this from the outside, then tied to the garment. Later, eyes were soldered to the backs of buttons, as well as on the backs of otherwise unaltered

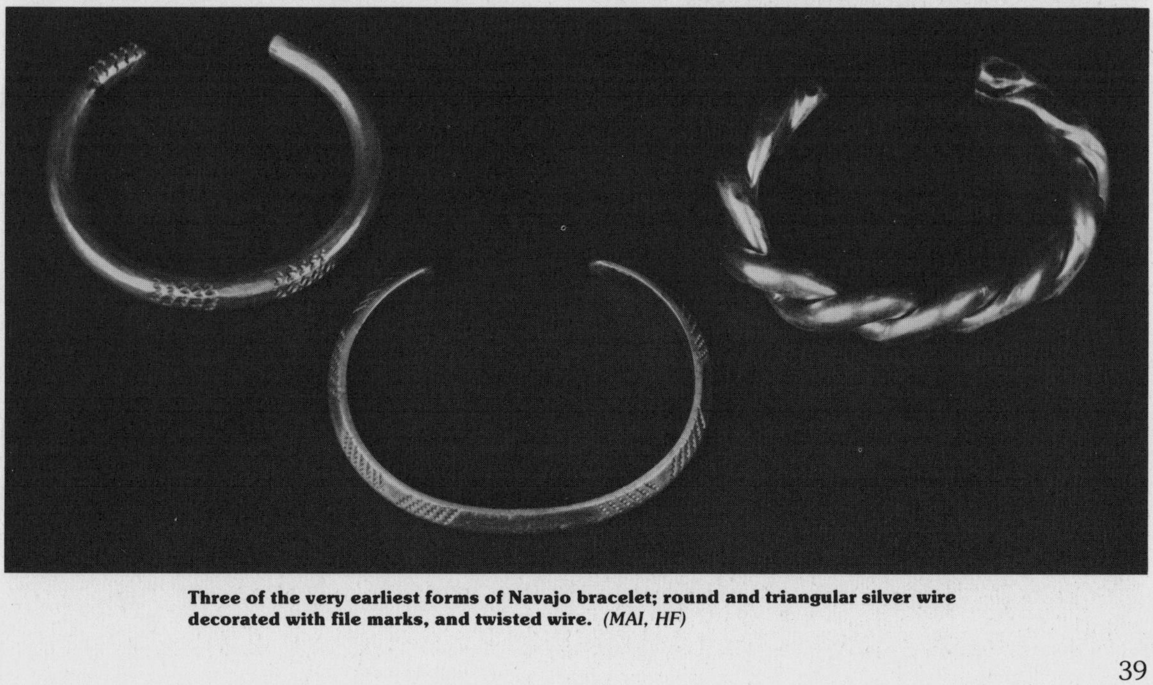

Three of the very earliest forms of Navajo bracelet; round and triangular silver wire decorated with file marks, and twisted wire. *(MAI, HF)*

American silver coins, a custom that remained in use well into the twentieth century. Coins of any denomination were used, depending upon the affluence of the wearer. For years it was common in the Southwest, particularly on or near the Navajo reservation, to receive a coin in change which still showed a drop of solder that had once affixed an eye to it. If the wearer needed change and was short of ready cash he—or more likely she, since the women most often wore these on their velveteen blouses—simply removed a button or two to make up the deficit. Men used coin buttons on their leather pouches or other accessories. Like all forms of Navajo jewelry, buttons could be cast as well as wrought, often in a starburst design with knobs on the ends of the rays—much like a flattened jack used in the children's game. (Cast rings also had this design.)

Bridles were among the first metal ornaments made by the Navajos. No matter when he learned to work silver, there is no question that Atsidi Sani was creating iron bridles before the Long Walk to Fort Sumner; it is possible that the first silver horse gear was not made until after the return from there. Mexican smiths and plateros were trading their wares to the Navajos long before the Indians learned to work metal, and it is likely that bridles were among the first objects traded, for the Navajos valued their swift war and hunting mounts more than any other possession. The headstall of the bridle was the part which received the most attention, with the straight silver bar relieved by the presence of round conchas on either side of the face and a naja, to ward off the Evil Eye. Earlier najas often came closer to the traditional Old World design form, that of two boars' tusks placed stump to stump.

Buckles for cinches on bridles and saddles probably were the inspiration for the first belt buckles, which were cast or wrought, or both. Buckles were very simple and functional in design to begin with and only later became more decorative. Cast buckles usually had a soldered bar to which the unpunched end of the leather was attached; a slightly bent prong on the other side of the buckle was inserted into the hole in the belt.

A few smiths in the late 1870s and early '80s were making the tobacco canteen (Matthews reported that most smiths at the time lacked the skill to make these). This was made in the shape of the contemporary army canteen—the Boy Scout canteen of later days—except that the Navajo version was only 3 or 4 inches across.

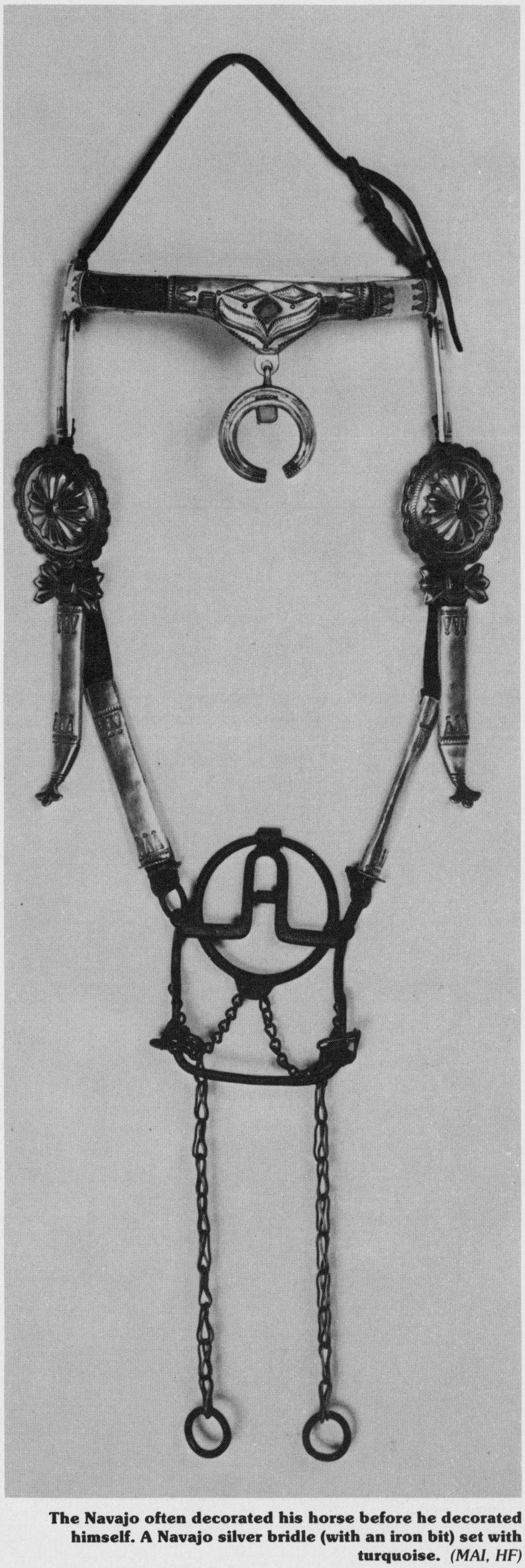

The Navajo often decorated his horse before he decorated himself. A Navajo silver bridle (with an iron bit) set with turquoise. *(MAI, HF)*

It was round and its sides were somewhat convex, and it had a round neck and stopper. The stopper was held to the canteen by a short silver chain. Although it has been stated that these canteens were used to hold gunpowder, Navajos say that they were much too small to have been used for such purposes, the traditional cow or buffalo horn being the preferred object, and that powder could not have been poured from them while a man was running or riding at a gallop. Powder chargers such as Matthews describes were made in the 1870s and '80s and along with canteens their manufacture has been revived from time to time, but today they must be regarded as novelties rather than standard items of jewelry.

By 1880 all of the now-traditional forms of Navajo jewelry had been introduced; a number of new fads or items would be made in later years, usually at the instigation of traders to accommodate the tourist or eastern trade. Overall, the two main characteristics of all such jewelry were simplicity and mass. Turquoise and other stones were yet to be set in silver. Solder was in use, enabling smiths to make hollow beads and to join two or more elements of silver. Shape and form were as described in the foregoing passages. The presence of much die stamping would argue against an early age for any article of jewelry. However, while silverwork might be simple, it was not likely to be sloppy or inept; for what it was, considering the means available to the smiths of the time, it was made very well and very carefully.

If you were considering purchase of a purportedly early piece of Navajo silverwork, could you make absolutely sure of its authenticity? The answer is no, not absolutely, but you could stifle most reasonable doubts. In the first place, the criteria given above could be used. In addition, the sheen of the metal might be of some value in judging, although laboratory analysis of the alloy would be most conclusive; the silver would have to have the same composition as the Mexican pesos or American silver dollars of the period. At best, laboratory analysis often proves only that an article of jewelry could *not* be what it is represented to be; science cannot always offer positive proof.

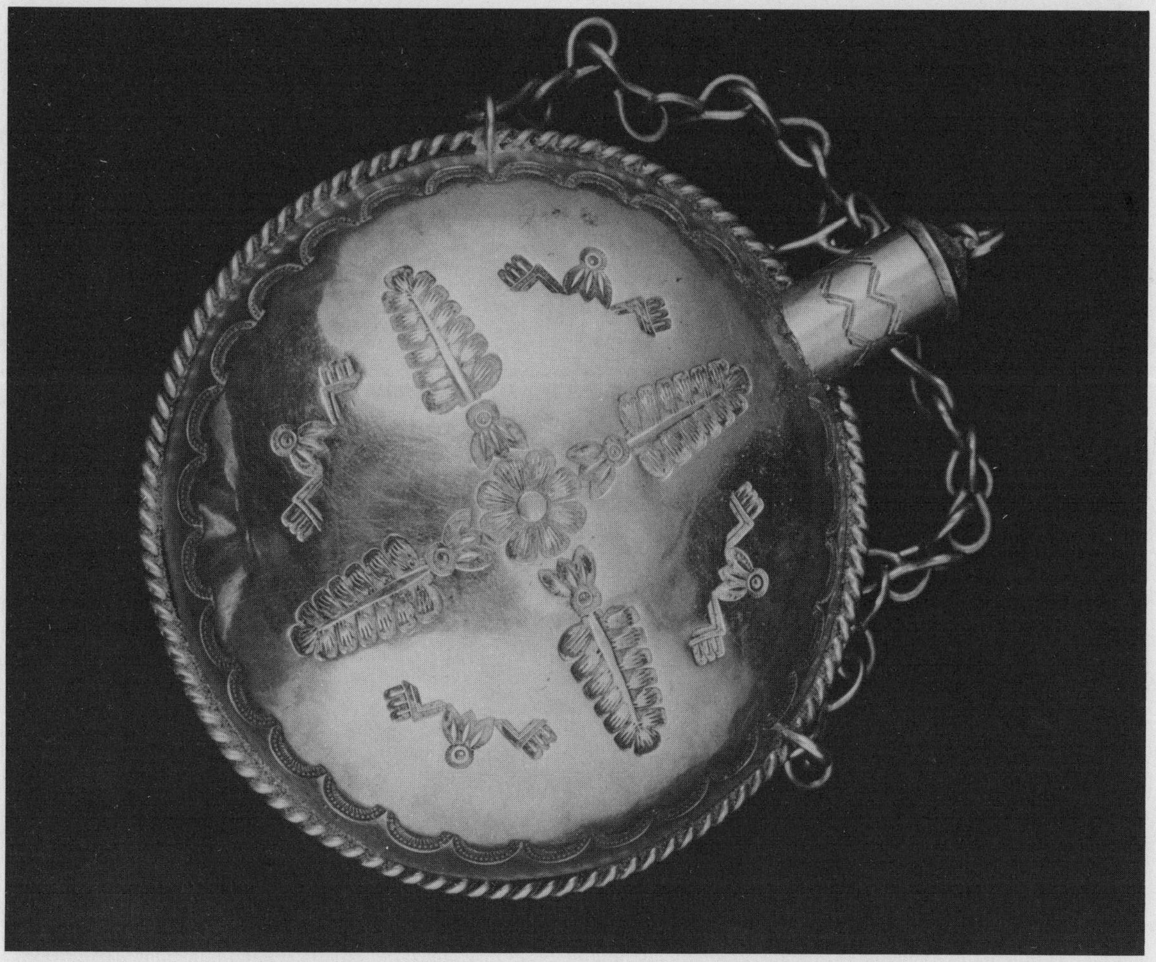

Navajo tobacco canteen with ornate stamping, c. 1910. *(MRMM, Al Abrams)*

A group of silver dress pins, conchas, buttons, and butterflies. The large concha on the right was originally part of a bridle; at center is a concha wristband. *(RT, Richard Polson)*

Patina, or surface appearance, can be faked. In fact, a mint-condition example of early Navajo silverwork would be most unlikely of all to find.

How do counterfeiters fake a piece of early jewelry? In the first place, they use only the kind of silver available to smiths of the period, and they allow themselves to use only the simple tools described, say, in Matthews's 1880 report; the same is true of forges and anvils. Given these materials, tools, and conditions, the faker would then do the best job he could with them; he would not make deliberate errors. (John Barrymore once said that for an actor to imitate a man with a limp he must twist his leg into an almost unbearable position and then try to walk as normally as possible.) Elements and designs would be only those known to have been used by the early smiths. In fact, the author personally knows of two non-Indian smiths in New Mexico who make superb "early Navajo" jewelry by using precisely the methods just described. The point is that while a buyer might be fooled by a less-painstaking fake, the good curator, dealer, or appraiser won't be; the item must be authentic in every detail, down to the composition of the solder. The hardest things to duplicate are the patina and use marks which can only come from long years of being worn; it is in this area, guided by his instinct and feeling, that the expert can most easily separate the fake from the genuine old piece of jewelry.

Once an article is finished it can be "aged" in an unbelievable number of ways: buried in damp earth or manure, treated with acids or other chemicals, towed over rocky ground after being fastened to the bumper of a car—the list of tricks is endless. Once aged, the jewelry will be polished so that it appears to have been normally used and cared for over the years.

The best guarantee of authenticity in Indian jewelry is the word, or written pedigree, of a reputable dealer. Where value warrants, the dealer will supply a statement saying that he acquired the piece from a certain individual or collection. But if a seller can give the name of the smith who made a piece of true old pawn or its first Indian owner, you have the right to be suspicious unless its subsequent history substantiates these alleged facts.

The early smiths did not use hallmarks, and even as late as the 1930s no one dreamed that the jewelry being made then or earlier would acquire the value it now has. Discerning individuals bought examples of good workmanship; records simply were not kept—which makes it easier for counterfeiters—and harder for today's reputable dealers.

Another caution: it is not illegal to make copies of early pieces of Indian jewelry. Many contemporary smiths do this, and the pieces usually don't last long in the showcase. What is illegal, of course, is misrepresentation, since an authenticated original commands a much higher price than the best-made copy.

To return to our history of early Navajo silverwork, the development of the tourist trade was to bring about the manufacture of some new items by silversmiths, but before this came about the craft was revolutionized by the introduction of turquoise sets for the heretofore plain metal.

Navajo silver pin with dangling loop of beads. The ornate effect of this piece is achieved with relatively simple stamps used over and over again. C. 1910. *(MRMM, Al Abrams)*

6

THE MAGIC STONE

When the first turquoise stone was mounted on silver by a Navajo smith no one may have known it at the time, but that smith was creating far more than a piece of decorative jewelry. He was, in fact, creating a tradition, a mystique, a style, and an art form that would grow to unimaginable limits—if, indeed, there are limits, for the silver and turquoise jewelry of the Indians of the Southwest is still evolving, still taking turns and striking out in new directions often far removed from what we now think of as traditional Navajo or Zuni or Southwestern Indian forms and styles.

We have spent some time speaking of prehistoric Indians and of the Navajos generally, especially since their return from Fort Sumner. This is not an oversight or digression. This jewelry cannot be separated from the Indians, and even though its history does not go back relatively far in time, silver and turquoise jewelry is inextricably linked with the Indians; it was accepted by them and became as much a part of their lives as the chants they sang, the horses they rode, the clothes they wore, the food they ate. Other stones and materials have been set in silver by Indian smiths, often with telling effect, and certainly silver—and the art of working it—is a recent gift of modern Europeans to the Navajos and other Indians. But the distinctive forms created by early Navajo and Zuni smiths from silver and turquoise were adapted so readily by their tribesmen that no one who has known Southwestern Indians over the years can think of them without thinking of the jewelry they wear. This is not costume jewelry; this is a part of their lifestyle. To see a piece of traditional Navajo jewelry is to be reminded of remote hogans set in scenes of mesas and cliffs and juniper trees—of a stark and harshly beautiful land with all the colors of the rainbow—of blue skies flecked with white clouds, of herds of sheep, of warm brown skin and velveteen clothing, the pungent smell of juniper smoke, of falsetto chants rising into darkened night skies—and always the flash of sun and fire upon silver, the glow of turquoise, the metal and the stone taking life from their wearers.

From its beginning, silver and turquoise jewelry was made, and acquired, to be worn. A Navajo might not wear every bit of jewelry he owned—in fact, he usually did not—but he wore a great deal of it; he wore it in quantities that would seem in bad taste if seen on a white man or other non-Indian, but on the Navajo or Pueblo Indian it seemed perfectly fitting, utterly natural.

Today Indian jewelry is sold in elegant shops, in department stores, in bus stops and airports and roadside curio stands—in scenes often far removed from the Southwest and its Indians. But it all stems from that area and those Indians, and to one who has grown up in that milieu there often arises a feeling of unreality at seeing this jewelry in unlikely places and in highly evolved styling. But ultimately the mind drifts, memory and the senses have their way, and one is back again in the trading posts of earlier years, in arid canyonlands, and among people who speak strange languages in soft voices and whose faces —far from impassive—reveal a dignity enhanced by flashing dark eyes, whitest of teeth, colorful clothing—and always the silver and the turquoise.

Turquoise came first, for it was native to the Southwest and had been worn for centuries—as beads, pendants, and mosaics and carved into fetishes which played central roles in the religious and ceremonial lives of prehistoric and historic Indians. Turquoise was set into the walls and floors of ceremonial chambers, deposited in shrines and caves, as offerings to the gods. This was only natural, for turquoise was regarded as a gift *from* the gods; it was the Sky Stone, as enduring as the heavens, a reminder of myriad myths and legends of creation and of survival in a bold and unforgiving environment.

Although turquoise is found sporadically elsewhere in the United States—even as far east as New Jersey—its main known deposits are in Nevada, New Mexico, Arizona, Colorado, and California. The fact that turquoise is little known in natural form in what is now Mexico perhaps had a great deal to do with the development of mining and with trading ties between the prehistoric Southwestern culture areas and the great civilizations of central Mexico. Turquoise was treasured by the Mexicans, as well as by the Mayan peoples of Yucatan; a mosaic plaque containing 3,000 pieces of turquoise was found by archeologist Earl Morris at Chichen Itza, Yucatan, and Morris concluded that the stones came from New Mexico. (Subsequent laboratory analyses of these and other turquoise stones used by artisans of the great prehistoric Mexican civilizations substantiate this.) Southwestern turquoise also has been reported from the West Indies and from California east to the state of Mississippi and as far north as Ontario, Canada.

In its natural form, turquoise appears most often in arid climates, as witness its Old World occurrence in the Sinai Peninsula (the mines there were worked by the Egyptians as early as 3200 B.C.) and in Persia, central Asia and Tibet, Peru and Chile, as well as our own Southwest. It is a secondary mineral in that it is formed by the percolation of surface waters through rocks containing apatite (source of phosphate in its chemical makeup) and copper minerals, plus aluminum and some iron, calcium, and silica. The chemical formula of turquoise can vary somewhat, depending upon the presence of other minerals, but Northrop's primary formula (see *Turquoise*) is, for those who care: $CuAl_6(PO_4)_4(OH)_8{\cdot}4H_2O$. It is a hydrated basic phosphate of copper and aluminum. It is found at relatively shallow depths, seldom exceeding 100 feet. The matrix, or host rock, can be igneous, sedimentary, or metamorphic—that is, any of the three basic types of rock on earth. When taken from the depths of a mine, turquoise often displays a breathtaking shade of blue, but on exposure to air and light the stone's color may fade rapidly; this is thought to be the result of drying out. The blue color of turquoise is probably due to the presence of copper, the green to the presence of iron.

The matrix found in turquoise can be brown, black, red, yellow, gray, or white, and it often enhances the value of the gemstone, particularly in the case of so-called spiderweb turquoise, which gets its name because the matrix is thin and veined delicately throughout the stone.

Other than the thin traceries of spiderweb, turquoise matrix is likely to be chunky and irregular in shape. The most expensive turquoise today is either of the spiderweb vaiety or else it has no matrix at all in its worked face. In earlier days—and here we are speaking in generalities, not stating immutable rules—the Sky Stone was apt to show a lot of matrix, and its color varied from greenish blue to the robin's-egg color, with most stones falling somewhere in between the two. The earliest sets, utilizing locally mined stones, especially those from Los Cerrilos, New Mexico, often displayed a greenish cast distinctive of that area; when, in the 1890s, traders began to import quality Persian stones robin's-egg-blue became more common, and much sought after. As Indian jewelry came into favor with tourists by the turn of the century, other mines were opened in the Southwest, and color and hardness became more important—and more divergent. Even within one mine the quality of turquoise could vary greatly—as it still does—and multiple-set jewelry often lacked perfectly matched stones. Many of the early stones were relatively porous; such turquoises were called oiling or chalk quality, meaning that an agent such as artificial color or oil or animal fat had to be added to make them salable. Santo Domingo Indians preferred to oil their stones; today these early treated Sky Stones have taken on a mellowed patina that actually adds greatly to their value. The superb collection of early Navajo silversmithing on display in the Laboratory of Anthropology in Santa Fe shows the whole gamut of shades of green and blue stones, and the author can remember, as a boy, seeing as much greenish stone as blue being worn by the Navajos and other Indians. Again, when in the 1930s true clusterwork, needlepoint, and channelwork began

Early Navajo bracelet set with jet and turquoise. *(MRMM, Al Abrams)*

Navajo coin silver bracelet with filed grooves, c. 1890s. The appliqué mounting may have been added later if the bracelet band was made before soldering was learned. In this period turquoise ear bobs and other drilled stones were often reset in silver. *(FHFAC, HM, Al Abrams)*

Early Navajo bracelets with irregular-shaped stones. In the early days of turquoise setting a smith's skill in lapidary work might not be the immediate equal of his silversmithing. *(Laura Gilpin)*

to be made, it was rare to find that all of the stones in one piece matched. It was common then, and not impossible now, that one or more stones in a needlepoint bracelet would turn, usually to a greenish hue as foreign matter penetrated the soft turquoise. Some owners might choose to have the offending stone replaced, while others preferred to keep the original sets, letting each stone "age" as it would. This is still a matter of taste and of debate among collectors.

Atsidi Chon, the smith who first taught a Zuni to make silver jewelry, was among the first to use turquoise sets. It may be that he was the first to do so, but there is no way to be sure of this. The practice did not come into widespread use until after 1890. It was not until the first commercial boom in Indian jewelry, during the 1890s, that commercial mines in Nevada, Arizona, and elsewhere began producing stones for the trade.

Turquoise sets were first introduced to Navajo silverwork in the 1880s, although they did not become common until 1890 and after. Because the earliest stones were often mined, cut, and polished by the Indians themselves, they were crude in finish and either flat or cabochon (convex) cut in shape. In fact, frequently polishing would be delegated to wives or apprentices. Later, the lapidary work was done increasingly by the Zunis, but today the stones are also imported in finished state from Persia or obtained from commercial gemstone companies.

In outline, viewed from the top, the stones of the 1890s and later tended to be square, circular, lozenge-shaped, or mildly free-form; in cross-section, cabochon was perhaps the most popular finish, but stones could also be flat if they were large enough, with a primary faceting around their outer edges that amounted to a bevel. All this is to say that the shape of turquoise sets is no determinant of age; the Indian smiths and lapidaries did what they could with them according to the equipment they had and depending upon the hardness and natural form of the stone. Often turquoise which had been shaped and pierced for use as pendants was reused for setting in silver, and it is not uncommon to find pierced stones set in older jewelry. However, since this is well known to modern copyists, contemporary stones set in traditional forms of silver are sometimes deliberately pierced to give the finished piece an aspect of age.

The first gems were crudely finished, because the smiths could not obtain professionally polished stones then, and—owing to the lack of sophistication of their silverworking tools—crudely set. Stones usually are set on silver with *bezels*—strips of metal which are cut to fit the gem—soldered on the basic silver piece, then bent around the stone. The tops of the early bezels sometimes were serrated or scalloped; they were cruder than they are now because the smith's limited tools would not allow him to do the fine, precision work necessary to obtain a sure fit. Bezels were cut from thin sheet metal; after they were soldered onto the ring or bracelet, before the turquoise was set in place it was cushioned with a piece of cardboard cut from a matchbox (nowadays tissue paper is often used). This is done for two reasons. First, turquoise cracks relatively easily, so when the bezel is bent or tamped around it the cardboard has just enough give to prevent the stone from breaking. Second, when worn, a jolt to the metal from a tabletop, or desk, or doorway is transmitted to the stone unless it has a bit of cushioning beneath it.

Navajo silverwork, as we know, originally tended to be classically simple and imposing, and the first turquoise sets conformed to their mountings. In the beginning, one stone was considered sufficient for a single piece of silver jewelry, but multiple sets were soon common; however, generally the stones remained large in relation to their mountings, and this is characteristic of the traditional Navajo style.

Although the Zunis since prehistoric times have been excellent lapidaries, they apparently did not set their silverwork with turquoise until around 1890, some ten years after the Navajos first began using it. As turquoise became more plentiful, the Zunis became increasingly skilled at working and setting it in silver.

At first the Zuni smiths copied the Navajo forms of turquoise as well as their silverwork, but their lapidary skill in making fetishes, beads, and pendants, which far predates the appearance of the first Europeans in the Southwest, soon asserted itself; large, simply shaped stones became smaller and more exquisitely ground and polished. Gradually, the earlier, extensive silverwork was abandoned in favor of light frameworks which were no more than platforms upon which large quantities of delicately cut stones were mounted, in clusters of varying designs, in geometric patterns, set by the Zunis in bracelets and necklaces whose weighty feel and appearance stems from the incredible amounts of hand-shaped, uniform turquoise sets. But this was a refinement that did not come to full flower until the twentieth century with the advent of more sophisticated tools and power-driven equipment. Today, typical Zuni styles are clusterwork and needlepoint, as well as inlay, which developed, according to more than one authority, in the early 1930s, and channel work—a heavier, deeper form of inlay—which also became popular in the middle to late 1930s.

Ultimately, two forms or styles of silver and turquoise jewelry were to develop: the heavier, more imposing Navajo style and the lighter, more delicate and complicated Zuni style. If one wished to wax lyrical over such things, one might be tempted to say that the Navajos wrought in the manner of Beethoven while the Zunis ultimately would compose in the style of Mozart.

Again, however, generalizations serve only as guides; they are anything but infallible, and one cannot look at a given piece of jewelry and say, "This was made by a Navajo." One can only say, "This is made in Navajo style." As in any profession or field of art, over the decades each master watched his competition and borrowed or imitated or improvised as he saw fit. Professional excellence and beauty were the goals—along with earning or supplementing one's income—and the smiths of each tribe copied from the others. From almost the beginning, then, we encounter a problem that will recur in modern times when non-Indian smiths create silver and turquoise jewelry in traditional Indian styles: does art transcend all boundaries, or is there a racial or tribal copyright? Is it fair or ethical for others to capitalize on what American Indians have so painstakingly created? And if it is unfair, then what of the *fin de siècle* European painters who borrowed with unabashed enthusiasm from Oriental and African art? And what of the Indians: from whom did they borrow or learn? Turquoise was long known to them, for it is common in the United States Southwest, but the art of working silver was taught to them by Europeans, and the tools were supplied by non-Indians as well. Working by themselves on their reservations, the Indians received little outside encouragement at first; alone, they developed their own art form, and they sold or traded their jewelry to other Indians or, much more rarely, to soldiers, traders, government employees, and occasional visitors who braved the rigors of those still wild lands. In the late nineteenth century and until the post-World War II era, Indian jewelry was classed as a curio, along with pottery and the old-style Navajo blanket (but not the Navajo rug, as we know it today) and childish souvenir tom-toms and bows and arrows. But just as Pueblo potters were master ceramists, and Navajo women were to develop the Navajo blanket (itself a work of art) into the magnificent Navajo rug, so the Navajo and other Southwestern Indian silversmiths were developing an essentially folk art into a true art form, the work of master craftsmen. But this did not occur spontaneously; it took the Atchison, Topeka, and Santa Fe Railroad and the perceptiveness of the Harvey House people to create the first nationwide interest in Indian jewelry.

Early Navajo coin silver bracelets with stamped and filed decorations and early turquoise sets. All of these bracelets were made before Indian silver was sold in any great quantity to tourists. Note the very simple repoussé on three of the bracelets. Variations in surface height in all these bracelets were made by filing down part of the surface, not by adding silver, as was done later. *(FHFAC, HM, Al Abrams)*

7

STEEL RAILS AND SILVER BANDS

By 1880 the Santa Fe Railroad had reached Albuquerque, New Mexico, but despite its name the line's main branch bypassed the state capital because the mountainous terrain made it economically unfeasible to follow the route of the old Santa Fe Trail south and west from Raton Pass. Thus, the historic Santa Fe Trail came to an end after sixty years of use, and Albuquerque soon outstripped Santa Fe in size and economic growth.

While one branch of the Santa Fe pushed south to join with what is now the Southern Pacific Railroad, an affiliate of the Santa Fe, the Atlantic and Pacific, extended westward across New Mexico and Arizona in a more direct route to southern California. In 1889, Gallup, New Mexico, with its nearby coal mines, became a division terminal of the new transcontinental rail line. Gallup also became the focal point for all mercantile activities on the vast Navajo Indian Reservation, even though the greater part of the reservation lies within Arizona, whose state boundary runs about twenty-five miles west of Gallup. Although Flagstaff, Arizona, draws a sizable amount of trade from the western portion of the Navajo reservation, Gallup is still the acknowledged Indian Capital of the World, as it takes pride in describing itself. Window Rock, Arizona, the Navajo capital, is twenty-five miles north and west of Gallup, just across the Arizona line, but administrative as well as economic mainlines flow through Gallup.

With the trains along the southern edge of the Navajo lands came the line of Fred Harvey Houses where, before the advent of Pullman cars, weary travelers could stop over for a night's sleep, hot meals, and a taste of Western atmosphere in surroundings genteel enough to soothe the most timid heart. The Navajos had been peaceable since their chastisement at Fort Sumner ended in 1868; the Apaches to the south had been forced permanently onto their reservations by the late 1880s, and the Pueblo Indians, whatever they may have thought privately, had long since ceased to be overtly hostile to white intruders. Tales of the stark beauty of the Navajo country, and the strange rites of such Pueblo peoples as the Hopis (whose reservation is surrounded by Navajo territory) acted as a magnet to curious Easterners, and they came to the wild country in greater and greater numbers to observe the Navajos and—in late summer—to watch the Hopi Snake Dances. It was customary to detrain at Gallup and to engage horses or wagons to travel north and west to the Hubbell trading post at Ganado and thence to Keams Canyon, the administrative capital of the Hopi reservation.

By now the great traders were already established on the Navajo and Hopi lands, and they quickly assumed a role among the Indians of much more than simple storekeepers. They were bankers, suppliers, advisers, and counselors during a period when the Indians were feeling the first sustained pinches of government bureaucracy and regulation, often administered in a peremptory and totally incomprehensible manner by government employees who rarely ventured from their official residences, knew nothing about the Indians' traditional lifestyles, and cared even less. Under such circumstances, it was natural for the Indians to turn to the traders, who dwelt among them, often spoke their language, and were familiar with their customs. It was the traders who read and explained to the illiterate Indians the bewildering directives from Washington, and it was the traders who counseled their clientele to send their children to school so that they might learn to read and write and ultimately assume the leadership of the tribe. It was the traders, too, who bought wool, skins, and other products, including jewelry, from the Indians, frequently advancing them money on future deliveries. The earliest traders began the custom of accepting jewelry as pawn, not as a form of loansharking, but as collateral against which a line of credit could be extended until the next year's wool crop, or money from other sources, could redeem it. The traders charged no interest on loans against pawn jewelry, and, although not required to do so, most of them would keep a piece pawned by a regular customer for years. When it had to be sold, it often was placed on the "dead pawn" rack so that the pawner or his relatives could see and redeem it; if they did not do so within a stated period of time, it usually was sold to merchants in Gallup or elsewhere, since it irritated an Indian to find his former personal jewelry being worn by another Navajo in the area. Often an Indian would pawn a piece of jewelry he did not like, with no intention of redeeming it; he simply used it to establish a draw against which he could purchase necessary supplies. In such cases, a trader had to take care that he did not "buy the bracelet"—that is, advance more money against it than he could receive when he sold it. Jewelry was pawned at a percentage—usually no more than 50 percent—of its off-reservation retail value, depending upon its workmanship, the weight of the silver, and the quality of the turquoise in it, as well as the integrity of the pawner.

The Navajos could, and did, pawn anything they owned, but jewelry was the most universal and convertible asset among The People. As late as World War II there were many Navajo families which never handled as much as fifty dollars cash in an entire year; theirs was still a barter economy, and at the poverty level. But they could trade for jewelry from Indian smiths, or buy it at prices which are unbelievable now, and only the most abjectly poor failed to own at least a few pieces of jewelry, which could be pawned at a trading post. Until World War II, when a modicum of prosperity came to the reservation, every post had a sizable pawn room. The walls were usually lined with filing cabinets which contained rings, bracelets, earrings, ketohs, and other small items of jewelry. From the ceilings hung concha belts, necklaces of shell, turquoise, and silver, and larger items like bridles. Pawn jewelry did not (and does not today) represent a distinctive style; it was simply the jewelry worn by Navajos of the time, and if it differed from commercial jewelry the difference lay in the fact that it was more likely to be of classic Navajo style, heavy in silver and rich in turquoise—and sometimes in better taste than that which was made for the outside market. A significant percentage of the jewelry that was sold in Phoenix, Tucson, Albuquerque, and Santa Fe made its way to those cities from the pawn rooms of the traders on the reservation. Wholesalers made the rounds of the reservation posts once or twice a year, buying up dead pawn; traders sold it to outlets in towns like Gallup, where it was resold to retail stores over the country. Collectors from museums toured the reservation from time to time, buying up outstanding examples of jewelry and other handcrafts, and private collectors who could afford it (and who could withstand the hazards of reservation travel in those days before paved roads and motels) also showed up at the posts.

As the Depression eased on the reservation, big traders there opened their own shop outlets in the tourist centers of the Southwest. But as times got better for the Indians, pawn got scarcer too. Pawn rooms became bare and no longer were there the gorgeous festoons of necklaces and belts hanging from the ceilings. As supply diminished, demand increased, and "old pawn" is almost a fetish with some collectors today, although each collector has his own definition of what constitutes "old" pawn. In those dusty, dirt-road days of the 1930s, however, pawn represented the plight and the economic lifeblood of a depressed people. It was beautiful to see, but there was a bit of heartbreak in nearly every piece of it, and many of the great traders would keep an item of pawn for decades after it had gone dead legally; it was a cherished possession of a good customer and friend, and not to be sold impersonally to some passing stranger. But we have gotten ahead of our story.

By the end of the nineteenth century, jewelry was becoming more popular with whites around the fringes of the reservation, as well as with tourists passing through Gallup on the trains, and the traders supplied dealers there with dead pawn

A Navajo silversmith, c. 1920s. His anvil is a section of steel railroad tie, his forge puddled adobe. Note the array of dies and stamps at lower left. *(Museum of New Mexico)*

or with new silver pieces made especially for the tourist markets. In addition, traders were supplying the smiths with metal saws, vises, commercially made die stamps, and increasingly modern tools and equipment.

In 1899 Herman Schweizer, head buyer for the Fred Harvey Company, conceived the idea of obtaining silver and cut turquoise and turning these over to the traders, who in turn farmed them out to smiths in their area. The smiths would manufacture jewelry from this, being paid by the ounce for the silver they worked, plus the stones. Although Adair says the smiths in the area of Thoreau, (pronounced *threw*), New Mexico, were the first to be employed in this manner, Katie Noe of Gallup believes the Indians of Manuelito were probably the first to turn out jewelry on a commercial basis. Both communities are in the Gallup area.

The Navajo jewelry obtained for the Harvey Company was sold aboard the trains and at the Harvey Houses along the line, including the big hotels in Albuquerque and at the Grand Canyon. It was also being shipped to retail outlets in other areas of the West and Southwest. While still classed as a curio, along with crude pottery and Navajo blankets, Ruth Falkenburg Kirk, a member of a distinguished Indian trading family, notes in *El Palacio* (1946) that tourists were amazed to discover that their silver souvenirs of the Southwest had intrinsic beauty of their own, and they came to be prized by their owners and sought after by others in the East who saw them.

Although she does not cite her authority, Mrs. Kirk says that Schweizer's venture met with little success, for he "was not getting new jewelry from that [the piecework] or any other source." Adair, writing a few years earlier than Kirk, does not seem to share that opinion, and it is certain that by the early years of the twentieth century the first upswing in silver and turquoise Indian jewelry had begun. In fact, by this time turquoise mines were being worked commercially and the stones cut and polished by professional lapidaries.

To handle the boom which had developed by the early 1920s, Indian goods dealers in Gallup were hiring smiths to work in their shops, turning out jewelry for the tourist and Eastern trade on a volume basis. To meet the increased production demands and satisfy the buyers, two changes took place in Navajo jewelry that was destined for the commercial market.

First, up to this time, Navajo silverwork had been made largely for other Navajos, who liked heavy silver, simply made. They also appreciated well-made articles, which took time as well as skill. Large amounts of silver priced pieces out of the curio market, and speed in assembly was essential to volume sales, so the smiths were encouraged to use lighter silver and to pay less attention to perfection of detail. Although smiths traditionally preferred to cast their own silver, even when it was to be beaten into sheets for bracelets and bezels, traders now made sheet silver of various gauges available to the Indian smiths; turquoise sets were precut and polished. Thus, Navajo silverwork made for commercial markets became lighter and less carefully made. (For themselves, by and large, Navajos continued to make the solid pieces of silver jewelry that had become traditional, and most desired, among them.)

In addition, the Navajos loved the sheen of pure silver, sparingly decorated with die stampings in what had become classic styles. However, in addition to preferring lighter, less expensive jewelry, tourists and other non-Indian buyers liked more stamping and decoration on their silverwork —"authentic" Indian designs. Although the Navajo smiths had long since been making their own dies, or buying them at trading posts, in general these designs were simple and tasteful; but to meet the demand, the dealers obligingly created a number of "authentic" new die designs, with such symbols as the arrow, clouds, lightning, sun, moon, and many others. These were applied to the commercially produced jewelry, and, as noted earlier, a great deal of nonsense was written or rumored concerning the "meaning" of these symbols—when in fact, with few exceptions, they had none for the Indian. The arrow and the swastika held appeal to Indian tastes and were used more frequently until World War II when, for obvious reasons, the latter was discontinued.

Even by the 1920s, when Indian jewelry was passing from a native craft state to that of an art form (Mrs. Kirk calls Indian silversmithing an "art-craft"), there were probably less than 200 silversmiths in the entire Southwest, and their creations were by no means the basic medium of exchange among the Indians: sheep were.

The Navajo flocks had grown again since Kit Carson had destroyed them in 1863-64 (even today, Carson's name enjoys the same popularity among the Navajos that General Sherman's does in Georgia). The wool was sold each year to the trader, as well as excess livestock, although it is difficult to convince an Indian that he has excess livestock, since he reckons his wealth by them. Each year, part of the wool clip was held back to be cleaned, carded, spun, dyed, and woven into blankets, which in those days far exceeded silver as a source of income for the Indians. Again, it was the trader who saw the commercial possibilities in turning the traditional Navajo blanket into a rug and persuaded the women to use heavier materials and techniques.

In any event, the Navajo viewed an article of silver as being worth so many sheep (or horses or goats or cows), not the other way around. And the jewelry that was in pawn was just as likely to be redeemed by a handwoven rug as it was by cash, raw wool, or livestock.

In those days a trader lived a very isolated life; he had to like and take an interest in his Indian customers, for they were the only people he saw, outside of his family, for weeks on end. Many times he owed not only his livelihood but his life to his clientele, and the trader had also to be a diplomat, a psychologist, and sometimes a doctor to them in return. To survive, he had to be fair, honest, and consistent, for his every move was watched by his customers and his every word weighed against his actions. A trader who lied, cheated, or vacillated quickly lost the respect of the Indians—and their business as well; conversely, one who overpaid or otherwise showed that he did not know the value of the things in which he dealt was regarded with secret contempt and used until he went broke. An Oriental psychology prevailed: the trader must not lose face with the

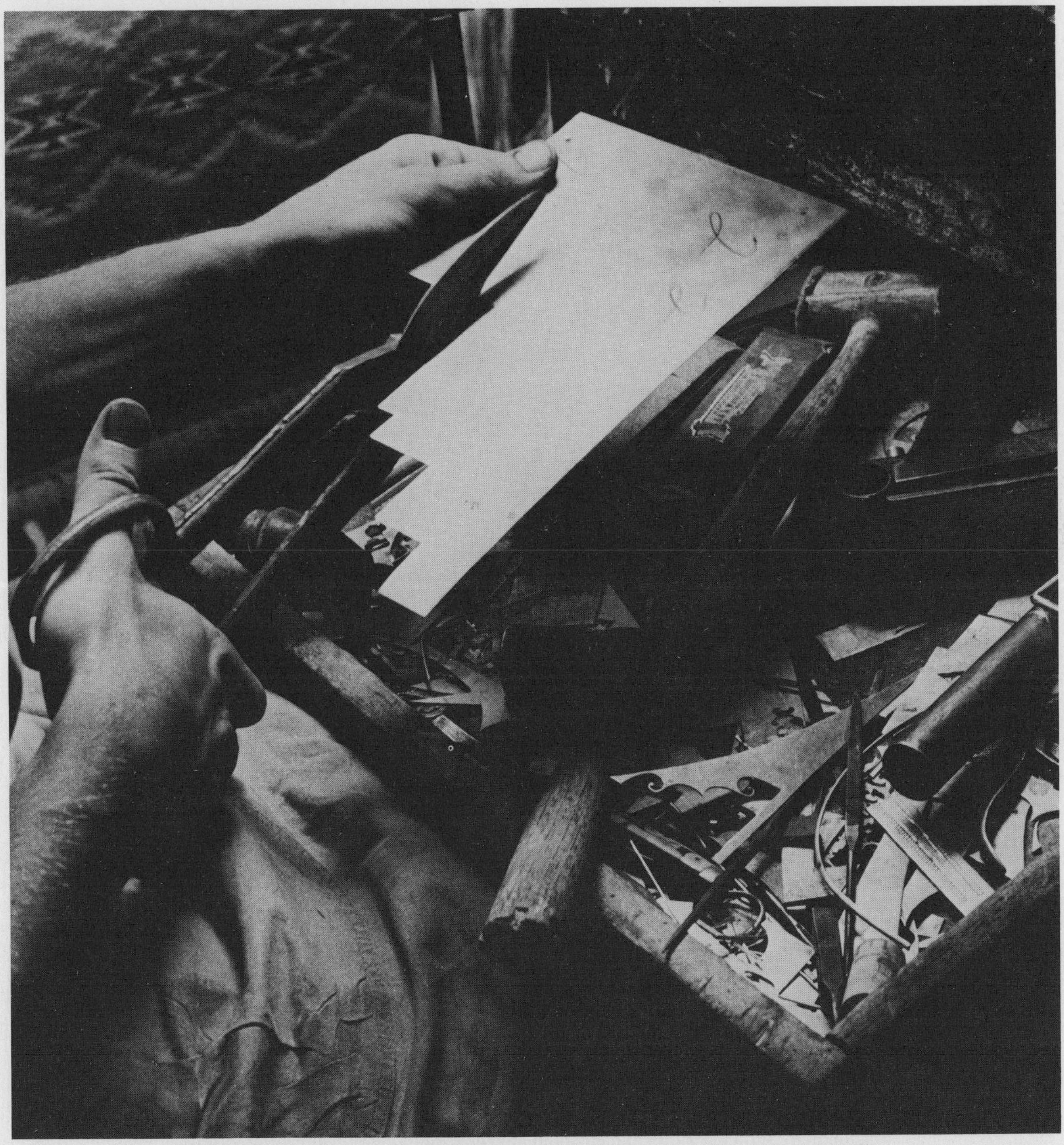

Since the advent of sheet silver, this is where the jewelrymaking process usually begins. Smaller scraps of sheet silver that cannot be used for other purposes are frequently melted down and made into sandcast jewelry.

Indians, nor must he do or say anything which would cause *them* to lose face with their tribesmen.

Until the 1920s, roads did not exist; there were ruts for the heavy wagons that brought in the trader's supplies from the railheads. A trader ordered his inventory months ahead of time, and if he bought unwisely he faced ruin. In the winter months he could be snowed in for weeks at a time; even in summer, if he were traveling, a cloudburst could turn the arroyos or washes into lethal torrents.

There are a number of books which portray the flavor and atmosphere of those early days in the Indian trading business. Among them are Frances Gillmor's *Traders to the Navajos,* Frank McNitt's *Indian Traders,* Clyde Kluckhohn's *To the End of the Rainbow*, Elizabeth Hegermann's *Navaho Trading Days*, and Joseph Schmedding's *Cowboy and Indian Trader*. To read any of these is a delight, for they recapture the Southwest and its Indians as no dull treatise ever can.

All the early trading posts looked very much alike on the inside. First, there was a U-shaped counter which ran around both sides and the back of the store. Behind the counter were tall shelves, stocked with goods, and hanging from the ceiling were saddles, ropes, buckets, pots and pans, pails, galvanized tubs—just about anything that could be hung from a nail or peg. In the middle of the store, or perhaps in the corner near the front, surrounded by wooden benches, was a potbellied coal or wood stove where customers could warm themselves in winter while they exchanged news and pleasantries.

But a Navajo did not walk into the front door, rush over to the trader, and begin buying things. It was necessary to enter quietly—preoccupied, perhaps, with those of one's family who had come along or with the merchandise on the shelves. Then one might suddenly notice one's friends in the post and go from one to another exchanging greetings. Once these amenities had been observed, one might approach the trader, and if the timing seemed right and the trader appeared to be affable, the trading might begin. If the wool clip had just been brought in or livestock sold, this was a good time to discharge one's debt to the trader, thus redeeming the jewelry and other items in pawn. The remainder of the allowance was spent on staples first and then other things. After each item was placed on the counter the trader would tell the Indian how much money he had left, not how much he had spent.

Looking back from the vantage point of today's business practices, the system may smack

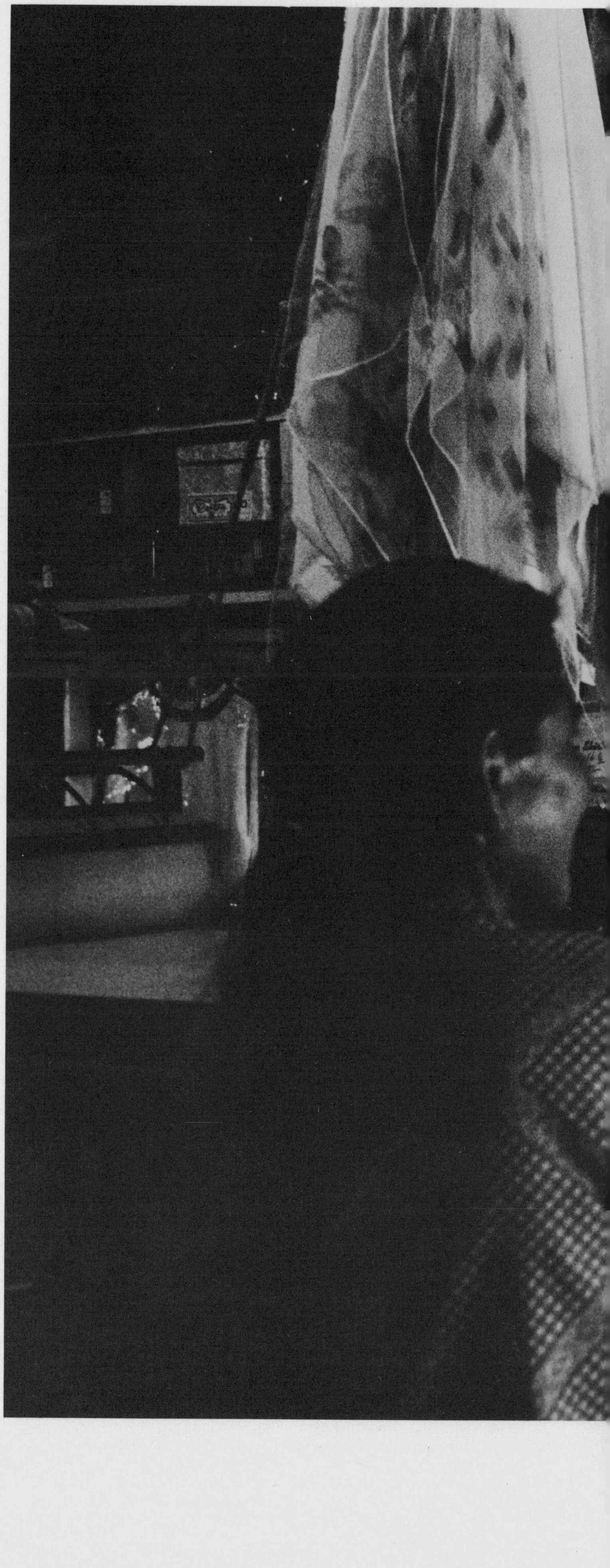

Scene in a contemporary trading post on the Navajo Reservation. Now, as in the early days, traders are often from families generations in their somewhat unusual trade.
(Michal Heron)

somewhat of economic bondage, but under the early conditions of trading (and they lasted well into the twentieth century) posts were often fifty miles or more apart, and the Indians had almost no ready cash (except weavers and smiths, perhaps, or those who lived off the reservation)—for that matter, neither did many of the traders. It wasn't until the late 1950s that a person could drive from east to west across the reservation without leaving a paved road, and it was the late '60s before a minimal network of hardtop roads was built up. The symbiotic relationship between Navajo and trader was one of history and geography as well as economics, and when conditions on the reservation began to change with the times, so did the economic system.

During the good times between 1900 and the 1920s, Navajo jewelry and blankets were becoming known and valued nationally, and the demand for them was growing, but the stock market crash of 1929 and the Depression changed all that.

Although few Navajos knew about it, the outside world shaped much of the economic life on their reservation; as the demand for wool and sheep declined elsewhere, so did prices on the reservation—and so did the inflow of cash. As for such luxuries as jewelry, few whites had the money for them; it is fortunate that there were so few smiths at that time, and that nearly all of these worked only part-time at their trade.

There was a rumor prevalent for years that during the Depression much Navajo silver pawn was melted down and sold as ingots. Yet no one who was active in the business in those days recalls such a practice, and it would seem foolish to do so, since almost any form of worked silver is worth more than the raw metal. What is true, as David Neumann points out, is that silver jewelry during the darkest years of the Depression was being sold for its weight in silver—which is not much different.

A great deal of the truly old pawn disappeared into museums and private collections during the Depression years, and even earlier. The plain silver jewelry of the 1870s and '80s and the early turquoise pieces were being buried with their owners. (Usually at least a part of a Navajo's jewelry is buried with him; what is left must be purified by special sings before it can be worn safely by its inheritors.) The growing preference among Navajos for silver jewelry with more and more turquoise sets was another factor in the disappearance of old-style Navajo jewelry; traders regularly stocked Zuni-made pieces for their Navajo customers. But the most avid customers for the fine old Navajo jewelry during the first few decades of this century were the collectors, private and institutional, who bought the pawn whenever it was available. A lot of it was for sale, especially in the Depression years, for the Indians were forced to pawn or sell it outright in order to buy the necessities of life. As we have noted, not only had the market for Indian jewelry and other crafts shrunk dramatically, but wood and livestock prices had hit bottom, too.

Another factor made life even harsher for the Navajos: they reckoned their wealth in sheep and other livestock, but the tribe had grown astoundingly in numbers (in the 1930s there were 40,000 Navajos, compared to the 6,000 or 8,000 who peopled the reservation in the days just after Fort Sumner). Each Indian had his own flock of sheep and goats, some had herds of cattle, and all owned horses. Although the reservation in that era contained nearly 16 million acres, most of it was marginal in its grazing capabilities, and a long drought was creating an erosion cycle which destroyed large chunks of what land had been available for livestock. To halt overgrazing and restore the rangeland the federal government issued edicts limiting the total amount of livestock that an individual could own. (However, the government also introduced better stock, and the policy was certainly of benefit.) This was the equivalent of telling white Americans that no one could possess, say, in excess of $2,000 in expendable cash, and its effect on the Navajo way of life was enormous, causing a great deal of bitterness against the government, especially as few Navajos were familiar enough with the principles of animal husbandry to understand the philosophy behind the regulations.

The government continually bewildered the Indians (not to mention the whites) by its inconsistencies and reversals of policy. Since their confinement in the nineteenth century to reservations, all American Indians had been considered wards of the government; they did not have the right to vote in state and national elections, they were not allowed to purchase alcoholic beverages, on or off the reservation, even after Prohibition ended. But they could be drafted for military service (thousands of Indian volunteers, as well as draftees, served with great distinction during the First and Second World Wars, and later) and were subject to off-reservation taxation.

The thrust of government thinking since the

Indians' subjugation had been that the Red Man must be turned into a Christian American citizen and the reservations broken up into individual landholdings, which meant that unsophisticated Indians could be cajoled or tricked into selling their bits of land; oil companies, large cattle outfits, and mining interests acquired lease rights to reservation lands all over the country on ridiculously easy terms.

During the Depression years, the Department of the Interior under Harold Ickes and his Commissioner of Indian Affairs John Collier took a number of actions which reversed the long-time trends. The Indian Reorganization Act enabled tribes to incorporate, hold land jointly, and elect tribal councils which would enact and enforce laws governing on-reservation Indians. This effectively halted much of the attrition of tribal lands, and it gave the Indians a new sense of identity and purpose. But along with these innovations, another trend was operative: many who guided federal policy concerning the Indians felt—quite correctly—that much of the original Indian culture was good and should be retained; these officials wanted to stop the process of "Americanizing" (ridiculous term) or modernizing the Indian. Confined to his own sanctuary, the Indian was to retain all of his old cultural traits and not be "corrupted" by contemporary non-Indian influences. This policy, said its critics, tended to turn Indians into living fossils who were to be denied the genuine benefits that they could attain from white society. (It rarely occurred to anyone that under solid legal safeguards and benevolent noninterference the Indian could—as he always had done—decide for himself what he would retain of his own heritage and what he would adopt from the white man.)

The policy of keeping the Indian culture "pure" descended even to the setting of standards for silversmiths and their products. Only "traditional" forms of Indian jewelry could be made; experimenting with new styles and forms and methods of creating jewelry was discouraged—overlooking, of course, the fact that the silversmiths had created their traditional jewelry by borrowing and experimenting in the first place, and that many of its characteristics had been determined solely by the materials and tools available to them.

And of course, all genuine Indian jewelry must be entirely handmade by Indians. This was the rock upon which everything foundered, for no line could be effectively drawn concerning handmade jewelry. Smiths by this time were using acetylene torches to melt and anneal their silver; instead of laboriously hammering an ingot into a flat strip for a bracelet they were buying sterling silver sheets of appropriate gauges from traders; their stones were commercially cut and polished, often by non-Indians far from the reservations; commercially made screws for earrings and safety clasps for pins and brooches were universally used (they might be made of silver, but they were not handmade and certainly not made by Indians). Instead of filing silver smooth and polishing it by hand with sand and soft buckskins, smiths were trimming, smoothing, and buffing their finished silver pieces on grinding wheels, usually hand-cranked but driven by electricity where it was available. Sometimes commercially made sterling silver ring shanks were used; the smith created his own silver mountings and set them with turquoise by hand on the commercial shanks, but this was considered unethical and was halted, if and when it could be spotted. Carried to their extremes, these regulations meant that the smith must spend weeks making a bracelet that—even without otherwise modern aids—would take him a matter of days to create.

In those dreary days of the Depression, it was vital for the smith to produce handmade articles with regularity, if not in volume; and he needed such aids as he could get, so long as the actual jewelry was handmade of genuine silver and turquoise. In the late 1930s, John Adair estimates, the total amount paid to Navajo smiths on the reservation and its fringes for their labor amounted to around $100,000 annually. In 1936, admittedly a very bad year, a survey by the Department of Agriculture on the Navajo reservation and in Gallup reveals that $49,360 was paid to Navajo smiths for their labor and for jewelry sold outright to traders; the same survey shows $288,840 as being paid to Navajo women for their rugs. In those days a good smith—usually working part-time—might clear between $1,000 and $2,000 a year in income. Today, many full-time smiths earn between $20,000 and $30,000 a year, and not a few have incomes of around $100,000 annually.

As for the "cottage" aspect of Indian jewelrymaking, the New Mexico Bureau of Revenue estimated in 1976 that the Indian jewelry business in that state alone was a $750 million-a-year industry.

The railroad had done more than span a continent; it had linked two cultures with bands of silver as well as of steel.

8

NEW WAYS, OLD TRADITIONS

Looking back on Indian handmade jewelry since the early years of the century, a number of trends and changes are apparent. The first is that people everywhere, in Europe as well as in this country, became aware of Indian jewelry, and the better pieces made by master smiths passed from curio status to that of fine art. In steadily increasing numbers museums, private collectors, and tourists began to acquire them. Traders, wholesalers, and smiths themselves developed styles of the traditional jewelry which were specially adapted to the tastes and pocketbooks of Easterners and other buyers. Not only were new methods developed, but some old forms of jewelry died out and were replaced by new ones, also designed to please the non-Indian buyer. Tobacco canteens, powder chargers, and mother-in-law bells ceased being made; in their place appeared such items as silver cigarette boxes set with Zuni inlays or Navajo turquoise, shoe horns, salad forks and spoons, and other types of table service, pillboxes, napkin rings, ashtrays, coasters for drinks, silver hip flasks (during Prohibition), and money clips. Silver and turquoise trimmings were applied to women's ornamental hair combs, and special conical holders were made for ponytail hairdos. After World War II, when fliptop windproof cigarette lighters came into heavy vogue, smiths soldered silver plates to the commercially made products and set them with turquoise or overlay work. Another continually popular creation is the bracelet-watchband. One innovation which the Navajos developed primarily for their own use was the silver hatband, a strip of silver which was substituted for the grosgrain silk band on a Stetson hat. The silver band was adjustable in size, and the joint at the side frequently sported a turquoise setting. The bands were particularly suitable for Navajo use up to the '30s and '40s since the older men traditionally wore black Stetsons with the brims left absolutely flat and set perfectly straight on the head, the back of the brim resting securely on the bun of hair which the Indian wore on the nape of his neck, tied with string or yarn. In fact, in those days Navajos who adhered to the traditional customs and modes of their people were referred to as Long Hairs; young veterans returning from World War II largely preferred the GI or crew cut they were forced to adopt by the military. (It is not true, by the way, that Indians have no whiskers. Many Navajos sported mustaches—quite Oriental in appearance, even in the late nineteenth century; and facial hair, although sparse, led to the creation by Indian smiths in very early times of silver tweezers so that a man could keep his cheeks and chin smooth.)

Yet another Navajo invention—this one comparatively old—are the silver collarpoints which decorated the blouses of Navajo women when they were wearing the "traditional" Navajo dresses with long skirts, collars, and long sleeves, the blouses almost always made from velveteen. These dresses were, of course, not Navajo in origin but copied from Victorian fashions in the late 1800s. Use of these collarpoints continued

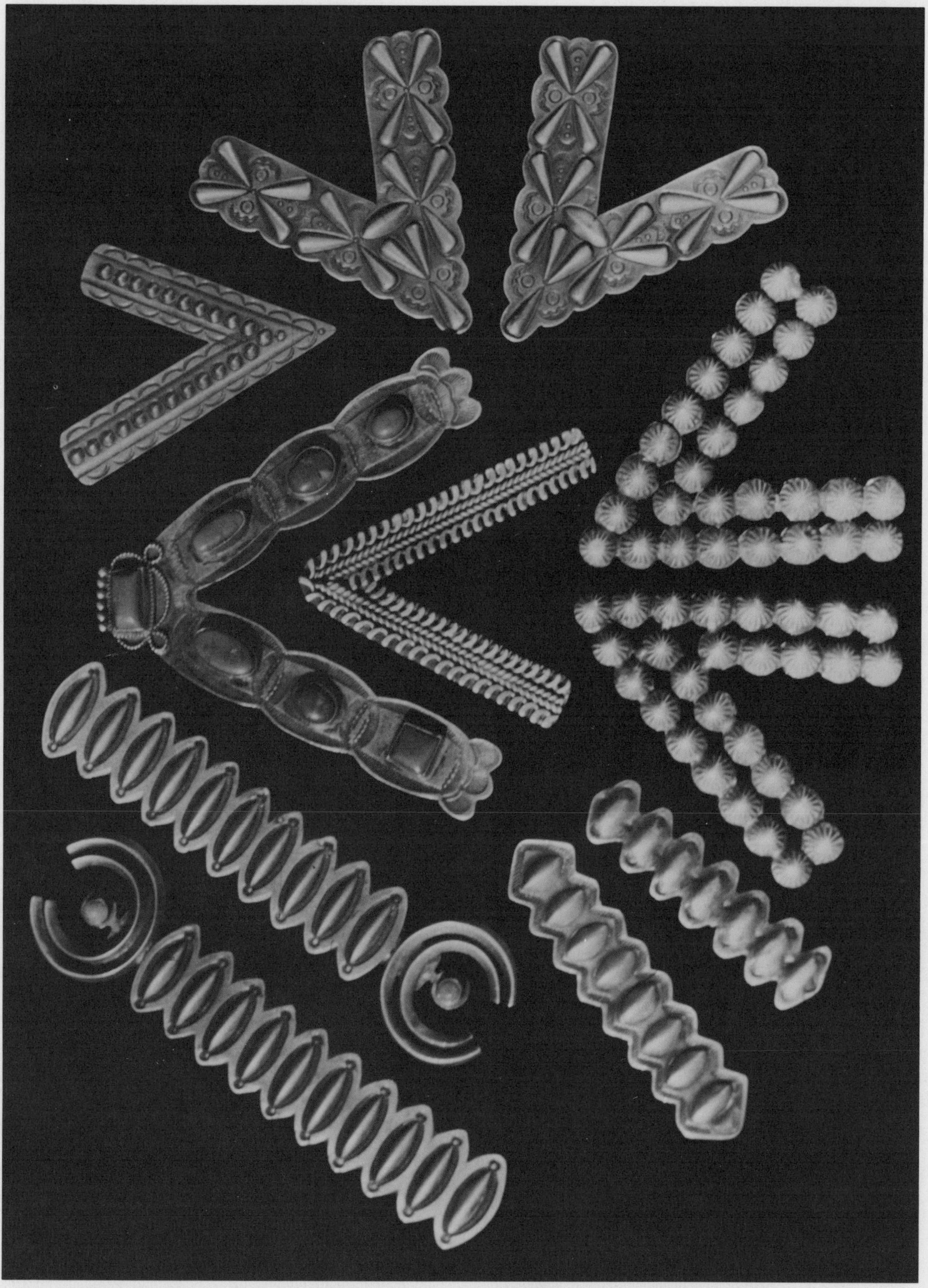

A variety of Navajo collar points, c. 1920s-1930s. *(RT, Richard Polson)*

Contemporary silver serving pieces set with turquoise, made by Kenneth Begay. One of many twentieth-century Anglo-influenced innovations in Indian silver.

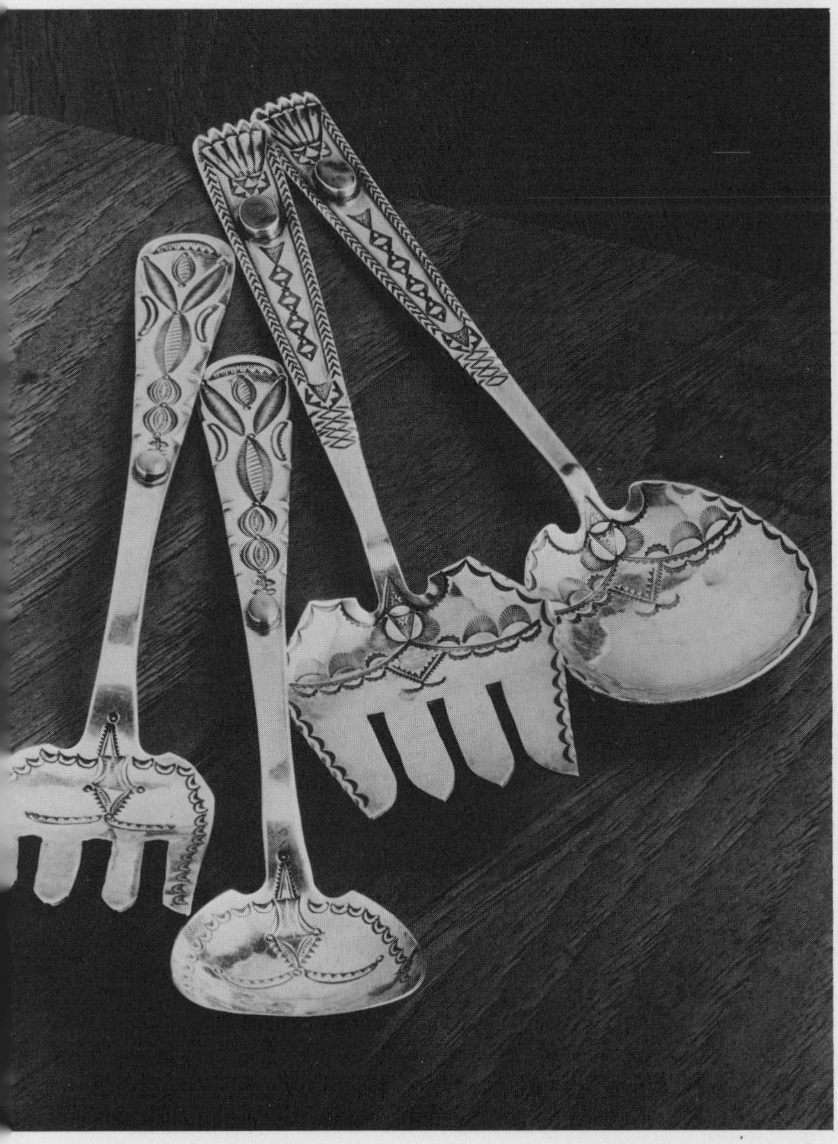

until well after World War II when modern women's fashions replaced the old styles; but they are still seen on ceremonial or state occasions when "typical" Navajo dress is called for.

We have noted that as better tools and more diversified materials became available to smiths, Navajos and Zunis developed their own tribal styles and preferences. Although each copied from the other to the point that one must speak in generalizations—with all their attendant risks—it is still true that the Zunis became increasingly known for their lapidary skills, while the Navajos generally were considered masters of the silversmith's art.

It is tempting to say that turquoise is more valued by the Zunis than it is among the Navajos, but that would not be true; it is simply that these Pueblo neighbors of the Navajos are more unrestrained in its use, to the point of abandon. Not only are they adept in cutting and setting delicate mosaics and clusters of the Sky Stone, but also wear it unmounted in necklaces of great natural chunks which are polished but only slightly shaped from their natural form; they are strung together in such a manner that they resemble Hawaiian leis. Zunis also make turquoise chokers and necklaces of graduated disc beads, as well as shell and coral neck ornaments. When they mount them in silver, Zunis cut their stones into flat forms which are separated with light silver ferrules, and the overall effect is not unlike cloisonné. Through the years the Knife Wing Bird, Dragon Fly, and Rainbow Man designs have become so common as to be synonymous with Zuni in the minds of many. These designs are made in the form of rings, earrings, or pins or are mounted on silver cigarette boxes. (The boxes often are made by Navajo smiths.) Mother-of-pearl, tortoiseshell, abalone, and jet also are used by Zuni lapidaries, and in recent years their inlay work has departed from traditional Indian designs to portrayal in natural form of birds, plants, and landscapes. Although it is meticulously done, it often lacks the "Indian" feeling of more traditional styles. Recently, plain silver belt buckles, adorned only with the inlay portraits, have become very popular. We have noted that Zunis often cut and polish the stones that are then turned over to Navajo smiths for setting; wholesale jewelry establishments—and some of the larger retail operations—employ artisans of both tribes who work on a sort of assembly-line basis in producing handmade jewelry.

One form that has typically been a cooperative intertribal venture is the so-called *channelwork*. This is really a heavier form of inlay, and Navajo

Cochiti woman wearing massive turquoise "tab" necklace (probably made by a Zuni) and a variety of other jewelry. *(Museum of New Mexico, T. Harmon Parkhurst)*

Navajo-made silver tweezers hang from the bottom of this Apache necklace of glass beads with brass brooch. *(MAI, HF)*

Zuni "sun face" bracelet inlaid in shell, spiny oyster, jet, and turquoise, and decorated with "raindrops." C. 1940s, purchased from a pawn basket in Gallup. *(HC, Al Abrams)*

smiths usually make the silverframes (most often for bracelets and large rings), whose central portions are laid out in rows of rectangles formed by silver rules set in with unflawed precision. The rectangles thus formed are filled in by Zuni lapidaries who cut each flat piece of turquoise to a near-perfect fit. The results, to say the least, are striking.

There is some divergence of opinion as to the difference between channelwork and inlay, since both forms use silver strips to divide, or contain, the design elements. Most people in the trade define channelwork as straight-line sectioning, while inlay can be curvilinear. Mosaic, of course, is like inlay but the different stones are not divided by silver rules.

Since World War II the use of coral in Indian jewelry has been encouraged, partly to offset the use of turquoise. Coral is not a natural American Indian adornment, unlike mother-of-pearl and other forms of shell, both fresh and saltwater, as well as jet, obsidian, mica, and other minerals and substances native to America. However, coral has been used in Indian jewelry, and though not traditional, it can at least be said that its use is common ever since traders first made it available to the smiths.

Coral came into relatively common usage during the 1930s, when traders and wholesalers such as David Neumann bought it in wholesale lots and made it available to Zuni lapidaries.

Turquoise and coral combinations are superb in the hands of a master craftsman (they have been used for centuries in the Far East). Coral is used in inlay work and strung in sections as necklaces, often interspersed with turquoise or jet beads. The red undercoating of abalone shell is sometimes mistaken for coral, and Neumann told me he once heard a clerk in a Phoenix department store tell a prospective customer that coral was "red turquoise."

In recent years precious coral itself, which comes from the Mediterranean waters off Sardinia, is becoming increasingly in short supply and thus more expensive.

Since the first decade of the century, Indian jewelry was being sought after by enough people that it was being machine-made by commercial jewelry companies which catered to the tourist-curio trade rather than to collectors or buyers of quality pieces. Concha belts, rings, bracelets, and necklaces were machine-stamped out of metal which often contained no silver at all and sometimes set with artificial turquoise which was so obviously fraudulent that only the most indifferent or ignorant buyer could fail to detect it. It was junk, and it looked it; but it was priced just enough below Indian handmade silver and turquoise jewelry that it took a good slice out of the bottom of the market. It was sold, and still is, in "trading posts" along the major transcontinental highways. Often it was labeled "Handmade by Indians," a claim which was substantiated by the hiring of Indians—or professed Indians—to operate the machinery which stamped out the junk. This same merchandise is sold today in the major cities and tourist traps around the Southwest, but other methods of creating spurious Indian jewelry—often using sterling silver and masterfully stabilized turquoise—have been developed to trap even the more cautious.

Imitation Indian jewelry of the 1920s and 1930s sometimes was made of genuine silver and turquoise. It could be produced more cheaply than hand-made jewelry because it was stamped out on die presses, often operated by hand and, of course, described as hand-made.

Cheaper imitations of earlier years, as well as today, are made of nickel and lack the luster of real silver. The designs are so contrived that a quick glance usually is enough to reveal them as imitations—and if that isn't enough the "turquoise" is plastic, or ground turquoise "reconstituted" with adhesive; it has a gluey dullness totally lacking the qualities of genuine turquoise.

Another form of imitation Indian jewelry popular in the 1930s was machine-stamped copper or copper-plated jewelry. Since Indian smiths did not work in copper there is little question of imitation here, except that tourists did not always realize this.

Efforts to make convincing fakes in the 1920s and 1930s did not achieve the near-perfection they have in the 1970s, perhaps because the Depression killed the market for Indian jewelry, and the need to imitate it.

Three very fine contemporary Zuni channel inlay bracelets. The bracelet at right is in triangle channelwork of coral and high-quality old Bisbee turquoise, c. 1960s. The ladies' bracelet lower left is "random channel" inlay in Morenci turquoise, c. 1970s. At top left is a raised rectangular inlay man's watch bracelet, with high-grade old Bisbee turquoise, c. 1960s. *(DNHC, Peter L. Bloomer)*

9
THE AWAKENING

World War II had a potent effect on the history of Indian jewelrymaking. Smiths who had scarcely ever been off their reservations suddenly found themselves in the great art centers of this country and of Europe and Asia; when they returned to their homeland they had seen too much to be entirely content with the traditional styles of jewelry, and while they kept the flavor they used new forms and new techniques. This came about partly through the use of new ideas and partly by employing tools and techniques which had not been available to earlier smiths. The marvelous inventiveness of the Indian craftsman was given free rein. Silver and turquoise were still the basic components of their jewelry, but beyond that all barriers were smashed; the limitations of the silversmith's talent and genius were his only fetters.

The most interesting aspect of this new experimentation by Indian smiths is that somehow a feeling of Indian-ness has been retained, but analysis of the components in a modern piece of Indian jewelry shows them to be remarkably liberated from traditional forms and styles. (Oddly enough, it is often the non-Indian smith, working by hand with genuine materials, who continues the old-fashioned Indian styles.)

And no longer are the smiths anonymous: Names like Loloma, Monongye, Golsh, Begay, and Yazzie command high prices for superb workmanship and a sense of artistry that may be expressed through Indian hands but is universal in its message—a message which begins with tradition and ends with creative art.

All of this is part of that same quest which led the great Hopi smiths to a style which has now become "traditional" Hopi—the overlay technique.

For many years Hopi silversmiths were content to copy the work of their Navajo neighbors, but in 1938 the Museum of Northern Arizona in Flagstaff began a program to develop a distinctive Hopi style of jewelry, which eventually was to become known as *overlay work*. This style was developed by two Hopis, Paul Saufkie and Fred Kabotie. World War II interrupted the development of this technique, but returning veterans who studied silversmithing

(Jerry Jacka)

Hopi silver overlay jewelry by Bernard Dawahoya. *(Jerry Jacka)*

under the GI Bill and in training with the Hopi guild brought about its revival. By the 1950s it had caught on well; its clean and simple styling made it a fine accessory to modern fashions. Since that time it has evolved into a superb art form—one, moreover, that has been copied by non-Hopi silversmiths.

In overlay, two identically shaped pieces are cut from sheet silver. The bottom piece remains otherwise unaltered, but in the top piece—the overlay—designs are cut with jeweler's saws; the two pieces are then joined, usually so skillfully that the weld cannot be detected. The finished piece is then blackened with liver of sulphur and then buffed and polished so that only the exposed surface of the lower piece of silver remains dark. Sometimes a bit of turquoise is set in the larger plain areas of silver.

The Hopi overlay technique is symbolic of what has happened to all Indian jewelry in recent years. In the first place, the tools and equipment of the old smiths, such as described in Matthews and Adair, have largely vanished—except when they are deliberately used to simulate the early traditional styles. No longer is silver melted in crude forges and hammered on makeshift anvils. Torches, fired by an assortment of gasses and chemicals, are used to melt or anneal metal; machine-driven wheels, saws and gravers shape and polish it. Turquoise stones are almost always cut by commercial lapidaries (except among specialists like the Zunis or Santo Domingo Pueblos).

Free-form or nugget-cut stones have led to free-form jewelry; what the best-known Indian smiths are liable to make today is classifiable as "Indian" only because of the ancestry of its smith, not by what the finished jewelry looks like.

Even working only with turquoise or shell, such as heishi, Indians have adopted modern equipment, power-driven usually, to help them in manufacturing. They have to do this; economically they cannot compete if they retain the laborious, fully handmade methods of their ancestors.

The Santo Domingans of prehistoric times were known for their *heishi* or *hishi* work—the manufacture of strings of discoidal beads made of shell; Indians of this pueblo also are known for their attempts to improve low-grade turquoise by treating it with animal fat or plastic substances. The Santo Domingans are known as the horse traders of Southwestern Indians, but there are now some excellent silversmiths at Santo Domingo, and interesting techniques used in the mass production of handmade jewelry have been developed in this pueblo.

But because it is prehistoric in origin (and so "classic" as adornment), heishi has come to be appreciated in recent years as it was not during the dark years of the Depression. This is a form of jewelry which has no borrowing from European

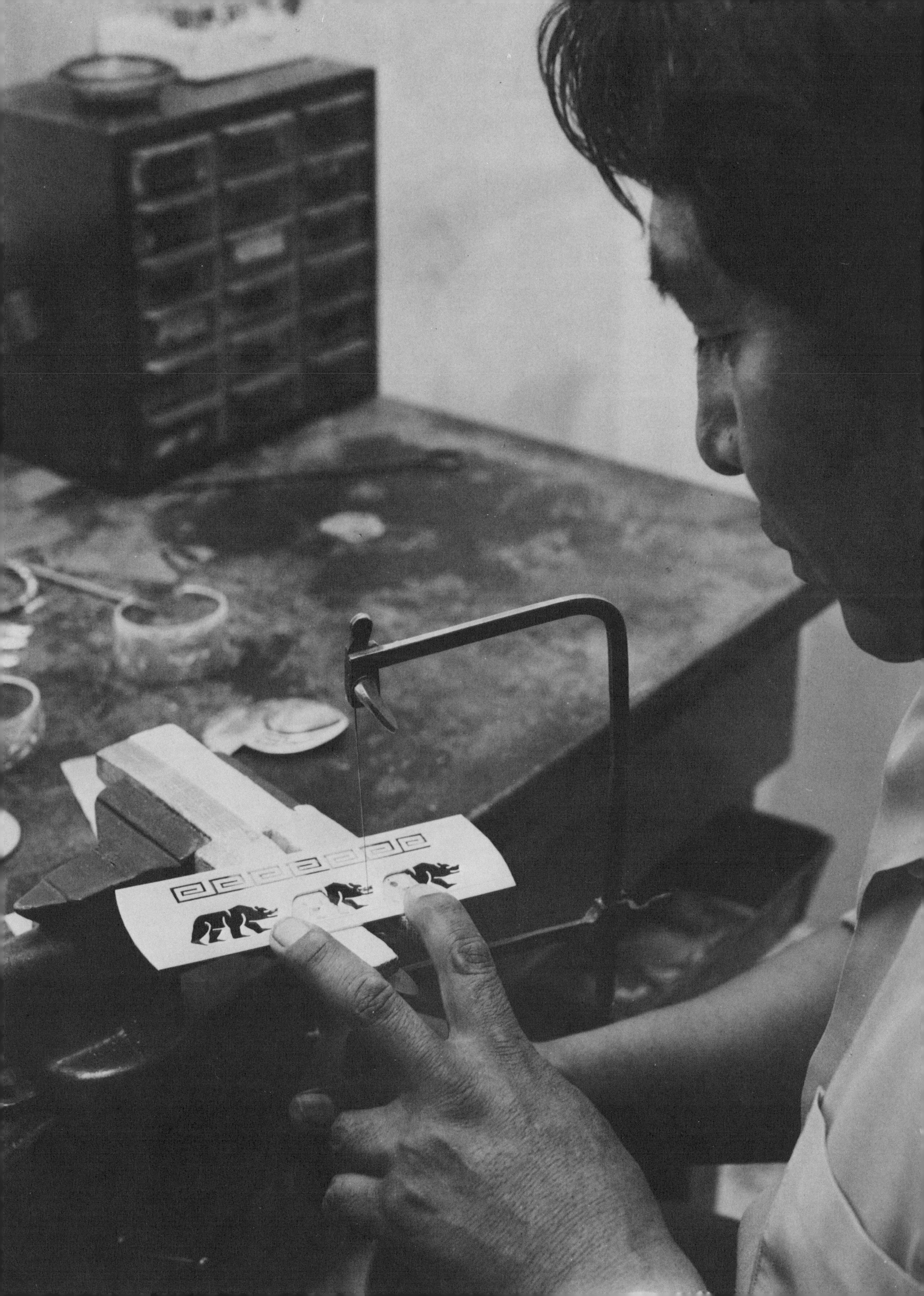

cultures; it was in use when the first Spanish came to the Southwest. It is interesting that such an age-old style has adapted so well to modern usage.

The 1950s and '60s saw a steady upswing of interest in Indian jewelry, not only in the Southwest but among discriminating visitors who liked what they saw on their trips to Santa Fe, Albuquerque, Gallup, Scottsdale, Phoenix, and Tucson. The jewelry was handsome, it was handcrafted, it went well with contemporary fashions, and it was made of precious metal and semiprecious stones. From any point of view it was, and still is, an excellent buy. Hundreds of people (mainly, but not always, from the Southwest), many of them possessing social and cultural credentials which placed their taste in fashion and art beyond reproach, had been collecting this jewelry for decades. It was a native American art form, it had the flavor of the Southwest—which was luring thousands every year as visitors or new settlers—and the genuine pieces of Indian handmade jewelry were far more valuable than the best machine-made costume jewelry turned out elsewhere.

Indian smiths, responding to the times, were departing from the traditional tribal forms and making jewelry that was perfectly compatible with any mode of high fashion and was to achieve social prestige for originality, good taste, and inventiveness. As the use of Indian jewelry grew, so did the appreciation of it; in fact, it has continued to grow over the years, not only among over-thirty adults but with the younger generation. These people like the jewelry not only for its esthetic value but because it was created by members of a race envisioned by younger whites as a pristine, exploited minority, a counterculture, as it were, whose concern for the environment and self-identification with nature were considered a refutation of the crass materialism of the "WASP" mainstream.

Many Indians—and traders as well—view such highly romanticized idealism about the native Americans as naive and amusing—and sometimes as infuriating as the old white-Christian-supremacy concepts of earlier generations. Indians, particularly those whose cultures are still viable and flourishing, refer to such non-Indian youngsters generically, and derisively, as "hippies," and their well-meant and usually sincere efforts to identify with, and partake in, Indian life on the reservations are often resented as patronizing and ill-mannered.

Many of the great Indian religious ceremonies have been closed, at least temporarily, to non-Indian visitors, largely because of the incredibly bad manners that some of them have displayed. A sign at the approach to the Hopi village of Old Oraibi declares the pueblo off-limits to whites without written permission from the village leaders; one of the reasons given is that "you do not respect tribal customs, including your own."

Ironically, while many whites go to great lengths to identify themselves with Indian culture, younger Indians in particular are avid to adopt the amenities and fashions of "Anglo" civilization which they see in visits outside the reservation or on television or read about in newspapers and magazines.

Lawrence Saufkie using a jeweler's saw to cut the design into the top piece, the "overlay," of a piece of overlay jewelry. *(Ray Manley)*

10

THE BOUNTIFUL SKY

Inflation and national publicity during the 1970s gave the craft we have been discussing a financial boost that carried it beyond the wildest dreams of those who watched it develop over the decades. It has been widely reported, in print and by word of mouth, that in 1972 the highly respected *Wall Street Journal* published an article which stated that next to land—other versions had it gold and diamonds—silver and turquoise Indian jewelry was the best financial investment an individual could make. In essence, the *Journal* article pointed out that genuine handmade Indian jewelry was a hard commodity made of precious metal and, like gold and diamonds, was a tangible asset not subject to the wild fluctuations of paper securities in times of economic insecurity. The superb craftsmanship of the better-made pieces further enhanced the value of the natural materials used, the article stated, and, all in all, investment in silver and turquoise Indian jewelry was an excellent hedge against inflation.

By now this endorsement from the *Journal* has been accepted as gospel. The only trouble is that the *Journal* never published such a story. In a letter to the Indian Arts and Crafts Association, published in its February 17, 1976, *Bulletin*, the *Journal*'s editors made an official disclaimer; but like the World War I rumor of Russian troops landing in England on their way to the Western Front, the *Journal*'s story has been so widely accepted that numerous otherwise reliable sources have referred to this article, with the ironic result that, even though it never was written, it has been worth literally millions to the Indian jewelry business.

(The *Journal has* published articles noting the expansion of the Indian jewelry business and pointing out the appearance on the market of a significant number of fakes and of Indian jewelry well made with genuine materials, but by non-Indians and not always properly identified.)

The original (nonexistent) article played no small role in the current craze for Indian jewelry which has benefitted Indian craftsmen and dealers alike and created new risks and problems for an industry that was not prepared for anything other than the leisurely, informal pace it traditionally has followed.

There is another rumor, almost as prevalent as the one involving the *Wall Street Journal*, which has it that turquoise, always classified as a semiprecious gemstone, has now been "reclassified" as a precious gem. Just how that would be done, or by whom, is hard to say, but the writer has heard this "fact" stated from New York to California. It is simply not true; there is no basis in fact for this report, which can easily be scotched by the following comparison:

According to a representative of a national retail diamond-selling chain, in early 1976 a 1-carat round-cut diamond sold for from $800 to several thousand dollars, depending upon its quality. At the same time, according to a Santa Fe dealer in Indian goods, a 1-carat cabochon-cut turquoise could be had for as low as $1, ranging to $25 for the finest spiderweb-matrix top-quality stones. According to a Scottsdale dealer, 1 pound of top-grade turquoise sells for $400. Obviously, there is a vast economic gap between turquoise and diamonds, and the Sky Stone—no matter how beguiling its qualities—has a long way to go before it becomes a precious gemstone.

However interesting rumors may be, the truth is astonishing enough. By the mid-1970s fashionable stores in every major American city were selling Indian jewelry; the great department store chains, whose clientele included customers in every economic range, ordered from Southwestern wholesalers in huge lots. Individuals in every part of the country—some of whom had never knowingly seen an Indian—bought Indian jewelry, and many who had dabbled in collecting such pieces over the years decided to combine pleasure with business and become dealers themselves. In the Southwest, banks found that they were considering more and more requests for loans from customers who put up the only collateral they had—their homes, cars, and other personal property—so that they could open Indian goods shops.

Under such stimuli, it was natural that prices would rise enormously; in addition, this trend was exaggerated by heavy nationwide inflation resulting in rising prices asked by silversmiths, either in wages or in craftsmen's prices to dealers; rising overhead in stocking, displaying, protecting, and selling the goods; and, certainly not least, huge increases in the raw materials that go into the making of Indian jewelry. Raw turquoise has risen enormously in value, and since there are not enough mines in the United States to supply the demand for top-quality turquoise large quantities are now imported from Persia.

Silver, like gold, has risen steadily over the years on the international markets. David Neumann observed that during the Depression of the 1930s it sold for as low as 28¢ per ounce; in the mid-1970s it was commanding about $1.25 per ounce. Many dealers are now quoting economists who predict it will reach $6 or even $8 per ounce by the 1980s. If this should happen, even inferior Indian jewelry will be worth its original price, or more, in the value of the silver it contains alone, not to mention its esthetic or historical value, or the worth of the turquoise it is adorned with.

No one knows for certain the total value of all Indian silver and turquoise jewelry sold annually in the United States during the mid-1970s. A 1975 United Press International dispatch out of Los Angeles quotes Mr. Jack A. Levin, described as a chief executive officer of Pueblo Traders, as saying that "authentic handcrafted American Indian jewelry is a $150 million annual business"; but this is surely but a minor part of the actual sales of genuine silver and turquoise Indian jewelry. Taking the process as a whole, from the cutting and polishing of raw turquoise and the wholesale supplying of raw silver, the preparation of various components and the wholesaling and retailing of all types of handmade or semihandmade jewelry, the figure would approach $500 million; add to this the dealers in junk and imitation jewelry and one can come up with a conservative figure close to $1 billion. But no one can be absolutely sure, for there is no clearinghouse through which such figures flow. It is estimated that in 1975 $1 million worth of Indian jewelry a week was going out of Gallup alone. The Navajo Arts and Crafts Enterprise estimated its annual sales for that year at $6 million. It was estimated that $750 million worth of business was done in New Mexico alone in 1975. With this in mind, the billion-dollar figure is far too conservative.

Small wonder that so great an expansion has brought with it a vastly increased number of pitfalls: more cheap junk jewelry, a great number of expensive fakes, genuine silver and turquoise jewelry made by non-Indians (but not necessarily sold as such), the appearance of a great many new dealers who do not know the business well—and an overexposure of Indian jewelry in many areas. But as Tobe Turpen, Jr., says, most of these are problems oldtime smiths and dealers have had to live with for decades.

There is a general feeling throughout the trade that it will have to level off somewhere, perhaps even decline in certain areas; but again the feeling is that the market for genuine handmade Indian jewelry will remain secure. It is the marginal areas that would suffer from any decline—including the fakers, the imitators, and the makers of and dealers in poorly crafted jewelry, even if it is made by Indians from genuine materials.

In earlier days, many traders and dealers policed their own industry by simply refusing to buy from smiths any goods that were sloppily made. But when demand is high, there is a market for any Indian jewelry, and the smiths know this, as do a number of wholesalers and retailers who are not concerned with the quality of the products they sell. As one dealer said, if a smith comes in with a poorly made piece of jewelry, he cannot be told to take it back and rework it until it is salable in a custom shop, and the dealer cannot offer him a reduced price for it; the Indian will tell the trader that if he doesn't want it, there are plenty of others who will take it as is, at the smith's price—and he is right.

Does all of this mean that the Indian jewelry market will collapse and that the buyer should wait a few years until he can pick up Indian jewelry at a fraction of its cost today?

The answer is no—not if he is talking about quality handmade jewelry made by Indian smiths using genuine materials. The inflationary trend has been with us since World War II and shows no signs of disappearing. The most optimistic economists are hoping only that it will slow down or—most desirable and most unlikely—that it will level off. No one expects prices to drop drastically; if they do, our whole economy will be in serious trouble, not just the Indian jewelry business.

Many American families are legally homeless today because they held off buying houses in the early 1970s in the belief that prices and interest rates would surely decline. They haven't, and homebuilding has been in a slump. What's worse, the prediction is that when it resumes at full volume, individual homes will be too expensive to build; apartments, town houses, and condominiums will replace the single-family unit—which will be more expensive than ever. A similar argument can be made for quality Indian goods.

There are, generally speaking, three broad markets in Indian jewelry today: the so-called junk trade whose products are so patently fake that they fool no one; the middle area—which is the largest—where decently made Indian jewelry is offered for sale, along with the majority of fakes, of which the dealer may or may not be aware; and the custom shops which deal mostly in expensive, genuine pieces made by established smiths. (But generalizations are very risky here: this is not to say that the most scrupulous dealers do not sell relatively inexpensive items of genuine Indian jewelry; conversely, the makers of spurious jewelry have long since learned that a high pricetag helps to sell the fake.)

The makers of imitation or—God help us—"Genuine Simulated Indian Jewelry" will always have a market. Hundreds of thousands of people visit the Southwest each year, and thousands of these tourists want to buy at least one piece of Indian-style jewelry for themselves or for friends or relatives back home. They do not wish to spend more than a few dollars per item, they get exactly what they pay for, and they really do not care a whit about the fine points of Indian jewelry. Many dealers in handmade Indian goods are infuriated by the makers and sellers of pot-metal synthetic turquoise fakes, but others take a more philosophical view.

"What the hell," said one dealer whose name is famous in the quality Indian goods trade. "Out of every hundred people who buy junk like that, at least one becomes interested in genuine jewelry and may eventually come to me. The rest of them I'd never see anyway."

It is not the blatant frauds which are the greatest threat to the market in handmade Indian jewelry, it is expert copiers and imitators who have moved in on the boom in Indian jewelry. Their products are so well made—utilizing genuine materials and sophisticated automated processes (as well as hand work)—that even the experts can be fooled. They go for the quality trade, and they keep honest merchants awake nights. The best of these imitations are made by centrifugal casting processes, which are variations on the lost-wax or *cire perdu* technique, except that machines do all the work. By this method a mold is made of a piece of handmade jewelry, and the mold is then placed on a machine, filled with molten silver and spun so that the liquid metal fills every line and every bend of the mold. As mentioned by so many traders and dealers, it is often difficult if not impossible to detect centrifugally cast jewelry when examining only a single item; it is only in the repetition of flaws or unusual markings that such a product can be detected and identified for what it is. Add stabilized turquoise to centrifugally cast silver and you have a completely synthetic piece of jewelry which often is as attractive as a genuine handmade item. When jewelry is being sold in wholesale lots of hundreds of items at a time it is easy for these to slip through. Every dealer and authority expresses concern over these fakes, and most of them are far more apprehensive over their effect on the market than they are about the effects of the national economy on their business.

Another group helping to cloud the picture are the non-Indian smiths. They often make their jewelry by hand, they use genuine silver and turquoise, and they work in the traditional Indian styles. Their work can be very good—excellent, in fact—and even if they are honest, once the finished piece leaves their shops no one will be the wiser.

The non-Indian smith creates things of beauty the equal of his Indian counterpart, using the same materials; and assuming that no misrepresentations are made, there is no moral or legal reason to exclude the products of the non-Indian smith from the marketplace, or from an assessment of esthetic worth. And again the question is raised of whether "Indian" jewelry can be made by a non-Indian, whether the collector or buyer will accept (if he is told about it) such jewelry for his personal collection.

Another outgrowth of the immense popularity of Indian jewelry today has been the appearance of Indian silversmiths who are neither Navajo nor Pueblo, although they are full-blooded Indians. There also are smiths who are only partly Indian. They create in all styles, from traditional to contemporary, and many of them are among the best of the younger silversmiths. Plains Indian

Two Navajo squash-blossom necklaces showing two of the many designs "plain" silver squash-blossom necklaces can take. The fleur-de-lis blossoms of the upper one and the hands on the naja of the lower one are just two of the many variations that exist. Note that the beads of the lower necklace are made from dimes. *(DNHC, Peter L. Bloomer)*

Navajo style squash-blossom necklace set with two turquoise rounds on the cast naja. *(PC, Marcia Keegan)*

Above: **Brass cross necklace probably from the pueblo of Isleta or Santo Domingo. The double cross with the heart has also been identified as a dragonfly. The red beads are glass Venetian trade beads c. 1870s.** *(HMC, Al Abrams)*
Right: **Early coin silver squash-blossom necklace made in the 1880s.** *(AG, Al Abrams)*

Right: Many '20s and '30s squash-blossom necklaces were combinations of two or more earlier necklaces. This one had coin silver beads and a few squash-blossom beads strung with a multistone naja and crosses set with turquoise. *(HMC, Al Abrams)*

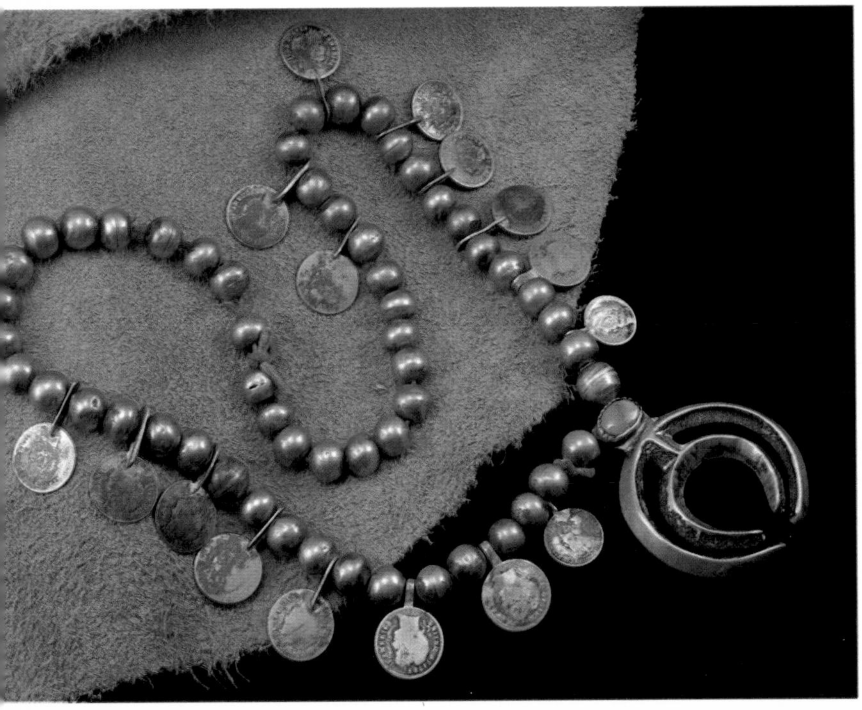

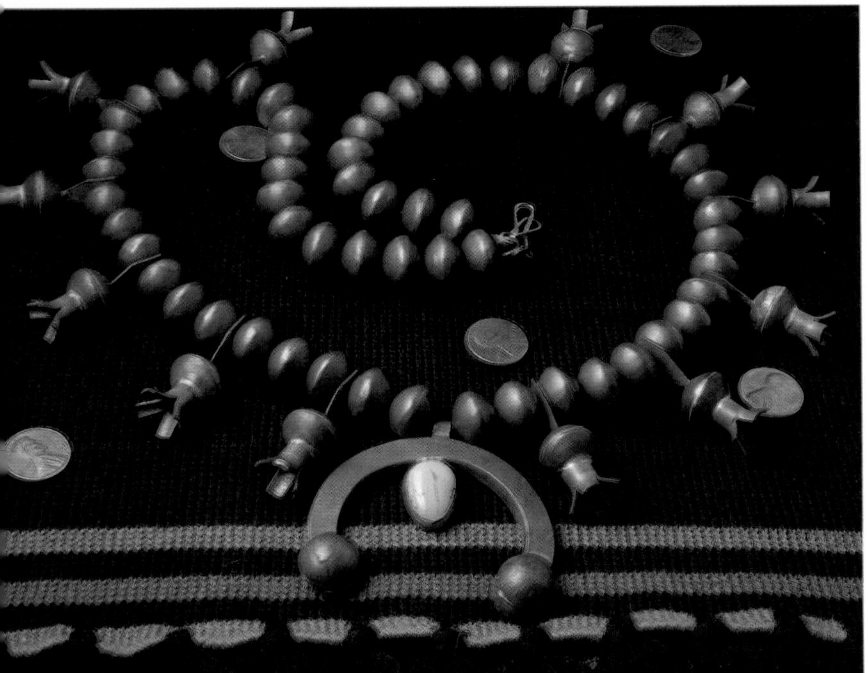

Top: Most necklaces made with coins were not made until the 1940s or later. This necklace was made about 1910 and is strung with both dimes and pesos. It is strung on rawhide and oiled cloth, not unusual for that time period. *(HMC, Al Abrams)*

Bottom: Squash-blossom necklace with beads made from pennies. This style was popular in the Gallup area in the 1940s and 1950s and many feel it was instigated by what Anglo traders thought older Indian jewelry should look like. *(HC, Al Abrams)*

Right: Squash-blossom necklace with beads made of quarters. This style was also popular in the Gallup area in the 1940s and 1950s. *(HC, Al Abrams)*

A Navajo child's necklace, c. 1920s. Indian children were given jewelry when they were toddlers, and in the case of necklaces, beads were added as they grew older. Most of them were on string or ribbon so they could be tied securely around the neck. *(HMC, Al Abrams)*

Navajo squash-blossom necklace with a Blue Gem turquoise mosaic pendant. C. 1950s. *(HMC, Al Abrams)*

Silver necklace set with claws from a small brown bear. *(HC, Al Abrams)*

Silver squash-blossom necklace with double squash-blossoms and a swedged naja. Note the small najas on the bottom beads. *(MRMM, Al Abrams)*

Choker necklace and bib► necklace made of restrung turquoise jaclahs and strands purchased to match. Many of the strands were gifts of Indian bead makers to the owners over the years. The necklace is draped over a Tulare basket from California. *(BTC, Peter L. Bloomer)*

Top left: **Contemporary turquoise and white shell heishi made and strung by Tony Aguilar of Santo Domingo.** *(BC, Markow Photo)*

Bottom left: **Turquoise and coral beads strung with large flat turquoise stones backed and bezeled with silver.** *(MRMM, Al Abrams)*

Top right: **Single strand of untreated high-quality Kingman turquoise nuggets. This style of nugget necklace has become popular since the late 1960s.** *(Jewel Box Collection, Markow Photo)*

Bottom right: **Turquoise and brass beads strung by Tony Aguilar.** *(BC, Markow Photo)*

Above: **Coral necklace with a Mexican silver cross and religious medals, pre-1900. Pieces such as this cross were traded into the Southwest and avidly sought by Indians who had been converted to Roman Catholicism.** *(MRMM, Al Abrams)*
Below: **White shell heishi strung with tab-shaped pieces of turquoise and shell. Pre-1900.** *(HC, Al Abrams)*

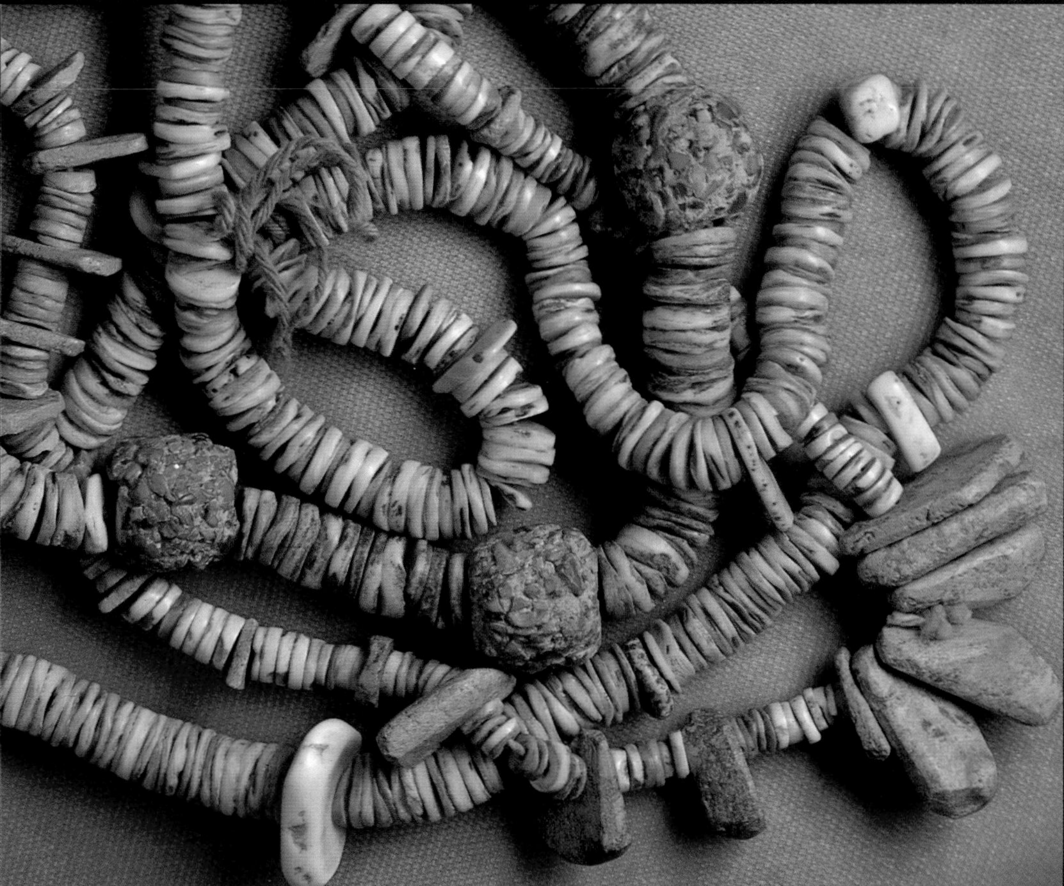

Right: **This tab style necklace contains 4½ pounds of mostly Cerrillos turquoise. The stones for this necklace were gathered over two generations by one Zuni family. Necklaces of this size are rare because they were usually broken into smaller necklaces.** *(MRMM, David Meunch)*

Below: **Navajo man wearing an old-style turquoise and shell necklace and old tab style earrings.** *(Michal Heron)*

This Zuni inlay figure, "The Old Bead Driller, Zuni Joe," in coral, turquoise, tortoise, mother-of-pearl, and jet is shown with a pump drill set with a nail tip. The figure was made by Teddie Weahkee and collected by C.G. Wallace in 1931. *(HMC)*

Left: Morenci turquoise jaclahs with white shell "corn kernels." *(HMC, Al Abrams)*
Below: Santo Domingo mosaic necklace of jet, turquoise, and shell mounted on shell tabs and strung on clamshell heishi. *(MRMM, Al Abrams)*

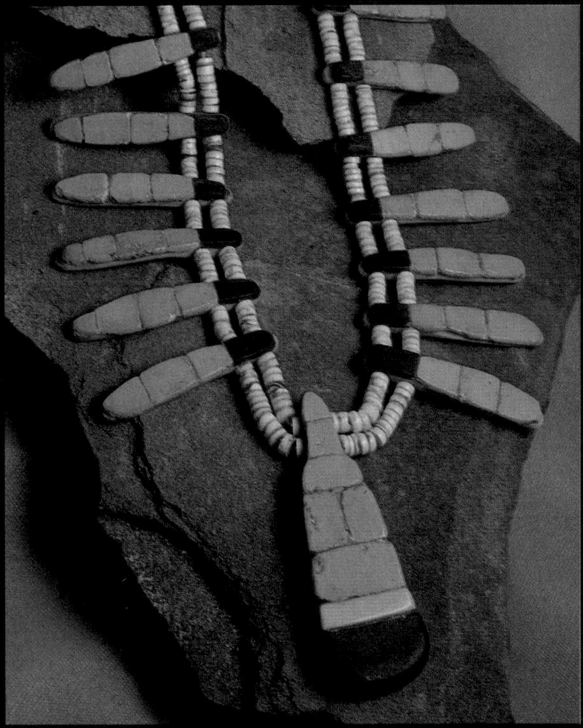

Above: Tab style turquoise nugget necklace strung on white shell heishi. Pre-1900. *(HC, Al Abrams)*
Left: Polished chrysocolla nuggets and silver beads strung together in a bib style necklace and matching earrings. *(BC, Markow Photo)*

Above left: **A selection of Navajo and Pueblo style necklaces shown as they might be stored between use in an Indian home.** *(PC, Al Abrams)*
Below left: **A Navajo woman wearing a coral and turquoise necklace and a Zuni cluster pin, two jewelry pieces that are frequently worn together.** *(Michal Heron)*
Above right: **A selection of nuggets and heishi of coral, turquoise, white clam, silver, and pipestone. The pipestone necklace in the foreground is made with a material which is more commonly associated with northern Plains Indians but has become popular with Southwestern Indians.** *(PC, Ray Manley)*
Below right: **Heishi of various materials, mostly from Santo Domingo. Note especially the fine light coral necklace at lower left, and the last three necklaces at right: liquid silver, prehistoric Mimbres steatite heishi, and very fine white olivella shell.** *(BTC, Peter L. Bloomer)*

Zuni turquoise bear fetish by an unknown carver, with bits of shell, turquoise, and rock tied on with sinew. Note the eyes inlaid in silver. *(PC, Markow Photo)*

Three-strand fetish necklace in turquoise. Many carvers use treated turquoise for fetish necklaces to minimize breakage. *(PC, Ray Manley)*

Right: **A three-strand Zuni fetish necklace carved by Sam Delano. The materials include shell, turquoise, serpentine, jet, and abalone.** *(PC, Al Abrams)*

Below: **A selection of small unstrung fetishes and carved figures from the C.G. Wallace Collection. Many were carved by Leekya Deysee, the master Zuni carver.** *(PC, Ray Manley)*

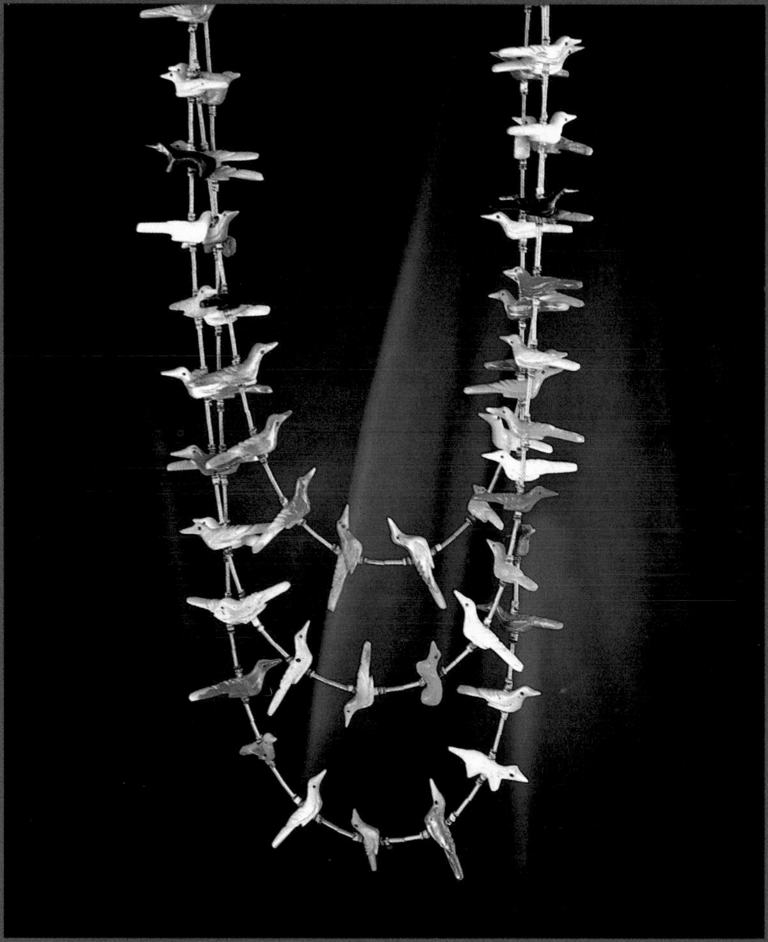

Above: **Four strands of a five-strand fetish necklace carved by the Zuni artist Sam Delano. The photograph shows the detail many carvers are capable of obtaining in their work.** *(HC, Al Abrams)*

Right: **Seven-strand bib fetish necklace by Lena Boone. Although this Zuni carver uses treated and dyed turquoise extensively, her necklaces are sought after because of the way they are strung. The red coral foxes at the top keep the strands spread apart.** *(PC, Peter L. Bloomer)*

This close-up of four Zuni fetish necklaces illustrates the variation in style and manner of stringing between individual carvers. The bottom two were made by Leekya Deysee. The lower one was carved in 1950 and the upper one in 1965. The two upper necklaces were carved by David Tsikewa and were both made shortly before his death in 1970. *(DNHC, Peter L. Bloomer)* ►

Single strand of flying bird fetishes, probably from Santo Domingo, possibly from Zuni. *(PC, Marcia Keegan)*

jewelry has enjoyed a new vogue in recent years, although it has nowhere near the popularity of Southwestern Indian jewelry.

The question of who is a true Indian smith also has created problems—among the Indians themselves and for others as well. The Palace of the Governors in Santa Fe, built in 1610, has since the early years of this century been part of the Museum of New Mexico, and it has been a traditional policy of the museum to allow Indians, particularly Pueblo Indians, to sit under the portal of the palace and sell jewelry and other wares to the tourists who throng the area in summertime.

These Indians police themselves; the museum assumes no responsibility for who may sit under the portal, nor does it vouch for the authenticity or quality of the items that are sold from blankets laid on the sidewalk. In recent years so many Indians have come to sell their wares that they overflow around the corner of the building or set up shop across the street. Disputes have arisen over who is entitled to sell his crafts there. Pueblo Indians claim they have first rights, and frown upon the appearance of Navajos or other Indians; all protest the presence of Indians who are not native to New Mexico, and the complaint has been made that some of the salespeople are not Indians at all. It is known that some of the Indians do not make all of their own items themselves but serve as "fronts" for dealers, often non-Indians. In addition, tourists and other buyers have complained that items were misrepresented to them. Since the goods are sold under the portal of the Palace of the Governors, the complaints are usually made to museum officials. Though the museum has repeatedly emphasized that it is not responsible for who sells under the portal, or for the authenticity of what is sold, museum officials are now reviewing their policy of allowing anyone to sell under the portal. (The Museum of New Mexico Foundation operates a Museum Shop inside the Palace of Governors; its merchandise is authentic and is fully guaranteed.)

Again, it is up to the collector to decide what he will accept as authentic Indian jewelry, for basically there cannot be a copyright on esthetics.

These are but a few of the growing pains of an industry—or craft or art—which is just coming of age, more than a century after it was born. It has reached dizzying heights for those accustomed to the leisurely ways of doing business in years past; no one is sure where the trade will go in years to come, except that it can never go back to what it was.

No prices have been cited in these pages for any item of Indian jewelry because they have increased so steadily that any price mentioned would soon be inaccurate.

A Zuni clusterwork bracelet that sold for $65 or $70 in Gallup in the early 1960s sold for ten times that amount, or even more, fifteen years later. One dealer estimates that in recent years the average annual increase in the price of handmade Indian jewelry has run about 18 percent. Roughly, this means that if you had bought an item of Indian jewelry for $100 in 1970, it would be worth almost $250 in 1975; by 1980 it will be worth well over $500.

But what if prices *don't* continue to rise? That is a possibility; but if they do fall, it will be a relatively small drop, and eventually they will resume their upward trend. Dealers are unanimous in their opinion that genuine handmade Indian jewelry will always find a good market and that over the years it will continue to appreciate in value, even if its present hectic climb levels off.

There is a scarcity of master smiths and a scarcity of top-quality turquoise; silver has been rising on the world market. There is greater and greater demand for genuine Indian jewelry, and even if the faddists, copyists, and fakers drop out, (and they haven't yet), that demand will continue.

11

COLLECTING INDIAN JEWELRY

The first collectors of Indian jewelry were the Indians themselves; they amassed and treasured it long before the white man took anything more than a passing interest in it.

We have concerned ourselves mainly with turquoise and silver, but we know that the Indians have for centuries used just about any material which would lend itself to personal adornment, from shell to eagle feathers to various colored rocks and earths which could be finely ground and mixed with water or animal grease and applied to the body and face; animal bones were polished, sometimes strung as necklaces or pendants, and sometimes mounted and strung horizontally for use as breastplates. Elks' teeth were attached to the buckskin clothing of the Plains Indians, as well as being worn in necklaces; bear claws, particularly those of the grizzly bear, were used by some tribes as necklace components, although other tribes, the Navajo included, regarded bears as sacred and would not kill them save in self-defense.

Before the white traders introduced the tiny glass beads which the Plains Indians sewed so adroitly to their clothing and moccasins, porcupine quills were dyed and sewn to garments and footwear in patterns which were the prototypes of the later beaded clothing. Designs were traditional, and one Indian could glance at another, a total stranger, and identify his tribal affiliation by the cut and design of his clothing.

In the Southwest, before silversmithing was introduced, we have noted that shell and stone of various kinds were used as jewelry; in today's Indian stores the shell heishi necklaces are direct survivals of a form of Southwestern Indian jewelry that is centuries old. Turquoise beads—sometimes flat discs, sometimes of greater thickness—also were strung for wearing around the neck, and these, too, were as highly prized in early times as they are today.

When the Indians first learned to work silver and then to set it with turquoise, this art form remained for decades a predominantly Indian craft. Photographs of Navajos in the 1870s and '80s show beyond doubt that the Indians of those days had come to prize it. Men and women alike wore not one but several necklaces, perhaps a strand of heishi or two along with a squash-blossom and naja set with turquoise. A ring might be worn on nearly every finger, and bracelets were often stacked, one upon another, on a person's wrist. person's wrist.

The wearing—and collecting—of such large amounts of jewelry told a great deal about the Indian wearer. First of all, it attracted attention by its esthetic qualities as well as by the sparkle of silver and flash of turquoise. Second, it marked its wearer as a person of affluence; only an individual of substance could afford to wear large amounts of silver and turquoise. (Of course, if one's personal collection was considered too meager to wear for a special event, it could be rounded out by extensive borrowing from friends and relatives.) In fact, bargaining over price could take a curious twist when one Indian bought jewelry from another: the more one paid for an item, the greater his (and the item's) prestige.

Precisely what prompts a person to acquire

"Indians have for centuries used just about any material which would lend itself to personal adornment"—a Cochiti man in ceremonial costume. *(Museum of New Mexico, T. Harmon Parkhurst)*

large amounts of jewelry—or any other commodity—would take a battery of psychologists to explain, but it undoubtedly transcends the simple motive of acquiring wealth. In fact, the early Indian owners of large amounts of silver and turquoise jewelry faced the same problem that today's collector does: often it has to be hidden, whether buried in the ground or locked in a safe-deposit box in a bank vault, and its presence confided only to one's most trusted friends and relatives.

Many of today's collectors acquired their jewelry almost by accident, with no fixed intention in mind; they acquired, over the years, a ring here, a necklace there, and a bracelet elsewhere until finally they became conscious of the fact that they were captives of the mystique of Indian jewelry. Some people have acquired jewelry through business transactions—and quite to their surprise have ended up as dealers in it, or collectors who thirst for that ultimate item which will put to shame all others in their possession.

There are those who say that today's collectors buy Indian jewelry because of their sympathy with the Indian and his long history of misunderstanding and mistreatment at the hands of the white man. While this argument may have some validity, people do not invest large sums of money in worthless items; an investment must have value, and to be of value it must have an intrinsic worth. In the case of Indian jewelry, this means that the basic materials that go into it have value in themselves, and that they are combined with the skill of a master craftsman and the soul (if you will) of an artist.

There is at least one other reason for collecting Indian jewelry, a very simple reason and certainly the overriding one: it has beauty.

Today, Indian jewelry has finally transcended the stereotype of an ethnic curiosity: it is admired by people worldwide for its esthetic qualities as well as its economic value. Everyone, it seems, wants to own at least one item of Southwestern Indian jewelry; many want to collect it, but they are uncertain about where to begin, what to buy, and how to tell quality Indian handmade items from imitations. They wish to know how to wear it, how to preserve it, how to protect it from all the perils which could conceivably befall it.

Starting a collection is like learning how to swim: you can read about it, you can watch others swim, and you can ponder on it at length, but eventually there comes a time when you have to get in the water. You may flounder a bit at first, but you'll learn to swim. When you decide to acquire Indian jewelry you may feel ill at ease or indecisive,

Juana María of Isleta Pueblo wearing Isleta cross necklaces, bead necklaces, and other ornaments. Traditional jewelry was often handed down for generations and worn *en masse* when the occasion demanded. *(MAI, HF)*

Two Navajo women c. 1950s in their everyday clothing and jewelry. For a Feast Day they would wear more, and more elaborate, jewelry. *(Museum of New Mexico, T. Harmon Parkhurst)*

Women of Isleta Pueblo wearing traditional garb, and jewelry. The more, the better, was the usual rule. (They are standing by an adobe oven or *horno*.) *(Museum of New Mexico, T. Harmon Parkhurst)*

but once you actually *own* any piece of silver and turquoise, or a string of heishi, your whole attitude will change, for you are now a collector; not only do you possess a tangible item of both material and esthetic value, but you have become one with those who share your knowledge and appreciation of such things.

You will be introduced to and learn to use a bewildering vocabulary: *gauge, spread, weld, matrix, bezel, carat, Lone Mountain, Bisbee blue, stabilized, oiled, machine-cast, hand-cast, pawn, old pawn*—and so on. But after all the glib terms have been bandied about and all the superficial motions of purchasing completed, one thing remains: you have acquired a work of art.

Silver is not the most valuable of metals, nor turquoise the most precious of stones, but there is a quality to them, singly or in combination, that seems to come alive when worn. Diamonds sometimes actually cheapen their wearers, and all the king's gold cannot disguise the fact of his mortality; but silver and turquoise make gentler jewels whose luster is awakened as easily by firelight as by crystal chandeliers. Their beauty is not dimmed when worn next to the dusty clothing of shepherds; neither do they lose their poise in sumptuous drawing rooms, sleek jetliners, or luxury resorts.

Perhaps it was these qualities that endeared silver and turquoise jewelry to its first Indian wearers—these and other things such as turquoise suggesting the enduring sky and silver taking on new life the more it is worn. These attributes, along with the honesty of patient craftsmen, are still the qualities that attract the collector.

But today's collectors are buying in a sophisticated world, and if you are among them you will want more definite guidelines, especially when you first begin to buy. Naturally, you will want to read everything you can about the subject; you will visit museums and examine their displays, and if you are thorough, you may even take notes. You will go to the dealers, and if you live in the Southwest, your problem will be that of deciding which of the thousands of traders there are worth your time. Do not hesitate to browse in shops which you suspect are not up to your standards; the best way to learn about imitation and poorer-quality jewelry is to see as much of it as you can, so you know what it looks like, what it feels like, and how it is priced. In the same fashion, go to the better shops and carefully look, touch, and examine; this is the only way you can train your own instincts and develop good taste and discernment. And in the long run, you will have to be your own expert, for

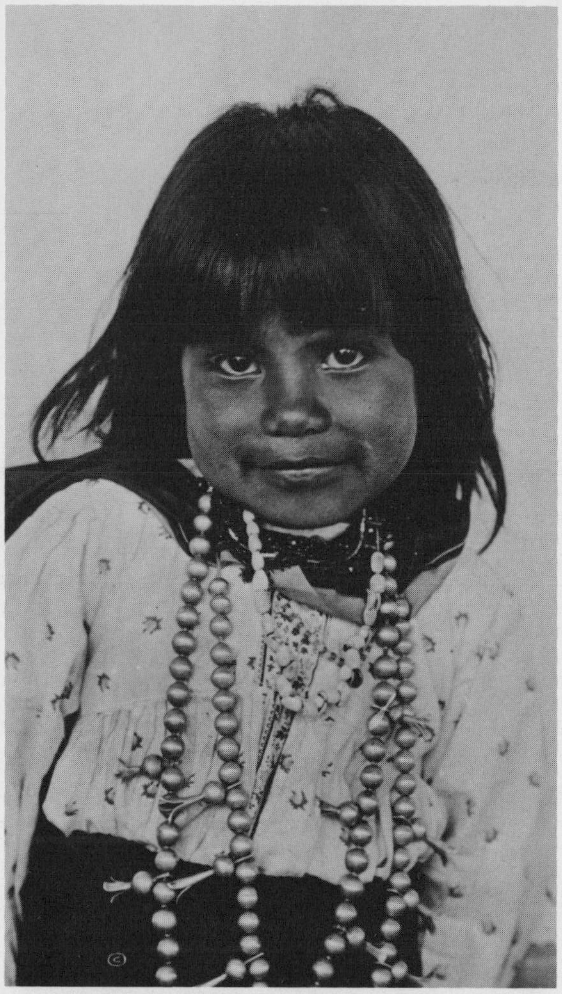

Even the children get silver: this little girl of Cochiti Pueblo is probably dressing up in her mother's necklace. *(Museum of New Mexico, T. Harmon Parkhurst)*

no one else can truly tell you what you want or need in Indian jewelry—or for that matter what is good or bad; honesty of materials and workmanship is your goal, and you must combine your own integrity with that of the smith.

Most people who deal constantly with Indian jewelry dislike being called experts; they know that they can make mistakes in recognizing and representing the quality of the materials in the items they sell, but they try to be honest and if they err they make good on it. They know, too, the literal meaning of the old saw that there is no accounting for taste; in the end, what is bought and sold is up to the collector. If the purchaser demands honesty and quality in Indian jewelry, and is willing to pay for them, he will get them.

There are probably three basic criteria which determine the purchase of silver and turquoise jewelry: desirability, authenticity, and price. *Desirability* is by all odds the most important factor: if something does not appeal to you, you will not want it at any price, no matter how impeccable its credentials. Because *you* have to look at and wear the jewelry, it is essential that you purchase only those pieces which will continue to give *you* pleasure.

Authenticity can be equated with honesty in that you should be getting exactly what you pay for. If you admire a certain bracelet in a dealer's showcase and he tells you the silver is hand-wrought but the turquoise is stabilized, you have no quarrel with him, assuming the price is commensurate with the materials and workmanship. Old pawn jewelry is very expensive; it still crops up with some regularity, but it quickly disappears into private collections and museum vaults. The individual customer is fortunate indeed who comes across a genuine piece of old pawn jewelry, since most dealers have standing orders from regular customers for such items. If you pay the price for old pawn, you should be sure you are getting it, and the integrity of the dealer is your only guarantee. Further, there is the question of definition: when does a piece of pawn jewelry become *old* pawn? Some authorities will insist that the jewelry must have been pawned and gone dead in the 1930s or earlier; others will tolerate a date from the 1940s, or even the '50s. Since it can be so relative, perhaps the word *old* should be dispensed with, but there is a further problem: pawn is not necessarily well made or esthetically pleasing. Is it better, then, to buy an inferior ring simply because it once was owned by an Indian, or would the collector be wiser to purchase a new ring of good quality and workmanship?

Another point: people often ask why laws are not passed which will regulate the manufacture and sale of "genuine Indian handmade jewelry." The answer is that federal and state governments have passed any number of laws which have attempted to do so—and all of them must be considered near-failures. The reasons are twofold. In the first place, while such laws may be put on the books, rarely do legislators appropriate sufficient funds to guarantee their enforcement, and other laws and legal procedures often make it difficult to win a case against violators. The second obstacle is the more serious: no one can agree on definitions. In legal, or even ethical, terms, how can one define *handmade jewelry*? Before an Indian smith ever lays hands on it, his sterling silver has gone through a succession of machined processes; the same is usually true of turquoise as well—and all of this work probably was done by non-Indians. Findings are almost always commercially made, and many processes in otherwise handmade jewelry are expedited by use of hand-operated machinery or motor-driven devices. Neither government agencies, legislators, smiths, nor dealers can agree on where to draw the line in defining *handmade jewelry*. In 1964 David Neumann wrote:

> In 1932 the Federal Trade Commission held that, in the public mind, "Indian jewelry" meant jewelry *hand-made by Indians*, and that jewelry, though made by Indian workmen, could not be described as Indian jewelry unless it was *hand-made*. Today little Indian jewelry is *hand-made* under this interpretation. All Zuni jewelry work is dependent on motor-driven tools; and all Navajo jewelry, while essentially hand-made, is set with stones from commercial (non-Indian) cutters and is finished on machinery by non-Indians. [*Masterkey*, Vol. 38, No. 2, 1964; italics Neumann's]

This does not imply quackery, or that Indian jewelry is not to be trusted. It merely means that the art of silversmithing has come a long way since the first smiths sat cross-legged on the floors of their hogans and used clay forges and scraps of iron to melt coins and beat out crude bracelets. It means that reputable dealers are still the collector's best bet, and that the buyer himself has to use common sense and good taste.

Take the matter of stabilized turquoise. This is *not* fake stone; it is real turquoise of low grade which has been treated to intensify its color and increase its hardness and impermeability. It will not fade in color, nor will it fracture as easily as run-of-the-mill turquoise;neither will high-grade natural turquoise—but it sells, or *should* sell, for a great deal more than stabilized turquoise. Since nearly every old-line dealer will admit that he can be fooled—on occasion—by stabilized turquoise, it is silly to pretend that a simple checklist will guide or protect the casual buyer. And color charts which purport to match the stone in your jewelry with that from various mines around the country are somewhat less than infallible; in the best of circumstances they can apply only to the characteristic top-grade natural stones from a given mine and not to the ordinary stones, even if they are not treated. And if your turquoise has been stabilized, all bets are off. Essentially, you are on your own, and that is where you should be.

If you are a Southwesterner the chances are that a wholesaler's shop is nearby. There you can purchase at nominal prices small bits of raw and stabilized turquoise; you also can buy samples of machine-cast or handmade components—or at least examine them—and you can see what commercial dies actually look like. If you wish to be the complete collector, you can familiarize yourself with every phase of the art, and you should know how silver is cast or wrought into finished jewelry and how turquoise and other stones are ground, polished, and set. Many wholesalers and larger retailers employ smiths who work in their shops; usually there is no objection to your watching, if you do not bother them.

We have mentioned that dealers generally like to talk about jewelry; many of them have spent their lives working with it, and they want others to know and love it as they do. In all the interviews we did for this book we found dealers, smiths, and everyone else connected with the business unusually frank and open. They are not reluctant to point out the pitfalls of collecting, because they want their customers to come back and because they feel —with justification—that the buyer already is aware of the immense esthetic and acquisitive pleasures of collecting genuine Indian handmade jewelry, not to mention its investment potential.

If your home is not in the Southwest, there are reputable stores in every area of the country which carry genuine Indian jewelry. They have their reputations to maintain, and they will stand behind what they sell. (But it is not reasonable to expect a salesperson in the East or Middle West to know as much about such jewelry as his or her counterpart in a Southwestern dealer's store.) And of course there are museums and libraries everywhere to help you learn more about your subject.

It is more difficult to view private collections. Generally, you will need a letter of introduction or some sort of credentials to prove that you are who you are, and not a prospective burglar casing the premises. Indian jewelry has grown so enormously valuable that private collectors usually do not like publicity. If they allow their collections to be photographed, they often insist that their names not be used since publicity can serve as an invitation to unwanted guests. Often, collections are kept in safe-deposit boxes in banks; this is sad to relate, for part of the fun of collecting is being able to handle your pieces and to admire and wear them freely. However, most collectors delight in showing their jewelry to people they can trust, people who also love and collect fine Indian silverwork.

What kind of collection can you specialize in? The possibilities are almost endless. You can specialize by tribe (Navajo,Zuni, Hopi,Santo Domingo), by period (although if you are after old pawn, you had better have a healthy checkbook and a very good knowledge of Indian jewelry), or by style (wrought, cast, channel, inlay); you can specialize in plain silver, in fetishes, in turquoise or coral beads, mosaics, or Singer-type (a form of mosaic chips developed by a Navajo family named Singer).

You will have to set standards for yourself: will you accept stabilized turquoise pieces? oiled turquoise? Where will you draw the line at "handmade"?

As for turquoise, remember that only about 10 percent of the stones produced by any mine are top-quality gemstones, and these command high prices. The rest of the stones vary in quality in their natural state, and this is why so many stones on the market today are oiled, stabilized, or treated in some way. The magazine *Arizona Highways* has estimated that 60 percent of the genuine stones appearing on the market are stabilized or treated.

Where price is concerned, comparison shopping is the only way to determine a fair price for a particular type or piece of jewelry—and again this means that you must become as familiar with the trade as you can. It doesn't take long to learn the value of good jewelry, and the truly good pieces are never sold at discount prices. Although every merchant may have special sales or sale items, you should approach with caution dealers who offer continuous high-discount prices. Usually, big discounts mean one of two things: the merchandise is not up to snuff or it was deliberately overpriced to begin with (so that the dealer could afford to offer large reductions). Once more, this is a generalization and should be taken as such. Ultimately you must depend upon your own discrimination and the reputability of the dealer.

How do you take care of your silver and turquoise Indian jewelry? As little as possible; the Indians never went to any great pains with it. Silver takes on a luster when it is worn, and the longer it is worn the more distinctively silver its patina becomes. If your jewelry is set away or is exposed to humidity it may tarnish a bit; a polishing cloth will bring it back again quickly. If you *must* polish your silver, do so sparingly; don't polish the low spots in the die marks, for they should be allowed to blacken in order to contrast with the rich silvery glow of the flat places.

The same is true of turquoise; most people who wear turquoise-set rings or bracelets daily take no finicky care of the stone. It was meant to be worn. There are a few obvious precautions: the Sky Stone, as anyone knows, is not as hard as a diamond, and heavy blows or hard knocks can chip or fracture a turquoise, especially the chalkier varieties. Another obvious injunction is that when you have paid a large sum of money for a quality piece of jewelry, whether of gold and diamonds or turquoise and silver, you must exercise reasonable care in protecting and preserving it. (You are not likely to be wearing it while you are working on your car or coming to grips with a heavy cleaning operation.)

Some turquoise stones are more porous and absorbent than others, and this accounts for warnings that you should never wear a ring while, say, doing the dishes and that turquoise will change color if exposed to anything from cold cream to perspiration. A chalky stone might well absorb the grease in dishwater and change color, but a good stone will not. While Indians reserve their finest and most elaborate pieces of jewelry for special occasions, they wear their favorite rings, bracelets, and other items day in and day out; until recently, at least, their lifestyles and environment could hardly be called comfortable, yet some of their stones have survived a half-century or more of hard wear without losing their color or their beauty. If anything, age and usage have given them a patina which some people consider even more desirable than the high polish of brand-new stones. The writer has worn one ring for nearly twenty years; it contains two stones, each about the size of a dime, in baroque cut. Neither the color nor the matrix is top quality, but over the years the stones have been exposed to dishwater, gasoline, motor oil, turpentine, oil- and latex-based paints, paint thiner, rubbing alcohol, drinking alcohol, perspiration, hand lotion, grease, and heaven knows what else, yet they have not changed their color in the least. They are the same average stones they always were, but they have drawn compliments everywhere.

Silver and turquoise jewelry was first made by Indians to be worn by themselves and other Indians; it was neither delicate nor effete, nor could it, in those strenuous and hard old days, have come anywhere near to being pampered. True, it was cherished and cared for, but it was *used*—in rain and snow, in torrid heat and bitter cold, while tending stock and while hunting and making war. Even though the Indians later made lighter, less craftsmanlike jewelry for the white tourist trade, they continued to make it in the traditional fashion for their own use—and it is this jewelry that is most sought after today by museums and serious collectors, along with the finest contemporary pieces. This jewelry also commands the highest prices.

Even if you have taken pains to comply with all the basic rules of buying and collecting, you are likely to discover that over the years you have acquired items which no longer appeal to you. There may be nothing at all wrong with them, but your tastes have changed, or you have come to

When this Navajo woman finished her weaving, she went inside her hogan to make fry bread and mutton stew, her rings and bracelet never leaving her hands.
(Michal Heron)

specialize in different areas, and they no longer go with your collection. If that is true, remember that if these pieces were salable when you bought them, they are salable now. Many dealers and collectors will trade items—and in fact enjoy doing so—or the pieces can be sold outright.

Obviously, you will come out better if you trade, rather than sell, your unwanted jewelry. A dealer can trade you on a retail-value basis; if he buys it from you outright he'll have to give you less than market value—because he must mark it up in order to sell it again.

If you wish to be sure of getting full retail value for your jewelry, sell it to another individual, who wants it for his own collection; he'll be willing to pay the full price.

If your collection is valuable—and almost any assemblage of Indian jewelry is valuable these days—it should be insured properly. Most homeowners' insurance policies on unscheduled personal property (meaning such items as jewelry) pay only on amounts in three figures, but one company's policy may vary somewhat from others'; if in doubt, you should read your policy carefully and check with your agent. Even if your collection is relatively modest, you may wish to have it specially insured; further, since prices on Indian jewelry have risen so dramatically, the value you declared only a few years ago may be far too low for its coverage under current market prices. Since no two pieces of genuine Indian handmade jewelry are ever exactly alike, you cannot replace items that are stolen or otherwise lost, but you can at least recover their going market value.

If you wish to know how much your collection is worth you may need to have it appraised. There are dealers who specialize in this, as well as full-time appraisers. Naturally, these people usually live in the Southwest, but they travel all over the country to appraise large or valuable collections.

12

TURQUOISE: MORE MAGIC—AND BLACK MAGIC

We have spoken of collectors and collecting. We will now speak of what must be considered the inevitable obsession of the Indian jewelry collector: turquoise. The demand for turquoise in the United States has been cyclic. When Navajos first began setting it in silver it was relatively scarce, even in the Southwest, and the call for it by Indians—and later by tourists—led to the reopening of a number of dormant mines. Reopening is the proper word to use since almost all the mines which are worked today are known to have been worked by prehistoric Indians.

We know that in the 1890s the Hubbells of Ganado sent to Persia for fine turquoises—but it is absurd to assert they would have done so if the Navajos had not already been using native turquoise in sufficient quantities and with sufficient artistry to warrant the Hubbells' doing so. After the early part of this century the demand for turquoise diminished, and it was not until post-World War II days that it rose again.

Nearly a hundred years after the first use of Persian turquoise we are again importing it in large quantities, partly because some experts believe it is superior to American varieties (although you can get any number of arguments on that score) and partly because in the last third of the twentieth century demand for turquoise is exceeding supply. In the Old World the gem is bought by the carat; in the United States until recently the purchase price of a stone set in jewelry was more often based on the piece as a whole, or the "spread" of the stone, unless there was a great deal of stonework or its quality was unusually high. The carat weight was not a factor. Because Old World stones are set in gold, light blue gems are most prized there; however, these stones do not show to best advantage when set in silver, and pale Persian turquoise is not used in Southwestern Indian jewelry, although darker Perisan gemstones are very much in demand by Indian silversmiths and lapidaries.

Turquoise is never faceted; since it is opaque there would be no point in it. Much of the best contemporary turquoise is nugget style (baroque) and not ground to any conventional gem cut. There are two reasons for this, the first being economy: since turquoise crumbles easily in grinding, there is less wastage in nugget cuts, and the process is not nearly as time-consuming. Another reason is that nugget cuts go better with the free-form silverwork which is most characteristic of contemporary jewelry. Such modern jewelry has been featured for years (along with more traditional styles) in the incomparable *Arizona Highways* magazine, which has furthered the acceptance of, and demand for, nugget cuts. In fact, *Arizona Highways* has done more than reflect contemporary jewelry styles: it has set them. This can be proved easily by attending any crafts fair from Scottsdale and Flagstaff, Arizona, to Gallup and Santa Fe, New Mexico, or Los Angeles: many smiths have copies of *Arizona Highways* on display along with their jewelry; traders and dealers commonly refer to it in discussing styles and fashions and trends. No doubt counterfeiters refer to it as well, although none has gone on record so far in admitting this.

But it would be difficult to overestimate the influence of this magazine in the Indian jewelry business during recent times.

Because the mines in the Southwest which produce turquoise are relatively few, many dealers claim that they can identify a stone's origin simply by looking at it and assessing its color, hardness, and matrix. While this may be true of a few dealers in relation to the highest-grade stones produced by each mine, as the quality diminishes the similarity increases and one lower-grade stone looks very much like another. However, there is little risk in anyone's stating (the more emphatically the better), "This turquoise is from...," since only the expert gemologist, or a laboratory test, is likely to prove him wrong.

The quality of turquoise varies within a given mine, although some mines or areas produce more top-quality stones than others. In recent years some of the best stones have come from Lone Mountain, Nevada, Kingman, Arizona (although the quality varies a great deal here), Bisbee and Morenci, Arizona, and Los Cerrillos, New Mexico. This last area has been in great use since prehistoric times, as we have seen, and much of the stone from there has a distinct greenish cast to it. In fact, the greenish stone is often more typical of Indian usage of the 1880s than the robin's-egg blue variety, which is preferred by most buyers today since it is more akin to the Persian gems in color.

The price of turquoise varies; in its raw state it is bought by the pound, but cut and polished stones are wholesaled by the carat, and top-grade turquoise now is sold retail by the carat with increasing frequency. But the price per carat varies considerably even among stones produced by the same mine, and it also varies depending upon its cut. (Many commercial lapidaries will not cut turquoise in cabochon form or in "snake-eyes"—small round stones; they prefer to cut and polish in free-form or nugget style, for reasons explained earlier.)

Despite its cyclic history, the current popularity of turquoise seems sure to endure; demand for it may dip somewhat, but there is too little turquoise and too many people who want it for that to amount to much.

In fact, the passion for the Sky Stone has created an entire new industry—that of faking, treating, "stabilizing," or otherwise altering or imitating turquoise. Other than soaking in water and oiling or greasing, treated turquoise did not become a serious factor until the mid-twentieth century.

The earliest way of treating turquoise, no doubt practiced in prehistoric times, was to soak it in water: stones often were held in the seller's mouth just before a deal was to be consummated. The moisture heightened the blueness of the stone, but the sharper had to have a quick means of departure, for as the moisture evaporated so did the color.

Grease was much more permanent. Animal fat was used at first, later various kinds of oils. Over the years, however, even oil will disappear, and the stone will resume its lusterless color. Alcohol or even detergent will remove grease and restore a stone treated thus to its natural state.

The addition of Prussian blue will stain a dull stone to a fine dazzling shade. Much chalk-soft turquoise, according to Neumann, at one time went to Idar-Oberstein, Germany, where color was added before it was resold. Ammonia will dissolve Prussian blue, but simple tests like alcohol and ammonia are useless in unmasking *plasticized* turquoise. This technique has been refined in recent years; at one time stones were simply dipped in a plastic solution which created a bright, hard, well-colored crust which was easily detected visually or when pierced with a pin or knife point; pressure from a pair of pliers will crumble the plasticized skin like a nutshell. Nowadays the foreign agent is injected into low-grade stone under high pressure. (The agent is plastic, but those who treat turquoise with it are unwilling to give an exact formula or to reveal the processes under which it is suffused into the stone.)

Another way of treating or stabilizing turquoise is by backing it with epoxy glue, a common practice in America nowadays. Epoxy in no way changes the color of the stone or its show-side hardness. What it does is to literally stabilize chalkier grades of turquoise so that the stone can be cut and polished easily, whereas without epoxy it might have to be discarded. Neumann, an old-time dealer in Indian jewelry, refers to the use of epoxy backing as a "lamentable" and "somewhat fraudulent" practice, and he points out that widespread use of the glue results in the purchase of epoxy by the carat; but he is essentially speaking of the wholesale trade, since retail buyers usually do not worry about the carat weight of their stones. Neumann adds that "the only decent aspect" of the use of epoxy "is that it has held down the price of cut stones"—which, of course, affects the retail buyer in the lower cost of an item of jewelry. Many dealers do not object to treated turquoise so long as it is labeled as such; the argument is that this turquoise is much cheaper to buy and sell than natural high-grade gemstones, and that otherwise unusuable low-grade stones can be salvaged to meet the heavy buyer demand. All of this is true, and again the operative and definitive clause must be *as long as the stone is identified for what it is*, there is nothing wrong with selling it or wearing it. In fact, this process makes good-looking turquoise available to buyers who otherwise could not afford the pure high-grade stones. Purchasers have the right to know what they are buying, and reputable dealers ultimately are the best guarantee of this. Some dealers in high-quality jewelry will not knowingly allow treated stones in their shop. Others, equally reputable, will sell both treated and natural turquoise, but they will carefully point out to the buyer what he is getting. There is a third class of dealer with whom anything goes.

It must be remembered that it is *not* illegal to make imitation turquoise; it is *not* illegal to stabilize it with plastic, or to back it with epoxy glue, or even to oil colorless low-grade chalky stone, which intensifies its color and increases its hardness. What *is* illegal is to misrepresent to the buyer the nature of a stone being offered for sale. Since silver and turquoise Indian jewelry is increasingly being purchased as an investment, the presence on the market of large quantities of misrepresented, treated stones can have an extremely adverse effect. Furthermore, some of the alterations can be done so competently under laboratory conditions that it is very difficult sometimes, even for an expert, to distinguish treated stone.

There are a number of other minerals which bear a resemblance to turquoise, and along with laboratory-made fakes these have caused problems over the years—and still do. The most common natural mineral lookalike is probably chrysocolla, followed by azurite and malachite. There are also certain forms of copper, known in the trade as *stains*, which bear a superficial resemblance, in their native occurrences, to turquoise. Generally, the trained mineralogist or dealer in turquoise can spot these lookalikes with relative ease, especially if they are still in their mineral forms. Besides, there are some simple tests which will identify them quite conclusively: specific gravity, hardness, streak, opacity, the forms in which they appear in their native state, and their reactions to certain chemicals or to heat. But these are tests which must, as a rule, be run on mineral samples; once the stone is cut, polished, and mounted in silver it can be much more deceptive, and dealers in Indian jewelry understandably are not sympathetic to the idea of unmounting a set stone and possibly ruining it in order to prove to a prospective buyer that it is genuine turquoise. Again, the reputability of the dealer is one's best guarantee of authenticity.

In fact, for anyone serious about collecting Indian jewelry there is no substitute for handling it as much as possible, for one develops a sense of discernment that cannot be put into words, and trial and error are necessary ingredients for this development. It is possible to buy chalk- or oiling-quality turquoise quite cheaply in its raw form, samples of various grades of turquoise in all stages of finishing—in the Southwest there are dealers who wholesale the Sky Stone and silver and the tools that are needed to work them. One thing hasn't changed in all the years of the Indian jewelry business—almost to a man (or woman), dealers and traders are friendly and open people. In addition to making a livelihood from Indian jewelry, they love their profession and they love the Southwest; if the crush of business does not prevent it, they enjoy talking to people about the trade, Indians, the quality of turquoise, and the way good silver is made. The newcomer should not be afraid to ask questions and to learn as much as he can by constant exposure to the profession. In the end, along with reputable dealers, one's good taste, common sense, and intuition are the best guides to quality jewelry.

And there *are* the tests. For example, Robert T. O'Haire, writing in the Arizona Bureau of Mines *Fieldnotes*, describes a simple test for determing whether a stone is turquoise, chrysocolla, malachite, or azurite. For the record, let us quote him in full:

Chrysocolla is mistakenly identified for turquoise more often than any other substance.

A drop of concentrated hydrochloric acid placed on your sample at room temperature will react immediately if the sample is chrysocolla. The acid will turn to a greenish-yellow color which can be more easily observed by blotting it with a white tissue. When the test is made on *fair to excellent quality* turquoise [italics supplied] no reaction will take place.

If the acid test is positive, meaning the acid turns greenish yellow, the sample almost certainly isn't good turquoise and probably is chrysocolla. But not all minerals that give a positive reaction are chrysocolla. For example, azurite and malachite will change the acid's color (but they will effervesce also—a distinguishing factor to watch for). Not all the samples that react negatively are turquoise, though. Knowledge both of mineralogy and other test procedures is obviously very useful. (ABM *Fieldnotes*, Vol. 5, No. 2, June 1975)

O'Haire, a mineralogist, adds that muriatic acid, a commercial type of hydrochloric acid that can be bought in drugstores and at swimming pool supply houses (a solution of muriatic acid helps purify the water in your pool), can be used for this test, provided the acid is clear in color. It should also be emphasized that you do not use this test on stones that are set in silver, and you do not use it on low-grade turquoise, whose impurities will cause it to react violently to the acid.

We have seen how the Sky Stone can be altered or synthesized, stabilized or otherwise treated. We have noted that there are look-alikes, and discussed how they can be spotted. We know, too, that some of the "handmade" silver jewelry on the market was really created on a machine. All misrepresentation is deplorable, but it is well to remember that such things as fake jewelry, machine-made jewelry, and treated turquoise would not be on the market if the genuine items had not achieved a value making them worthy of imitation. There is a message here:

The first Navajo smiths, whoever they were, learned to work silver from Europeans, combined it with Southwestern gemstones, and thus created a "native" form of jewelry. In its first decades it was, no doubt, primitive; but it is interesting to note that Navajo and other Southwestern Indian jewelry was "discovered" by Americans (and Europeans) at about the same time that the great French artists of the late nineteenth century were "discovering" the so-called primitive arts of Japan, China, Africa, Polynesia—and America.

The early Indian jewelrymakers took silver coin and rough-cut turquoise and with the crudest of tools, at first, fashioned objects that have grown in worth and desirability with every passing generation. Indian smiths today make jewelry in styles and forms that endlessly exhibit the Indian propensity for creativity. As the words of a Navajo song would have it, "Beauty walked before them." They followed it, and now beauty walks behind them as well. Like the rainbow it is above and below them. It is elusive, as all art is elusive; but to have seen it, to have touched it, is enough, even though it cannot be grasped. It began in beauty. It will end in beauty.

But like the rainbow, it will never really end.

Concha belt set with over 800 small rounds of turquoise. The belt was made in the early 1960s by a Navajo/Hopi silversmith. *(PC, Jerry Jacka)*

Above: Zuni cluster ring, somewhat unusual because of the shape of the center stone. C. 1930s. *(HMC, Al Abrams)*

Below: A Zuni cluster dress pin, c. 1930–1940. Note the serrated-edge bezels around the stones. By pressing these down with a light metal tool, a tight mount can be obtained without the danger of cracking a stone by hammering. *(FHFAC, HM, Al Abrams)*

Above: A selection of 1940s-style cluster jewelry by different silversmiths, collected at Zuni by C.G. Wallace. The bracelet at the upper left was made by George Martinez in 1941. Note that the stones in the squash-blossom necklace are not perfectly cut and polished cabochons, but in many cases only crudely smoothed from the original rough stones. The blossoms in the necklace are the style sometimes called "pollen pistil." *(PC, Ray Manley)*

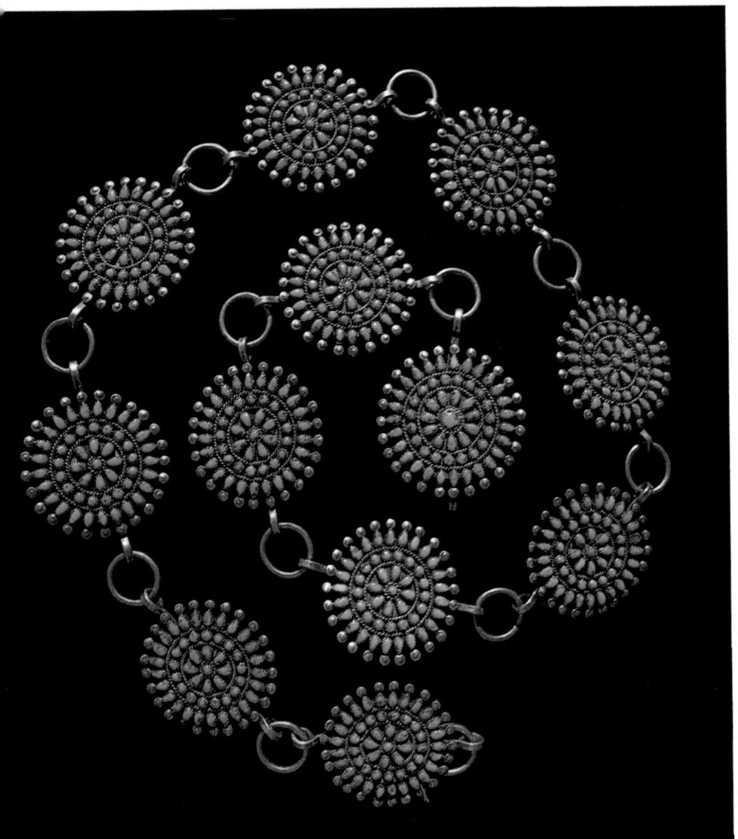

Above: A selection of 1940s Zuni needlepoint jewelry which shows that within the same general style, pieces of different design can be worn together. *(HC, Al Abrams)*

Left: A Zuni cluster medallion link belt made in the 1950s by an unidentified silversmith. *(RT, Richard Polson)*

A selection of Navajo and Zuni style dress pins made between 1920 and the 1940s, showing the great variation this one piece of jewelry took. Note the unusual baroque style of the center piece and the channelwork in the lower left, done in a New Mexico sun symbol design, with a silver dollar at the center. *(PC, FHFAC, all Al Abrams except lower right, Richard Polson)*

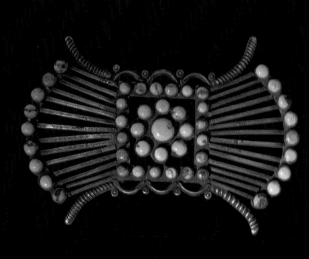

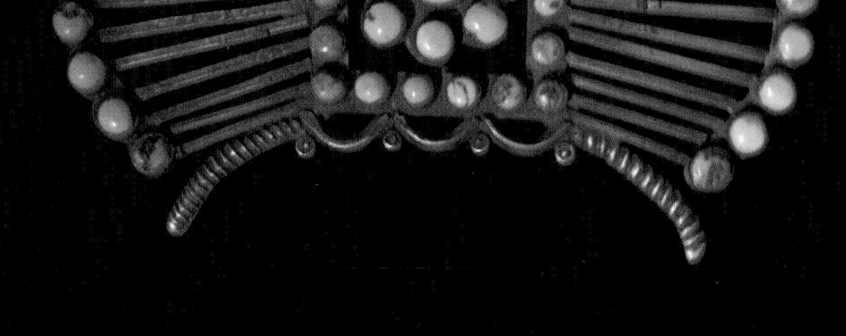

Zuni style squash-blossom necklace from the 1930s. The flat plate style, set with stones and, frequently, ornate stamping, reflected the increasing complexity desired by purchasers of Indian jewelry during that time, as well as the growing ability of the smiths to handle more complex work. *(FHFAC, HM, Al Abrams)*

Contemporary Navajo jewelry set of bracelet, ring, earrings, and squash-blossom necklace set with Blue Diamond turquoise. This set is typical of what is being turned out in large numbers by Indian smiths to satisfy a demand for Indian jewelry. *(PC, Marcia Keegan)*

Wallace Collection, is now in the collection of the Heard Museum. *(Al Abrams)*

Above: **Bear claw and Battle Mountain turquoise necklace made by George Stumpff, a contemporary Anglo silversmith. Although bear claw necklaces have frequently been made by Indians, they have become a popular Anglo-Indian style jewelry form.** *(RT, Richard Polson)*
Below: **Contemporary squash-blossom necklace and earrings with turquoise set in shadow boxes. The slab turquoise in the center is an intermediate form between the nugget in the rough and the finished cabochon.** *(PC, Jeffrey Kurtzeman)*

Navajo squash-blossom necklace with "pine cone" blossoms, a somewhat unusual form even for the 1930s, when unusual forms proliferated. The turquoise

Right: **An early large stone squash blossom necklace made in the 1950s.** *(HC, Al Abrams)*
Below: **A necklace set with green turquoise stones in contemporary style mounting by George Kee.** *(PC, Jeffrey Kurtzeman)*

Above: **An ornate squash-blossom necklace set with pale green turquoise carved into leaves, made by Teddie Weahkee in 1931. A relatively modest example of the baroque forms of jewelry that developed at Zuni in the 1920s and 1930s.** *(PC, Ray Manley)*
Right: **Channelwork squash-blossom necklace typical of a style popular in the 1930s and 1940s.** *(AG, Al Abrams)*

This Navajo woman is wearing a not uncommon amount of jewelry for a feast day (she also had on two bracelets that do not show in the photograph). If she were wearing more traditional attire, she would probably be wearing more jewelry. *(Michal Heron)*

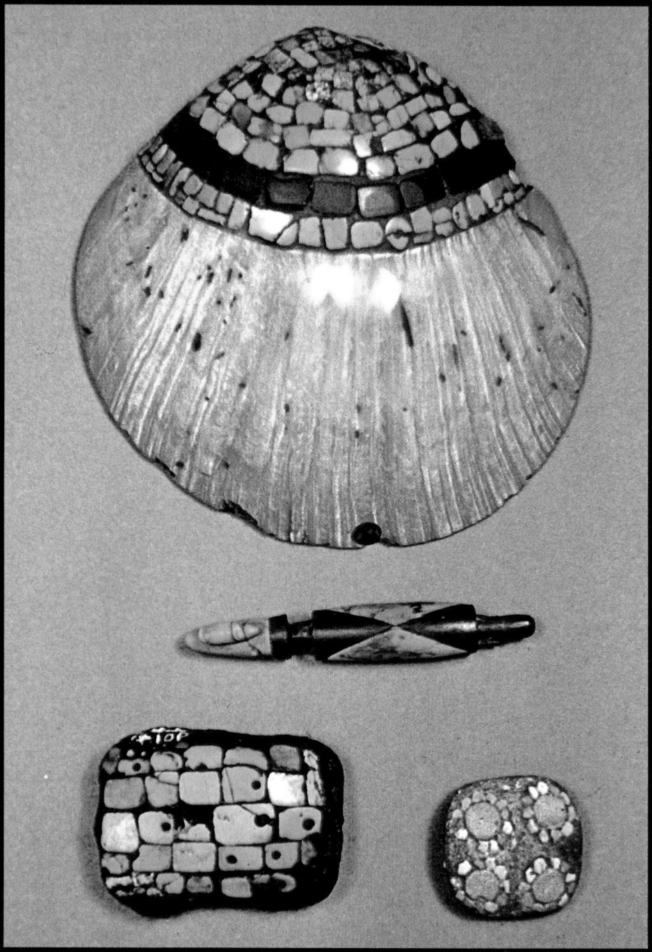

These three photographs show only a few of the many styles of turquoise mosaic jewelry created by prehistoric Indians in the Southwest. The items in the photograph at lower right were found at Hawikuh, New Mexico, a prehistoric Zuni site. *(Museum of the American Indian, Heye Foundation) (Jerry Jacka)*

Left: Contemporary Zuni inlay necklace of hummingbirds and flowers made by Virgil and Shirley Benn. Materials include abalone, mother-of-pearl, spiny oyster, and turquoise. *(GRIACC, Jerry Jacka)*
Below: Contemporary eagle dancer necklace, bracelet, earrings, and ring set made by Zuni artist Charles Poncho. *(Keams Canyon Arts and Crafts, Jerry Jacka)*

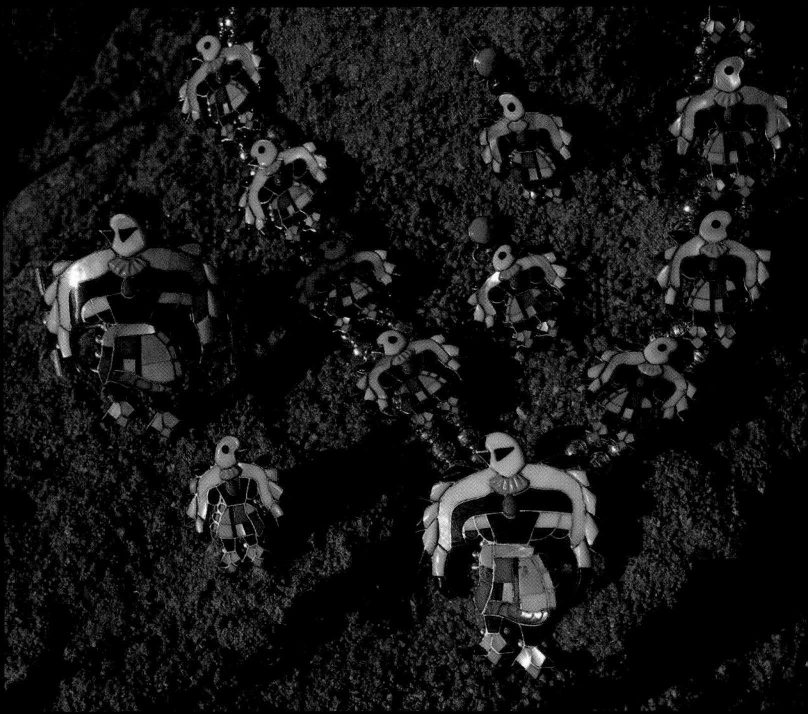

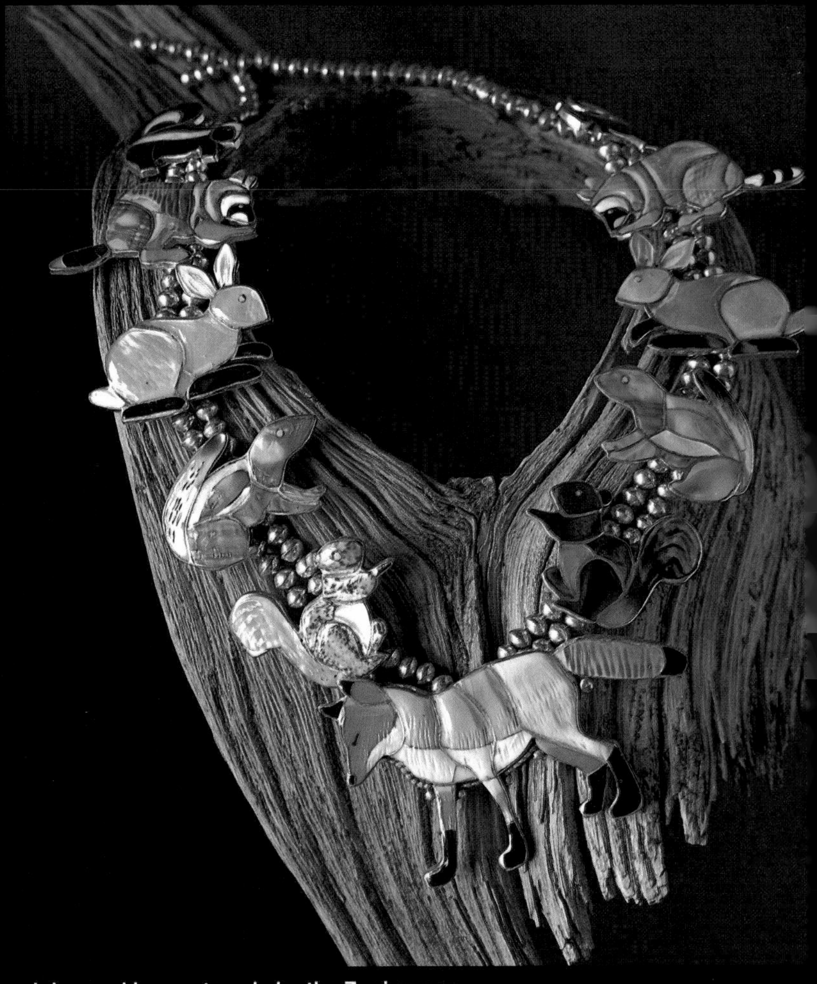

Above left: Contemporary butterflies and flowers inlay necklace set made by the Zuni carver Rosetta Wallace. Materials include turquoise, coral, mother-of-pearl, and jet. *(GRIACC, Jerry Jacka)*
Above right: Inlay animal necklace made by Virgil and Shirley Benn in 1965. By use of a variety of shells and stones, naturalistic colors and textures can be obtained by the carver.

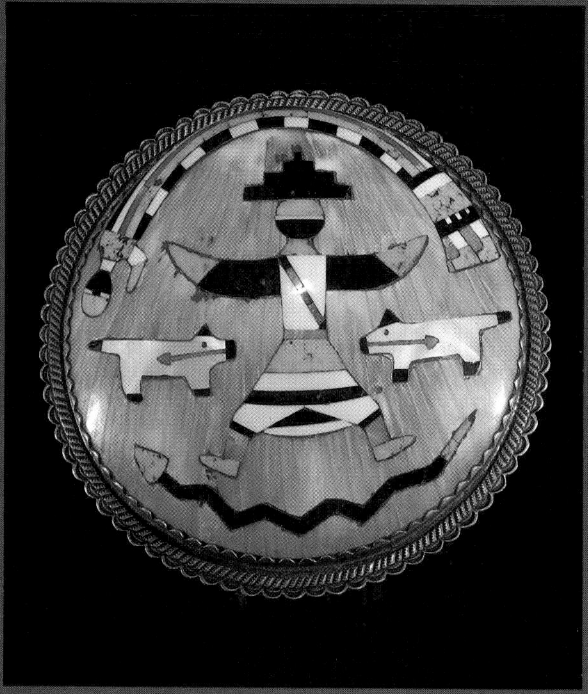

Top left: Zuni ketoh made by Juan Dideos in 1925. The hands are carved of spiny oyster. *(JFPGW, John Miller)*
Top center: Zuni inlay butterflies by Leo Poblano. These 1920s pieces are typical of one of the most popular forms of inlay animal ever created by Zuni smiths. *(James Fowler, Sr., Collection, John Miller)*
Top right: Silver tray c. 1935 with an appliquéd inlay figure of a woman in traditional dress making pottery (purportedly a portrait of Leekya's wife). *(JFPGW, John Miller)*
Above: Zuni ketoh set with an inlayed shell. The decoration was applied to the silverwork with a simple stamp. *(FHFAC, HM, Al Abrams)*
Above right: This Zuni inlayed shell, the insignia of the Priests of the Bow, was given to archeologist Frank Cushing in the 1890s after he was initiated into the society. He later had the shell mounted on a silver box. *(FHFAC, HM, Al Abrams)*
Right: Zuni ketoh with jet tadpoles and a white shell, turquoise, and jet frog. One of the finest examples of inlay art from the 1920s. *(FHFAC, HM, Al Abrams)*

Top left: Contemporary inlay of an Apache Ghan dancer (a figure that appears in Apache girls' puberty ceremonies) on a Zuni bolo. *(GRIACC, Ray Manley)*
Left center: Zuni inlay figure of one of the kachinas who accompanies the Shalakos in the Zuni Shalako ceremony. C. 1930s. In the best of this Zuni art, the figures have a life all their own. *(FHFAC, HM, Al Abrams)*
Left: A contemporary eagle dancer more complex than most, made by Virgil and Shirley Benn. *(ED, Peter L. Bloomer)*
Top right: A selection of Zuni inlay figures and pins (including both Pueblo and Plains Indian figures) that gives an idea of the broad range of these little figures. *(PCs, Peter L. Bloomer)*
Above: Turquoise eagle dancer made in the style of Edward Beyuka, a contemporary Zuni craftsman. *(PC, Markow Photo)*

Left: A selection of small Zuni inlayed and channelwork pieces typical of the variety made for tourists in the 1940s and 1950s. The dragonfly motif in the largest pin is more unusual at Zuni than it would be at Isleta. *(PC, Ray Manley)*

Below: Dennis Edaakie pin. The hummingbird is one of his favorite motifs. *(HMC, Al Abrams)*

A variety of jewelry from the master Zuni craftsman Dennis Edaakie, who pioneered this

Two contemporary Navajo silver boxes, entered in the 1973 Scottsdale National. The upper one was made by Bodie McKay and the lower one by Kee Benally. *(Jerry Jacka)*

A Zuni pin with both needlepoint and inlay. This contemporary piece is unusual for the combination of the two techniques in one item. *(FHFAC, HM, Al Abrams)*

A Zuni "tourist" inlay pin from the 1950s. Note cracked and poorly fitting stones, sloppy silverwork. *(PC, Al Abrams)*

Channelwork bracelet of a Zuni Knife Wing God. This figure was probably the basis of the belief that the "thunderbird" was an Indian design. A fine piece with intricate detail and high-quality turquoise. *(FHFAC, HM, Al Abrams)*

Zuni inlay pin of a flower, made by Virgil and Shirley Benn. Pictorial representations of things in nature, while not in the traditional repertoire of Southwest Indian designs, have become very popular in Indian jewelry. The materials used here are mother-of-pearl, abalone, and coral. *(DNH, Peter L. Bloomer)*

PART TWO

THE EXPERTS SPEAK

In any specialized field, the collector's instinct is to seek "the advice of the experts." Indian jewelry is not a field in which there are one, or two, or even a mere half-dozen "experts." From this book's inception, it was clear that for anything approaching expertise, it would be necessary to consult persons in "all walks of the trade," all phases of the art and craft.

Thus the following conversations, in search of insight and information, with a wide range of collectors, "experts", and appreciators of fine Indian jewelry. Together these people are a fair sample of the individuals who have influenced the past and are influencing the present of Indian jewelry; each in some way determining what the future will bring. Each has a unique vantage point to the romance—and the reality—of Indian jewelry.

"*Almost overnight the business expanded beyond our wildest dreams...*"

TOBE *(the "e" is not sounded)* A. TURPEN JR. *is the owner of Tobe Turpen's Indian Trading Co. in Gallup, New Mexico. He is a long-time dealer in Indian goods, and like many other traders in Gallup comes from a family which has been in the business for generations.*

Indian handcrafts have finally received the national and international recognition they have deserved for the past fifty years. The public has finally come to the realization that Indian jewelry is either the only, or certainly one of the few, crafts practiced in the United States which is really native to our country.

Indian merchandise has always sold well to visiting Europeans, because they are accustomed to handmade items and recognize both the quality and the value.

This has not been true of Americans.

As recently as five to ten years ago it was difficult to sell Indian merchandise to someone to give as a gift, because the buyer was always worried that the recipient would have no appreciation of the price that had been paid.

This seems to be one of the idiosyncracies of the American people: they are willing to spend money for gifts as long as the person receiving them is aware of their true value.

Today the American public has awakened to the fact that the merchandise really has value and is potentially a good monetary investment.

The more affluent citizens realized this to be a fact many years ago and bought Indian jewelry at that time. All these years they have enjoyed wearing their jewelry and as an added bonus have seen it increase in value many times over. Although they were many times looked upon as being eccentric or even placed in the oddball category by the average American public, they were far ahead of their times. A case in point would be the famous Millicent Rogers. [The Millicent Rogers Foundation of Taos, New Mexico, bears her name.] We had the privilege of supplying Mrs. Rogers with many fine pieces of jewelry during the 1940s and '50s. She preferred old pieces, but would purchase new items when they were quality and appealed to her personal taste. Today the Millicent Rogers museum, a privately endowed institution, is one of the most noteworthy of its type.

Of course, Mrs. Rogers was financially capable of making this type of investment, but there were many other people of moderate means who made their purchases, wore and enjoyed their jewelry, and paid no attention to other people who thought they were throwing their money away.

Many of the really fine collections are in the state of California. I suppose this is because the area was close and many vacation periods were spent in New Mexico and Arizona.

I many times had the feeling that the people doing the buying had been exposed to and probably owned other quality items such as diamonds and other precious jewels, but the desire for these had been satisfied somewhere along the line. It was as though they were turning to Indian merchandise, subconsciously, as a replacement, as something new to provide both prestige and pleasure. In short, they wanted to be different.

Many people who know the business as it was prior to 1965 have fear of such things as overexposure, imitations taking over the market, too many dealers in the business who are not really qualified to know exactly what they are selling, treated turquoise, manufactured jewelry, etcetera. Except for overexposure and a possible excess of new dealers, those of us who have been in the business for any period of time have always lived with the other factors. There has never been a shortage of imitations, treated turquoise, or machine-made items. I personally don't see a threat to the long-range picture concerning Indian jewelry. There are still many areas of the United States which have received very little exposure, and the overseas market is practically untouched.

For approximately forty years, from the 1920s through the '60s, the Indian jewelry market was identified almost exclusively with the Southwest. It was a sleepy but intriguing business, with low-volume sales and marginal profits. I would very much like to have seen it stay this way. We seldom failed to have a small yearly increase in sales, and the business was well in control of knowledgeable people who in many cases had been in the business for generations.

However, almost overnight the business expanded beyond our wildest dreams.

With prominence came the growing pains that come when any business expands so rapidly. You might say the business has finally come of age, and we are still trying to catch up with it.

For the short term it is obvious the business must slow down, possibly even quite drastically. Hardly anything can explode as the Indian business has without settling back to some semblance of a normal plateau. We will only know whtat normal is when we get there.

I don't think large-scale thefts have hurt the craft as a business. If anything, I think they have just added credence to the fact that the merchandise is valuable and can be sold with obvious ease.

Just a very few years ago, it would have been a waste of time to burglarize an Indian jewelry establishment: there was no place to go with the merchandise, and the value was considered negligible in most areas. Almost everyone in the business knew practically every other dealer, wholesale or retail, and stolen merchandise was usually very easy to trace and find.

Some treated turquoise can be spotted very easily by almost anyone with any knowledge, especially if it remains in nugget form. It will usually be quite vivid in color (usually blue, but occasionally green), and will be rather obviously coated with clear plastic or some other material of similar consistency. However, if the job of treating or stabilizing is well done, and the stone is cut and polished into a cabochon or mounted into a piece of channel jewelry by a good artisan, it is practically impossible to spot. This holds true for the expert as well as the amateur.

I would like to say we are one of the dealers who see no harm in using stabilized turquoise, as long as the buyer is informed as to what he is buying. We actually use stabilized in some of our finest pieces. If stabilized were not available, the price of good-quality natural turquoise could become absolutely prohibitive.

I suppose that if you go far enough back in the Indian jewelry business you would find that old pawn was an article that had been pawned to a trader by an Indian, had not been redeemed by the pawner, and was actually relatively old—at least twenty years or more. For the most part this still holds true today, with the exception of age. If it was never redeemed, it is often referred to as "old pawn" when the word *pawn* would be more accurate. The majority of pawn merchandise being offered to the public is relatively new jewelry. However, a reputable merchant should have no trouble in recognizing both quality and age.

There is lots of pawn available, but in my opinion very little of real vintage quality. If I were a collector, I would be more concerned that the article be of quality and have personal appeal. Just because an Indian owned the jewelry originally is no guarantee of quality. After all, he buys what is appealing to his taste and fitting to his pocketbook, just like anyone else.

The best assurance of authenticity a collector can get is the guarantee, verbal or written, of a reputable dealer, one who has been in the business long enough to know what he is selling and who will back up his sale if called upon to do so. It should be understood that even a reputable dealer could make an honest error in his representation, but you would have no problem in getting new merchandise or a refund. I place very little value on hallmarks, although they are often comforting to the buyer. It's not easy for the average buyer to spot a fake unless extremely obvious, and then the chances are very slim that the item is going to be misrepresented in the first place. I think it would be almost impossible for a buyer to gain enough knowledge through reading material and research to recognize a fake if the item was really well made —once again, a reason for the buyer to seek out a reputable source.

I feel it is possible to establish a person's being reputable by the appearance of the place in which you are doing business, the actions and manner in which you are approached by the owner or employees, and the sense of security and honesty projected by the entire operation. A reputable dealer is not going to be offended by being asked fair questions regarding his merchandise. I do not think organizations, trade unions, etcetera are an absolute guarantee that you are going to be treated fairly. I don't think it's a matter of avoiding certain types of dealers, but rather of seeking out the reputable dealer with whom you feel comfortable. I always like to feel I can return to the person or firm if I have a problem.

I think the Indian jewelry business has a great future, but on a more limited scale than the bonanza we have experienced during the past five years. I have a feeling the public is going to be more quality-minded and more particular about where they do their buying, and the successful dealer is going to have to meet the challenge of their wants and needs.

"When I first started there were not so many weavers, not so many potters, not so many silversmiths..."

KATIE NOE, *retired now after forty-five years in the Indian arts and crafts business, lives in a gracious home overlooking Gallup, New Mexico, and the beautiful country which surrounds it. She has worked for some of the greatest names in the trade, and for many years she ran her own establishment, the Zuni Shop, in Gallup. She has received two citations from the United States Department of the Interior for her efforts at encouraging authentic Indian arts and crafts.*

I think the greatest difference between the present and when I started out in the business forty-five years ago is that now we have many more craftsmen and many more crafts than we had originally. When I first started there were not so many weavers, not so many potters, not so many silversmiths. Now everyone is doing it, and some of the effects are bad. They're not doing the quality work they used to. They don't take the time. They know that somebody will buy their work, regardless of the quality, regardless of the materials, regardless of the workmanship. I think that's kind of tragic, because they don't take the pride in it anymore. They want to have something ready because somebody's going to be standing at their door to buy, and they want to make it right away and sell it.

The best way people can collect Indian jewelry, I always tell them, is to find something they like and make sure that is from a well-established and reliable dealer. There is no easy way a person can identify good handmade jewelry. It used to be, years ago, we never questioned the fact that if an Indian brought it in to sell, it was handmade. But I don't think anymore, because of centrifugal casting, machine casting; that's very hard to identify. The materials used in it could be real turquoise and sterling silver; it's the method that makes it difficult to tell. When they used to press it out, you could tell, yes; but they have new and modern methods of doing it now, and it's not so easy.

It's hard to get laws to assure higher standards in selling jewelry, very hard. I worked with the Zuni tribe and the All-Pueblo Council up in Santa Fe, and Dean Kirk and Al Ribek here in Gallup. Bills have been introduced and become law, but the state can never get together on enforcement. It's pretty hard to pass a law and then actually enforce it. The Federal Trade Commission was involved in this area for a time; you can take action on misrepresentation, but to prove it is very difficult. Enforcement depends entirely now on the integrity of the craftsman and the dealer.

Misrepresentation is the real problem—not only the materials but the handcraft and the silversmith. We have a lot of Spanish people making jewelry and a lot of Anglos making jewelry, and it's just as beautiful and well made as an Indian would make; and if a dealer buys it, it would be very hard for him to do anything but take the word of the wholesaler who sold it to him. I think enforcement would be *real* difficult.

I'm wholeheartedly in agreement that turquoise should be identified, because if you went into a store and bought a wool suit and you found out it was part cotton, there's a law to protect you in a situation like that. If they're going to have any kind of a law to protect you, it should protect the genuineness of the turquoise. Of course, stabilized turquoise is all over the country. It looks better than some of the real turquoise, as it's mined, but I think it should be identified for what it is. You could tell your dealers or your retail customers that this is stabilized turquoise and not genuine—as it is found; but it's attractive and it holds its color and it matches—and then people would know what they're buying. But sell it as genuine? I've been in the business too long for that. We always had all the good turquoise we needed. It was high, and it's still high.

I don't think the well-made, better-quality pieces of jewelry on the market will ever go down to where the market has been, but I think that there's so much jewelry today that they're going to have a hard time getting their price. I think they're far overproduced. There are a lot of big chain and department stores buying it now, but I also think that when the market slows down and the purchasing relaxes, they'll be the first to quit. I worked at the old Gallup Mercantile Company, and we used to service some of the big eastern department stores. We got into a little recession and they were the first to leave all the dealers out here with big orders to fill, and they didn't want them. I saw that happen.

Is there such a thing as old pawn today? Well, I think there's still some old pawn left, but I don't think it would be offered for sale by the traders holding it. I think the people who have this nice old pawn—what *we* would call old pawn—I think these dealers are reputable enough to keep it for the people it belongs to, regardless of how long it takes. A lot of the newer jewelry that's been pawned will be sold.

A lot of people have capitalized on the fact that old pawn had a reputation for being something very special, something that was considered a little better than if you walked into a store and bought it. I think a lot of people who have bought old pawn really thought they were getting a forty- or fifty-year-old piece of jewelry. I don't think that's been the whole pattern, but I think there's been some of that. But old-time ethical dealers that I grew up with kept jewelry twenty-five or thirty years.

[I asked Mrs. Noe about the adverse publicity that Indian traders have received in recent years, adding that I felt that—with a few individual exceptions—the old-time traders had been among the best friends and advisers the Indians had.]

You're looking right when you feel that way. I was raised here and I grew up with all these traders. If it hadn't been for a lot of these people, you wouldn't have had any of the crafts that are on the market today. I've known a few that would take advantage and abuse the privilege of doing business with the Indians, but they were so few; you're going to find somebody that would take advantage of you,

I don't care where you go. It was the traders, the older traders, who found the markets for Indian crafts.

I think Fred Harvey was the first major market for Indian jewelry. As I recall, it was the Indians around Manuelito who were the first to sell to Harvey. The smiths all lived in that area then. Now they're all over.

I would say that a million dollars a month in Indian jewelry goes out of Gallup alone. Nowadays I imagine there are quite a few silversmiths down in Zuni who are making a hundred thousand dollars a year.

Take a pair of cufflinks with a nugget set, and a nugget ring and a bolo tie and a belt buckle—possibly a five-piece set. It sells for $2,500 from Indians. They can make it very easily in three days, four days—make two or three sets a week. But one thing about them: they don't work when they don't want to.

Twenty years ago everybody thought the good work was high-priced—it was about one-tenth of what it is today. But when you think about what inflation we have, and see that $2,500 set for five pieces, and think about twenty years ago when the market wasn't inflated as it is now—it was *still* high-priced for the average person, the better-quality jewelry.

But the Indians are really capable people, and they're entitled to get a good price for a good piece of jewelry. I think we bought it very reasonably for many, many years. Even five years ago you had to find your market to sell jewelry. Now the market finds you.

But it was never hard to find people who appreciated good Indian jewelry; not the kind of people who came to me. Sometimes the prices were higher than they felt they could afford, but they always appreciated seeing and hearing and talking about it.

I'm sorry to see it like it is today. It was a real joy and pleasure when everybody wasn't selling Indian jewelry. I think the better-quality jewelry will always command a good price. The real nice pieces, with nice turquoise—I don't think the prices on those will ever change very much. But I'm sure that the good businessman will prepare himself for a drop in the market. It's just overproduced. You'll find, too, that the old, well-established, conscientious dealer that has always been there will still be there, and these new people who have got in on the demand—well, they'll be doing something else.

As for stolen Indian jewelry: it's so hard to identify. You could take a picture, but there may be twenty pieces made just alike. I noticed that article in *Arizona Highways* about C. G. Wallace [August 1974; C. G. Wallace was a long-time trader at Zuni Pueblo south of Gallup until he retired a few years ago] that said he could identify every piece he owned. Well, in his time you *could*. I worked five years for him. Every piece that came in, we knew exactly which family had made it. But you can't do that any more, because the last fifteen years they've copied each other's work, and they can do it to perfection. You can take a certain pin that was made by a certain family, and maybe they'd made ten of them; then you've got another family, because the pin sold well, making ten or fifteen, and maybe you've got five different families making that same thing—and how are you going to identify it?

"No piece of jewelry should be bought strictly as an investment but as what's to become part of your life..."

PAUL HULDERMAN *owns the House of the Six Directions on prestigious Fifth Avenue in Scottsdale, Arizona. He not only sells quality Indian arts and crafts but is a serious student of them as well. In addition to handling the work of established craftsmen he seeks out and encourages promising younger artists.*

What is the greatest boon to the collector of Indian jewelry today? In the first place, I wouldn't call him a collector, I would call him an investor because unfortunately the purchases of Indian jewelry are always preceded by the question of how good an investment they are. In my opinion, no piece of jewelry, Indian or otherwise, should be bought strictly as an investment but as what's to become part of your life.

The greatest boon, I think, is that so many people are buying it, the common psychology being that you should have *some* piece of Indian jewelry. People nowadays buy items as "Indian jewelry" and don't pay any attention to style—that is, traditional style or new developments; they just want to buy the turquoise as an investment.

The greatest threat to the craft is the outright fakes by non-Indians, the quantity of people who are entering the business on the wholesale and retail levels, and the complete ignorance of these people regarding prices—and the Zuni is an excellent illustration.

Zuni jewelry has probably gone higher percentagewise than any other type of Indian jewelry, and since not all of these people who are now entering the business actually knows the value of a piece of authentic design or of the turquoise by actual carat, the business has gone completely out of kilter. I don't think anybody should be in this business just for money's sake; I think there should be a love affair with the turquoise and Indian arts and crafts. This is an element that has gone completely out of the business but was prevalent in years gone by with everybody involved.

It's very hard to tell how long the present boom will last, and it's something that is partly up to the public. It's hard to understand, for instance, why someone who is interested in buying Indian jewelry will go to a place that offers discounts. There are only two explanations for discounts: one is that the merchandise is not very good and was bought, therefore, cheaply; the other is that the merchandise is fair or good and that the prices were raised before the discount was taken off.

If the public were to be more selective and not just buy on the spur of the moment in the discount shops, the present boom would not go on very long. Another element that affects the boom is the department stores, and since they don't know very much about the actual background of Indian jewelry they are not equipped to sell it. But as soon as the sales go downward, I'm certain in my own mind, the department stores will get out of the business. Basically this business is a small privately owned business, and there's nothing that you buy by the dozen nor do you buy it to sell by the dozen. Under the present conditions the element of creativity is bound to fall by the wayside.

The layman who has bought very little Indian jewelry during his lifetime is really not equipped to look for authenticity, because he doesn't know enough about the background elements of this business. So there's really only two choices left to him. One is to go into a number of stores and see where he has confidence in the owner and let the owner guide him. Or, he can look around and see who has bought where and let these people guide him.

The average buyer cannot spot a well-made fake. In some cases, yes; but more often he has to have some sort of help and advice.

Old pawn is something that was actually pawned to a trading post or an individual and carries a ticket saying how much money was paid. Unfortunately we are getting nowadays pawn tickets attached to more recent jewelry or to items that were not made by Indians or jewelry that never was pawned. There is very little available today, but occasionally you can come across it by sheer luck—which does happen once in a while. A good piece of old pawn would be twenty years old or more.

I don't think the collector should be concerned about old pawn too much. It's like collecting antiques, in that you buy whatever strikes your fancy. You like to get involved in it, and if you get involved in buying old pawn it's a fascinating thing to collect, but not everyone can afford it.

Up until the present avalanche of buying Indian arts and crafts, these—for some reason that I cannot quite explain—were looked upon as aboriginal arts and crafts and not, somehow, considered as a part of the total American art scene; they were placed in a niche off by themselves. Now, fortunately, that has changed.

The question has often come up; will the young Indians continue this art? My answer is that the Institute of American Indian Arts in Santa Fe has always had a waiting line for students who want to learn the craft. There are many young people who want to make this their life's work.
people who want to make this their life's work.

Another point is that I don't think that any Indian can live without creativity. This feeling is supported by the fact that Indians in prehistoric times made things like jewelry and pottery and other decorative things. There always has been a need for the Indian to be creative in an ornamental sense. I think the art is here to stay; there just has to be a thinning-out process.

There is a desire on the part of young people to enter this business; and as much as it is desirable that they do enter it, it should be borne in mind, too, that things have changed considerably. In years long gone by, when we started, you could start a store of this type with fairly small capital, but nowadays your initial inventory demands much more. It's very difficult for young people.

It always has been my contention that Indian stores should get more and more into the hands of Indians instead of non-Indians, which involves the big task of educating the Indian in the economics of the non-Indian society. I think Indian shops should evolve to the point where they specialize in one particular aspect of Indian arts—Indian jewelry for instance—and when we get to this stage of "specialty" shops then we will have a much better climate.

I'm a firm believer that any form of arts and crafts has to evolve, that it has to take on other forms. This word *traditional* Indian jewelry is really

very inaccurate because it doesn't describe anything. There is no form of art that is traditional. There may be traditional design elements, but if arts and crafts are to stay alive, they must explore new areas.
I realize that a lot of people—customers—will say, "This doesn't look Indian to me." My answer is, "Well, it may not look Indian to you, or to your tastes, but it was made by an Indian, and consequently it is Indian jewelry." And who are we to determine what is traditional, what is contemporary, or what is anything in the case of Indian jewelry?
Whatever the Indian makes, that is Indian jewelry. We're always looking for new talent, and in that respect you are more likely to find it, not on the reservations, but in urban areas where the younger Indians have been exposed to new ideas. When you work with young people you not only are helping them to find new means by which to earn a livelihood, but you also have a very enjoyable experience, apart from the buying aspect of it.

By way of illustration there's a young Navajo boy who has incredibly beautiful ideas about creation of jewelry, and he has advanced on his own to the use of other materials than jet or shell or turquoise or coral; he uses lapis lazuli, he uses old ivory, he uses pipestone— anything that lends itself to expression. In working with these young people it helps us because we can learn new ideas that are going around in their minds, and on the other hand, we hope, of course, that we can be helpful, too.

"Indian jewelry is still the best buy in the world..."

JOE TANNER *operates Tanner's Indian Arts on West Highway 66 in Gallup, New Mexico. Tanner is a famous name in the Indian goods business in the Southwest, but not all Tanners are related, nor do they necessarily work in cooperation with one another. Joe Tanner's shop is not small, but neither is it large; his items are carefully selected, and the tourist looking for an "Indian style" ring would find himself out of place here.*

I've been in this business for the last fifteen years. I got into it because I was running a supermarket here in Gallup and the Indians would come in to me trying to sell the things they couldn't sell anywhere else; what they wanted to do was trade for groceries. But most of the things they had were not good enough, and that's when I started going to Zuni and getting in touch with the better Navajo smiths.

The year 1960 was a comeback year that began this present cycle, although it wasn't anything like the tremendous market it is now. I would go to dealers and ask them what they wanted, and I would order it from the smiths. I set it up so that they were all given profit-and-loss statements. I would say to them, "I'll give you so many dollars worth of raw materials for you to make such-and-such with, and I'll pay you so much money for the finished product." It was understood that the product had to be of quality standards; everything was on special order, and it had to be good or it wouldn't sell. Nowadays any piece of garbage that an Indian might just have looked at will sell.

Will the present cycle continue? It will never return to the low of what it was a few years ago, and the situation right now is that Montgomery Ward and the service station owner and the beauty cosmetics salesman in Atlanta are selling Indian jewelry, but at least they're introducing people to Indian jewelry and it has caught on nationally like it never has before.

I was listening to Vincent Price on television not long ago, and what he had to say about buying art is true. If you become interested, the thing to do is to rush down and become involved. Usually you buy the wrong piece to start, but then you trade up. Out of every hundred buyers, one or two become serious collectors.

Now there are museums and books where the serious collector can do research, and the subject should be approached like buying a fine diamond. If you're laying out a lot of money, you find a good dealer. As Joe Stacey says in *Arizona Highways*, if you don't want to do the research, find a dealer you can depend on the same way you trust your doctor.

Fakes hurt the business, and they hurt the Indians themselves to a tremendous extent. We call ourselves Tanner's Indian Arts, and that's exactly what we sell. We won't even handle a piece that has manufactured beads. Now the findings—earscrews, things like that the Indians never have made—we don't consider that cheating. But I think one reason people are so anxious to buy Indian jewelry is that they are sympathetic toward the Indians and want to help them. When they took the silver out of coins, the next step was for people to buy silver jewelry, and they went to Indian jewelry to help the Indian. If you compare high-quality Indian jewelry with other silver jewelry anywhere, Indian jewelry is still the best buy in the world. Naturally, not all pieces are good investments, but every penny I have in the world is invested in Indian jewelry.

Buyers of Indian jewelry are becoming a lot

more sophisticated. Tom Bahti (an Indian goods dealer in Tucson, now deceased) once said that it is impossible to overestimate the enormous bad taste of the average buyer, but that isn't true anymore. It's easier to buy good jewelry here in the Southwest; I'd say that 60 percent of the shops out here have quality jewelry to sell. *Arizona Highways* has been a real important factor in presenting pictures of good Indian jewelry and showing that it is available.

When you're buying you should, above all, insist on something you like and don't just follow the fads. A few years back, squash-blossom necklaces were all the rage; that's all women wanted to buy. They proliferated on the market, and many of them were not handmade, most were not well made, and a lot of them were in bad taste. And the trouble is that while one good piece of jewelry will create ten new customers, one bad piece will destroy ten. As long as the demand exceeds the supply you'll have junk on the market, so if you don't *want* it, don't buy it, no matter what anyone says.

As for old pawn, we sell it, and we have excellent sources. But ten years ago, pawn belonged to the Indian, and he cherished it; it was his fortune. Today, pawn is often a piece of jewelry that a smith couldn't sell; he pawned it, but he was really selling it because he had no intention of redeeming it since he couldn't sell it any other way. There's still a lot of quality pawn, but today, more so than ever, it's a case of let the buyer beware.

There are a lot of Arabs dealing in Indian jewelry today. I don't deal with them, and I don't know any of them personally. But they practically live down at Zuni; they go to bed with them at night and they get up with them in the morning and they're there to buy anything that's for sale. They've driven prices up and quality down. They say that the Arabs ship the quality goods out of the country and sell the low-quality things around here—Albuquerque, Phoenix, the West Coast; but again, I really don't know about that.

Every trader has certain families he deals with; it's a one-to-one rapport. We've developed about thirty Navajo families with whom we deal. All the smiths know each other, they're related, or they're friends, or they learned the trade from one another. They know that we supply them with quality turquoise and materials, and that attracts quality people; when you treat them right, they know it. It's the same with customers.

We insist on hallmarks on all our jewelry and, wholesale or retail, we put the artist's name down. It's a double-edged sword: if the smith does a lousy job, he knows he'll get it back.

Gallup is the real "Indian jewelry capital" of the world, but the title of "Indian jewelry *style* capital" would have to go to Albuquerque or Los Angeles. They make a lot of fake jewelry in Los Angeles, and by that I mean jewelry that is not handmade and not made by Indians.

Centrifugally cast jewelry can be very good jewelry, but it's just not handmade. For example, take a genuine handmade ring that would sell for $36. You could sell a centrifugally cast ring of the same quality for $18 and show the same margin of profit. It's a tragedy we don't have the kind of market where each piece has to be labeled. In the meantime, though, the buyer had better depend on his dealer.

Indian jewelry guilds depend entirely upon the people who run them and the standards they set. If they insist upon quality workmanship from their members, that's what they're going to get. Not everyone does, and when that happens the guild is meaningless.

Indian jewelry has increased in value an average of 18 percent a year in recent years, and as much as 50 percent for quality pieces. The other goods, lesser quality, are dependent upon what the price of silver does. Some economists are saying that silver will be selling for $10 an ounce by 1980, and in that case these pieces will increase in value just on the worth of the silver alone.

"There are people running around now selling turquoise who, a few years back, couldn't even spell it..."

JIM GODBER *operates Godber's Jewelry in Scottsdale, Arizona. He is third-generation in the Indian jewelry business, and his two boys are working with him now. He's been active in the trade for twenty-five years.*

I think the greatest change in the business over the years has been price, and on the whole there's not as much top-quality jewelry as there used to be. There was such an undersupply for a while, with the department stores buying up jewelry, but some of the larger stores are very selective and they are selling good jewelry. Some of the discount houses are selling jewelry that I think is not of the greatest quality.

The best advice I can give anybody is to go to an old-line dealer; if he's been in business fifteen, twenty years, he knows what he's doing. If he's got a reputation to maintain, he can't afford to misrepresent anything. Occasionally, now, he'll get hold of something that was misrepresented to him, like the synthetic turquoise. Yesterday, a man came in to me and he had a bunch of turquoise. It was Bisbee turquoise and it was stabilized, but I would defy anybody to say, "This is stabilized." They've got the art advanced to the point where even the oldest dealers in the business can't tell the difference.

I don't think anybody uses oiled turquoise much anymore because the new stabilizing processes are so good they don't need it. They used to use mineral oil or paraffin, and now they're using plastics and I guess they've got stuff out that is even newer than that. You can take a snow-white nugget and treat it and it'll bring off a nice shade of blue. In fact, when they overdo it, it almost gets to a purple, but of course that's easy to spot. I don't think there's a thing wrong with selling stabilized, as long as it's not misrepresented. I mean, if you're going to buy a $20 ring with stabilized turquoise, the same thing with genuine turquoise from a good mine would probably run $50, $75, or $90.

Generally you can look at a stone and tell how good it is, but a dealer can't check every stone he sells. Occasionally you'll get a soft turquoise which will absorb foreign substances like butter, cold cream, even perspiration. But that doesn't happen often with your top dealers, and when it does they'll replace it or make good on the piece immediately.

People come in here and want to sell us turquoise; we find the stone is too thin, or it's not right in some other way. Sometimes, when they want to sell us silver, we find it has too much alloy in it. The same is true of some of the big Indian events; a lot of people who sell jewelry there aren't even Indians. I've had people come to me with a ring they bought at [he named a well-known Indian gathering], and they want their ring sized. They say, "I paid $13.50 for it." I could tell them that you can buy the same ring here in Scottsdale for $4.50.

Sterling silver is .093 fine, meaning that 930 parts out of a thousand are pure silver. That's what is used in Indian jewelry. Fine silver runs somewhere around .097, but that's used only for making bezels; it's too soft to use otherwise.

While most of the turquoise used now comes from the Southwest United States, I ran a mine in Baja California [Mexico], out of a little place called Rosario back in 1944, '45, '46, '47. Because of wartime restrictions in the United States we couldn't operate in Nevada—gas rationing and things like that. During that time we supplied most of the Southwest Indian business with turquoise even though the quality wasn't the greatest.

In finished jewelry carats aren't the usual way of determining price; it's what they call the spread. A stone the size of a nickel might be, say, a $10 stone, and even if the stone was twice as thick it would still sell for the same price. It's the amount of stone you actually see that counts. Cardboard, tissue paper, and nowadays sawdust are put under stones to protect them from shock when they're mounted. They also help to secure a good fit in the bezel, regulate the height.

It's not always easy to spot centrifugally cast jewelry. The best way to sell it is not to mix it with cast (as in sandcast) jewelry, and to label it plainly for what it is. As long as it's not misrepresented it's a nice way to get started. A person can buy a $5 ring and enjoy it and be complimented on it. Then he might buy a $10 or $15 ring. After that he may want to invest in actual handmade jewelry because the cheaper items have given him the desire to have better jewelry.

Even in centrifugally cast jewelry there are sometimes as many as fifteen steps that have to be done by hand, even though the basic piece is not handmade, and certainly not Indian handmade. But very often this can't be spotted. This is especially true of channelwork. A lot of so-called Zuni channelwork is actually centrifugally cast. In fact, there's a line of "Zuni" work that actually comes from Guadalajara, Mexico.

Zuni is the best jewelry, in my opinion, for collectors to invest in, the way the market has been lately. For example, four or five years ago I bought my wife a necklace for $230, and I just sold one last week and the same necklace was $1,050. Your real Navajo jewelry is very good, too, at holding its value, but I don't think it's advanced as much as Zuni. Not all Zuni jewelry is that good, of course; there's a big demand for it and they're making it as fast as they can, but there's Zuni jewelry and then there's exquisite Zuni jewelry. You can check the match of the turquoise and the silverwork and the gauge of the silver, and you can pretty well tell when the work is really good. They're doing some beautiful multicolor, coral, turquoise, jet, and shell. But the best investment, I would say, is anything over $100, for the good pieces. You're better off to gamble on $200, $300, $400, or $500 pieces. For instance, a piece you bought last year for $500 would probably sell for $550 today. So Indian jewelry is still a good investment.

I would say that there are definite rings that are stealing Indian jewelry and selling it elsewhere; it's going out of the area, and even though some of it is reported on in detail it never seems to show up again. To me, that's pretty good evidence that they're dismantling it and remounting the stones in new silverwork.

There are people running around now selling turquoise who, a few years back, couldn't even spell it. But your old-line dealers know their jewelry, and they know they're cutting their own throats when they sell bad jewelry. Of course, they can't always tell—for instance, about stones.

I think the main reward of this business for me is that I'm doing something I like to do. My boys and my wife work here with me, and we love to sell good jewelry. It's a lot of fun, not just a job; it's a hobby, and pretty well paying, at that.

"Uninformed people come in and look at the price of the good stuff and it scares them to death..."

DON and NITA HOEL *are proprietors of Don Hoel's Cabins and a fine Indian jewelry shop nestled in the heart of Oak Creek Canyon, Arizona. Don was raised on a ranch in Glendale, Arizona, and began trading jewelry with the Indians who worked there. Don and Nita insist on high quality in their shop and are diligent in assuring that end. The Hoel collection is probably the major private documented collection of contemporary Indian jewelry.*

Us experts? We've been in the business forty years and we're still not experts. There really are no experts in this field, I'm afraid. I see something different every day and I'm sure everyone in the business does.

Do we favor modern jewelry work, or traditional? What do you call traditional? Before forty-five years ago there really wasn't any tradition, just a stone and some silver to hold it, very little delicate work. I think a lot of the jewelry today is nicer than years ago; today we have some of the finest smiths ever.

That piece there is by one of the old-time famous smiths, Luke Yazzie. He does the very finest of intricate gold and silver work.

My folks were cattle people and farmers—we used both Mexican and Indian hands. I was raised in Glendale, Arizona, on a ranch. During World War I we had 102 Supai on our ranch at one time (there are only about 200 in the tribe), and we had Navajos over the years; they all lived on the ranch. I was trading, buying, and selling their things with them while I was still in high school, and I got to like the jewelry—you've got to, to stay in the business, though there are traders and merchants today who don't care what they sell, or how much they cheat people.

If I were buying today, starting a collection, I'd be very careful about the quality of the turquoise. The value is the turquoise; 90 percent of my merchandise is spiderweb. A thing has got to have good stones or I don't want it in my place. I can even stand fairly poor workmanship if the stones are good. With the good stones, who looks at the silver as much as the stones?

If I had money, I'd put it into turquoise—good turquoise is scarce, getting scarcer and scarcer. Turquoise from #8 mine, which only produced fine turquoise from 1936 to 1951, was some of the finest spiderweb ever mined, and today it is rare in the highest grades (and one of the highest-priced).

Up to three years ago it was true that the Persians didn't particularly value matrix turquoise—today they're keeping a lot of the good matrix stuff.

Just as with diamonds, the bigger a stone is the more it is worth per carat. So if I were investing, I'd invest in Navajo-style with good stones. With a good stone, you're almost assured good craftsmanship, because nobody's going to give a really good stone to a poor craftsman.

In the last ten years the workmanship is better in every class. Yes, partly because the tools are better, but also because the demand is for better workmanship, and they are realizing it pays.

We're seeing better needlepoint today than we ever got—in needlepoint you're paying nearly 100 percent for labor; in other types of jewelry you're paying mostly for stones. All the pieces we see that collectors really prize are pieces with very fine turquoise, and the price of good turquoise just keeps on increasing.

Sometimes the workmanship and materials are good but the design is not good. I'm sure there are good and bad tastes, but everyone has a different taste, so it is possible to sell nearly every design. I'm sure this is true because I'm afraid there is more junk jewelry sold today than good jewelry.

The very modern, I think, can get too far from Indian style. Then there is chip jewelry that is glued in, and I think this is terrible.

How do I feel about Mexican Indians doing "Indian jewelry"? I feel very strong against it. I've heard some people explain they're really American Indians with Mexican names, but I think Indians should have the respect that they deserve. If jewelry is made by a hippie, a white, or a Mexican, it shouldn't be called Indian jewelry, it should be called "Indian-style" jewelry.

How do I keep control over authenticity? I'm careful who I buy from, and I only buy from about four different people. I do this because I know where their jewelry is made and by whom.

Uninformed people come in and look at the price of the good stuff and it scares them to death (because they have been looking at low-grade stones and treated stones). There's always the collectors, and people wanting quality; but the others, they've seen it somewhere for half the price.

"Curiously, foreigners, especially Europeans, appreciated good silver more than most Americans did twenty years ago..."

AL PACKARD *runs Chaparral Trading Post on Santa Fe's historic Plaza. He is extremely knowledgeable about Indian jewelry and other crafts, as befits the head of the Ethics Committee of the Indian Arts and Crafts Association, whose 700 members work together not only to promote knowledge and appreciation of genuine Indian arts and crafts but to maintain standards of quality workmanship.*

In acquiring Indian jewelry there are two things the buyer should look for: the quality of the turquoise and the quality of workmanship. He should be suspicious to excessive regularity in stamped designs, and of repetition of minor flaws when designs are repeated, as they are in a concha belt where the same die mark will be repeated on each concha. Also, when a drop press has been used to stamp the designs they will never be as deep as they are in hand-stamped jewelry.

An experiencd dealer can almost always spot stabilized turquoise, but it's an instinctive thing with him, something that's just about impossible to put into words. It's harder to spot stabilized turquoise when you are dealing with just one stone than it is when you are looking at a batch of them. In a batch of stabilized stones the regularity and consistency of color immediately attract the trained eye.

Present laws regarding the labeling of Indian jewelry are unfair. For instance, the non-Indian smith who makes jewelry by hand, using genuine materials, must mark his products "Indian Imitation." But there are people in New Mexico producing copies of jewelry by centrifugal-casting methods, and they should also be made to mark their items "Indian Imitation."

There are two real offenders when it comes to selling spurious jewelry: first, the shops that are casting it centrifugally but not telling anyone that they are, and second, the foreign countries which are producing copies of Indian jewelry and other crafts, using cheap labor and materials and exporting them to the United States. The government should put a high embargo on such imports, to protect the Indians. The Santo Domingo Indians, for instance, have long been noted for making heishi. It's an arduous and time-consuming process when done by hand, but at the rate they're importing cheap foreign-made heishi there will be a lot of Indians at Santo Domingo who will have to go on welfare.

Anyone who is serious about collecting genuine handmade Indian jewelry should by all means buy from established and reputable dealers; sometimes local museums and Chambers of Commerce can be helpful in this respect. In addition, the serious student should spend at least a year studying the field and getting to know it first-hand.

Caring for quality jewelry is very simple: treat it as you would any other jewelry. Good turquoise won't change color no matter how long you wear it, and soap or cold cream or perspiration won't affect it at all. Nevada turquoise is probably the most durable.

Silver keeps its shine by being worn, but it if is stored away and tarnishes a bit, it can be brought up quickly by using rouge cloths or polishing cloths; if it gets too dark, you can take it to a jeweler's and have it buffed up on a polishing wheel.

Indians have a real feeling for their own good jewelry, but not for the trade stuff. The best smiths create art, but they want to make money, too.

There is a religious quality to the turquoise, too. At Santo Domingo they love oiled turquoise; it turns bluer and demands a higher price. It's better than stabilized; the oil makes it bluer at first but it gradually changes to an olive green at times, with each stone having a separate color. The varicolored necklaces appraise at high prices after they have mellowed. They don't oil all of their work—some of them use good natural stones that don't need oil.

It is true that some smiths are putting out fake old pawn jewelry, but this is relatively easy to spot because the authentic old jewelry bears true wear marks which can only come from long years of being worn. Steel wool and oxidization can't duplicate these marks.

Today you find the ironic situation where non-Indian smiths are creating jewelry in the traditional Indian styles of the early part of the century while the Indian smiths are doing contemporary work in what I would call the Scandinavian style.

People today, in general, have better taste in Indian jewelry than they used to. The new-style Indian jewelry being made has lost us some of the old collectors, but we've gained new ones. This new interest has made people aware of Indian jewelry as art, and a great percentage of them know the good jewelry.

Curiously, foreigners, especially Europeans, appreciated good silver more than most Americans did twenty years ago.

I can't agree with anyone who thinks of handcrafted Indian jewelry as costume jewelry; that's what you find in the dime store with rhinestones and nickel silver. It's not handcrafted jewelry.

"There's a saying here in Gallup that anybody with a day off and twenty dollars in his pocket is a jewelry dealer..."

PHIL WOODARD *operates the Indian Jewelers Supply Company in Gallup, New Mexico. He comes from a family long associated with the Indian trading business. His showroom is full of silver of all gauges and shapes, turquoise, and the tools needed to work these materials. Phil Woodard began his career in 1952 helping his father after school and on weekends; upon graduation from college in 1961 he went to work full time.*

Our operation is quite a bit different than when we originally started. We developed a manufacturing facility, with Indian silversmiths working at benches here, making pieces some of which they designed, some of which I designed, or my brothers. In 1965 this place came almost exclusively under my control, for design and construction and cost accounting.

We had smiths at the shop, but there were more who preferred, for one reason or another, to work at home, so we issued them stones and silver and they worked at home.

The business changes every day, every day. Volume is astronomical in comparison to when we started. In those days, each piece had a lot more individual care and inspection than is currently possible.

We almost never turned out second-rate merchandise and sold it. At that time, if it wasn't first-class we made it first-class. Dealers policed the quality and pricing, and if a smith felt he should receive more money for a particular piece he had to show that there was good reason for it. This is not the case any more. There are too many dealers involved these days, and there is virtually no control on quality of the product, or of quantity.

The demand for Indian jewelry used to be about commensurate with supply, as recently as fifteen years ago. Quite frequently we might have one good piece which, for one reason or another, wouldn't sell; there was nothing wrong with it—it just wouldn't sell. Again, this is not the case any more. People who are now involved in the retailing of Indian jewelry across the nation are not as knowledgeable as they were fifteen years ago. The situation has changed in that many dealers want to go into the business when the only credential they have is their bankroll. Consequently there are a number of people who have bought just about whatever was offered to them—at whatever price it was offered at. Through the years a number of these people with, say, five years' experience have learned the hard way that there are certain places you must go to get quality pieces at reasonable prices.

The demand got to be such that there was a lot of imitation; some of it can be made of materials that are just as good or better than those used by the Indian craftsman, and with as much skill as the Indian craftsman possesses himself. They are good pieces of jewelry, but they are not made by Indians.

The Indians are not dumb, by any stretch of the imagination, and if prices are extremely high they will jack their prices up, and they have been able to jack them up so high that imitations could be sold for substantially less than the Indian would accept for *his* product. Consequently, we saw the flourishing of products of Indian design made by non-Indians. These worked themselves into the marketplace in one fashion or another and were sold as Indian handmade products—which is fraudulent on the part of the dealer who sells it to the customer. And the customer has virtually no recourse.

In fact, it's almost impossible for the retail customer to help himself. People who are involved in this business day in and day out—*they* make mistakes. Unless you stand over a man and never blink your eyes once while he is making any given piece of jewelry, you cannot unequivocally say that this man made this or that piece of jewelry. There have been cases where a maker's hallmark stamp has been reproduced by people other than the craftsman himself. The situation is such that as a buyer you have to couple yourself with good, reliable dealers and depend upon their skill and expertise, and that of all of their employees, if you want to get consistently good products at fair and reasonable prices.

The retail buyer definitely should familiarize himself with the market and make enquiries of the dealer: his background, how long he's been in the business. Ask him straight out: "Do you have any imitation Indian jewelry or do you not?" and "Are all of your items Indian handmade to the very best of your knowledge?" If the dealer can give good sound assurances to the customer he might well go ahead and buy from that dealer.

My function is at the bottom end of the entire Indian jewelry business: I supply metals, stones, tools, and supplies, but I currently am not involved personally in any production or buying or selling of Indian jewelry.

There is no one particular group of smiths we deal with; being open to the public we have to sell to anyone who walks through the door, and we do sell to both the Indian and the non-Indian craftsman.

The mission of findings, being parts and attachments used in Indian jewelry, has got to be very narrowly defined. To a purist, the finding means strictly nothing more than an earscrew or the catch and joint on a pin stem on the back of a brooch. It does not mean that that brooch can have any premanufactured element that is part of the design element itself. This has been a rub that has come about lately as a result of centrifugal casting —we refer to it as lost-wax or centrifugal, it's basically the same thing—in that design elements are now available not only to the retail market but directly to the Indian craftsman himself. Machine-punched beads, blossoms, silver heishi—virtually all these elements are now available to the craftsman fully machine formed, so that all he does is an assembly operation. Even silver cups for setting stones in are quite prevalent, so that there is no creativity.

In years gone by this sort of thing could be policed by dealers such as myself not offering this type of product to the Indian craftsman, although it was available. It has been my position that I do not, will not, and have not offered to the craftsman reproduced design elements such as cast beads, bracelet shanks, ring shanks. I have had to compromise my position somewhat in that we do offer a machine-punched hand-soldered bead to whoever wants to buy it—whether it's an Indian or non-Indian; likewise we offer a line of machine-made bolo tips and necklace cups. These are sold here as such—they are not sold as Indian handmade goods—and each package is labeled so that there is no doubt in the purchaser's mind what he gets when he gets it from me. Beyond that—what *he* represents his products as—I have no control.

I do offer identical products in both handmade and machine-made items, such as bolo tips, with the machine-made being about 20 percent less expensive than the handmade items. And the economics of the craft being what it is, even the Indian craftsmen sometimes prefer the machine-made products over the handmade line. They take the machine-made bolo tip, put it on the handmade bolo tie that they have made, and away they go.

During the winter of 1974 there was a definite recession in the handmade Indian jewelry business. Dealers did not sell what they anticipated they would sell, and they didn't buy any new jewelry, to speak of, in January, February, and March of 1975; consequently this backed up all the way down to the hogan.

Now jewelry can be produced, handmade, in sufficient quantity to supply the big department stores; consequently there are dealers who do make genuine Indian handmade jewelry to supply these stores. It may be a repetition of the same design over and over and over—a simple bracelet, for example. It is handmade, hand-soldered—everything is done by hand, including shaping and polishing the turquoise. On the other hand there are other people who are supplying these same stores because these stores do not buy everything from one supplier—they simply cannot buy all they need from the same supplier—and you are getting something other than handmade merchandise mixed in with the good stuff.

As for foreign money in the Indian market, there are a group of Arabs—I don't know whether they are foreign-born, naturalized citizens or not, but they are particularly aggressive in the area of Zuni. They will go down there and stake out the pueblo and buy everything there is to buy. As I understand it, they do sell virtually everything they buy right here in the Gallup area. But as far as their shipping what they buy to Iran or Iraq or wherever, I don't think there's anything like that.

It's just the last few years they've got involved in the business, they were down there at Zuni selling Arabian and Mexican tapestries, which the Zunis are fond of, and they discovered that people down there offered to trade them jewelry for their tapestries, and they found that they could dispose of the jewelry readily, so the next thing they knew, they were in the jewelry business.

There's still a great deal of barter that goes on around here; automobile dealerships will take jewelry in payment toward cars, and things like that. There's a saying here in Gallup that anybody with a day off and $20 in his pocket is a jewelry dealer. Space for stores is hard to come by, and if a phone booth remains empty for twenty minutes somebody puts a sign up and it's an office.

Indian jewelry falls into two basic classes—fine-quality jewelry and costume jewelry. For years, even the best handmade jewelry was priced so low it fell into the costume jewelry class—just about anybody could afford to buy it.

During World War II the United Indian Traders Association was able to see that, even though metal was in short supply, silver was available to the smiths here in the Southwest; consequently Indian jewelry continued to be made. In those days there was a lot of travel through here—not tourists, really, but soldiers, people passing through on their way to jobs elsewhere—and they were still able to buy genuine handmade rings three for a dollar and bracelets for a dollar apiece—items that were made expressly for the tourists or costume trade. Now, of course, prices have gone up and up and up, and the net profit that a smith is able to realize from a piece of jewelry gives him a much better and fairer share of what that item is worth. And even though much of this jewelry is still being made for what you would call the costume trade, there is no comparison between prices today and during earlier days.

Nobody knows how much silver is sold from this area each year, but it runs into the millions of dollars. Dealers around here rightfully are reluctant to disclose their figures, and since we also are the largest volume dealers in this area, I have to take into account the amount that goes out of here. We sell to rock shops, hobby shops, colleges, manufacturing shops—even back in Massachusetts.

As for the bloom falling off the market, when you're speaking of quality goods and talking about the millions of ounces sold and the dollar value, it's still a good, healthy industry and probably will remain so for a long time to come. The quality pieces are commanding very good prices and are being bought up at a very good rate. On the other hand, the less expensive merchandise, I anticipate, will peak in demand.

If the collector wants to obtain good merchandise, some of the best places he can look are the shows that are put on around here every year—things like the Intertribal Indian Ceremonial in Gallup and the Scottsdale show. These shows are judged by professionals who really know their stuff, and they are judged on the basis of workmanship and the quality of the material that goes into the item. On the other hand, there are shows on the West Coast—you can hit two or three of them on just about any weekend—where the merchandise is laid out like a flea market, and these shows—well, let the buyer beware. The same is true of buying from a stranger on the street or in a bar.

The buyer is likely to come to grief with turquoise. In the past five years we have seen the appearance on the market of stabilized turquoise, and in some ways stabilized turquoise is superior to natural turquoise in that it will not change color, where as natural stones might, depending upon their absorbency factor. Some turquoise is more absorbent than others, and this is true of stones coming from the same mine. It's a play on words to try to tell someone that stabilized turquoise is not an adulterated stone: it *is* adulterated. It is not *simulated* in that it has not been reconstituted from chemical elements that appear in natural turquoise. But it has been impregnated with both color and binder under both heat and pressure; it's generally low-grade turquoise, but the process does what it's intended to do. It's not fake turquoise. However, what difference whether it's stabilized or boiled in animal fat? It's treated or adulterated in one form or another.

For a stone to be considered unadulterated it must not be subjected to any process that will in any way change the natural color and appearance of the stone. The generally accepted technique is to grind turquoise in a water bath, whereas with harder material such as agate they will use an oil bath. But turquoise will absorb the oil and change color, so that cannot be used. Then you polish the stone, and the most common way is to use tin oxide, which has been used for centuries. There are other agents, too, but these do not change the color—they just provide a final gloss. It's extremely difficult to look at a stone—a person would have to be a gemologist—and say that *this* stone came from *that* mine and is untreated. A layman is at the mercy of the dealer. And many dealers are at the mercy of their suppliers. I myself am not qualified to unhesitatingly spot every bit of treated turquoise; as I say, only a qualified gemologist can do that. But if I am buying a batch of turquoise, and I spot one treated stone, then I turn down the whole batch; the only alternative is to go through the whole batch stone by stone and judge each one individually.

But as long as the buyer is looking for costume jewelry and the stones are not misrepresented to him, what difference does it make to him—since he's not looking for absolute top quality—whether the stones are stabilized or not?

Epoxy backing simply increases the amount of yield that can be gotten from raw stone. It used to be, before epoxy was used, that you could get 600 to 800 carats of turquoise per pound. Now, when epoxy is used—in small quantities—the yield goes up to double that amount. In years past, the cost of raw turquoise was $35 or $40 a pound; now it can go as high as $400, so with epoxy backing the net effect has been that the dealers get more stones per pound and the price of turquoise has been relatively stabilized.

"It's the merchandise in the middle that has been hurt..."

ROBERT NADLER *is a dealer in contemporary Indian arts and crafts in Scottsdale; he has been a collector (and appraiser) of Indian jewelry for more than 15 years.*

We moved out to Arizona about sixteen years ago and started collecting in a rather serious way all kinds of Indian arts and crafts of the Southwest. About seven years ago we decided to go into the business full time and started by doing the shows throughout the United States. At that time there was a group of about thirty dealers, all considered very legitimate—people who had top merchandise—the best in every class, whether Southwest, Plains, Northwest Coast, whatever. We dropped out of the show circuit when it became overgrown both in the number of dealers and in the number of shows. It had gone from 30 dealers once a month or so to 300 dealers every other week. Of course, we believe that there aren't 300 dealers of any caliber, so we decided to open the shop.

We handle basically traditional-style jewelry by Navajo, Hopi, and Zuni smiths. Mostly the pieces are modern, but occasionally we have an old piece. The majority of the pieces are signed because we try to deal with the top artists that are signing their pieces. We are going for first-quality by buying from those we consider the best smiths. Some of these people don't sign their work, however. And today a signature means very little, because for $5 any silversmith can buy a stamp that signs his pieces.

We have found that people are becoming suspicious of even signed pieces. We have gone to the point of getting pictures of some of our craftsmen taken with the piece of jewelry that we buy from them. Some of our customers who do not know us are very nervous about the whole thing. They have seen the articles about how things like heishi are made in Albuquerque and Taiwan, but they don't know how to tell the difference. The whole situation is hurting the dealer as well as the customer.

You can tell good heishi from bad by the look and feel of it if you know what you are looking at. No machine has been developed that can make heishi as fine as the finest of the Santo Domingo craftsmen. A good heishi maker can use any kind of material: serpentine, rocks, minerals, ivory, turquoise, shell—even coral, which is about the hardest to work with because it is so brittle. I think that heishi is one of the things that there is still a demand for in the high-quality type. Unfortunately there is also a demand for the junk. It's the merchandise in the middle that has been hurt. People will spend a lot of money for the best quality, but if they can't afford that they seem to slide right down to the cheapest junk and don't look at the material in the middle.

My basic philosophy is that you can get a nice piece of well-made Indian jewelry for $15 to $50. But it's hard to explain to the customer, because when you get down into that price bracket, they feel that it is either machine-made or not Indian-made.

We pride ourselves in the people we deal with. In some cases, the only way you know is by the people you deal with. If they slip something on you, it's sometimes difficult to tell. We're very careful nowadays. We used to look at a lot of merchandise. But there are fewer and fewer traders who are handling the top merchandise. We don't even look anymore.

We look for two things when we buy for the shop, the craftsmanship and the quality of the turquoise and other stones. Design is also important. There are a lot of silversmiths who can do good work if they are told what to do. Unfortunately in a lot of cases the design and silverwork is good, but with the lack of good turquoise around some of the smiths are going the easy way and using treated stones and stones of poor quality. Then we look at the completed piece, if all of the quality is good, to see if it hangs together.

We are traditionalists in what we handle, and this may hurt us if we don't change because the trend in Indian jewelry today is definitely toward contemporary styling. Also, it is becoming more individualized. You can recognize an individual's work, and that is what more and more people are looking for—the jewelry of artists like Charles Loloma, Larry Golsh, Preston Monongye. Of course, there are a lot of imitators, but the top quality will out, I think.

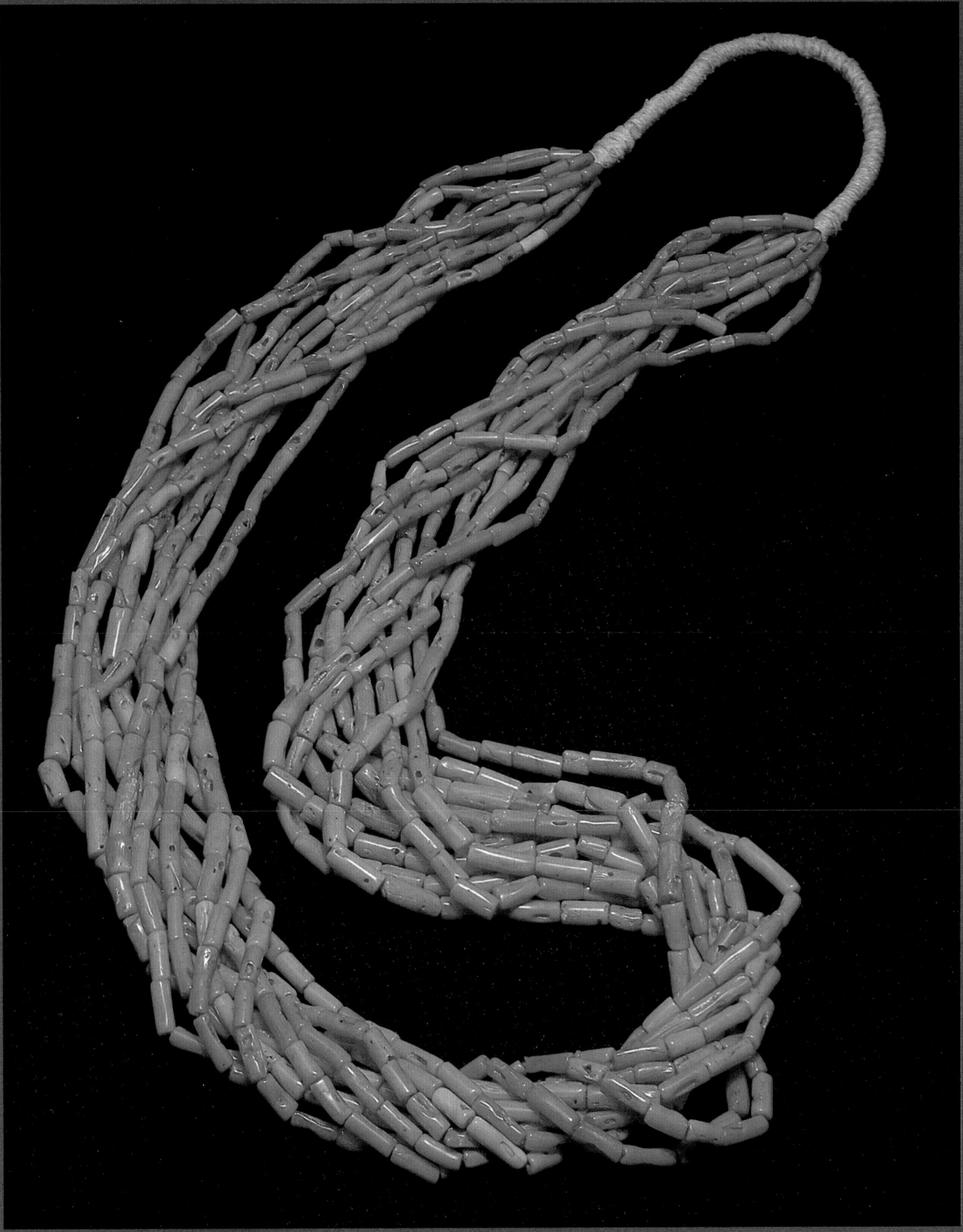

Nine-strand coral necklace bound with a string wrapping. This necklace is a nice mix of the mid-range of coral colors available. Pre-1920. *(HC, Al Abrams)*

Multiple strands of coral strung with turquoise and tubular silver beads. The two nuggets tied on are "sing" stones: stones added to commemorate the owner's participation in a religious ceremony. *(FHFAC, HM, Al Abrams)*

These two necklaces show two of the forms in which coral can come. In the outer necklace, chunks of coral are polished enough to give a shine but not enough to destroy the shape. The interior necklace is made of smaller branches strung crosswise, a more contemporary style. *(HC, Al Abrams)*

A massing of coral in various► contemporary pieces of jewelry. This photograph illustrates the many forms that coral comes in, from cabochons perfectly matched in color and size, to needlepoint, a rare occurrence in coral, to semi-shaped free-form pieces that still retain some of the shape of the original branch. The combination of turquoise and coral is a contemporary form in Indian jewelry. *(BTC, Peter L. Bloomer)*

3elow. A selection of Zuni
channelwork from the early 1930s.
The turquoise is all Blue Gem.
(JFPGW, John Miller)
This massive (the bottom cross is
5 inches long) necklace of
channelwork crosses and restrung
aclahs, all of Blue Gem turquoise, is
one of the best early large
channelwork pieces. *(Collection of
Mrs. James S. Fowler, John Miller)*

Large crosses of this sort have become popular in the past twenty years. It is strung with round and pinion beads, named for their resemblance to the pinion pine seed. *(HC, Al Abrams)*

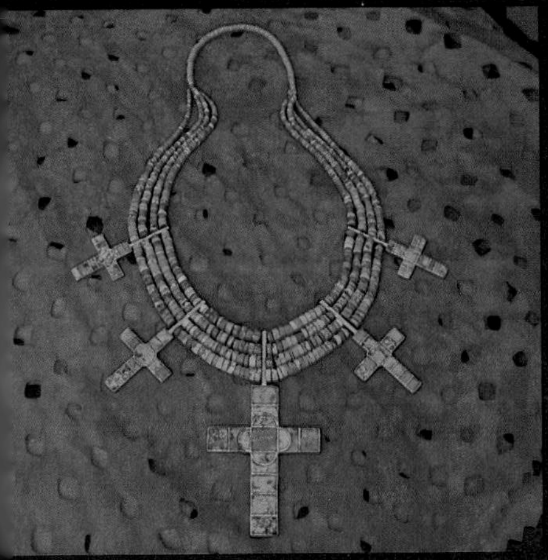

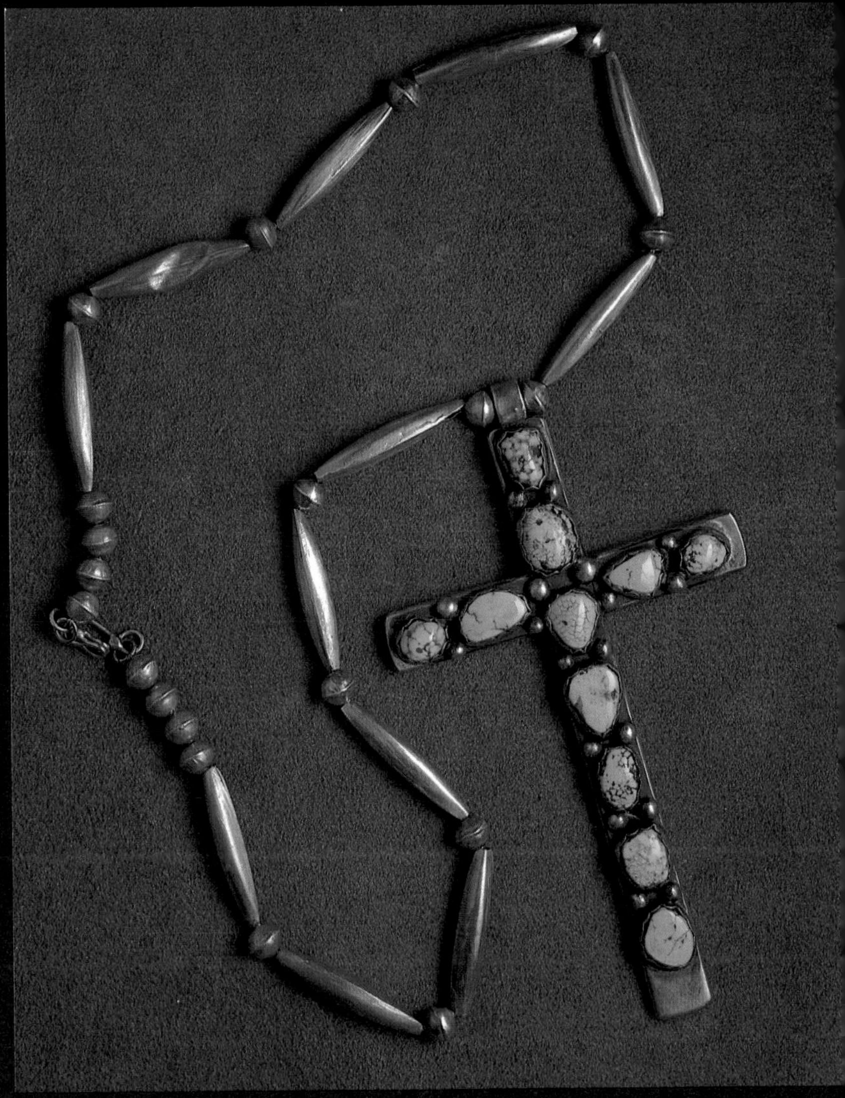

Isleta cross necklace in silver with red glass trade beads, pre-1880. The designs in this piece were done with a file and a punch. Even with those primitive tools, the silversmith who made it was able to create a strong visual statement. The design of the smaller crosses was based

Left: **Navajo woman wearing contemporary silver and turquoise earrings and an older Zuni style cluster pin. Mixes of this type are very common, as Indians add what strikes their fancy to what they already own.** *(Michal Heron)*
Below: **Older Zuni Knife Wing God earrings. The Zuni made many pairs of the long dangling earrings, both for themselves and for sale. The Knife Wing God was a popular design motif, both in plain silver and set with turquoise.** *(JFPGW, John Miller)*

A selection of rings from the 1940s. Note the cracked stone in the ring at lower right. *(FHFAC, HM, Al Abrams)*

Three rings made pre-1902, before Indian silver was made in quantity for sale. *(FHFAC, HM, Al Abrams)*

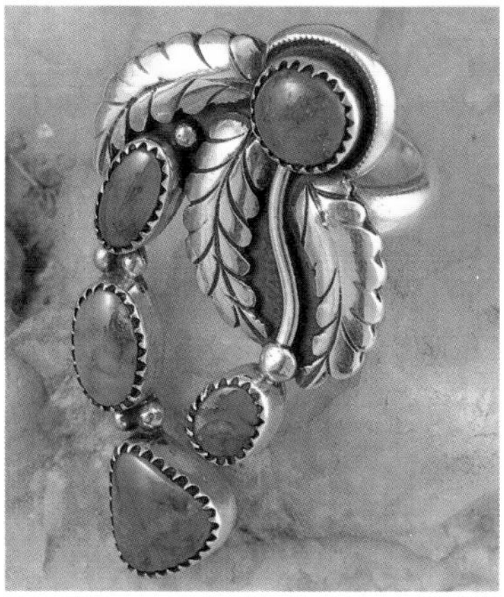

Left: Contemporary ring of turquoise and silver which shows how an Indian artist, by varying the placement of the traditional Indian turquoise and silver leaves, can design a very modern, almost "non-Indian" piece. *(R. W. Mullen Collection, Neil Koppes)*
Right: Zuni multistone ring typical of the 1930s. Note the one changed stone, and the ropework between the stone rows. *(FHFAC, HM, Al Abrams)*

Three contemporary Zuni bracelets. The silver bracelet with the Knife Wing God in inlay was made by John Bedoni, the center cluster by Ondelacy, and the large turquoise and silver leaf bracelet by Jake Hawalarne. *(McGee's Indian Den, John Miller)*

A selection of modern rings typical of what one could find in any reputable Indian jewelry shop. *(Half Red Man Shop, Ray Manley)*

A Navajo child starts wearing jewelry at an early age. If a piece is►

A selection of rings from the 1940s. Note the cracked stone in the ring at lower right. *(FHFAC, HM, Al Abrams)*

Three rings made pre-1902, before Indian silver was made in quantity for sale. *(FHFAC, HM, Al Abrams)*

Left: Contemporary ring of turquoise and silver which shows how an Indian artist, by varying the placement of the traditional Indian turquoise and silver leaves, can design a very modern, almost "non-Indian" piece. *(R. W. Mullen Collection, Neil Koppes)*
Right: Zuni multistone ring typical of the 1930s. Note the one changed stone, and the ropework between the stone rows. *(FHFAC, HM, Al Abrams)*

Three contemporary Zuni bracelets. The silver bracelet with the Knife Wing God in inlay was made by John Bedoni, the center cluster by Ondelacy, and the large turquoise and silver leaf bracelet by Jake Hawalarne. *(McGee's Indian Den, John Miller)*

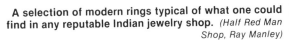

A selection of modern rings typical of what one could find in any reputable Indian jewelry shop. *(Half Red Man Shop, Ray Manley)*

A Navajo child starts wearing jewelry at an early age. If a piece is outgrown, it is frequently handed down to the next child. This child's bracelets are at least one generation old. *(Michal Heron)* ►

Left: Navajo woman wearing contemporary silver and turquoise earrings and an older Zuni style cluster pin. Mixes of this type are very common, as Indians add what strikes their fancy to what they already own. *(Michal Heron)*
Below: Older Zuni Knife Wing God earrings. The Zuni made many pairs of the long dangling earrings, both for themselves and for sale. The Knife Wing God was a popular design motif, both in plain silver and set with turquoise. *(JFPGW, John Miller)*

Left: A grouping of contemporary earrings that could be available in many reputable Indian jewelry shops. *(DNH, Peter L. Bloomer)*
Right: Two other examples of older Zuni earrings. *(FHFAC, HM, Al Abrams)*

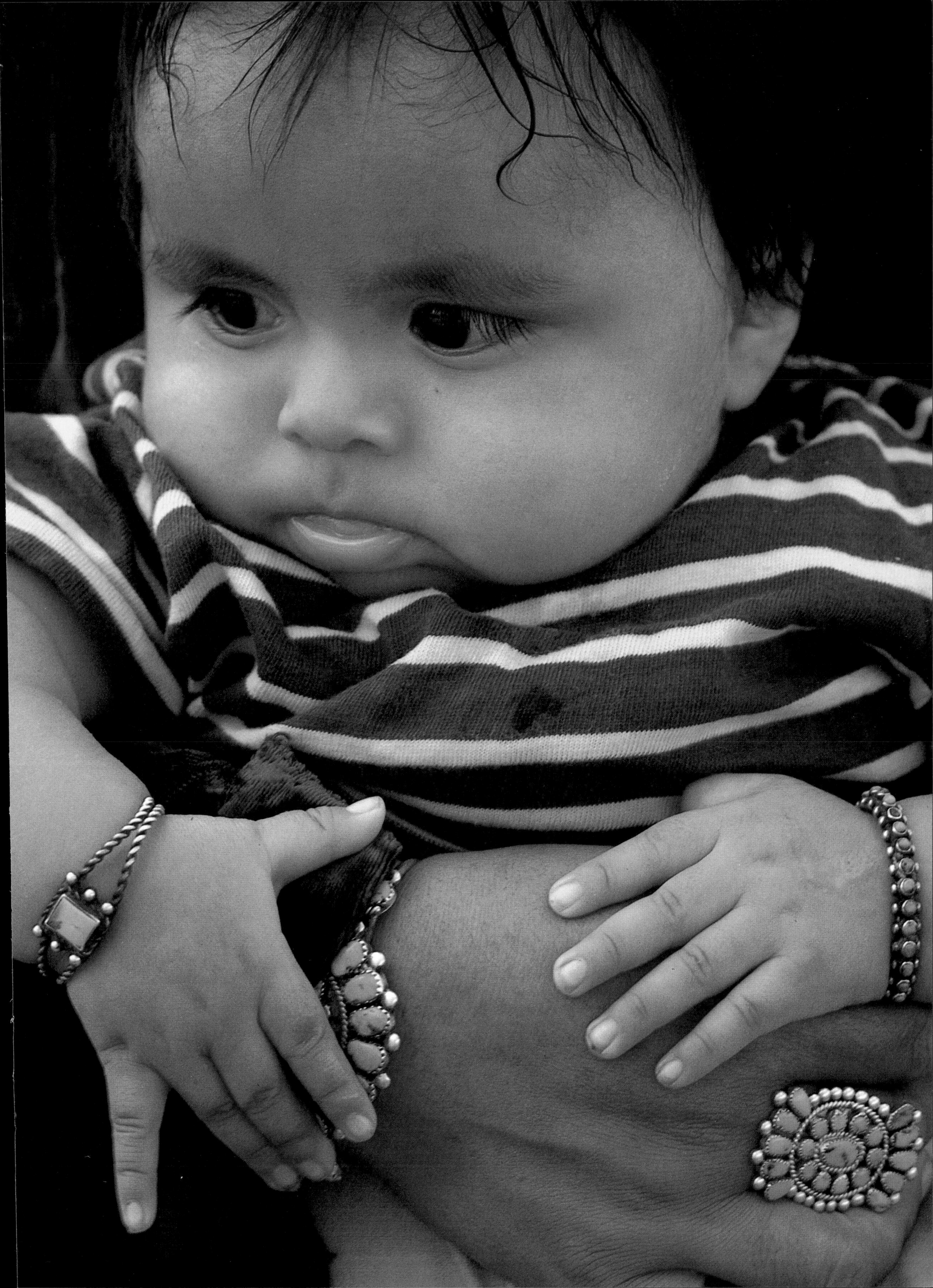

One of the most popular forms of bolo tie is that with a figure. This photograph shows four common types of figures used. From left to right: Navajo Yei, butterfly, eagle kachina, Apache Ghan dancer. *(PC, Markow Photo)*

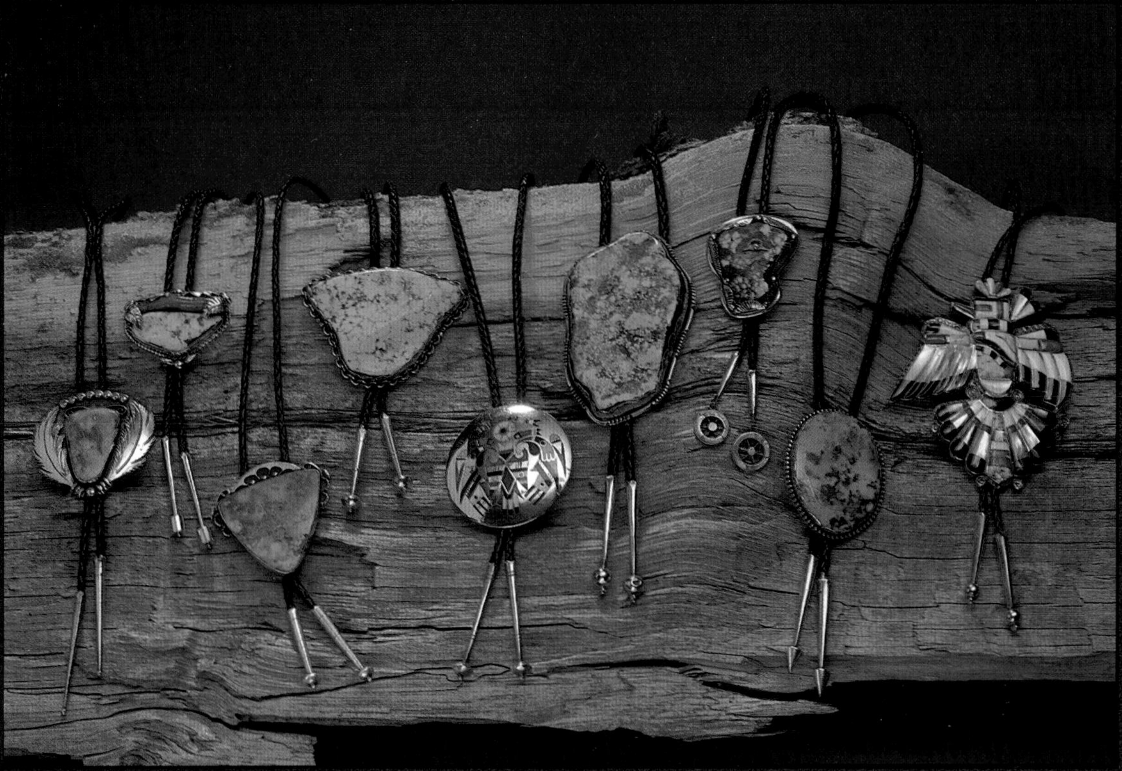

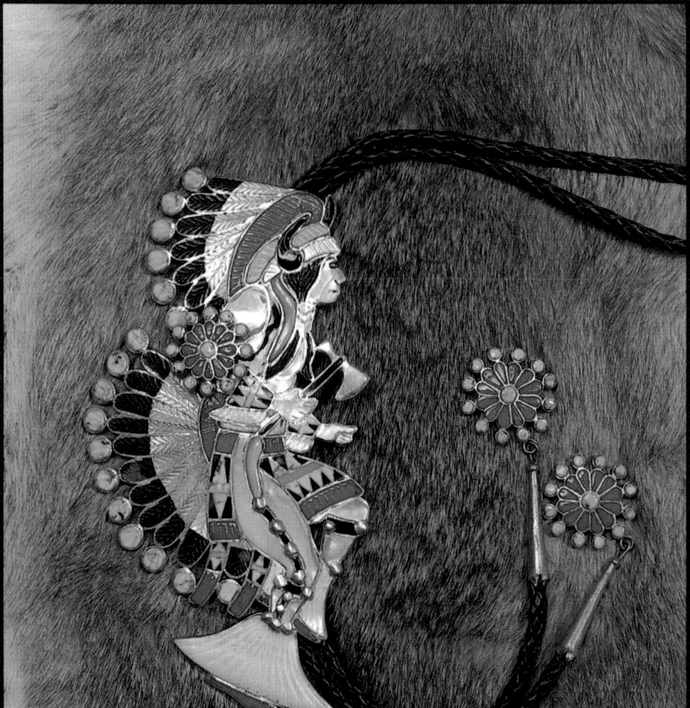

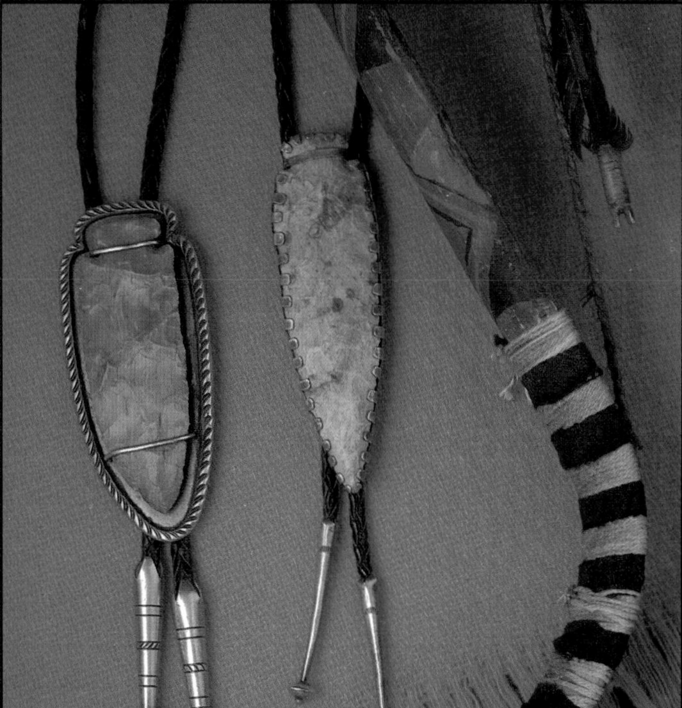

Top: **A variety of contemporary bolos. Slabs of turquoise cut as large as this are difficult to work, and ties such as these are relatively rare.** *(PC)*
Left: **Contemporary bolo tie made by Dixon Shebola, a Zuni craftsman known for the detail he carves into the stones and shells he uses.** *(DNH, Peter L. Bloomer)*
Right: **These two projectile points from the St. Louis, Missouri, area have been mounted in Indian style silverwork to form bolo ties.** *(HC, Al Abrams)*

"Nugget" and "Sea foam" style stones have become popular since the mid-'60s. A selection of this very contemporary jewelry by various smiths. All of the turquoise in these pieces comes from the Lone Mountain mine, except for the two pendants by Sedalio Lovato on the left side; these were made with high-grade Kingman turquoise. *(DNH, Peter L. Bloomer)*

Contemporary jewelry set with Nevada Blue Wind turquoise and bear claws by Navajo artist John Hoski. *(DNH, Peter L. Bloomer)*

"Sea foam" Lone Mountain turquoise set in 18-karat gold. In this set the turquoise has been combined with 1¼ karats total weight of diamonds for an ultra contemporary look. The artist was Andrew Kirk, a Navajo. *(Goldwater's Indian Jewelry Department, Jerry Jacka)*

The two canteens in this photograph were made after tobacco canteens ceased to be made for Indian use. The one at upper left is set with Stormy Mountain turquoise; upper right, with Morenci.The contemporary box has a large slab of Lone Mountain turquoise on it which has only been slightly polished. *(DNH, Jerry Jacka)*

A collection of Navajo pieces all made in the 1920s and 1930s. Pieces such as these often form the nucleus of a long-held and treasured collection. The silver spurs are a somewhat anomalous piece—when made, they were worn for rodeo and dress occasions. *(BTC, Peter L. Bloomer)*

This photograph shows the kind of eclectic mixture► of old and new jewelry that a collector will usually end up with after years of collecting, each piece a well-worn and much loved favorite. *(DNH, Peter L. Bloomer)*

**A wide
semi-p
comin
Indian
shows
spectr
and az**

**Nine s
Persia
stones
are ex
highly
impor**
(Jeffrey

**A sele
high-q
Numb**

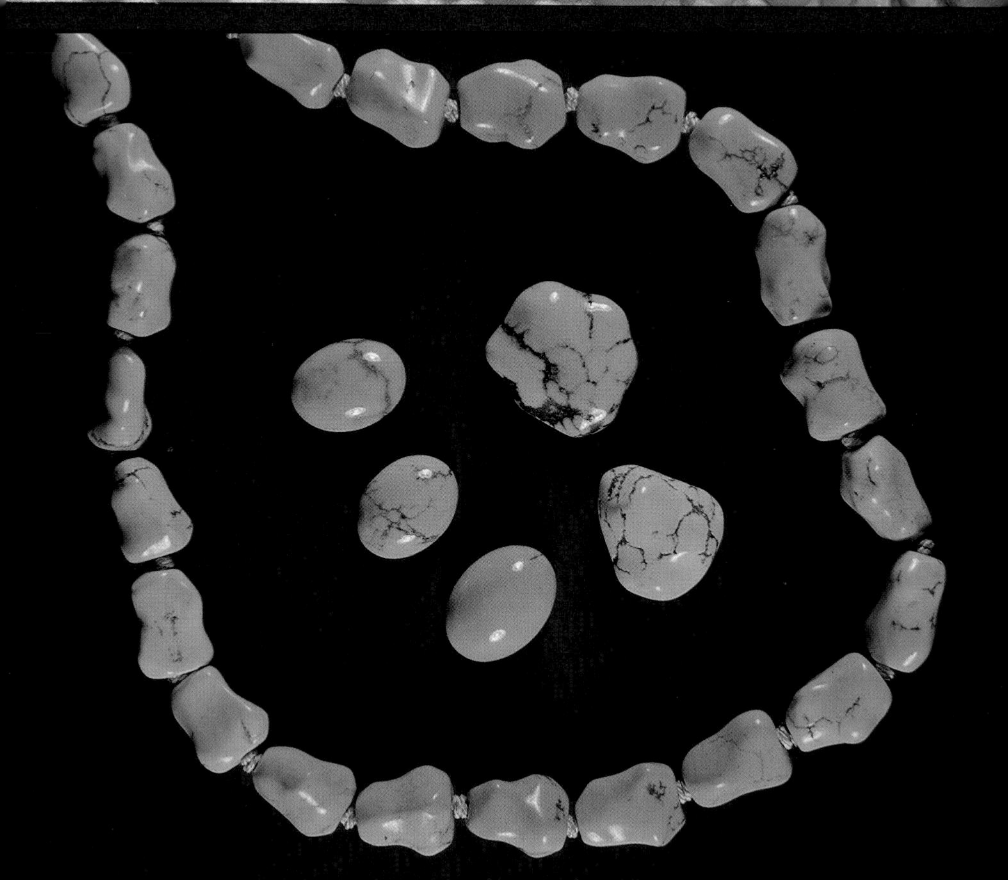

Top: Cabochons of gem quality chrysocolla, one of the stones most commonly mistaken for turquoise. The masking tape they are attached to shows the way cabs of turquoise and other stones to be set in Indian jewelry are carried to prevent damage to the stones.
Bottom: Cabs, nuggets, and a string of polished pieces of turquoise from the Mongolian province of China. The necklace in this photograph is of the variety [illegible]

Then there are the modern smiths who are doing very-high-quality work who are not Indian but who are using the same materials. I find in the high-quality pieces it doesn't make that much difference whether the item is Indian or not. We are an Indian shop, but we do carry the work of a few who are not Indian. Johnny Foutz, for example, was born and brought up on the Navajo reservation with Indian smiths. He is not Indian, but his work is as good or better than most. We are getting back to the quality of the individual work. Foutz's work is accepted because it is of extremely high quality, and his background makes his a rather special case.

I think laws should be and eventually will be passed to protect the consumer, the shopowner, and the Indian—they have to be passed to save the Indian jewelry business. Otherwise we will be forced into dealing with only established people that customers can recognize. This will hurt young Indian smiths just coming up. The fight for recognition just will not be worth it, and they will turn to other work.

There was a dealer in Scottsdale who was caught importing heishi and other material from Taiwan, ripping off the labels, and selling it as Indian-made. He is now subject to fines and has had a number of things confiscated. We are looking for more of this to happen, which will better the industry, the creator, the craftsmen, the dealers, and ultimately the consumer.

We also appraise Indian jewelry. Ninety percent of all appraisals are done for insurance. With the high rate of theft of Indian jewelry, people are worrying about replacement; and we make this very specific, that we are appraising this at replacement value—what it would cost to replace if the piece were lost or stolen tomorrow. We name the turquoise if possible, or list it as "origin unknown." We keep a copy in our files so we can enter the picture if there is an insurance problem. So for this reason we want to establish it as a point of appraising good jewelry that we are not ashamed of trying to equate dollars with what was lost in case of a claim. When we are appraising something that is irreplaceable or would be hard to replace, the only way we can look at it is to say what it would be worth *x* number of dollars if it could be replaced. Since I deal and appraise mostly in contemporary material, most of it can be replaced.

If someone wants to know what a piece is worth to a dealer, that is a completely different story.

I'm cutting down on appraisals now because it places us in a very difficult position. Someone comes in with an item to be appraised and they say, "Well, it has a value," and I say, "But I am in the Indian business; I have an Indian shop. Your piece is made by machine. It is not worth the $600 to $700 you paid for it, but only $150 to $200." Then they get mad at you and that leaves a bad taste in everyone's mouth. I never appraise jewelry over the phone; I have to see a piece first. In a lot of cases I will just tell people that I have not seen anything like it and therefore I can't appraise it.

I usually charge $25 an hour for an appraisal, which I feel is pretty reasonable. There are some dealers who charge a flat $50 plus $1 per item, and I am sure there are other methods. We have a minimum charge of $25 for one item—unless, of course, we sold that item to the customer, in which case we provide an appraisal at the time of sale free and any other time the customer requests it.

"The flavor of the West is half the fun of collecting..."

BOB WARD *owns the original Indian Trading Post in Santa Fe, New Mexico, and he also has acquired another long-established store in the same town. He is enthusiastic and knowledgeable, and many motion picture and television stars and other celebrities are among his clientele.*

What does the term *old pawn* mean to me? It's the fine, early jewelry, forty years old or more. In those days that's all the Indians had to pawn. Today, they'll pawn anything—radios, TV sets, saddles, some jewelry. Actually, there's very little pawn on the reservation today; what there is nowadays you find on the periphery of the reservation, towns like Gallup and Flagstaff. A few dealers still have a little, but it's hard to find. You suggest that maybe when people refer to old pawn today what they actually mean is collector's-quality jewelry, regardless of age or whether it's actually been pawned. To some extent that's true: it means fine jewelry. But authentic old jewelry has been pawned at least once and probably many times.

The most serious threat facing dealers in Indian jewelry today are the fakes and reproductions. Since 1974 they've done tremendous damage to the market. With the price of jewelry what it is today, buyers are afraid to put out that kind of money when they can't be sure, especially if they've been burned once. Obviously, the best way to protect yourself is to buy from reputable dealers.

How do you find a reputable dealer? For one thing, you can go to the Chamber of Commerce; here in Santa Fe, for instance, they'll give you a list of recommended dealers, people who will stand behind everything they sell. Another thing, if a person has any doubts or complaints against a dealer, he can go to the Consumer Protection Agency. Every state has them, and they're usually a part of the state attorney general's office. Still another safeguard is the Indian Arts and Crafts Association—the IACA—headquartered in Gallup, which screens its members to make sure that they practice authentic representation of what they sell. If they don't maintan IACA standards, out they go.

Starting a collection is a matter of taste and budget. Generally speaking, reputable dealers have always charged higher prices, but that isn't always true these days. People who make fakes or imitations have found out that their stuff sells better if they price it higher. A prospective collector ought to avoid buying from people who sell from motel rooms and offer open discounts. Another good rule is not to buy anything except in the Southwest, unless you're buying from the big department stores. These stores have their reputations to maintain, and if there's any valid complaint you get your money back.

But the flavor of the West is half the fun of collecting, and in addition to the trip you get better prices and the assurance that you can buy from dealers who know their profession and will stand behind their reputations.

How can you spot a fake? The worst fakes show signs of repetition: you look for exact repetition of design, because many of the fakes are turned out in factorylike operations, using the same die stamps on item after item. On a concha belt, for instance, take one concha and examine it carefully, look for some imperfection; if you find one, hold it up next to another concha. If the same flaw is repeated, you can be pretty sure you've got a fake. The same is true with bezels: no two handmade bezels are ever exactly the same. If things are too regular, or a flaw is repeated, then it's probably not handmade.

Oiled turquoise is oiled all the way through; scratching it with a pin or a knife won't show it. Plastic or plasticized turquoise is visible to the naked eye; it doesn't take long to learn to spot it. One test for treated (oiled) turquoise is to hold a paper match under it, with the flame just touching. It will turn black and the foreign matter will drip out of it. It won't damage the stone; you can rub the black off with your finger. But no dealer would take kindly to anyone scratching his good turquoise with a penknife.

There are factories now that turn out fake jewelry, copying genuine old pieces. They don't call it fake, they say it's "derivative": *that's* a unique term.

My best customers are—well, wealthy people, sure—but generally people in the $10,000- to $15,000-a-year bracket. They'll sacrifice in other areas of their budget to buy what they want for their collections. When their collections get big enough they like to trade: they cull what they don't want from their collections and trade them for new things, especially if they get overextended. A lot of collectors will buy on charge or layaway, too. Collectors can't help collecting. I'm like that: my psyche tells me I need to collect. I'm compulsive about collecting; I don't know why. In fact, dealers themselves are the biggest buyers and collectors. They're always visiting each other's stores and buying or trading for whatever catches their eye.

When you buy from an Indian who makes the rounds of bars and restaurants hawking jewelry, you've probably got one chance out of a hundred of getting a good buy. It's colorful and all a part of the Southwest, but it's no way to buy.

The big boom in Indian jewelry shows signs of dying down somewhat, and that's a good thing. It means that serious collectors can get down to business, and it's going to drive all the fakers and counterfeiters out of the market. They'll be making fake Oriental or Mexican stuff, or whatever the next craze happens to be. The fakers got into this business for what they thought was quick money, but that isn't so—there's no way to make quick money in this business.

To some extent guilds have helped to preserve the traditional arts of jewelrymaking, but they tend to discourage experimentation in nontraditional designs and techniques. This craft is never static; it's always changing and developing, and all you need to do is look at the work of such craftsmen as Tony Da, Charles Loloma, and Popovi Da. Guilds hold craftsmen to more traditional lines. Economically they don't help much and have never really been successful. And whites tend to dominate the guilds. At the recent South West Association for Indian Affairs fair here, the Zuni Cooperative Guild sent whites up to man the booths, although that's against the rules and they had to be told to leave. But none of the Zunis wanted to come up for it, since they were having the Gallup Ceremonials at the same time.

How would I define handmade Indian jewelry? It's hard to draw a line, but the only things not produced by Indian hands are the stones; they're cut and polished by machines. Grinding wheels are acceptable for trimming and smoothing or polishing cast and wrought iron silver, since to do these things by hand takes ten times as long. The Santo Domingos have things pretty well mechanized and organized. They still do things by hand, but there are families of jewelrymakers and each member specializes in a certain task: one will rough-cut a bead, another will grind it to shape by hand, another will pierce it. The same with silver mountings: it's like an assembly line.

Now you can buy what they call jewelry components: the bezels are precut, the najas are precast, the beads are precast and soldered. They're called bench-craft beads. And there are stones that have been precut to fit these. In one day a smith can turn out a $300 squash-blossom necklace. This does the business no good and needs to be stopped.

"Would you want a Persian rug made by an Eskimo?..."

JOHN and PATRICIA WOODARD *have been collecting Indian jewelry for twenty-six years, and have offered a fine variety of jewelry and other Indian crafts in the Bear Track Trading Company in scenic Sedona, Arizona, since 1968. "We opened our shop because we had so much of it we either had to open a shop or a museum."*

Why isn't Anglo "Indian-style" jewelry the same as or "as good as," genuine handmade Indian jewelry? It's neither fish nor fowl, neither Anglo nor Indian. If an Anglo is a good silversmih, he should be using his own imagination and, therefore, his own designs. Anglo "Indian-style" jewelry could better be called pseudo-Indian jewelry.

If a person is starting out to collect Indian jewelry, he should be collecting Indian jewelry, not copies made by Anglos. Would you want a Persian rug made by an Eskimo?

One of our favorite types of Indian jewelry is drilled beads. Drilled beads are made by the oldest known method, yet are among the least appreciated, almost ignored forms (perhaps because they're not flashy). Yet an Indian would prefer them over all.

Heishi neclaces are prized by collectors for their silky feel and sheen. Hours spent drawing the finished work over an abrasive stone are followed by many more pulling the strand through buckskin to achieve the final polish. Heishi are made from olivella shell (white), pipestone (red), cameo shell (pink), serpentine (green), tortoiseshell (brown), pure white shell, coral, and turquoise. The finer the bead, the higher the price. Turquoise is by far the most expensive bead material, depending on the mine from which it came and the silkiness. A good turquoise heishi strand should feel like a snake's skin. The pure white shell called "chief's heishi" is very special, for this shell is virtually extinct at this time, and has always been very hard to get.

A heishi necklace should be routinely cleaned with a soft brush stroked over a bar of Ivory soap. The string on which it is strung should be examined frequently for signs of wear—it is imperative that the beads be restrung before the string breaks, so that they may be restrung in exactly the same sequence as originally. One bead turned can ruin the whole piece.

Good inlay work should be carefully fitted with no visible sign of "fill"—surfaces of silver and stone or shell should be glassy smooth and flush. In inlay work, the labor, the skill of execution, is more important than the specific materials (with the possible exception of coral and turquoise), because they do utilize smaller scrap pieces, which are much cheaper. Integrity of design and execution are very important also. Inlay, since it seems to lend itself to various excesses, requires more design judgment on the part of the purchaser. On the other hand, however beautiful, a design poorly done would have little value.

"Old Navajo" is one of the areas we have chosen to specialize in. This jewelry is distinctive for its weight and simplicity of design. The Navajo liked his silver heavy, and turquoise set in generous pieces. He did the all-silver pieces better than anyone because he carried on a love affair with the glistening metal from the moment he first laid eyes on it.

Describing the special beauty of an old primitive Navajo piece is difficult, if not impossible, because it is much akin to trying to describe a fine old piece of furniture, with all the nicks and scratches, the shine of use, that give it its character.

Silver ketoh with stamping and repousséed leaves, c. 1890s. *(FHFAC, HM, Al Abrams)*

We are partial to the older, heavier, elaborately die-stamped pieces, because in this period the Navajo silversmith was making silver for sale to other Navajos. They seem more pure in their overall "Indian feel."

A squash-blossom necklace is a very special and dramatic piece of jewelry. A person has to dress "around" a squash-blossom. It may be a little more limiting than certain other pieces; however, it can also be the core of a wardrobe; it could be that person's trademark or signature. Selecting a "squash" from the great variety of types available is very much a matter of taste. From the standpoint of investment, there's no better investment than a truly fine needlepoint squash made by a known maker. There are few Zuni alive today that can do the superfine needlepoint work.

Many women who consider Indian Jewelry ostentatious will collect and enjoy Indian earrings. In the past, the jockla, or drilled nugget, was what the Indian himself preferred. The demand of the Anglo market has encouraged new concepts and designs in earrings. The bola tie has become the official neckwear of the State of Arizona. It's masculine appeal is undaunted by the most elaborate designs and colors. Many are works of art which should be framed and displayed as such.

Fetishes can be strung to order. Our specialty is the "collector's necklace," featuring fetishes by all the noted carvers, deceased and living.

As for the opinion that in many styles of Indian jewelry "the older work is better, more persistently pleasing,"—this is a misconception. It's as if you were to say that the first surgical procedures were superior to the sophisticated methods of today's surgeons.

Some of the current Zuni silversmiths are doing astonishing inlay. The tools and electrical equipment available today have opened wide the artist's doors of imagination and all things are possible.

The beginning collector should do his homework by frequenting museums and libraries, and not be afraid to ask questions of people in both places and also in shops of good reputation and long standing, to firm up his own taste and preference. And then shop carefully, always getting a specific receipt for the authenticity of what he's purchased.

When you deal with the same Indian families over a period of years and come to know them well, you also know their work. It would be very hard for a silversmith who is known to pass off somebody else's work as his own. This background is essential to both the dealer and his customer.

We're a classic case of the hobby that got out of hand. We spent money on Indian craftwork that should have been spent on necessities. It wasn't because we ever thought they'd be the investment that they turned out to be, it was because we'd rather have them than the washing machine, the car, the vacation.

"We buy what we like, and it sells..."

ROBERT ASHTON *is a dealer in American Indian art who specializes in older jewelry as well as new pieces by name craftsmen. He is also publisher of* American Indian Art *magazine.*

The old jewelry interests me the most, especially those items that were made by the Indians for their own use. There is a feeling about items made by Indians for their own use—the polish, the wear, maybe a little bit more personal concern of the artist who is making the item, knowing that it was going to a friend or perhaps for his own use all show through.

This is, of course, not a native craft. The Indians in the Southwest had turquoise before European contact, but silverworking was learned from the Mexicans, and the ways stones are set in silver certainly is not Indian. Most of the old traditional jewelry is not even really traditional but reflects the influences of the newly arrived Spanish or Anglo-Americans. The pomegranate, for example, is Moorish by way of Spain and Mexico. Isleta cross necklaces are visually exciting and nice to have, but their crosses are obviously from the Spanish culture. So it's a combination of these influences with the way they view ornamentation which makes Indian jewelry both exciting and what it is today.

An item has to be esthetically pleasing, though. Just because it is old doesn't mean that it is good; it might well be old and ugly, too. How well an item is put together designwise and how well the parts balance are both important. I look for the creativity the artist was using, the polish, and the wear it gained from being used. I also look for simplicity in design, but that's a personal taste.

Then there are a number of recent contemporary artists who are designing some incredible items. Some of these are reflecting earlier traditional designs, some are not. Larry Golsh, for example, is combining the traditional materials in a very simple way that is sculptural in form, not really jewelry.

I don't make any distinction in the jewelry

that I buy for myself and that which I buy for the shop. When I first started in this business eight years ago, people told me, "You can't buy what you like, you have to buy what sells." Well, for 90 percent of our purchases in the shop, we buy what we like, and it sells. Those that don't sell, we don't mind having around for a while because we do like them and don't mind living with them.

"I have to keep coming up with new ideas all the time..."

CHARLES LOLOMA *is perhaps the best known of all Indians working in jewelry today. Mr. Loloma is a Hopi who has formal training in art, taught at the Institute of American Indian Art, in Santa Fe, and now resides at Hotevilla on the Hopi reservation. He is well known for the unusual materials he uses and the way in which he combines them into fine-art jewelry.*

I am not versed in the exact date that I started working in jewelry, but my guess is it was in 1947 when I was a student at Alfred University. I was working in pottery and silver, and after moving to Scottsdale and opening up a shop in the Kiva Craftsmen Court I started doing more jewelry than pottery. I spent three years at the Institute of American Indian Art as the head of the Plastic Arts Department of the school. By that time I felt I had succeeded in helping to get the school started and felt that I could make it on my own, so I left and came here. Six months later I built this little home and then started expanding.

From the first, people seemed to like the type of thing I was doing. When I was in Scottsdale, I had lots of publicity; I was one of the few Indian people who was running my own concern and making it work. We got in quite a number of national magazines—*Time, National Geographic,* and lots of Western magazines. I was also participating in various shows.

When I first started out there were a number of people who were stimulating to me—Oleg Cassini and others in the fashion world. I was aware from that point on that my jewelry needed to be something special, to go with other special things like clothes.

In order to create a unique presentation one must work from his background. This is the primary reason I live up here at Hopi—to be involved with the ceremonial happenings that are our background. Anytime you remove yourself from it, the farther away you get, the less you live it and the less important it becomes. You have to be with the people there and in the surroundings. That is why I am objecting to some of the newer things that will bring about change that will not benefit our people, that will only cause interruption.

When I was in a private show in Paris, a famous architect told me to stay with my background, and not to lose sight of it. He said not to try to be influenced by other cultures. I think if you stick with your background all of the time, you will be a bigger person. This is what I have followed through with. I still use the silver and turquoise that is Indian jewelry but I've added my own things to it. If you take the kachina doll cult, and understand the color schemes and all, and hold one of my pieces up to a doll, they will fit together very well.

You have to understand other peoples' way of life, too, to be able to create jewelry with universal appeal. I am arriving at the point that I must travel to do this. On one trip to Egypt I felt I had to be on location, on the spot, with their roofs over my head and me walking around inside their houses. In Japan it was the same way. We went into a shrine which has a great depth to it and I felt that the spirit of who we are exists in ancient cultures as well as our own. I felt it in Korea as well. One must go there, because books just don't do it for me. Someone else could get the full richness out of them perhaps, but since a book is a very personalized type of expression it reflects only one person's way of seeing.

Have any of my travels or any of the jewelry I have seen anyplace had a major influence on my work? No because I have not seen any good pieces anywhere in the parts of the world that I have been. I am not saying this because I think I am the best jeweler in the world, but I have seen nothing that has any depth to it. People are aware of the highly commercialized aspect of jewelry. One famous man designs the pieces and then they are knocked out by other people. In France, for example, the best jeweler there was designing mice and poodles with diamonds and rubies and emeralds. These are high-priced items, but they are not original. They don't have any depth in the cultural world they come from. I think Southwestern people are probably the greatest designers in the world.

Do I think of myself as an artist or as a Hopi artist? I consider myself an artist and I am Charles Loloma.

How do I go about achieving a creation for one particular person? Each of us is very individualized and concerned with our own personal things. I think this is good because the richest part of man's personal concern should be himself. When a person has a strong image of himself, the work is easier. Over a period of years I have developed a very sensitive approach to people. I have to read people—I have to try to realize who they are, who they think they are, and who they want to become so that I can make the piece farther than they realize they will go. If I limit it only to their personal taste, then it is no fun. They can't appreciate it beyond when I make it for them because to be great, they have to go on discovering new things about it and through it about themselves. I find in the letters that people write to me that their experience of wearing one of my pieces has influenced the way they experience life.

Some people don't like to talk about themselves, but from the way they present themselves I can detect what they are trying to say. That is where I come in as an artist. My interest in doing this is heavily psychological. My fun comes in seeing a person's reaction to a piece or in reading letters from the people who have my pieces.

I am creating for people all of the time even when a piece is not meant for just one person. I am creating for myself because I know that people who buy my pieces will reach the imagination that I have at this point if they are to enjoy them. If they don't reach that imagination, they won't like the piece for very long. Take the single long earring I designed [a single 6- to 12-inch earring of turquoise heishi with silver or gold dangles at the end]. That happened almost twenty years ago, but it is just now starting to be sought after. People are accepting it now.

I am working with a person's inner thoughts and experiences, and the more they have on the inside to appreciate things, and the more strength they have inside, the better they can make anything of mine perform. Even the littlest people can wear some of my big jewelry. In one case a very small girl is enjoying a ring that is three inches above her fingers. There is no reason for anything to project out that far, but there is no limit and no rules in what will work for a person, especially now that men are wearing jewelry. It's a beautiful game, and I just don't want to be anything else.

Then there are people who want a richer effect and have the right to it because it is their environment. So I go all out and don't economize on stone or metal or whatever. The piece doesn't have to be big, just rich.

I have been working a lot in gold recently. The reason is that I can now afford to put more money in my materials. If I had had more money a while ago I would have been working more in gold sooner. I like silver because of the way it feels and works, but recently I have been reinterpreting some of the things I have done which I felt were great in silver and discovered that in gold they are even greater.

The question is whether you can take all kinds of material and make them work. I think you can—expensive and inexpensive materials can be really great together. It depends on how much you use of one against the other. You must also make a piece rich in depth, not necessarily in terms of money, but in terms of the greatest mystery you can give it.

Is there a way that I go about looking at my materials that makes me combine them in the way I do? I had formal design and color training at Alfred University, and you have to look at how materials fit together and balance each other. I feel that I have to make each material interpret itself as richly as I can by the amount of that material that I use. It's like the blocks I played with when I was a child. I could balance them one on top of another, but when I got daring and would pile more on top, I had to balance everything or the blocks would come tumbling down. This applies to materials—you have to be aware of it. I ask myself, how can I make this look as rich as it can? Sometimes you use too much of one material and it kills it. You have to arrive at a balance. The fewer materials you use, the harder it becomes. On the other hand, the more materials you use, the surer you have to be about your design. But when you finish and it balances out, it looks great.

As for some of the more unusual things I use, like pearls—any stone you have to experiment with. Having the pearls come from the Far East is another reason I had to go over there to realize how these people work with them and how they view them, and why they treasure them. Any Indian person not familiar with them could see a whole basketful of them and not care less. I think I understand pearls enough to make them work. Using a material in an unusual way—bracelets and jaclahs—results in a more sophisticated, a more formal piece of jewelry. They won't go into every situation, but if they were for sale in any fine jewelry company, they would all sell out.

I have a deep feeling of responsibility for teaching other people. If I am going to teach someone I have to see them all of the way through.

I am not just going to have classes and then let everyone go out and do their own things. I have discovered that I have not ever taught anybody enough. And vice versa—I have not ever learned enough from other people. I believe in an apprenticeship system, but you have to start with someone who is good. You can't just apprentice anyone and have them turn into a fine jeweler. They will be in jewelry for the rest of their life, and if they can't grow it creates frustration. They have to have a good grounding in basic design, because this is where they discover the imagination that they have and what it can do. You also have to teach how to sell. Someone has to do the dirty dishes. You can't just teach someone to make jewelry without teaching them the business aspects, too. It is because I am so concerned with the teaching part of it that I am not teaching now, because if I were it would be a full-time job and I would not have enough time for myself and my work.

I am still in touch with the people I have trained and we talk about things. If I see a bad piece or a piece that doesn't quite work, I tell them. If I see a particularly good piece, I tell them that, too. My feeling is that if one wants to learn, one should see the top people and discover what makes them tick. I've done this, so I know that this is where you have to come from.

An artist must work from his background, and whatever depth there is, the artist must understand and work with that to the best of his ability. An artist can discover this depth through education or just getting to know himself. The sources are endless. I am still finding out things. The more I am involved in it the better I can interpret what things mean to me, and that is what feeds the work that I am doing. I laugh at craftsmen who are just copying, because the depth can never be there, can never interpret itself. It is hard to do something and right away someone else is doing it. Sometimes I have not worked on a concept long enough and have not tested it out, and when someone else does it, it becomes very negative and I won't do it again.

Great things are only done if you are happy with yourself. You have to exercise yourself in the role you are taking—whatever role that is, just like a runner or a tennis player. The same thing happens to a silversmith. You have to know the craft well and keep working at it. You have to create a happiness within yourself by being nice to yourself—doing nice things like eating popcorn and listening to good music.

People think I can pump this stuff out any old day. It doesn't work that way. If I am feeling negative, nothing works. I can get an idea and it may take as much as ten years before it works, sometimes longer. And I have to keep coming up with new ideas all the time.

"Don't work yourselves to death, I've got it all made up..."

ANITA DA—pronounced "day"—*is the widow of famed Indian craftsman Popovi Da of San Ildefonso Pueblo, New Mexico, and the mother of equally well-known artist Tony Da. She also is the daughter-in-law of the incomparable Maria Martinez, the Potter of San Ildefonso. Mrs. Da continues to operate the Da Popovi Studio of Indian Arts and Crafts in the heart of San Ildefonso Pueblo.*

Today we have probably hit a peak as far as Indian arts are concerned, but it's regrettable that so many times non-Indian experts feel they know more than the Indians. Many non-Indians may know a great deal, but the Indians have lived with all these things; so much of it relates to our way of life—the jewelry, the pottery, the painting. All of these were, in one way or another, created and brought along with our way of life. In the past, certain Indian people did certain things and traded them with others, who did other things well, for the things they needed. They didn't all make designs; how could they survive just making designs? Like today, the Indians had their hunters, doctors, lawmakers.

Now, with all the mechanically produced goods on the market, we do not rely on our pottery or use it, except for ceremonials; the same goes for paintings. In the past a lot of our Pueblo designs were not allowed out for commercial purposes; it was not until fifteen years ago that they began to draw kachinas for the [non-Indian] public to see. Some things still cannot be painted, some kinds of pottery still cannot be sold—and some designs have appeared, in jewelry and other crafts, that should not have appeared.

We are losing quality in Indian crafts today, no doubt about that. It's the pressure, the demand; the top craftsmen can't keep up with the demand, so they work a little faster and the quality suffers. We do have some fine-quality work coming out, but there is so much competition from the outside world, from non-Indians and from foreigners.

Many leading Indian citizens are trying to help out by keeping quality in the market and by working for legislation to make people in the business identify the crafts that they sell—precise labels such as "Indian handcast." The non-Indians claim they are not trying to compete with Indian craftsmen, but it's not so.

It's very frustrating, the way things are today; it's hard for our Indian people to be honest about everything they do. A turquoise dealer from Nevada will come to Santo Domingo Pueblo—Santo Domingo is one of the few tribes that work with rough turquoise—and the dealer will say, "Here is natural turquoise right out of the mine. We've come to sell direct to the craftsman." The Indians will buy it and find that the "right from the mine" turquoise has already been treated.

I blame much of this on the non-Indian, who introduced mechanical aids, machine-made supplies centrifugal-cast parts, turquoise already cut—all of these things were brought to the Indian by the non-Indian, who said, "Why bother to cut your own stones, why take the time to cast your own metal; we've got it all made up. All you have to do is polish it, trim it, put the turquoise in it." It wasn't the Indian who went to the big companies and said, "Hey, you guys, do all this so we won't have to work hard."

The non-Indians should keep their new ideas to themselves, and there would be more traditional work. Myself, I like the traditional styles, but then I'm older. I grew up with them. But the world is changing, and the Indians are changing like everyone else.

Tourists who come here often are disturbed because I wear pants, have my hair done; they don't stop to realize that the Indian lives today in a white society. We're trying to preserve our culture, but we are a minority surrounded by a modern society. You cannot expect us to be as we were a hundred years ago.

The Indians are not all artists; their art is just one of the things that they *show*. Indian art is different, so it is noticeable.

The surge of interest in Indian art has made Americans more aware of the Indian people; they have come to realize that there really are *live* Indians. Non-Indian Americans are among the least-informed people in the world. They may have traveled all over Europe, but they've never heard of the Pueblos.

Customers today are more conscious of Indian jewelry, but they complain more about the prices (overall, prices have at least tripled). Often now Anglos are demanding the same kind of prices for Anglo-made pieces of jewelry. These people are infringing upon the Indian world; Albuquerque is the biggest center of mass production of Indian-style jewelry in the country. With this situation, naturally, you get mediocre Indian craftsmen who can probably do a little something; but before now they wouldn't have thought of going into making Indian crafts.

I think I'm in daily contact with more buyers for people going into business than I am with ordinary customers. Those who have entered the business in the past five years are in it only for the money. But Indians are charging retail prices now like everyone else, like the shops.

Indians, like anyone else, look for the fine workmanship when they're buying jewelry. If they can't afford them, they'll buy cheaper things, but they know the difference. They're not proud of it, but they have a good sense of humor. They'll say, "Look here at my lovely handmade Japanese necklace."

In the past, certain Indian people did certain things and traded them wih others, who did other things well, for the things they needed. They didn't all make designs; how could they survive just making designs? Like today, the Indians had their hunters, doctors, lawmakers.

Of course, the best jewelrywork is what an Indian makes for himself or for a relative. Sometimes he will have a special piece of turquoise and make something special with it. He may sell it, but only if he's hard up. But it isn't always the case that because an Indian is wearing a piece of jewelry it's the best (Indians are not dumb, either).

I'd say that Indian craftsmen today are getting the profit, instead of the middleman or the shop. In the Southwest this business has been overrun by amateurs, and it's getting very hard to distinguish what is genuine. The Japanese heishi, for instance, the Philippine heishi—we resent the importation of these things very much. You can say this: the best Indian jewelry is not bought in motel rooms, at public auctions, from people selling door to door or on the street.

Many old-time traders and pioneers came out here to make money. The whites are always commercially minded; they think in terms of money all the time. They traded with the Indians to make a profit. The Indians were used to bartering, to trading this for that, but they did not think of a trade in terms of profit. Many of the traders, whose fathers had been traders and collectors before them, are probably very well off now.

When it came to pawn, the trader, always money-conscious, would say to the Indian, "What do you have?" and take the best they had.

The Pueblos have done very little pawning compared with the migratory Navajos. The Pueblos, as settled farmers, were more or less united groups who took care of their own. The Navajos have brought about some changes recently on their reservation in how pawns could be handled by traders. In the past there were sometimes some illegal transactions made by traders.

The Navajos and the Plains Indians always did the most pawning. I'd say the Indians are much wiser now, regarding pawn, than in the past. The better things are no longer pawned.

Recently we had a non-Indian man stand up at a meeting in which we were working for stricter controls on authentic Indian jewelry and he asked how we could try to say this was ours alone when all of our designs came from Europe. To him I say, you haven't been in our kivas; you don't know what is there.

I blame much of the confusion on what is authentic and handmade on the non-Indians who say, "Don't work yourselves to death, I've got it all made up." And I blame it on the non-Indian who recognizes that a piece brought to him is not truly handmade and he gives the Indian less money (and the Indian takes it because he knows he did not put all that much work into it anyway). The trader then turns around and sells the piece for a price as if it were handmade. It is the non-Indian's place to discourage bad work, it is his place to say, "This isn't good enough; go back and bring me a real sandcast piece."

The non-Indian must help.

"This spring I learned how to make a bead..."

PHIL NAVAYSA, *a young Hopi jeweler from Old Oraibi Village, M.F.A. in Contemporary Art, University of Montana, represents the new generation of jewelry designers emerging from the traditional Hopi lifestyle.*

Three springs ago I was living in the Flathead Indian country of Montana. The weather was changing from cold to warm. The soft breeze that comes with the early morning light would awaken me and I would be drawn to walking the rivers and into the mountains. I felt very fortunate to be living. I could think of nothing but this feeling of love for all things. The land is vast with mountains and the sky even greater, but what was surrounding me was the scent of living things, their greenness, their warmth, smothering me, filling me. I felt honored by their gift of love. Now was there growth and inspiration, celebration, great ceremony within me, now to be shared and a gift prepared in return.

Great love and respect for my Grandmother Alice James, Corn Clanwoman at Old Oraibi Village made the choice for me, and a necklace of silver beads handmade by myself was to be the gift. This was the beginning of my involvement in creating "Indian-style jewelry."

It always seems to be the grandmother in Native American tradition who teaches and guides with various subtle and mystical means. I think grandmother has been melting the snows that surrounded me for so many seasons, and with this spring I learned how to make a bead.

I had been amazed at the high prices Indian jewelry was going for. Simple strands of beads and squash-blossoms that don't take that long to make were selling for a lot of money. Then I tried making that strand of beads for my grandmother and found that there's a lot more that goes into the beadmaking than I had thought, but still not enough for what people were paying.

In the old days, a half-dome impression was made in a piece of very hard wood and a punch with a round end like a ball-peen hammer was used to shape the metal into the form by hammering or applying pressure to it. Holes were punched in each half of the bead and the edges filed down so they would make a tight solder joint. Today we use a dapping die and punches—about the same thing, but they are smaller and more sophisticated. They have diameters that get smaller and depths that get deeper, and you form a bead by moving the metal from one hole to another until you get the right diameter and height. The two halves are then soldered together to make the completed bead.

Jewelry started out as a hobby for me. I'd taken courses in college to fill requirements but never really thought I'd use the skill. I'd been working in sculptural forms with wood and cast aluminum, and the silverwork was a natural extension. I guess I still think of it as a hobby because I am still exploring my ideas about it. In jewelry I'm interested in good craftsmanship and clarity of thought and design.

Everyone who is caught up in the creative process ideally wants to be known as an artist. They want that identity, so they spend a great deal of their time convincing themselves that they are artists and neglecting what *artist* really means. I think it must be like a marriage where you love something dearly, you almost can't live without it, you have to participate in it with your daily life, your dreams, your visions. I've been a student of art for a long time. It isn't important that I have a paper from an institution saying that I'm an artist. I'll be a student of art as long as I live.

An artist has a never-ending stream of training and discovery coming into him. It's a learning process you have to take hold of and work at. Some of the younger artists have been able to take the time to read and investigate—they have been able to take their time.

I think background is more important than training. I seem to draw from my background a lot more. If some person wanted me to make a piece of jewelry for them, I would look at them and then look at something else. They reflect something, but what I see in them might be what I see in a cottonwood tree when the wind is blowing and the leaves are reflecting the sun. I look for something there in that one person and maybe I'll receive inspiration from the dancing leaves.

I hope my jewelry is an entity unto itself. I don't like to look at a person and say that the piece should reflect him. I don't even like it to reflect myself. Yet jewelry is very personal. If you know where your jewelry is, you keep track of it and find out how the people are doing with it, how they are developing a relationship to it. These creations are like little children in that they should be watched over. It gives me a very good feeling to see the old pieces that I have made. It's like seeing your family or relatives after a long absence.

Phil Navaysa, Hopi, polishing a modern silver bead necklace set with rings of inlaid turquoise and coral. The bracelet he is wearing is his own design in cast silver. *(Forrest Stroup)*

I like to see my work on graceful young people—that's one of the reasons I changed my policy on pricing. It's sad so many people can't afford good jewelry till they're older.

Gold is a fantastically beautiful—an elegant—an important material, especially in its purest forms. The metal itself has a pre-Colombian philosophy behind it—more than a philosophy—a presence. It evokes very old and primal civilizations, mythological peoples. People think of turquoise as always traditionally combined with silver, but in the Southwest it's only been since the late nineteenth century.

I like to use gold more than silver because there is a certain quality to the surface finish of gold. It's the overall form of a piece with which people are first impressed, then it is the surface quality of the metal. Gold doesn't tarnish or oxidize because the metal is pure. With silver you have to alloy other metals with it so it can be worked. Copper, which is the most often used, tarnishes very quickly. This patina of oxidation is good in traditional jewelry, or where there is a sandcast piece with texture it can be incorporated into the design to give it depths and highlights. I try to give my surfaces a very fine finish quality that includes reflection, not patina—a reflection of the world around incorporated as movement in a mirror.

"Progression...is what the new Indian jewelry art is all about..."

PRESTON MONONGYE *of Third Mesa, Arizona, is a well-known Hopi/Mission silversmith, innovator, sculptor, and teacher. His craft and direction have transcended the mainstream of Hopi jewelry.*

It has been said that the Indian started making jewelry at the turn of the century when the Spaniards came, making jewelry, ornaments for their horses, and trinkets for barter.

If we go back into the discoveries made by anthropologists who dug up many ruins throughout the Southwest, we find magnificent pieces of shell, stone, and bone, dating back to the Hohokam era. Gold and silver were worked by the Indians in Mexico, Central and South America, so it is really hard to put a date on just when the Indians started making jewelry. Some authorities will say the 1870s, some the 1890s; but for now let's just say it all started. It happened!

Now, in the 1970s, there is a new art emerging from the old art—"The new Indian jewelry of the Southwest." The Indian silversmith can no longer be stereotyped. He has branched out into many avenues of jewelrymaking. Such artists as Charles Loloma; Kenneth Begay; the Plateros—a large Navajo family of silversmiths; Roger Tsabetsya of Zuni; Mary Tsikewa—a very fine fetish carver; Robert Leekya; and the Navajo brother and sister team of Lee and Mary Yazzie. These are just a few. There are others from Santo Domingo,Cochiti, and in the last few years there have been very fine overlay pieces coming from Taos, New Mexico. These tribes are taking the jewelry into a new dimension...a new degree of silversmithing.

Some people like to compare old pawn with the jewelry being made today: "Old pawn is better than new jewelry." I disagree! Some of the techniques being used today are far superior to the techniques that were used in the past. I can recall at the age of nine, being out on the Hopi Mesas in the village of Hotevilla with my uncle, pumping bellows to melt down Mexican silver pesos or American silver coins, and hammering them into small bracelets that took days to make. We didn't get one-tenth the quantity or quality that we get today. Now we make highly refined items, beautifully decorated with polished turquoise and other precious stones, even using diamonds, rubies, emeralds, star sapphires, ivory from the walrus and elephant, ironwood from southern Arizona, obsidian, onyx, and coral—just to name a few.

During World War II, money was hard to come by for the Indian whose income at the time was less than $300 a year on the reservation. Turquoise was scarce and very expensive, so petrified wood was used because it was readily available and the Indian could find it on the reservation. Cutting was difficult in those days. We had to use a hammer to flake off the petrified wood and then grind it with an old hand-cranked grinding wheel. Polishing was even more difficult because electricity was not available to us. We would hone the stone down on a piece of buckskin with wood-ash grit, and the finishing polish was done using natural facial oils and rubbing the stone on our pants for hours to achieve a sheen. Even then it was dull.

If you look at the jewelry received by museums ten or twelve years ago, then look at the pieces they are receiving today, you will see that there has been an improvement in the quality of Indian jewelry all along the line. The Navajo technique used both hammered silver and heavy clustered turquoise. This was probably the earliest recorded concept in jewelry design. Now the Navajo has progressed to finer pieces with highly cut stones and cabochons.

There are people today who say that a lot of the stones are by non-Indians. This really doesn't make that much difference since most other jewelrymakers around the world do not cut their own diamonds and emeralds. Another thing, there is not electricity on all parts of the reservation. Therefore, for Indians to continue making jewelry, and since the general public demands high quality, Indians do buy a lot of precut turquoise. There are many good stones today, however, that are cut by very fine Indian lapidarists, such as Lee and Mary Yazzie who work for Tanner's Indian Arts and Crafts Center in Gallup, New Mexico. I use their stone cuttings and incorporate them in my style of silver jewelry. I also know of many Zunis that do very fine stonecutting. It's what happens to that stone from the time the Indian gets it to the time it ends up as part of a beautiful piece of art that is important.

There are fewer silversmiths coming along now than there were, say, fifteen years ago. This is caused by industry coming onto the reservations and assimilating Indians into the mainstream of American society. Indians go off to various metropolitan areas and work in factories and do other things to earn more money. Nowadays it takes $2,000 to $3,000 annually to live on the reservation. When I was a boy, it took only $250 to $350. I might add, however, that an Indian who has stayed with the arts can really make a fine living today.

Of the 800,000 full-blooded Indians in the United States today, only 10,000 to 15,000 are silversmiths. Of that number only about a dozen or so have taken the "traditional" Indian style and have gone beyond to where it has taken on a new look—something that you can say is modern or contemporary. I'm sure that these artists did this because they wanted to evolve a new look, to take on a new identity.

The Institute of American Indian Art in Santa Fe, New Mexico, pretty much teaches a free-form type of art. They have been turning out some beautiful work. I think the basic reason Indian jewelry is classified as "Indian," even though it might be very contemporary in its looks, is that it still has an Indian feel to it. "Indianism" is the basis for this art form. In the beginning, during the Hohokam period and the Basketmaker period, Indian arts were painted pictographs on rocks and decorated pottery. They used man and animal stick figures and many abstract forms. Today we call those abstract forms "modernistic." When one speaks of our modern artists, like Maria Martinez of San Ildefonso Pueblo with her famous black pottery, and her grandson Tony Da, who combines turquoise and fine cuts of shell along with silver in his new pottery innovations, you will notice the type of designs they use are still that basic modernistic form.

When designs of this type are put into jewelry, the pieces take on a feel which is both very old and very modern. One reason for this feeling is that many Indians are still using proven old methods while branching out into new fields. Personally, I still use the traditional method of honing down tufa stone, which is a volcanic ash, and carving a negative mold. My design is in negative form and I pour to get a positive. By using old designs and old techniques, combined with modern cuts of turquoise and other precious stones and then adapting each to the other, we have a new form of jewelry—an art jewelry! You can't really say a new style, because it's just going along with Indian progression...the individual getting deeper involved with his true "Indianism," his religion, his traditions. If anything, this jewelry has evolved because of the way the Indian artists are dominated by non-Indian society.

Some silversmiths use the lost-wax method, sculpting in wax, encasing it in casting plaster, burning it out, and pouring into the negative mold to bring out the positive piece. Charles Loloma uses both wax and tufa stone methods and makes many one-of-a-kind pieces. This comes not so much of choice, but is caused by the undercuts in the mold which are necessary in the design of our jewelry. After you pour the molten silver into the mold, it cools. When you pull the jewelry out, it automatically destroys the mold because of the way it clings.

When you are buying this jewelry, remember that the method is old but the jewelry is new. As "Indianism" extends deeper into the art world, the new Indian jewelry of the Southwest will be accepted as a distinguished art form.

Many pieces have multicolors. The turquoise comes in colors from green to aqua and from a very sky blue to a robin's-egg blue. The dark streaks are matrix—a natural formation in turquoise. I like to use it that way because it lends character to the kind of jewelry I design. Most of the turquoise being used comes from the Morenci and Bisbee mines in Arizona; Lone Mountain spiderweb from Tonopah, Nevada; deep jade green from Battle Mountain, Nevada; and various shades of blue and green from the Blue Gem Mine, also in Nevada. Most of these mines, I might add, are not now in operation. Coral from the Mediterranean is deep rich red. Pink coral is known as angelskin, and there is also a white coral. White and yellow shells are mother-of-pearl. Some whites and off-whites are ivory. Black is generally jet, a hard, compact coal substance, and the iridescent colors are abalone or clam.

The new trend of Zuni inlaying goes into the more delicate and matched stones, such as those done by Lee and Mary Webothee. They do very fine clusterwork and have refined their techniques into cabochon cuts which when used with the old cluster method achieve a very unique look. Another fine Zuni inlayer is Eddie Beyuka. He is well known for his Kiowa and Comanche war dancers and the Taos hoop dancer bolo ties. Eddie also does figures in gold, blending his inlays with turquoise. Lambert Homer, Jr., Zuni, has a very fine touch in his inlaying. I have him inlay my mudhead, fox, and rabbit bolo ties and pins. So the Zuni, too, is breaking away from the stereotyped traditional Indian jewelry.

When you talk of new art in paintings and baskets and pottery and certainly in jewelry, you are not talking traditional. Much of this dates from the late 1800s, and that is recent time. So we progress from that point...and that is what the new Indian jewelry is all about, progression! An old piece of philosophy given to me by my father and other men of the Hopi Mesas is, "If you can progress without hurting your tradition or your religion, you should do so." I believe all Indians do this whether they are quite aware of it or not. It is because the Indian culture is so beautiful, I feel, that it shines through in their art.

Gold is now being widely used by Indian jewelrymakers. I don't know of any record showing when Indian goldwork got started. However, it has become quite renowned through the decorations that were done on platero-type watch bands and bracelets. Charles Loloma, Kenneth Begay, and I have done much work in solid gold. In competitive Indian shows, such as the Inter-Tribal Ceremonial held in Gallup, New Mexico, every August; the Scottsdale National held in Scottsdale, Arizona, each spring; the Arizona State Fair; and the New Mexico State Fair, gold was very well received.

Most of the gold used by the Indian artists is 14-kt gold. There was a little 10-kt gold in the beginning. The alloy was changed a little bit by mixing 14-kt and 16-kt and 24-kt with the backs from old watches and melting it along with the 10-kt gold alloys. But today, only 14-kt gold is being used. It is harder and has a very good color. Gold, however, is quite difficult to use. You can use the same techniques as with silver, but 14-kt gold sheet plate is a lot harder than silver sheet plate. Also, in pouring gold, it reacts and handles with difficulty. Because it is very expensive to use, we try not to make the massive pieces that would do just as well in silver. When we work in gold, we also use the best of other materials and stones. All this causes the price to be higher than an equivalent piece in silver. But gold certainly has a high value and will remain that way. I definitely encourage buyers and collectors to look at the new items in gold.

There is very little goldplating in Indian arts. We have little technical know-how in that area and there is also a great expense involved. When we get special requests for plating they are taken to people who can do it. All gold items in most of the stores throughout the Southwest are either made from rolled sheets of gold or from solid-casting gold nuggets.

"Navajos should make jewelry like Navajos and Zunis like the Zunis..."

KENNETH BEGAY, *instructor at Navajo Community College, Many Farms, Arizona, (the only all-Indian college in the U.S.A.) is a Navajo silversmith who has been concerned with high quality silverwork for over thirty years.*

I started playing with silver when I was about twelve years old. My great-uncle worked with silver and I watched him and played with the silver when he wasn't around. I went to the school at Crystal, New Mexico—Fort Wingate Vocational School. I learned metalworking there and then started learning silver. Fred Peshlakai, the son of Slender Maker of Silver, was the teacher.

We started learning with copper, filing and chiseling—and then went on with silver. We used scrap silver and melted it down the old way at a forge and hammered it out into the shapes we needed. We learned to make our dies out of steel. I still have all of the dies I made, but I don't use them any more. I make the ones I use now out of tempered steel.

Fred Peshlakai taught us the old Navajo style that he learned from Slender Maker of Silver. I like that style and still work in it. My designs are different from others. I see the designs on potsherds and on Navajo rugs. I dream about designs at night and then write them down and use them. Now it just comes naturally. I don't look at anyone else's jewelry except for the old things. I like to create something new and still use the old Navajo design style.

When I was still in school I went to the national parks at Bryce Canyon, Zion National Monument, and the North Rim of the Grand Canyon and worked demonstrating silvermaking. I worked for Babbit Brothers in Flagstaff. I've done a lot of work for the White Hogan in Scottsdale and taught silversmithing at Navajo Community College. Now I am out on my own, but sometimes I work seven days a week to get the things done. I make jewelry, hollowware, plateware, and a lot of things like boxes, lamps, church silver.

The stones and other materials I use are the best. I like blue turquoise the best—good spiderweb, and high-quality Persian turquoise. In rough turquoise if I can't tell which is the best, I ask for the highest-priced. That's usually the best. Bisbee and Morenci are the best in Arizona. I only use natural turquoise—none that has been treated or stabilized. I like a stone with a nice matrix. I used to use jet, but not so much anymore unless someone wants it. While I was working at the White Hogan I started using ironwood. Then everyone started using it. Ironwood, coral, and turquoise look nice together. I like to combine materials for special looks.

I'd like to be able to work at my family home in Steamboat Canyon near Ganado, but there is no electricity or running water in that area, which makes silverwork hard. I have a home in Window Rock, and I work there. I've walled in the carport and put in a fireplace. My daughter and son-in-law work with me. They have their own way of thinking about silver, and now and again I teach them a little bit. My son has a shop in Steamboat Springs, Colorado, and does very good silverwork. He used to work with me at the White Hogan while he went to school at Arizona State University.

I began marking my jewelry in 1951 or '52 using a *"KB"* as my mark. While I worked for the White Hogan I stamped it with a small hogan

I liked teaching silver at the college. Many of the students graduate from other colleges and come back to learn about themselves and the Navajo. They ask a lot of questions about the early ways, and so I have to demonstrate these

Kenneth Begay, foreground, working on silver church candlesticks.

techniques. I show them the old ways of melting silver, from mining the coal to making the fire in the forge and keeping it burning with the bellows. And the right way to pick sandstone for casting. The Navajos have a legend that you have to give a fine white horse to the Navajo smith to get him to show you how to pick a good sandstone. You have to pick one that is between medium and fine in grain, and it has to be cut right. Then you have to let it dry in the sun or in an oven to get all of the moisture out of it before you can use it.

My students still start with copper to learn because silver is too valuable. When I think they are ready they start working with silver. Some are slower than others, but it usually takes a whole semester. A lot of what is being made today is just junk because the maker knows very little about it. They take a few lessons or just start fooling around and think they know it all.

The chip inlay of Tom Singer is a good example of competent work. He used good turquoise and a good cement to glue the pieces in—you couldn't see much of the glue. Now everyone is copying his things and not doing good work at all. They use cheap glue which dissolves when you get it wet.

It takes five to ten years to be pretty good and another ten years to be very good. I'm still learning. I keep looking at the old jewelry to get ideas about how things were put together.

The way I feel about it, Navajo, Zuni, and Hopi smiths should each stick to his own style. Navajos should make jewelry like Navajos and Zunis like the Zunis. The Puebloans in New Mexico and a lot of other Indians who are trained smiths do Navajo-style jewelry. I'd like to see them stick to their own work.

"It was just a job to them, translating tradition into junk..."

LARRY GOLSH *is part Pala (California) Mission Indian and part Cherokee. He is a far cry, in one sense, from Atsidi Sani, for unlike the legendary Navajo smith he did not sit quietly in the background, watching the white and Mexican smiths to "learn a few things." Although his parents were Indian, he attended Anglo schools; his education is better than that of most whites in the field of art. He has combined formal education with good taste, respect for tradition, and the knowledge that what he creates is a product of all of these plus his own artistic skill.*

I was born in Phoenix, but my family moved back to California and I've lived equal amounts of time near San Diego and in Phoenix.

I took the back way into working with Indian arts and crafts. My grandmother worked at the Phoenix Indian School and my mother has worked there and at the Indian hospital.

During high school we were living near Los Angeles and San Diego, and I never went to an Indian school. After high school I studied art at El Camino [California] College and at UCLA, which I didn't like. I was concerned about design and quality but not about Indian art, as such. I'm still not.

In 1968 I was back in Phoenix and I enrolled at Arizona State University to study sculpture, design, and fine art. Initially I wanted to enroll as an architecture student but I would have had to wait a year, so I entered as a sculpture major. I'm glad I did.

During this time I visited the West Coast galleries and found them very exciting. I also became an apprentice to Paolo Soleri, a visionary architect who designed cities, and I studied under him, setting up, planning, and installing an architectural exhibit that was shown in galleries throughout the United States and Canada. All of this was indirectly connected with Indian art, but I didn't see it at all then.

Back in Phoenix I had to make ends meet, so I studied under Manfred Susunkewa, the Hopi artist; at first I did silkscreening on fabric. By that time I had decided that I wanted to make my living in some form of art and that I wanted to work for myself, not someone else. In painting or sculpture it takes a long hard time. So I thought jewelry is a lot more saleable, it's a practical thing. Manfred brought his tools down and we started working in jewelry part of the day. He taught me all the basic things—cutting and sawing and soldering. Through him I entered the national show in Scottsdale with my work related to Indian designs. I became concerned with the backgrounds of Indian art.

I began to study some of the old Indian things; they weren't bad or wrong, but I couldn't take advantage of the old things. I had to be an artist, good or bad.

I remember my grandfather telling me of the very violent things that were done to change the Indians' way of life. I suppose things had to happen that way, but later I went up to Hopi and there's a lot of tradition left there; it really impressed me. I also studied Plains Indian beading and costume: how could they have had all that time to spend on them? I also admired them for the way they lived close to the earth, not wasting anything. But today life is in the cities and you can't go back to a situation no matter how good it was.

Then Charles Loloma walked in. I had never seen any of his work before, I'd never heard anything about him. I went out to see some of the things he did and was amazed. I'd been looking at old jewelry, concho belts, bracelets, etc., but I also was seeing all of this new jewelry popping up and the new places opening up. There was the fine jewelry and all the awful things. In talking to Charles about this he told me how he got into it—how he used to be a potter, and he was trying to break away from what was being done but still appreciate the good of what had been done. And that's the feeling I was getting. The first time I went up to see Charles he told me "People always imitate my stuff. I'll show you anything you want to know but if you really want to do something you'll have to do something distinctive that people can recognize."

This is becoming more clear today. There are so many people doing Charles Loloma type jewelry. I think I am doing different things. I'm using casting techniques and I could never even try the inlay like Charles does, even though it is very salable now.

I have come into the Indian thing because I respect some of the artists—Fritz Scholder, and Tony Da, Joseph Lonewolf—the craftsmanship is incredible. These people have broken away, they have gone past the point of doing something for a sale.

I can also appreciate the older, traditional jewelry, from 1910, '20, '30. I like the workmanship, the quality. I'm inspired to do something equally as good—but not copy.

It's very disturbing to me today to see people doing traditional work but with less and less quality, compared to what was done in the 1930s.

The popularity of Indian jewelry has destroyed traditional feelings about how things were done. The trade has been monopolized only to make money. I don't see anything wrong with how it started, with the traders helping the Indians to make a better life for themselves by selling jewelry. I've never had to live without heat or running water, but it's no good—only if you have the choice of not living with these things can it be good.

The early traders took only the very finest things. Four to eight years ago they started taking everything, and even the Indian craftsman was turning out junk. It was just a job to them, translating tradition into junk. But if you live without a washing machine and want one, it's important to have the money to buy it; if you've never had one, you're tempted.

Talking about non-Indians turning out Indian jewelry doesn't upset me so much. What I feel sorriest about is that many people aren't knowledgeable to tell what is good and what is bad in total design. Many people in the United States have no sense of quality, but I see that changing somewhat. Non-Indians are fooling a lot of people who have no sense of quality. Popularity is destroying the whole meaning of Indian arts and crafts. Treated turquoise and cheap rings—only the profit motive is moving people to make more so they can get more. I see this destroying the pride and heritage of Indian crafts.

It helps for people to know how Indian jewelry is made; it's important to be able to tell an original sandcast from a centrifugally cast wax buckle. Craftsmen should be encouraged to sign their pieces and become known, to work with established dealers.

It's all good and fine to talk about these things, but what do you do? You do quality things so you can be proud of everything that's done.

I reach my own designs by various means: the shape of the turquoise stones I happen to have, or the other materials. I make drawings. Some of the basic things just creep into my work. Take a line on my cast silver. Is that really a rug design or from a pot design or is it from the actual spark of inspiration to the first weaver doing it? In jewelry, too, any time you have a change of style that is true innovation it's impressive.

Everything I do I make myself. Machine-stamped beads destroy the whole thing. I've had special dies made to make my own beads from. My production is very low—two pieces, or three at the very most, a week. Even the catches I make myself.

We started an innovative art program at St. John's Indian School near Laveen, Arizona. We had some of the nicest young people I've ever met. I didn't think of myself as a teacher. We set up a studio on the second floor of an old adobe building at the school. We had some fairly good equipment to start out and were able to get better things. We talked about the materials the old smiths used, how to cut stone, where the turquoise came from, annealing. We would go to Phoenix and eat at posh places, or to the openings at the Heard Museum or the Phoenix Art Gallery. This

Silver overlay box and lid with a procession of stylized petroglyph figures for designs. Even though the designs are quite old, the artist's treatment of them makes this one of the best examples of the new silverwork being done by Hopi artists. This box was created by Bernard Dawahoya. *(PC, Jerry Jacka)*

Below left: **A selection of silver and turquoise overlay jewelry created by Hopi artist Lawrence Saufkie. The Greek key variant and the bear are two of the designs he is best known for.** *(PC, Jerry Jacka)*
Below right: **An overlay necklace of Anak'china, or Long-Haired kachinas. This piece was made by the McBride twins in the 1960s.** *(HMC, Al Abrams)*

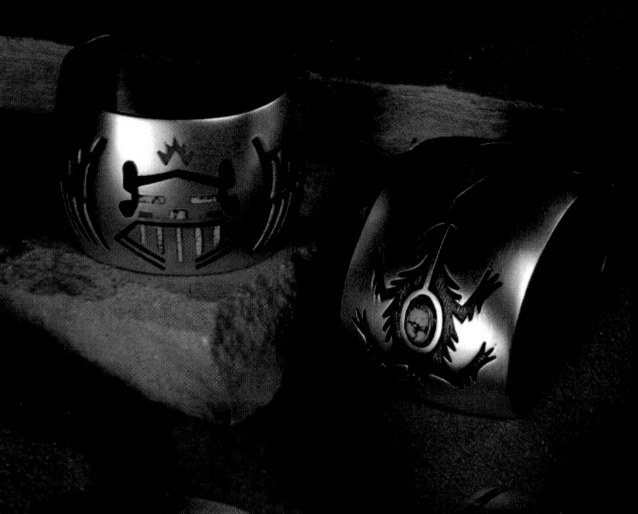

These four bracelets are made in what has come to be called the "singer style" of jewelry, named after the Singer brothers, Navajo smiths who originated the technique. The stones used in this process are inlayed in a chip mosaic held in with glue. Designs used in this style of jewelry are drawn from all of the jewelrymaking traditions. *(PCs, Jerry Jacka)*

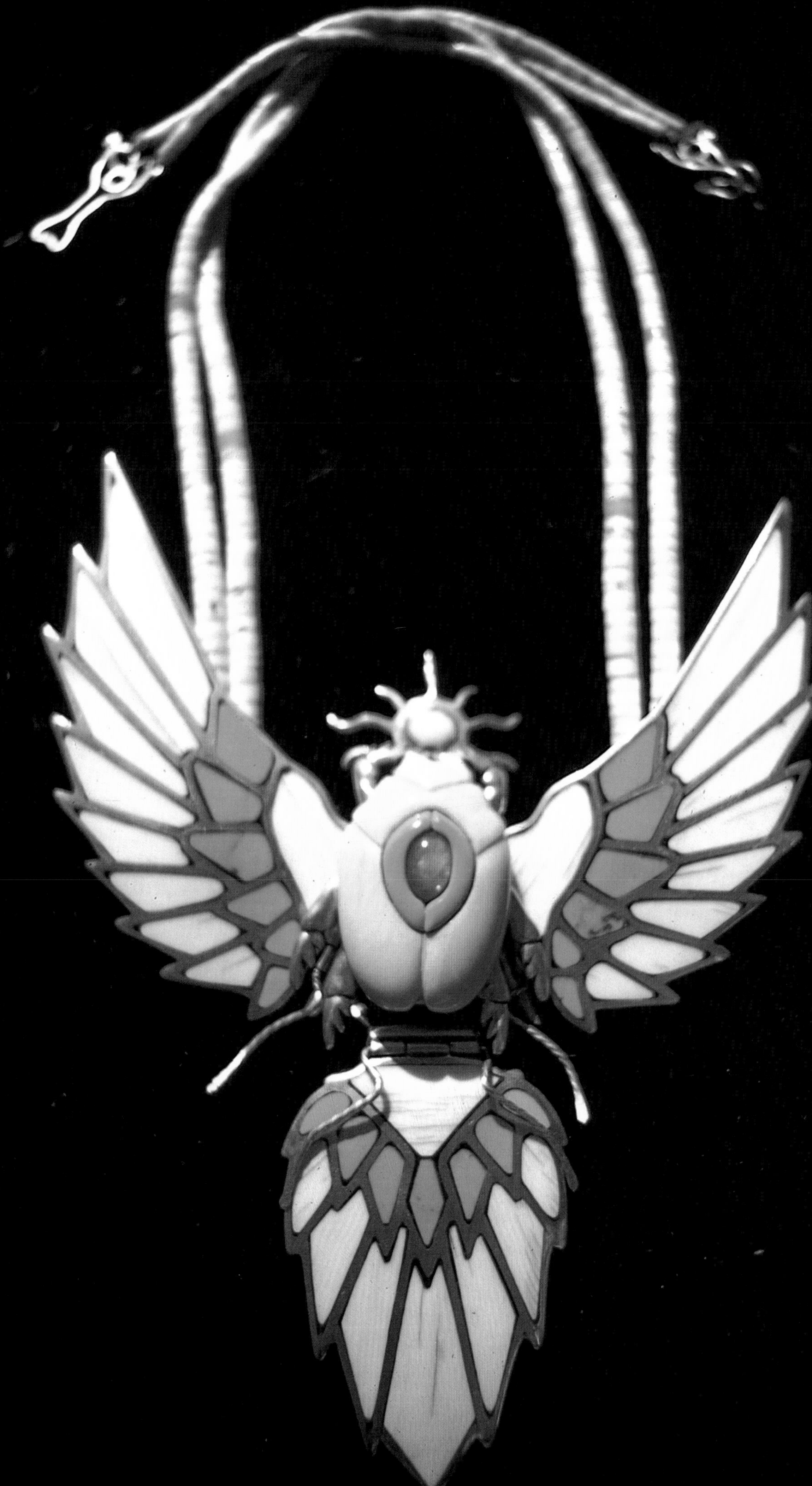

All of the jewelry on this page was created by Lee Epperson, an Anglo silversmith working in the traditional Southwestern materials. The better non-Indian craftsmen develop a style of their own that is accepted for what it is and not confused with Indian jewelry, even though the materials may be the same. *(Jeffrey Kurtzeman)*

This contemporary silver, turquoise, eagle claw, and ironwood necklace was created by Michael Durkee, one of the better known of Anglo Southwestern craftsmen. The thin pieces of turquoise set on edge he describes as a "mother water" concept, whereby the turquoise takes on the movement and sparkle of running water. Morenci and spiderweb turquoise from Number 8 mine were used. *(PC, John Miller)*

One of the best known of Anglo Southwestern craftsmen is Dee Morris, who made this contemporary bolo tie. Many jewelry wearers are now demanding pieces that can be worn with the most formal outfits. A piece such as this could even be worn with a tuxedo. *(Peter L. Bloomer)*

Increased interest in Indian jewelry has sparked interest in matrix turquoise even in more conventional recent jewelry forms. This "organically styled" lost-wax cast necklace in 18-karat gold is set with Persian turquoise and facet-cut diamonds. *(Paul Johnson's Jewelers, Jerry Jacka)*

Right: **Many older pieces can hold their own with those of contemporary design. This Zuni inlayed pin made in the 1940s has a boldness of design and a quality of execution that can be compared with the best jewelry being made today.** *(FHFAC, HM, Al Abrams)*

Below: **These carnelian and gold earrings by Anglo craftsman Clare Yares have the clean lines and exciting design that the best of Southwestern jewelry exhibits.** *(PC, Neil Koppes)*

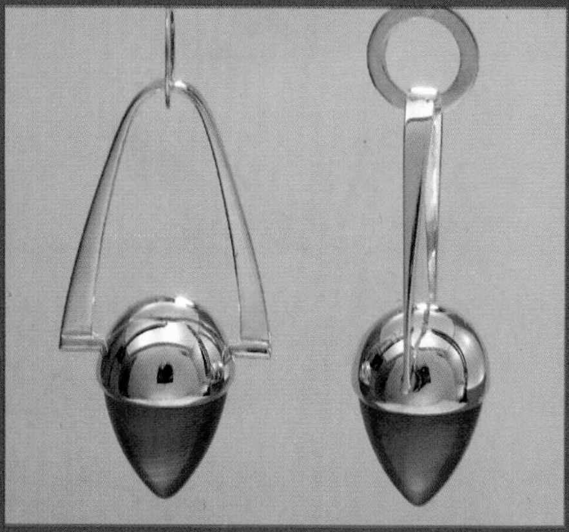

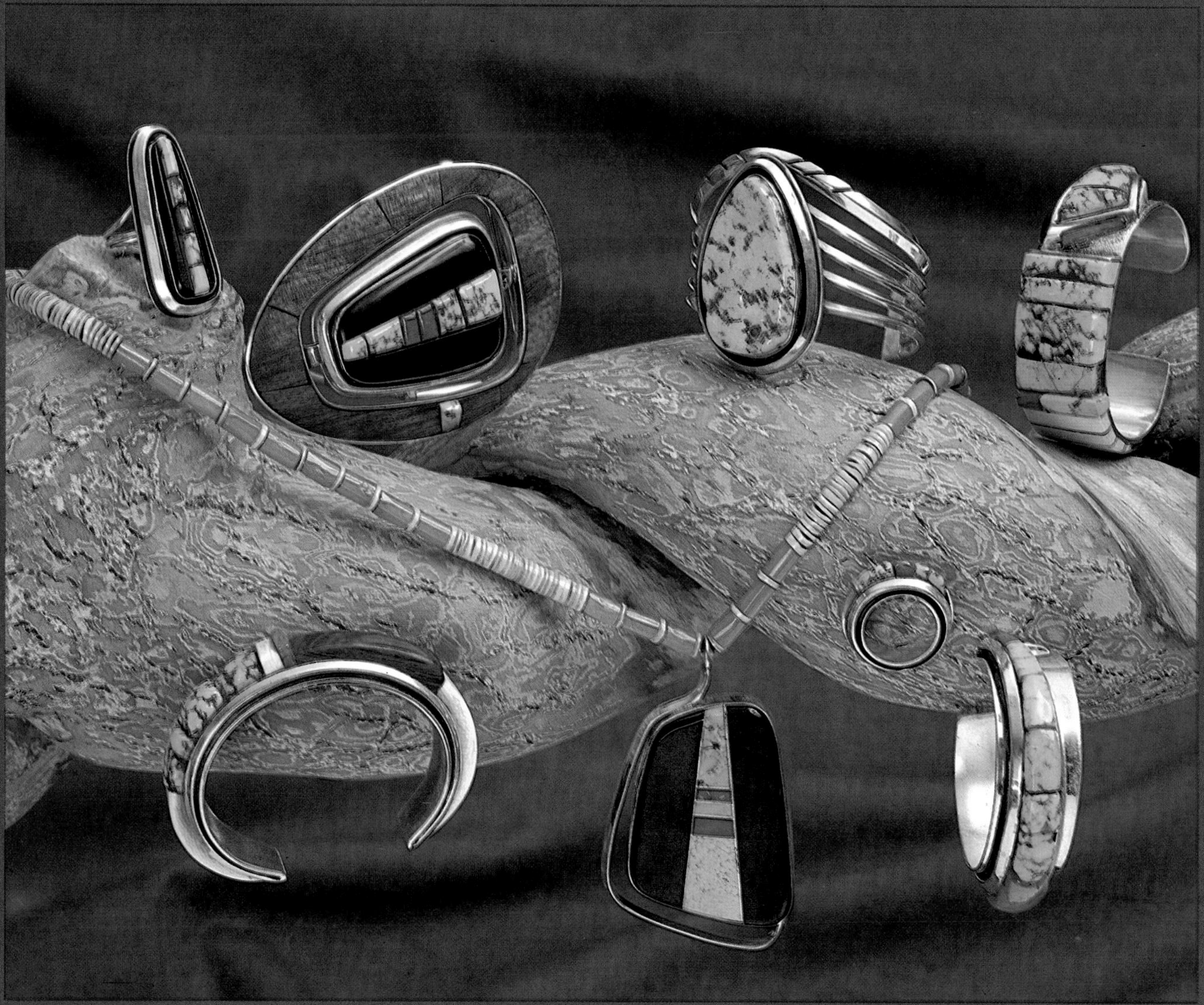

Victor Beck, a young Navajo silversmith, is known for the clean designs and quality materials that he combines in a strikingly nontraditional manner.
(Artist's Collection, Peter L. Bloomer)

Charles Loloma was one of the first Indian artists to break the Indian design barrier. Working in gold as well as silver and a variety of traditional as well as nontraditional materials, he has created a style that is much admired and copied. The bracelet at upper left is called a "sculptural" bracelet. The bracelets in the foreground are inlayed on the inside to reflect the "hidden inner beauty of the wearer." The modern ketoh at upper right is inlayed with turquoise and green abalone. *(PC, Jerry Jacka)*

Charles Loloma, contemporary Hopi jeweler. *(Jerry Jacka)*

Silver and fire opal ring by Charles Loloma. This large free-form silver and stone ring was made to be worn as a living sculpture. *(PC, Jerry Jacka)*

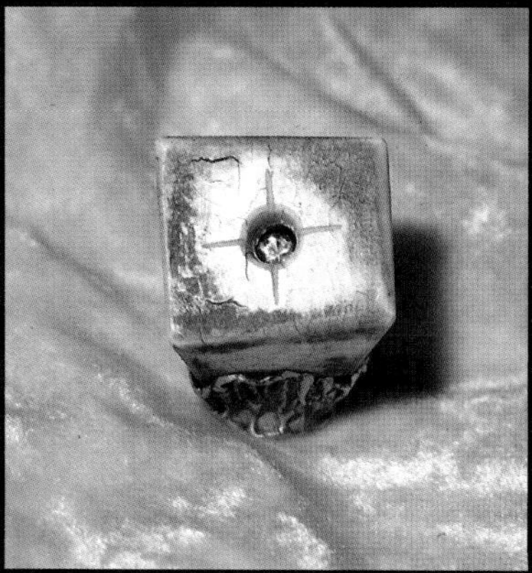

This fossil ivory, diamond, and turquoise ring set in gold by Charles Loloma is an example of the way nontraditional materials can be combined with the traditional. *(PC, Jerry Jacka)*

This cast silver pendant by Charles Loloma is inlayed on the visible side with turquoise, coral, ivory, ironwood, lapis, and abalone. The reverse side has the cast outline of a man, shown in the sand next to the pendant. *(PC, K. J. McCullough)*

Two silver belt buckles by Charles Loloma with inlays of ironwood, turquoise, rosewood, ivory, lapis, and abalone. The buckle at the bottom is a view of the Hopi mesas with turquoise buildings and an ivory sky. *(PC, K. J. McCullough)*

These bracelets and pendant were designed and created by Preston Monongye. The bracelet in the center has a long-haired kachina inlayed in it; the design of the bracelet at the bottom represents corn. *(Bea and Gene Gordon, The Eagle Dancer, Peter L. Bloomer)*

◄A group (ring, choker pendants, and bracelet) of cast silver pieces set with Lander turquoise. Designed by Preston Monongye, another very well-known Hopi jewelrymaker who has become a contemporary artist in his work. *(PC)*

These bracelets and the ring were also created by Larry Golsh. The top bracelet is a combination of sheet and cast silver. The bottom bracelet is a contemporary rendition of the old-style row bracelet. The ring combines nontraditional jasper with polished silver to create a feeling of mass without the weight. *(PC; American Indian Art Magazine, Roger Buchanan)*

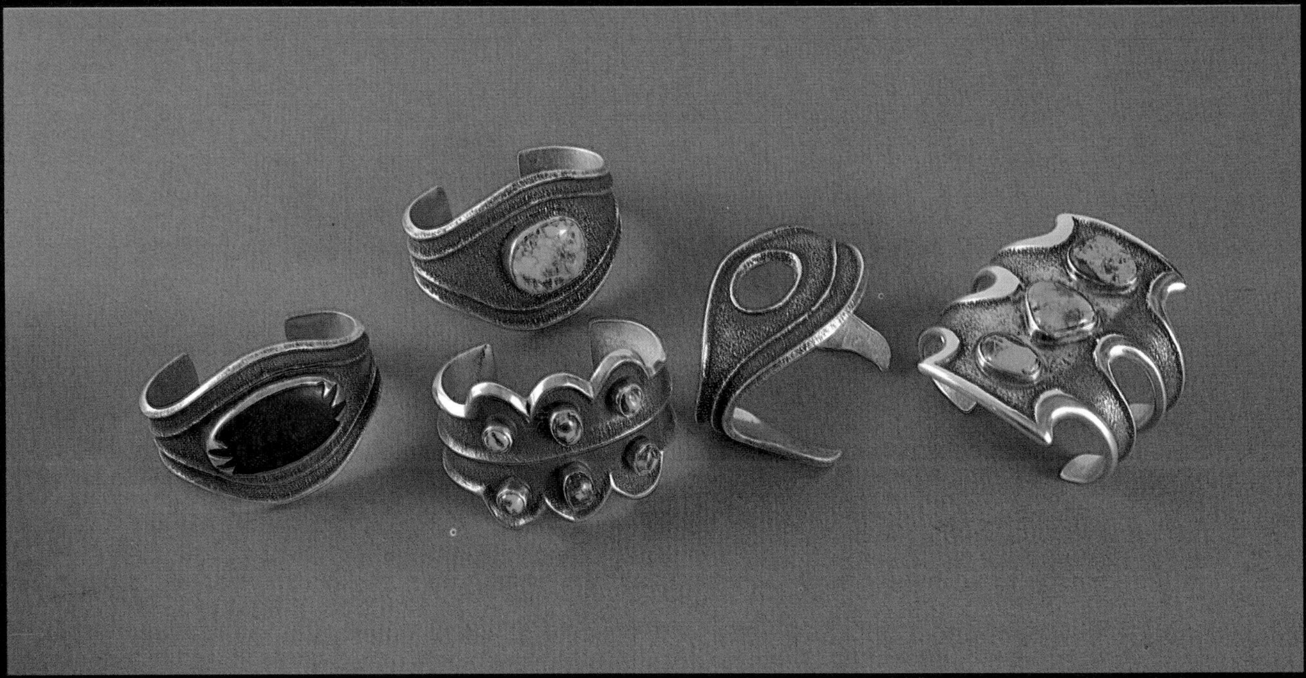

This photograph of a selection of bracelets designed and made by Larry Golsh shows the wide range of styles he is able to obtain by changing a few elements of space and materials within the basic bracelet form. *(PC, Guy Monthan)*

was all new to many of the young people and they were stiff at first but they got used to it. Anita Da [widow of famed San Ildefonso, New Mexico, craftsman Popovi Da] came out and talked to us at a special assembly, and Lucy Lewis [Acoma Pueblo potter]. We got old people, who were just sitting around all day, into the art programs.

Some of the students started selling their silverwork, making as much as $20, $30, $50 dollars a week. But some of the girls had trouble welding, so we worked with them a lot; since welding was difficult for them, we taught them to make twisted-wire bracelets, as they made in the old days.

When summer came, I didn't try to find jobs for anyone. I said, "If you want to work bad enough, you can find jobs at the big shops in Phoenix and Scottsdale. You can learn while you work, doing the simple commercial things, but you'll discover that it's not what you will want to do forever."

"If it wasn't for my parents, I'd probably be designing circuits for the moon..."

JOHNNY and MARLENE ROSETTA *are a young Indian couple who work together on very fine bead necklaces, in a style originated by John's parents Ray and Mary Rosetta of Santo Domingo Pueblo, who brought the art of "heishi" to great refinement.*

JOHNNY I am a full-blooded Santo Domingo Indian; my parents are Ray and Mary Rosetta of Santo Domingo Pueblo. Santo Domingo is located halfway between Santa Fe and Albuquerque.

In 1968, after my graduation from high school, I joined the Army, where I was an electronics technician for three years. In 1970 I met my wife Marlene, and a year later, after my discharge, we were married. At first I wanted to complete the electronics engineering course I had started while still in the Army, but my parents' desire was for me to pick up where I had left off in 1968 as their most skilled necklace maker apprentice. If it wasn't for my parents, I'd probably be designing circuits for the moon.

Santo Domingo has been known for centuries for necklace making. There are also many fine silversmiths in the pueblo, but that came in the late 1800s. Necklace making has been done for centuries.

Now everything is called heishi—the real term for *heishi* is *shell heishi* (*hesche* is the word for shell in Santo Domingo Indian language).

When the Santo Domingos first made heishi it was ceremonial—they wore it at dances, etc. (there are many things I cannot divulge in regard to religious and ceremonial meanings and uses); but as things progressed heishi started going on the market. For many years everyone in Santo Domingo did large-diameter heishi and nugget necklaces—basically the same necklaces that were worn long ago. In the mid-'50s, my parents changed from the usual bead necklaces (quarter-inch and larger in diameter) and made them much finer—one-sixteenth inch in diameter.

March 1972 was the year the trademark "JMR" [for Johnny and Marlene Rosetta necklaces] came into being, but I actually started working on fine [small-diameter] bead necklaces in the late '50s, as soon as I was old enough to work.

MARLENE I was born in Second Mesa, Arizona, on the Hopi Reservation. The languages (Hopi-Santo Domingo) are very different, but the cultures are much the same. When I married Johnny he needed help in making necklaces so he had to teach me. (His pueblo's crafts differ from mine; they make necklaces out of turquoise and shell, and pottery; my people make silver overlay, baskets, carvings, and pottery.) So I had to learn how to cut, drill, polish, and string in order to help him.

Since 1972 Johnny and I have both been working with what he learned from his parents—making necklaces from turquoise, shell, coral, and liquid silver.

JOHNNY Marlene and I each have our respective jobs in making the necklaces. Marlene does all the drilling and stringing; sometimes she does some preliminary grinding of the beads. I do all the rough-cutting from the raw materials, grinding, polishing, the hand-drawing of the silver and cutting of the silver tubes, and finally the finishing touches, such as putting on the cones and hooks and eyes (all of our cones, hooks, and eyes are made by us—we do not buy them commercially).

Turquoise and heishi necklaces were first made in Santo Dominto with tools such as the pump-type drill with flints. As time progressed they started using sharpened files with manually operated stone wheels (turquoise and heishi were ground down on a flat piece of stone). They used this method up until the middle or early '60s when came the motors for lapidary work to Santo Domingo. Today, for many of the necklaces being made, these tools are used—but all these tools still are operated by hand. Natural turquoise still is drilled with pump drills.

We use these tools because they are faster and because (some people won't say it, but the truth is better) we've had to, to combat the thousands upon thousands of foreign-made heishi necklaces. Today thousands around the world (and across the country) are making so-called Santo Domingo-style heishi, which ruins the market for the people who are really known for it in the first place (as I said earlier, the necklaces did have some religious significance and were used only as ceremonial pieces); it cheapens their work.

All foreign heishi should be marked. By "foreign" I mean heishi made outside the country, or in this country by Anglos, Spanish nationals, or Indians other than Santo Domingos.

My parents were also the originators of Liquid Silver (fine silver-tubing necklaces). There may have been silver-tubing necklaces before this, but it was the finesse, the cut, and the feel of the finished necklace that gave these the name—Liquid Silver. The person responsible for the name Liquid Silver is Mrs. Lillian Young of Albuquerque. As she handled a necklace in 1957 she said that it felt liquidy in her hands.

Liquid Silver, as people know it today, is mainly machine-made from very-thin-gauge (30- or 32-gauge) silver. All RMR or JMR Liquid Silver has from the beginning been made from hand-drawn 28-gauge sheet silver. This process is started from sheet silver cut to a certain width, half-rounded, points put on one end and pulled through a draw plate (steel plate with a series of holes from large to small) forming a tubing, then cut, strung on wire, and several processes after that to complete the silver necklaces.

In 1963 *National Geographic* interviewed my parents, with the help of Dr. Florence Ellis, a professor at the University of New Mexico. I admire my parents for what they have achieved and for what they will still achieve, and therefore I call them the "King and Queen of fine necklace making."

You can tell if a necklace is Rosetta-made by looking for two things: (1) the initials RMR or JMR on the cones, and (2) a piece of coral in the necklace. The coral in the necklace has a long history behind it. When my parents first started making fine necklaces they used one coral bead as their trademark, thirty beads from the top. Then when a few people in Santo Domingo realized how successful they were getting, they would break off the coral bead and claim it was their necklace. So in the late 50's my father made cones, hooks, and eyes, the cones having three circles running perpendicular and three arches on the bottom. But that didn't work either, so in 1960 my father had a stamp made in his handwriting of the initials RMR and with the circles still on the cones. In the mid-'60s my father did away with the circles, and today his stampings are RMR three times on the cones or the RMR with leaves. With all the changes the cones went through, the one coral bead trademark remained in the necklace, but not in any specific place, just anywhere in the necklace.

Our JMR stamp was made for us in June 1972, when we started to sign our pieces (using also the one coral bead). The stamp was very small (sixteenth-inch letters), so in October of 1972 we had our present stamp made. However, we used the small stamp for eight months.

People ask: "How long does it take you to make a necklace?" but we cannot really say because we work on several pieces at the same time (you can get frustrated working on only one thing at a time—you work on one thing, then maybe put that thing down and work for a while on something else).

When I make something for our own people I make it well because it's our work and it will stay in the family. But I try to put the same feeling into a necklace that I make for you. (You don't just put together a necklace and give it to someone; you give it to someone else first—the Spirits, let's call them. I let them wear it first—the same goes for clothing and shoes.) If I have no buyer for a necklace, I wish and hope for it to catch your eye and please you. But the Spirits wear it first, and I ask them for their beauty.

The thought of taking nature's own resources from land and sea—turquoise, shell, silver, gold—and putting them into fine bead necklaces, so different in shape and form from the raw materials and yet so beautiful, can be intriguing to the mind.

We do all of our stringing (except Liquid Silver and Liquid Gold, which are strung on fine wire) on nylon bead cords, which are very strong, equivalent to about a 30-pound-test fishing line. When my parents first started to make necklaces, they strung them on regular cotton string.

Cleaning and care of fine bead necklaces is important, especially the silver, because it does tarnish. Ordinary soap and water will keep all the necklaces clean, including the silver. Liquid Silver bibs should always be handled by the cones. Be careful not to drop the necklace because the beads do overlap and are very hard to put back in their original position if the necklace breaks.

All beads are breakable, with the exception of the Liquid Silver—that is, if you were to accidentally drop them and then step on them. But it is highly unlikely that they would break by themselves.

I like best to work with my new styles, the newer creations are sort of a challenge. Sometimes I make something and I don't know how it's going to turn out till I finish it. There are many things I've sketched out, but haven't done yet.

In 1972 I started making Liquid Gold necklaces from 18- and 22-kt gold. Liquid Gold is made exactly the same way Liquid Silver is made but with a slight difference in price, both per ounce and the finished product!

Right now I am doing inlay on ivory, bead by bead, and double inlays. In 1974 I bought four elephant tusks and had them for many months, thinking about what to do with them. The idea of inlaying came into my head, an idea that brought the necklaces into contemporary jewelry. I took the ivory and made them like the regular necklaces, except that I inlaid each bead with tiny inlays of gold, silver, turquoise, various shells, coral, serpentine, pipestone, lapis, amber, jet, etc. I had troubles like the inlays popping out during grinding and polishing, but soon I was able to master it. The first piece took about three months to complete.

These new contemporary necklaces I am making are all in series limited to twenty necklaces (or less) per series, depending on how hard the series is to make. The cones on them are marked with our initials, the series (in roman numerals), the number of the necklace, the month and year.

"Metal is one of the finest sculptural materials..."

MICHAEL McCLEVE *is a sculptor who creates jewelry. He has worked with Paolo Soleri on the Arcosante project and is unusual among Southwestern artists who work in metal for the feeling of space and form in his work.*

The jewelry that I make is innovative in that I use materials not universally used by Indian craftsmen working in jewelry. I'm only slightly more than one-quarter Indian, but my work has somewhat of an Indian feel to it and I've become better known by entering things like The Heard Museum Indian Art & Crafts Fair, and The Scottsdale National Competition.

I consider myself a sculptor; that's what I have my training in from Glendale Community College. I think metal is one of the finest sculptural materials to use. The same metal can look chunky or airy, sit there or flow depending on what you do to it or how you finish the surface. In working with small sculpture you get a feeling of encapsulating what you want to express in a limited area. I guess that is the principle at work when I do jewelry.

All of my pieces are wrought pieces—I bend the metal and join it together to produce forms that I see as small sculpture. I'm now toying with the idea of creating a sculpture which has a piece of jewelry as part of it. You can take it off and wear it and put it back when you are through with it.

But the distinguishing thing about my jewelry is still the materials. I combine steel and other metals with an industrial solder that gives the pieces great strength. I can match any metal with a solder so you can't tell where one begins and the other ends. Most of the time I finish the pieces off very well so you can't see joints at all. And then the treatment of the surface is what makes any piece unique. Metal surface can be colored with chemicals for effects from the blue of a revolver to a warm brown and hundreds of colors in between.

I like turquoise, but other stones such as agates, jade and other non-precious stones seem to go better with my work. But the stones have to lend themselves to the design. Too many artists *add* stones to pieces.

"Design is really easy when you have a lot of interesting material to work with..."

VERONICA ORR *is a Colville Indian who has taught jewelry at the Institute of American Indian Art in Santa Fe, New Mexico, and has been working in the medium herself for twenty years.*

I guess you could say I came to the Southwest to take advantage of the unusually favorable environment for Indian craft; I started making jewelry when I was twelve years old. At the time I was growing up on the Colville Reservation in Washington State. It's a large rural area that ranges from ponderosa pines to farmlands. Until I was seventeen, all of my jewelry was made to give to friends and relatives. Then I started selling my things. I prefer to merchandise my things myself because I like to get to know the people who will be wearing my jewelry. It also looks better when it is out where people can touch and feel it, rather than in a showcase in a shop, because it is really very tactile.

My jewelry is contemporary but has a strong feeling of tradition behind it. The designs I use are traditional basket, beadwork, and petroglyph designs from Washington. But the traditional things in that area are usually rather crude-looking, which my jewelry is not. Also in that area there is no metal involved. On the northwest coast there is etching of silver done; but more inland, they work the raw materials, antler, bone, and stone into the finished forms.

My design style is very different from the Southwest. The Navajos have their own style that the majority of them use. Many of the people in the Southwest get into that style, which is very popular, and the market is so saturated now that a person would be better off to use his own imagination rather than to do the same pieces over and over again.

I work mostly in silver. Other materials are walrus ivory—I like all of the different colors and textures. It's creamier and nicer to work with than bone and antler or elephant ivory. I like the red earth tones of the pipestone and the natural greens of Canadian jade.

I also like to use buffalo horn when I can get it. It has a movement and flow in the grain that I can use in my style of jewelry. I work with the material and then inlay stones in the cracks and rotten areas which I clean out. By inlaying these areas I don't have to cut into the material and cause waste when I make channels to hold the material I am going to set into it.

Design is really easy when you have a lot of interesting material to work with. I don't sit down and draw up a design. Rather I look at the materials and see how they would fit together and work from there. I look to find a shell or something that will turn me on and work from there. I've never had design training in an art school, but I have such a strong sense of design that it doesn't matter.

The color tones of the materials are important to me. Some artists and craftsmen put things together and they have no concept of how colors work together. This makes their pieces very heavy. I'd rather leave mine simple.

Simplicity is important to me in design. I will sometimes add complexity with the texture of tufa stone casting. This gives the pieces the feeling of being carved out of stone—and many of the pieces I do remind me of the texture of some of the older traditional pieces I've seen that were actually carved out of stone.

My pieces are almost body decorations. I add things onto them—fringes and beads. My people like to add things onto their costumes when they dance. I like things that move, things which add color—like old brass beads and glass trade beads.

"Just putting it on is what is important..."

LAURA GILPIN *is one of the great photographers of the Southwest. Her most recent book,* The Enduring Navaho, *has received tremendous acclaim not only for its magnificent pictures but for its clear and incisive text as well. She has an intimate knowledge of the Navajos, and they have learned to trust and respect her.*

To a Navajo, jewelry is his most important possession. It's hard to tell exactly how he feels about it for there is so little we know about the Navajos, really. They never tell you anything.

I don't think the jewelry has any religious significance for the Navajo; just putting it on is what is important. Whenever you photograph them they always have to put on all their jewelry first; that's very important. Perhaps it's because they want to appear well-off. But Navajo religion is a state of being. I'm not really sure that the symbols on their jewelry have no meaning for them; they can fool you about such things. They take good care of their jewelry when they're not wearing it and have special places they keep it in. I've never seen a Navajo polish his silver; wearing it keeps it in good condition.

I like to tell a story about Navajo jewelry that happened many years ago, in the 1930s during the Depression. A friend of mine and myself were at Red Rock, near Shiprock, New Mexico, looking for jewelry for another friend who had a shop in Colorado. From the Red Rock trader's stock we bought a pawned concho belt—which had gone dead three years before but the trader had refused to offer it for sale before then. Not long after we bought it, the Navajo owner rode in for it from his hogan near Round Rock, Arizona, a long ride. He was heartbroken to find his belt was gone, and so was the trader. He wrote to inquire if the belt had been sold. We discovered that it had not been, and we got it back and sent it to the trader, who returned it to the Navajo. I think the story illustrates not only the great love a Navajo has for his jewelry but the attitude of the traders, who will do anything they can to help the Indians.

Two Navajo women photographed by Laura Gilpin in the 1950s.

Navajo medicine woman photographed by Laura Gilpin "at a Squaw Dance up on the mountain" in 1934.

Even the younger Indians love their jewelry. I don't think they will ever abandon their love for it, although they are leaving their traditional costume behind. I was at Navajo Community College and they asked me if I would lecture about the period between 1930 and 1940 to a class of about forty youngsters sixteen to nineteen years old. There were about twenty-five girls, and not one was wearing a skirt. They all wore bluejeans instead.

It always changes, the Navajo way, and it always will. They took what they found useful from the Pueblo Indians and from the Spanish and Mexicans, and now from the Anglos. If they have any feeling for esthetics, then they have it in regard to their jewelry; it's so important to them. They are very sensitive to the beauty of their landscape, and their jewelry is very close to them. Of course, the taste of the trader has influence on them, especially in regard to their rugs; each region has its own distinctive style, but the jewelry is universal among them.

[Miss Gilpin opened a copy of *The Enduring Navaho* and began turning its pages, commenting on the pictures, the circumstances they were taken under, and the fact that nearly every Indian was wearing at least some silver and turquoise jewelry and strands of turquoise beads.]

See here: children wear it, and this very old man—over 100 he was—wearing all his jewelry while herding sheep. Here is a blind man, wearing jewelry even though he couldn't see it himself. And they wear it at the Squaw Dances; they put everything on.

This picture here of two women: they insisted they wash all their clothes before I could photograph them, and after they were dressed they put all of their jewelry on. And these women inside the hogan are wearing all their jewelry: if they have their blouses on, they put their jewelry on as well.

And look at this pawn room at a trading post; it's festooned with jewelry. Pawn simply means that the owner needs money.

Here's a medicine man; medicine men always have jewelry. There are medicine women, too, and they wear a lot of it.

These pictures were taken at the Gallup Ceremonial: lots of jewelry there. It's hard to find *any* Navajos in there that don't have jewelry on.

Not long ago a Navajo man came to my house [in Santa Fe]. I didn't know him, but he asked to see this book. He said he had heard about it and wanted to look at it; he said he wanted to learn about the old ways of life. There was plenty of jewelry there then and it is still there now.

A well-to-do young Navajo mother photographed by Laura Gilpin in her everyday finery near Red Rock, New Mexico.

"The Indian race has a special bent toward artistic expression..."

SALLIE WAGNER *has a practical knowledge of Indians that comes from day-to-day contact with them; at one time she was the owner of trading posts at Pine Springs and Wide Ruins, Arizona, and now she is active in the South West Association for Indian Affairs in Santa Fe, where she makes her home. John Adair did much of the research for* The Navajo and Pueblo Silversmiths *at Pine Springs, and Alberta Hannum's minor classic* Spin a Silver Dollar *centers around Wide Ruins.*

Jewelry meant prestige to the Indians, as it does now. They pawn their best pieces to make sure they are kept safe; it's like putting them in a bank vault. When they needed to wear them, they would borrow them and then bring them back and put them in pawn again.

When the trader took in pawn it was kept indefinitely, especially if it was quality jewelry that the Indian valued. Legally it was necessary to keep it only one year, but usually it was kept much longer; no interest was charged.

We usually gave one-half to three-fourths of actual value on pawn jewelry; it was the Indian's security, his bank balance. We wouldn't give full value because we wanted the Indian to redeem it. When it finally came out of pawn it was put on display for a month, and if the owner still didn't redeem it, the trader sold it.

Most people don't realize that it wasn't only jewelry the Indians pawned—they also pawned wool, rugs, blankets, buckskins, tools. We used to tease them and put pawn tickets on their babies. They are very astute.

It's not stylish to compare differences between races, but I think there are inherent differences. I don't mean that these differences imply superiority or inferiority; there are just differences. The Indian race, in my experience, has a special bent toward artistic expression and oratory.

It used to be that it was illegal to buy directly from an Indian on the reservation. You had to have a trader's license to do so; that was true of wool and silver, at least. Besides, most of the silver the smiths used then was issued to them by a trader, along with turquoise. The smiths made it into jewelry and returned it to the trader, who paid them for their work.

Is it wrong for non-Indians to copy Indian jewelry? My gut reaction is yes. But after all, the Indians copied in the first place, when they were learning the art and developing their styles. Why shouldn't the non-Indian copy? Besides, one who copies doesn't have ideas of his own—and for that matter, not all Indians have original ideas. People like Charles Loloma and Tony Aguilar are innovators, truly creative artists, but not all smiths are.

The South West Association for Indian Affairs tries to regulate the things that are sold at their annual fair here in Santa Fe, but it's an impossible job. We try to see that everything sold is handmade by Indians, but things are always being sneaked in on us. If the SWAIA becomes aware of fakes or imitations, we write letters of protest; sometimes these help. As far as new laws are concerned, there already are laws on the books which attempt to prevent the manufacture and sale of fakes and misrepresentations. What is needed is enforcement of these laws and prosecution of those who are obviously violating them. But never is enough money appropriated to hire enforcement officers.

In the long run, the whole question is up to the buying public; they have to insist upon genuine quality jewelry. But the public doesn't have much chance to become educated as to what's good and what isn't.

"It's hard to pin down a first source..."

DR. BERTHA P. DUTTON *is the former director of the Museum of Navajo Ceremonial Art in Santa Fe, New Mexico. She is an archeologist who has done extensive fieldwork in Mexico and the United States Southwest, and as an anthropologist she is an authority on Southwestern Indians, particularly the Navajos. She also is the author of numerous scholarly and popular books which have sold in the tens of thousands of copies.*

The Navajos were certainly making metal jewelry during their stay at Fort Sumner (1864-68). They worked mainly in brass and copper and most of what they made was pretty crude, but they were making it. They surely knew all of the principles of making silver jewelry before that, because they learned the processes involved either as slaves of the Spanish or as visitors or traders at the Spanish settlements. But they couldn't make it for themselves because they lacked the materials and the tools, and they weren't allowed to do much more than to haul wood for the forges, But after Fort Sumner, when they had the means and the time to do so they quickly became skilled smiths. As you would expect, their first efforts tended to be clumsy, but they learned fast.

The Navajos may have picked up some of

their ideas from the Plains Indians, but they were completely familiar with the Spanish designs and motifs, such as the crescent characterized in the naja. The Spanish were using the naja on their horses' trappings when they first came to the Southwest; they got it from the Moors, who in turn had picked it up from the Muslims in North Africa and Arabia. In fact, the crescent is a worldwide symbol. The Spanish also were using the pomegranate element—which came from the Moors—and, as you know, came to be referred to as the squash-blossom by the Anglos.

But in these as well as in other aboriginal design motifs, it's hard to pin down a first source because they occur again and again, all over the world.

As with all such ideas, they originate with the environment: the earth, sun, moon, stars, clouds, lightning. Their awareness of these elements affected their lifestyles, simple things like the annual harvest, the passing of the seasons, the solstices of the sun; the cyclic nature of these things was represented by the circle, or the crescent, such as the rainbow, and these were reflected in the design motifs they used.

The earth was the symbolic mother, the sun was the father, for the sun impregnated the earth, which brought forth the plants and animals that the people lived on. Directions came into the picture—the six directions being the four points of the compass and the "Below" or underworld and the "Above" or sky. Snakes abide in the ground; therefore, they are the messengers to the Below; the Great Bird—of whatever specific name—was the messenger to the Above.

The symbols were more fixed with the Pueblo peoples, and the Navajos got much of their religion from the Pueblos, who made paintings on the walls as well as the floors of their ceremonial chambers. The Navajos used what they could use —not wall paints because they didn't adapt to Navajo dwellings; but the floor paintings, done in colored sand, did. Pictographs on the walls of cliffs or caves were the Navajo equivalent of the Pueblo wall paintings, done by people who were thoroughly familiar with Pueblo ritual. But the sand paintings on the ground—inside hogans, or outside—were easier to make, and they could be obliterated afterward, destroying evidence of what had been done there.

But the design elements the Navajos use are, in a sense, universal. Moroccan silver jewelry is set with garnets—which the Navajos used in early times because garnets are common on the reservation. Some of the Moroccan jewelry is almost identical to early Navajo jewelry. They use

Detail of a Navajo sandpainting. Design elements from many forms of Southwest Indian tradition have in modern times been reflected in their jewelry, and other silverwork. *(Michal Heron)*

a Great Bird design, like the Thunderbird; and the crescent, of course, is a common Islamic decoration. Even the Navajo bracelet shape is a crescent—a broken circle. The Navajos don't like to make a complete circle because that represents life. and when the circle is completed life is done. The doorway of a Navajo hogan breaks the complete circle of the dwelling's shape. The doorway faces east, but not always true east. The swastika element represents the whirlwind, and the Navajos use it frequently in their sandpainting designs—and it can face either way.

Traditional Navajo jewelry is dying out fast. They're going more and more to baroque designs, and so they appear just like jewelry that anyone could make. Again, they have adapted to modern trends and modern demands, as with fiesta clothes, which are modern versions of the traditional Navajo dress. While they are suggestive of the earlier Navajo styles, they can be worn anywhere, and so can the modern jewelry.

"The whole Hopi culture is so visually oriented..."

MARGARET WRIGHT, *the author of* Hopi Silver, *published by Northland Press, has worked with Hopi silversmiths through the Museum of Northern Arizona for twenty years. Her research into Hopi silver hallmarks and the documentation of silver work among the Hopi are important contributions to the field.*
BARTON WRIGHT *is Curator of Anthropology at the Museum of Northern Arizona and an expert on Hopi kachinas and religious ceremonies. He has written several publications about the Hopi culture.*

MARGARET The Museum of Northern Arizona has been involved in Hopi silversmithing since the 1930s. Up to that time Hopi silver was almost indistinguishable from Navajo and Zuni silver. In 1931 the museum sponsored the first Hopi craftsman show, though members of the staff had been working with craftsmen for a year or so before. They started the show because there was a need for an outlet for the people to bring their work to, and at that time—that was during the Depression—there was no other market.
BARTON The craftspeople would have to take their wares to Winslow and Flagstaff and sit by the roadside to sell them. There weren't as many tourists coming out, so the craftspeople were really hurting for a market. That first year they had all of 200 items in the show.

MARGARET In 1938 Dr. Harold S. Cotton and his wife, Mary Russell-Ferrell Cotton, began developing a project which would make Hopi silver unique. Virgil Hubert, who was the assistant curator of art at the museum, created sample jewelry designs drawn from designs on other Hopi crafts. These were distributed to various Hopi smiths. Several of them made pieces in this new style for the Hopi craftsman show that year. As the project continued, they enjoyed relative success, considering the kind of situation that existed then. The smiths had to use hand-hammered silver to get the Arts and Crafts Board stamp, and the tools were a great deal different from what is used today.

Then, of course, World War II started, and museum personnel couldn't travel out to the reservation. The Hopis were busy either off the reservation in war work or taking the places of the ones who were off the reservation in the ceremonial cycle and with the crops. There was one Hopi craftsman show during the war, in 1942, but the silver project was not continued.

At the time, it looked bad for the project, because the museum felt continued involvement was necessary. I think it turned out to be a good thing, though, because it gave those who were working in silver a chance to think about it. The early designs as a whole are quite different from what is done now. This was the idea, to give them the suggestion of doing silver with their own designs and let them evolve something with it. There was never any intention of just having them copy. Different smiths worked on commission for the museum. Some of them made it; some of them didn't. Some of them tried one piece, and when it didn't come out well, they said, "We'll go back and try again."

Then, after the war, classes were started under the GI Bill to train Hopi servicemen. Paul Saufkie, an old-time smith, was hired as the technical instructor, and Fred Kabotie as the design instructor. The museum designs served as a starting point, but the styles developed from there.

The whole Hopi culture is so visually oriented. They have a tremendous fund of designs—all graphic—more than many other people's. I think it is the consistent exposure to this that gives so many of the craftsmen the artistic flair behind their work.

As far as I know, there isn't any way of telling earlier pieces of Hopi from Navajo silver. This is one of the reasons I think people tended to feel that the Hopi weren't as good smiths as

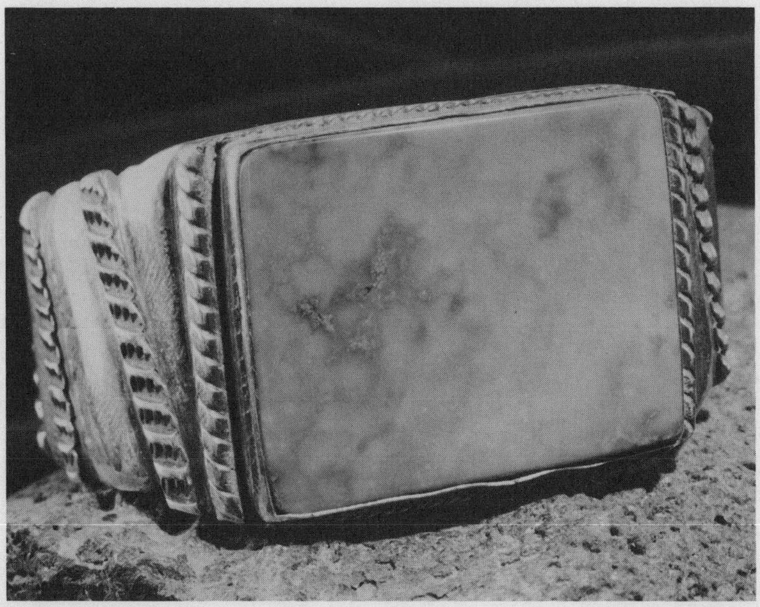

Hopi silver and turquoise bracelet, c. 1930s, showing how similar Hopi jewelry was to Navajo before the Hopi started doing overlay. *(HMC, Al Abrams)*

the Navajo, because once the jewelry left the Hopi reservation, there was no way to tell which was which. There were quite a few good smiths working from 1900 to the 1930s in what is considered Navajo style.

I have a feeling, though, looking at the few examples of bow guards from that period of time, that if we had a large number of them all together we might be able to pick out the differences. But, since we don't have a large number of them, well.... You have to also take into consideration that as far as design is concerned, silver design isn't a traditional form that they are bound to. In pottery and baskets they are somewhat, but not in silver.

At one of the recent Hopi craftsman shows at the museum, we could pick out examples that illustrate this. There were three pieces depicting long-haired kachinas. The first was a very realistic portrait with the long beard and hair. The second one was a little abstract, but you could still tell what it was. And, the third was completely abstract—all triangles. But when you put the three together, you could see what each was. I think they are unequaled in this ability to do design, both representational and abstract.

Tools were as available to the Hopi as to the Navajo in the early years, but there were just not that many tools. The older smiths still make many of their own. Most of them were pretty proficient blacksmiths, because to make a die is no easy thing. You have to be able to temper it just right. If you don't, it falls apart, or it shatters.

BARTON What collecting policies does the Museum of Northern Arizona have to document this cultural process that we started? We try to have a representative collection—we're not trying to collect every other item the Hopi smiths ever made. We try to collect those items which tell the story of silversmithing. It's not very easy to do, because many times you don't realize you are holding an innovation in your hands, and then six months later you think, "Why didn't I hang on to that. It would have been ideal for the collection." By that time, it's split, developed, or varied and well on its way. Then you're in the position of competing against the rest of the market to get one of the items back.

Then, of course, any museum depends on donations, and you usually get things other than what is in your master plan which you have to work with.

MARGARET We also try to collect examples of different smiths—both good and bad. And the stamps. We also collect on copper an example of the trademark stamps and the dates during which each one was used, which is harder than it seems.

BARTON First, you go out to see some smith and he's out herding sheep. The next time you go out to see him he's in Flagstaff; and it goes on and on and on.

MARGARET It's funny. Many of them just don't remember. There are two or three smiths from the first class who are dead, and their very close relatives don't remember how they signed their silver. It just isn't important to them. Something else I felt was terribly important was to record the dates that smiths used the stamps, because they changed them.

Bernard Dawahoya texturing the background of a modern Hopi silver design.
(Jerry Jacka)

In one case, we were looking for one of the smiths from Fred Kabotie's files, and he'd changed his name. He got a different name when he was initiated, and then, like so many others, he took that name, so you end up looking for the wrong person.

The Hopi Silvercraft Cooperative Guild was an outgrowth of the silversmithing classes. When the subsistence payments to the smiths ended at the end of the classes the smiths no longer had cash to buy silver with. The guild provided a place for them to get tools and silver on consignment. Actually, I don't think they ever had to put out any cash for the silver. They would get the silver and then they would turn in their jewelry, which was sold, and the money taken out for the silver, so they never had to put any cash out for the silver.

It also provided a place for the smiths to work, which was important because many of them didn't have electricity in their homes to run the tools with. And then, of course, it provided a place to market the goods.

The Hopi Silvercraft Guild is very active in training smiths because they simply need people to work, and they can't get enough people to work for them. They have always had more orders than they can fill.

BARTON The process is ongoing. Once a smith reaches a certain level of competence, he can see opportunities that exist outside the guild. One of the opportunities many of the smiths see is owning their own business or at least working for themselves. If a smith leaves and goes into business for himself, he will probably be involved in training other smiths. A large group of smiths that have banded toghther as a private, rather a tribal enterprise is the Hopicrafts Cooperative. The business was formed in Phoenix by Wayne and Emory Sekaquaptewa, who hired another brother, Eldon James, and Bernard Dawa'hoya as smiths and Peter Shelton, Jr., as a designer. The business soon moved to New Oraibi.

One innovation from the group was that many of the Hopicrafts pieces were not crafted individually, but by several smiths, each doing one job on a piece. But overall, Hopicrafts has resulted in a great improvement in Hopi silver.

Peter Shelton is a good designer, but it is difficult to design on a day-to-day basis and keep coming up with something new that is still Hopi. After a while, designs with eagles, longhorns, roadrunners, and other things started to appear—designs drawn from other sources.

MARGARET What type of craftsmen are developing now? Well, there are a lot of young silversmiths who, if confronted with some silver dollars, couldn't make jewelry. All they know is how to take a piece of sheet silver, cut it out, and solder it together. They don't have the basic techniques. There are a lot of others who are really excellent smiths, developing styles of their own, but it is not fair to mention some of them to the exclusion of others.

BARTON Since World War II, silversmithing has been very important to the Hopi economy.

MARGARET It gives the Hopi a good cash inflow and the men can live on the reservation . That's one of the nice things about it as far as a job opportunity goes. They can live out there and are free to take part in the ceremonies and plant their fields and still get the cash they need to live.

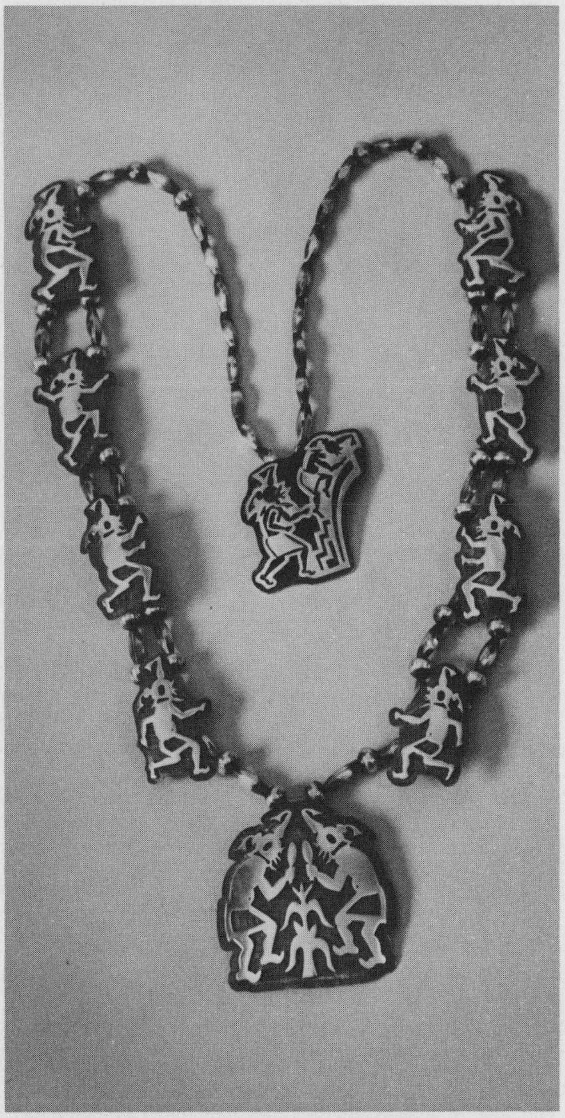

Overlay necklace and pin by Bernard Dawahoya. *(Jerry Jacka)*

"With their own two hands, they will keep the art of silversmithing alive..."

DAVID L. NEUMANN *has not forgotten the art of conversation. It is always a pleasure to talk to him. He has the traditional western knack—shared by Indian, Anglo, and Spaniard alike—of injecting wry humor with a straight face, so that its full significance sneaks up on the listener. Mr. Neumann also writes. He is quoted or referred to at length in the parts of this book which deal with Indian jewelrymaking from the 1930s to the present. His booklet* Navaho Silversmithing, *though relatively short, is probably the most informative reference of its kind on Navajo and Zuni silversmithing between 1930 and 1955. (The booklet is a collection of articles which Mr. Neumann contributed to* El Palacio, *the quarterly journal of the Museum of New Mexico, during that period.) Mr. Neumann has been by profession a wholesale dealer in Indian handmade goods for more than forty years. He is particularly knowledgeable about Indian jewelry, and any dealer of long standing is likely to tell you: "See Dave Neumann about that, he'll know the answer if anyone does."*

I came West for reasons of health and got interested in Indian jewelry and decided to make a career of it. I first went to the Navajo Reservation in 1930, scarcely a propitious time for a young man to enter a business that in its best years has more than its share of pitfalls for the unwary. In those years, as I do today, I bought raw turquoise—by the pound or carat, depending upon its quality—and took it to the Zuni lapidaries, to be cut and polished. I then sold or farmed out the worked stones to Navajo smiths, who set them in silver, and I wholesaled the finished products to dealers.

By this time, the Zunis had emerged as lapidaries—stonecutters and stonesetters—without peer, a talent they have exhibited since prehistoric times. Their silverwork consists of little more than thin sheeting and filigree on which small, perfectly matched stones are set in stunning clusters and inlay and channelwork. The Navajos, of course, were unrivaled as silversmiths, and although they and the Zunis sometimes copied one another, their styles remained distinct. The Navajos became very fond of the Zuni needlepoint and clusterwork, and traders on the Navajo Reservation regularly bought Zuni jewelry from dealers in Gallup to sell to the Navajos.

During the Depression days I and many another trader like myself would begin a buying trip on the Navajo Reservation with only a couple of hundred dollars in capital. There were no paved roads on the reservation then, and it took a long time to make the round of all the trading posts and the hogans of the working smiths. By the time you paid your expenses and sold your jewelry you could count yourself fortunate if you had cleared a hundred dollars in a month.

To save money, I often camped out, or if the weather was bad I put up with the traders at their posts. In Gallup a room with running water but no bath could be had at the new El Navajo Harvey House for $1.50 a night. I remember with fondness an occasion when I and the late Dr. Henry P. Mera of the Laboratory of Anthropology in Santa Fe toured the reservation on a grant to collect jewelry for the laboratory. On that trip, we obtained a deluxe room with twin beds and full bath, and it cost the princely sum of $6.

The Depression was at its height and silver was worth 28¢ an ounce; concha belts were being sold for their weight in silver (That means a traditional Navajo concha belt, 1930 vintage or earlier, could be purchased for about $20; that same belt today would cost well over $1,000—if one could be found.)

You can't identify the source of a turquoise stone simply by looking at it, except possibly for the top-grade gems from certain mines. Morenci, Arizona, turquoise, for instance, is characteristically studded with tiny bits of iron pyrite, but for the most part turquoise cannot be distinguished visually, especially as one descends in the scale of quality. Persian stones have a distinct color which makes them easier to identify.

It is also difficult to spot stabilized turquoise when only one stone is being examined; in a batch of stabilized stones there will be a uniformity of color which is not found in natural stones, even when they come from the same mine.

Plastic-steel backing on turquoise stones is being used frequently; I first noted this when a magnet on my desk drew to it several stones which happened to be lying there. Backing, of course, reduces the friability of stones, making them easier to cut and allowing stones to be used which otherwise would fracture on a grinding wheel.

When Navajo smiths first began setting their silverwork they used the stones which were immediately available, which is why many of the earliest pieces have garnet settings: it could be obtained locally. The same is true of turquoise, and the Sky Stone soon eliminated the garnet as the preferred gemstone because it could be shaped, it came in larger pieces, and it already had a well-developed role in Southwestern Indian cultures.

Some of the best turquoise in the Southwest

today comes from Pilot Mountain, Nevada—the same geological formation which has produced some of the other fine Nevada stones such as Lone Mountain and Battle Mountain.

Many stones are cut and polished in Manassa, Colorado, which became a center for turquoise working when a rockhound named King in 1912 discovered a lode of the Sky Stone, which produced well during World War II days. Manassa, a Mormon settlement in the southwestern part of the state, has become a center for stonecutters; the small community, set in lush mountain pastures, is otherwise famous as the hometown of Jack Dempsey, the "Manassa Mauler" of prizefighting fame. It is also the site of the Burnham or Godber turquoise mine.

Turquoise is a geological associate of copper, and since Arizona is one of the great copper-producing states of this country a great deal of the gemstone comes from the mines at Morenci, Bisbee, Globe-Miami (the Sleeping Beauty Mine at Castle Dome), and Mineral Park near Kingman.

Much of the Kingman turquoise is porous and chalky in nature and cannot be worked or sold unless treated; the town of Idar-Oberstein in Germany used to receive much of the Kingman stone, where it was a community endeavor to color it with Prussian blue for resale as a gemstone back in the United States Southwest.

Many stones are now cut in Hong Kong, and shell heishi (the round disc beads which are strung as necklaces and chokers) commonly comes now from Taiwan because it is cheaper to have it cut, ground, and pierced there than by the Pueblo Indians of the Southwest, traditionally those of Santo Domingo, New Mexico.

Another product of Taiwan is imitation Zuni inlay, done so well that it is difficult to distinguish it from the Indian-made jewelry. However, dealers and traders know the sources and pipelines for this type of merchandise, and those who sell quality handmade Indian jewelry simply shun the entrepreneurs who peddle the foreign goods.

Another problem in the overall picture is the definition of what constitutes handmade Indian jewelry. At one time smiths manufactured their own clasps for necklaces, and earrings were made with a small gap so they could be inserted into pierced ears. But the demand for earrings with screw attachments was solved by obtaining commercially made screws, which the smiths soldered to their handmade pieces. The same was true with pin clasps and catches for brooches. A ring shank is the circular part of the ring which fits around the finger and can be made easily, in graduated sizes, by commercial casting, using genuine silver. The artisan then makes his own mounting for the shank and sets the stone, all by hand. But this is frowned upon by those who insist an article (earscrews and pin clasps excepted) be entirely handmade by the smith. Dealers who guarantee their merchandise to be fully handmade will not stock such items.

Silver beads are now made commercially in great numbers. They are stamped by machine out of heavier-gauge silver sheets and soldered and ground smooth by hand. Beads can be turned out much more rapidly and cheaply in this manner, and besides, Indian smiths often use such thin-gauge silver for their handmade beads that when they are buffed the silver tears. This is in addition to the fact that making silver beads by hand is a time-consuming operation; the buyer who insists upon his jewelry being entirely handmade must pay the price for such material.

Furthermore, machines are used in grinding and polishing silver, and in buffing, as well as for cutting and polishing stones, but this is almost never looked upon as a violation of the "handmade" code. Thus, there is a large area where definitions play an important role in labeling a piece "handmade," and the industry as a whole has never been able to agree upon an inviolable set of definitions.

In 1975, 50,000 ounces a week of silver components were being shipped out of one establishment in Albuquerque, and 80,000 ounces of so-called silver heishi (tubular silver beads) were being sold in a month. This bespeaks the immense demand for silver jewelry—and the problems of drawing a line between handmade and assembled or component products.

I look with amused exasperation upon a great many "experts" in Indian jewelry who have never troubled themselves to learn the step-by-step processes of making jewelry or the properties of silver at various temperatures of high heat. I recall with considerable glee a trial which took place in Albuquerque a number of years ago in which an "expert" took the stand and described a Navajo smith energetically hammering a piece of cherry-red silver into shape. The joke is that when silver becomes cherry red in color it is just at the melting point, and when pounded flies to pieces; silver is best wrought at its annealing temperature of 900 to 1400°F, when it assumes a dull red color. (The trial, incidentally, concerned a dealer who supplied his smiths with machine-made graded-sized ring shanks of sterling silver; the smith then welded and stamped by hand his own silver designs on the shank and set it with turquoise. The government charged that this violated the "handmade" definition of genuine Indian jewelry, and it won its case.)

The advent of sophisticated techniques and power-driven equipment have added to the difficulty of defining handmade jewelry; little, if any, Indian jewelry today is completely handmade from start to finish. The smiths themselves are probably as responsible for this as anyone; they are fully as aware as any Anglo that time means money—although culturally the Indian concept of time is totally different from the white man's—and as long as the Indian chooses or is compelled to compete in Anglo society he will adopt the Anglo viewpoint, at least to a limited extent. Because of this, the smith sees little point in laboriously fashioning by hand such things as findings, or in hand-buffing and polishing silver when he can use a machine for this; he prefers commercially cut turquoise for the same reason.

The overall problem lies in allowing the smiths themselves—the master craftsmen—to develop their own styles and methods of making silver and turquoise jewelry. Since they are artists, they must not be confined to "traditional" or "modern" jewelry; with their own artistry and intuition, and with their own two hands, they will keep the art of silversmithing alive and flourishing.

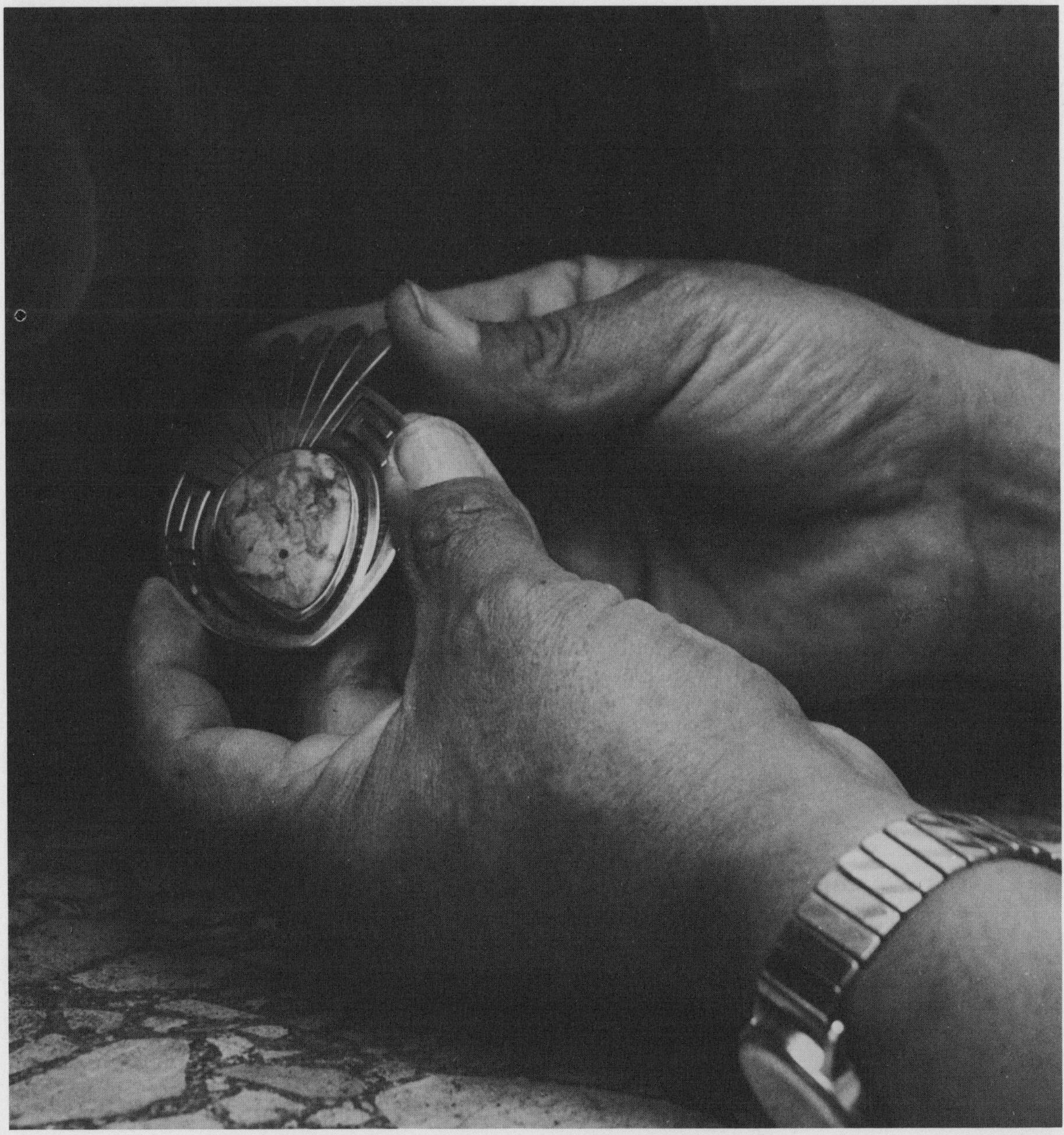

Little if any Indian jewelry today is completely handmade from start to finish.
(Ray Manley)

"Silver deserves a sheen, not a shine..."

BETTY T. TOULOUSE *is curator of anthropology collections for the Museum of New Mexico in Santa Fe. She has written a number of articles and papers in her field and has served in an editorial capacity on a number of publications.*

Being curator of a large collection of Navajo and Pueblo silver and turquoise jewelry produced in the late years of the nineteenth and early years of the twentieth centuries dulls your sense of appreciation for the silver and turquoise jewelry being produced by the Indian silversmiths of today. From one point of view this is most unfortunate because some of the "modern" jewelry is designed by true artists who are also expert silversmiths. The visual comparison of silver in the old and in the new could be made by putting a swatch of silvery grey satin of the earlier years, spun by silkworms and woven in China, beside a square of unwrinkled aluminum foil.

However, the fault is not always with the silversmith. In the early years all silver had to be crafted from coins and other silver sources into the form of bracelets, beads, and conchas with handmade tools. Even the most expert smith couldn't achieve the perfection which is possible with the jeweler's tools of this age of mechanization. Also, techniques for polishing are so vastly improved that a shine akin to that of chromeplating can be produced. This is regrettable because silver deserves much more; silver deserves a soft, deep luster that is reserved only for silver. Silver deserves a sheen, not a shine. The real artist in metal knows this and designs his creations with this aspect of silver in mind.

Eventually the new shiny jewelry will gain the thousands of minute scratches needed to give the surface of silver the satin finish treasured by devotees of the lustrous metal. The beauty of those pieces exquisitely designed and expertly crafted will be enhanced by the wearing thereof. Even pieces of mediocre design will be greatly improved.

As the products of the present day come into the collections, this curator is finding it difficult to work with them. They are so shiny every contact of the hands leaves its mark, and the first scratch, however small, gives one the feeling experienced with the first dent in the new car. Handling them with "clean, white cotton gloves" as recommended for the handling of works of art by the curatorial manuals would certainly keep them in mint condition, but this would be an exercise in futility when working with a collection intended for study, exhibit, and photography. Much of the beauty of the older pieces came about by being handled with bare hands and worn under all conditions. Also, jewelry has to be handled, as well as seen, to be fully appreciated.

My deep admiration for the old does not imply a complete rejection of the new. There is always awareness of the fact that once the old was the new and a certain amount of wear will add beauty to even the most average piece of jewelry. Squared edges soften, silver areas which are untouched by wear darken, and areas which are touched by wear have highlights that cannot be achieved in any other way.

Nevertheless, it isn't easy to be the one to start the process of "aging" which all jewelry must go through, sooner or later, even though you know it can only be for the best.

When you are working with a large collection of silver Indian jewelry, cataloging, evaluating, selecting for exhibit, you do handle it continually. A favorite piece will be contemplated with admiration and then buffed with the palm of the hand to bring out the highlights, and soon your hands begin to take on a grey tinge and you are aware of the distinctive odor associated with old, slightly tarnished silver. Although museum collections of Indian jewelry are protected with maximum security and away from sulphur pollutants, a slight tarnishing is inevitable when silver is not washed or polished frequently, and this is transferred to the hands when in contact with it.

This is only a minor annoyance to a curator because it is part of what working with Indian jewelry is all about. This slight annoyance can be a valuable tool in these days of so much imitation and fakery, because when in doubt in identifying the metal in a piece of jewelry, old or new, which has an excessively high polish or is slightly lighter in tone—which might indicate it is made of an alloy not containing silver—just rubbing the surface vigorously with the fingers will give the answer. Silver is self-revealing.

Another characteristic aspect of Southwestern Indian jewelry is, of course, the turquoise embellishment. This curator has mixed emotions when the "old" and the "new" turquoise settings come into view. As you pull out the cabinet drawers in which the "old" bracelets are stored, row on row, you see greens of every shade, blue-greens, blues of many hues, the browns of the matrix, all the colors of turquoise, hand-polished, soft-toned, muted, but strong and with great depth. You sense that the stone has substance beyond the beautiful color of the surface. The effect is that of a tapestry of ancient fabrication in greens, blues, browns, and greys. Then, as you walk into a modern trader's shop, you also see bracelets displayed, row on row—"new" bracelets with highly polished, mechanically polished, intense blue turquoise settings all of the same color and tone. This is the bright blue color decreed by fashion of the moment —the color the experts say you must have. The intense blue color indicates that the stone is "hard" and will therefore not change color. This curator has been wearing, continuously for some thirty-five years, a lovely green turquoise that hasn't changed color or deteriorated in any way.

The fashion of the moment also seems to require that the stone must have been mined at a famous turquoise deposit, and that the seller must know this source and advise the buyer of its location. With great pride the wearer, in turn, passes this information on to anyone who mentions with favor this particular piece of jewelry. This information seems to be essential in establishing authenticity and great worth. In days gone by when someone complimented another's jewelry, the usual return was a quiet "Thank you," acknowledging a sincere admiration for its design and quality of workmanship and its wearer's good taste in jewelry. No one was concerned with the color of the stone or where it was mined. How times have changed!

Turquoise with a pedigree is more valuable, of course, and usually is very beautiful. Sadly, though, the high polish in vogue today concentrates the gaze of the viewer on the surface—only on the surface—and you are unaware of the depth of the stone. Fortunately, the high polish will soften with time and wear, and these fine, hard stones of deep, intense blue will become even more beautiful as the quality of turquoise, the depth of the mineral, becomes visible once more.

With the widespread demand for the intense blue color, the green shades being spurned, doubtless this demand is responsible for the current doctoring or outright fabrication of turquoise in the color so desired today, a color which is not in unlimited supply naturally. Perhaps green will be popular some day. It could happen.

A curatorial admiration for Indian jewelry parallels the curatorial quest for knowledge. A large collection can satisfy this desire to know because of its great scope and diversity, but it can frustrate, too, because all knowledge is not visible in the collection alone; it must often come from other sources.

"Collections" are assembled for many reasons. High on the list is the desire to have the most outstanding, the best, the most unusual, the largest. Also high on the list is that of investment, speculation. Someplace in the list is an interest in objects themselves, their history, use, and diversity or similarity. These reasons imply that articles will be chosen with great care and a discriminating knowledge of quality in design, workmanship, and materials. Jewelry collections have the same attributes as any other collection because they come into being for the same reasons.

When a collection begins to take shape, enthusiasm is high, memory keen, the facts of acquisition—dates, places, makers—are unforgettable. If the Fates decree that a jewelry collection will eventually become a part of a museum's assets, so often by the time the fateful destination is reached the memory of the collector is dulled, the facts vague because few records are kept, and the museum receives a collection of superb bracelets, rings, and necklaces which elicit exclamation of "oh" and "ah" from any viewer; but anyone doing research, although not insensitive to the beauty, will feel a keen disappointment because of the lack of information.

Nothing so delights the heart of a curator, researcher, or writer than a date, a place, a silversmith's name. Occasionally a piece of jewelry, a collection, small or large, for which all the facts are known will find its way into a museum. Such a piece or collection can sometimes be a Rosetta stone when comparisons are made with undocumented collection items—comparison often reveals similarities of design, style, workmanship. As a museum collection grows, such instances of documented material being made available can add much to the overall knowledge of the entire collection. Such is the substance of research, whether concentrated or in bits and snatches as a curator has occasion to be working with the jewelry, choosing items for exhibit or photography, and returning it to storage.

Such is the way one curator sees a collection of Southwestern Indian jewelry.

A variety of Navajo cast ketoh designs, pre-1900.
(All photos, Museum of New Mexico)

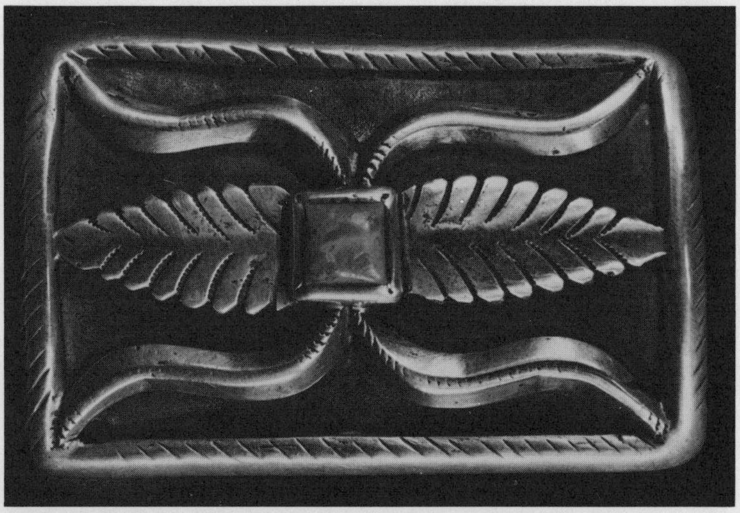

This curved leaf and flat leaf combination (the leaves are said to have been originally modeled after tobacco leaves) is a classic design that has been much copied.

Curvilinear design is somewhat unusual in ketohs of this period.

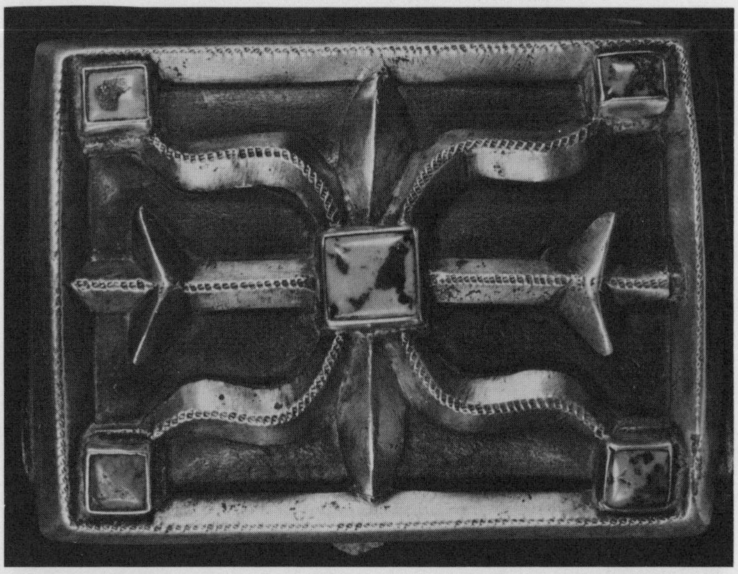

As soon as turquoise became available, it was a popular embellishment.

The use of such a large stone is rare for this period. Note the one darker stone, and the way the bezels on the smaller stones curl over the stone to hold it.

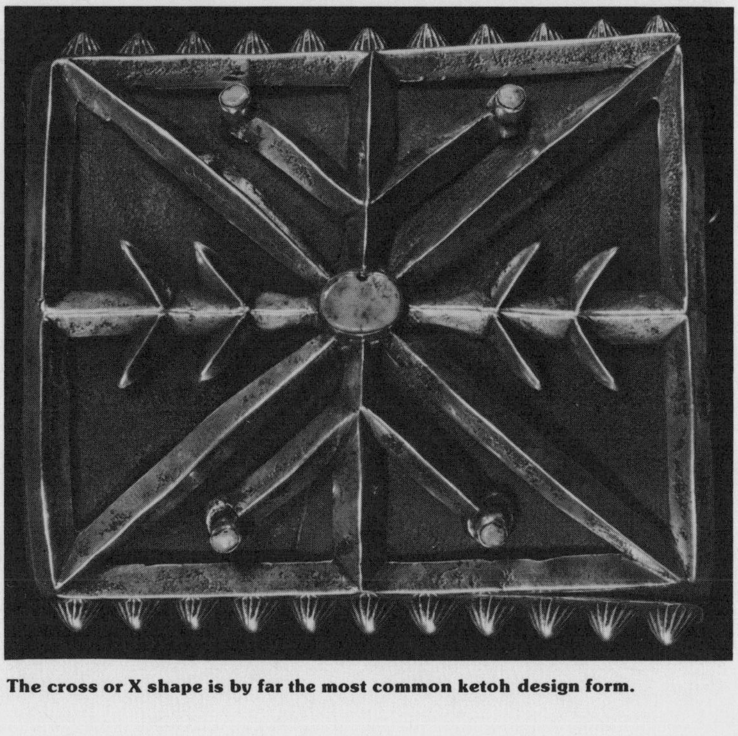

The cross or X shape is by far the most common ketoh design form.

"If God is good, I will die in this state with a better silver and turquoise ring around my finger..."

MAGGIE WILSON *is a native Arizonian who is a well known feature writer for* The Arizona Republic. *Her writings have dealt with both the problems and the pleasures of the Arizona Indian scene, and the ways the native and Anglo culture mix.*

It used to be that when you moved to the Southwest you had to do two things to really "belong." First you had to learn to eat chili, and second you had to get Indian jewelry.These announced that you identified yourself as a Southwesterner. Today there seem to be two groups wearing the jewelry: those trend-setting women who set fashion and wear the finest of the jewelry, and the gal who wears the polyester pantsuit and the standardized-design squash-blossom necklace. Those people who don't truly love their Indian jewelry, who don't understand the tradition behind it, are now leaving it in the drawer with the rest of the out-of-fashion jewelry they own.

Indian jewelry, for all that it is sold nationwide, is still very much a Southwestern tradition. Many Easterners I've talked with bought Indian jewelry out here and when they got home would take it to a major jeweler to be appraised for insurance. Then the jeweler would have to send it back out West to get that appraisal. It made the buyer wonder just what the value of his pieces were.

Also, before the Indian jewelry "fad," turquoise seen on the East Coast came mostly from Persia and was a lovely clear blue with no matrix in the highest quality turquoise sold. Then it began showing up in many colors and with a variety of matrixes. Many people who might otherwise have purchased Indian jewelry weren't able to relate to the other colors and to the matrix. What many of the shops in the East carried was "Indianesque" jewelry styled to what they thought Eastern taste was—much of it done by Anglos and a lot of it in poor taste. No wonder people from out of the area have been suspicious.

It's almost come full circle. When I was growing up here, we felt undressed if we didn't have at least one piece of it on somewhere—sure we wore it as costume jewelry, but we all wore at least some small piece to announce ourselves as Southwesterners. Then these pieces spent twenty years in the drawer after they went out of fashion. In the sixties with the concern for nature and the sense of things historical, the interest came back. Some people are calling the '70s the decade of the Indian, and people aren't looking at it as costume jewelry this time. Especially in the Southwest, collectors are getting very selective in what they buy, insisting on the highest quality and knowing about what they buy. Anytime you admire a ring the wearer will come back with the type of turquoise and who the silversmith was—things it is not necessary to know for enjoying a piece.

Indian jewelry can be worn so many ways. Some pieces look better with a more casual look of jeans and a shirt, but others—with gold and high quality turquoise—look just as well in a formal situation. Many of the fine older pieces too are worn formally and no one out here thinks it strange.

Today you are making a statement about yourself when you wear fine Indian jewelry. First of all you are saying that you are "in"—that you know what you are wearing and that it is the "best you've ever seen." Secondly, it's a statement of wealth. But then, man has been using jewelry to define status and position and knowledge for a long time. Then there are those people who will only collect one thing or another—the old jewelry, jewelry that has been worn through a sacred ceremony, or jewelry made by an Indian for Indian use. They are all forms of the same type of snobbery. The most sensible are those who want a piece of jewelry because it's the best piece they have seen.

Of course there will always be the "bomber" jewelry around—those great big pieces that defeat the purpose of adornment, which is to make the person wearing it look better. When you see those pieces you see the piece first and the person second, if at all. The majority of these are in really poor taste—like a stuffed pheasant under a glass dome and just as useful.

I think that on the whole Indian jewelry is gorgeous, exciting, and exotic. It has a mystery that is really hard to define. As a girl who was born in this state with a silver and turquoise ring around my pinkie, I hope, if God is good, I will die in this state with a better silver and turquoise ring around my finger.

"It turns out not to be so gaudy after all..."

JERRY JACKA *is a photographer who has been one of the major contributors to* Arizona Highways *issues dealing with Indian arts and crafts. His book* Turquoise Treasures *is one of the finest pictorials of Indian silver yet published.*

My interest in Indian jewelry started when I was living with my folks on a ranch north of Phoenix. There were a number of Indian ruins on the ranch and I began collecting things from the ruins. I developed an interest in Indian art through that and it just kind of grew and grew.

I got interested in photography in high school and after graduation I got a job working as a photographer's apprentice in a local portrait studio. After that I went into law enforcement where I was able to exercise my interest in photography.

The fact that for ten or twelve years I was constantly photographing things from the aspect of presenting them in court—recording minute detail in objects that were evidence—gave me an awareness and sensitivity to detail that I carried on when I eventually became involved in photographing Indian art. I realized there was more to Indian art than just an object, that normally there is a combination of design elements and/or a combination of materials, and I try to represent that in the photographs I take.

When I photograph Indian jewelry, I try to make use of my instinct and knowledge about the jewelry. I try to pick things that relate to one another—by time period, by materials, by artist, or whatever. I try to avoid mixing apples with oranges, if you will, and put things together that fit together for a purpose.

Normally I get to pick the pieces of jewelry I want to photograph unless it's for a specific assignment. I don't think there is any one best style of Indian jewelry or any one best Indian jeweler. There are a number of exciting and excellent Indian silversmiths and jewelers—all equally good in their own fields. I like to show both the old and the new. Obviously I look for quality in workmanship and design and materials.

I usually use natural materials in the backgrounds of my photographs even if I'm shooting in a studio situation. I hate to see a piece of Indian jewelry on velvet. I think even the very contemporary artists such as Charles Loloma still have built in their jewelry a lot of tradition and awareness of their environment. I think that if you photograph a piece of Indian art you need a naturalistic environment. It works better with the jewelry.

I also collect Indian jewelry, but the jewelry I like to collect is different from the jewelry I like to photograph. In collecting, I prefer the old jewelry, the simple, bold jewelry of the early 1900s. To me this represents to some degree a continuation of the prehistoric jewelry but it also has the flavor of some European contact. I pick a piece for its simplicity and its being characteristic of its time period.

I used to think that Indian jewelry was an informal type of jewelry, but not any more. Now that you see it with diamonds and gold it can be very formal. People are wearing quality Indian jewelry of many styles to the most formal gatherings and its acceptable. Years ago I would have said it was an informal thing, but that has changed.

But you can get too informal too. Some jewelry is bought and worn with no sense of proportion, or of what it's worn with. I see a lot of people wearing jewelry that might be fine jewelry but it is gaudy because it is too large or there is too much of it. I think the same is true for any attire—it has to be worn in good taste. There is so much more "stereotyped Indian jewelry" being made today than there ever were Indians in the country to make it. When you compare what the good Indian craftsman creates as a gaudy piece to some of the garbage that is being turned out, it turns out not to be so gaudy after all.

"I grew up like many people believing that Indian jewelry was just costume jewelry..."

HELEN PINION WELLS *has been involved with Indian studies and Indian art in Arizona since 1968. She has a degree in archeology from Arizona State University and was formerly curator of the Fred Harvey Fine Arts Collection. She is now with Ashton Gallery in Scottsdale and is a contributing editor of* American Indian Art *magazine.*

I grew up like many people believing that Indian jewelry was just costume jewelry. My parents went through the Southwest in 1948 and purchased several items of Indian crafts, among them a few pieces of Indian jewelry which my mother wore casually the entire time I was growing up. I didn't think too much of it until a couple of years ago when she asked me what it was worth. When I told her, she was amazed both at the value I placed on them and that what she had taken so casually was now a highly sought-after art form.

I was lucky enough to move to Arizona just before the interest in Indian jewelry sent the prices sky-high and made the older pieces hard to find, so I was able to acquire a few pieces for myself. I look for workmanship, design, and materials, pretty much in that order when I buy for myself or for others. I much prefer simple jewelry, simple in design and simple in execution. A Zuni cluster bracelet can be simple if it's done right, but if you add all sorts of things like twisted wire bezel guards, silver balls, half loops, etc., it can get pretty complex.

With the amount of Indian jewelry being turned out today, quantitatively you see a lot less good design. Today with the Indian jewelry craze you can stamp the word "Indian" on the back of it and it doesn't matter about the design. People don't know enough about it, the buying of it. Mass-produced style is what you're getting. For example, many times bracelets sold as Indian jewelry have a stone or two on two wires forming the bracelet, with silver leaves on each side of the stones. The stones are cut in a predetermined size to fit precut silver bezels which are soldered to ready-made wire bracelets to which machine-made silver leaves are added. There is no design in this, and it only takes a couple of days to train an unskilled worker to put them together. There may be twenty workers in a back room: one person is bending the wire, another putting the stone in its premade bezel, and a third person is soldering the two leaves on it. A fourth person is polishing it. I would say at least 75 percent of all real Indian jewelry is made by the assembly-line technique. You can go into different shops and see 25,000 of the same type of Indian-made bracelet within a two-week period. There is absolutely no individual design in much of what you see, even though the craftsmanship may be excellent.

You probably had more items with good design back when the smiths were working a small volume, making items for themselves, their families, and little bit to sell to the trader. Even if a smith was making squash-blossom necklaces at the rate of, say, one a month for a trader, he still had to make the individual components by hand and fit stones to the design. In many cases he had to cut the stones, too, so he was in control of the design of each individual piece. When the designs weren't pleasing, the jewelry didn't get sold and the trader found another smith, and the family members found someone else to make silver.

Today design is extremely important if you are looking for good pieces. We purchased in the gallery a contemporary squash-blossom necklace with over 1,000 karats of Lander turquoise (an extremely fine stone) which was the ugliest squash-blossom I've ever seen. We gave it to Mark Chee to make into bracelets and rings in an old style, and the pieces came back simply stunning. Even though it was a new turquoise that has only been on the market for a few years and the setting was an old style, the design was such that a unity was achieved, and the pieces all hung together.

A lot of Indian jewelry that has been and is being purchased for Indian jewelry's sake is relegated rapidly to the owner's costume jewelry box. On the other hand, the older pieces that were made for Indian use, really stand up as fine pieces of jewelry.

Most of them are very simple in design, and you get the feeling looking at them, that the smiths were using their very best materials to make them because they, a member of their family, or a friend would be wearing them for years.

In traditional-style Indian jewelry it means a lot whether it's Indian-made or not because it's fraud if someone knowingly sells non-Indian-made jewelry as Indian-made.

In nontraditional jewelry the Indian-ness really takes a back seat. One can't call Charles Loloma an Indian artist, because the fact that he is Indian really is overshadowed by his artistry.

The business is reaching a point where a lot of the craftsmen are earning the title of artist. They are doing work that will stand up piece by piece in craftsmanship and design and execution to the work of any artist in any country in any time period. All of your really great pieces have to meet that criterion. These are the ones which will maintain their value. It doesn't matter whether it is the traditional style or contemporary style. It's the merit of the piece.

How do the craftsmen get their materials? Well, before the early traders started bringing material in, the Indians already had an incredible trade network built up. They were already getting turquoise from the Los Cerrillos mine, abalone from California, shell from the two gulfs. A lot of the red material taken for coral in early jewelry really is California abalone or spiney oyster with the outer shell ground off. An Indian would trade something for shell that another Indian had traded an Indian closer to the coast for.

These trade networks still work, but rather in an offbeat way. Friends, mostly Anglos, will bring what is needed when visiting. For example, Daisey and Sidney Hooee. Sidney is a Zuni silversmith and Daisey is the granddaughter of Nampeyo, a Hopi potter. I've been at their house when California friends came through bringing them abalone shells, seashells, feta cheese, Japanese soy cakes, and some commercial slip and glazes. Same results. They get the material they need, and the California friends get to buy jewelry from Sidney.

Whether symbols on jewelry mean anything to the Indian depends on the symbol. If it's something that is taken from his culture, yes, it would still mean something; they would abstract the meaning from the symbol. The awanyu, or water serpent, motif still is used in religious ceremonies. A bear paw might signify membership in the bear clan. Or cloud motifs would still bring to mind all the meanings of "rain" and what it is important for. A lot of them are taken out of context. Feathers, for example, make very nice designs but on jewelry they are out of context.

But many of the symbols are ones to which we have ascribed an Indian meaning—the bow and arrow, dart point, etc. These are easy to pick out because they are the white man's ideas of what Indian symbols should be—they have no meaning for Indians. These are ones they were encouraged to use in the early pieces made for resale, and they carried over through the Denver silver (earliest machine-made silver, made in Denver in 1905, 1910, with Indians running the machines in many cases). The earliest of this machine-made jewelry was in good, thick silver and set with real turquoise—in many cases as good or better quality than what the Indians were setting in their handcrafted jewelry.

Basically, Indians who wear jewelry look for the same things we do. A lot of what is worn is handed down as family heirlooms. Historically, the Indian preferred more massive pieces. They like the color of turquoise, and coral, jet, shell, etc., but the styles they have made for themselves have changed over the years, just as ours have. If they do wear new jewelry, they usually look for really fine material and good workmanship. Those who can afford it look for the best, just like we do. They can play the status game just as well as we can.

To some extent they've absorbed the Anglo esthetic values we have placed on what we buy. We feel that turquoise should match, for example, and now so do they.

As for Indian jewelry as an investment, I would put my money in signed pieces by the artists who are up and coming—Phil Navaysa, Larry Golsh, Preston Monongye, Kenneth Begay, and others.

It's rare to get a piece of jewelry with any sort of signature on it until you get to about 1972. Then you start getting it signed. I would also invest in older pieces made before the turn of the century, the old, traditional styles. I probably would not buy a squash-blossom necklace, unless it had incredibly good stones and a really fine design. In Navajo it would have to be a really good design with excellent craftsmanship. Certainly nothing with machine-made parts. Hopi jewelry is really undervalued and under-appreciated for the amount of work that goes into it. I would buy perhaps pieces by the best craftsmen. I would not invest in contemporary Zuni jewelry because they are still making it by the carloads and there's not that much originality in it.

I would collect the earlier pieces—perhaps a massive cluster squash with lots of turquoise on it. Some of them weigh up to 4 pounds. The next thing would be a cluster bracelet—with up to seventy-five stones in it. Then I would start collecting some of the inlaid shells from back around the early 1900s to the 1910s—some of them are set on silver boxes—then after that the earrings. For value's sake, earrings would be close to the last thing I would buy.

In many old Zuni turquoise pieces, the color of one or more stones might change under certain circumstances—oil, sweat, etc. To preserve its value as a collector's piece, my feeling would be to leave the discolored stone in, unless it really detracts. Since turquoise rarely discolors the same each time, though, it is a problem. In a bracelet that I have by Roger Skeet, the two side stones have turned green, even though the center one remains blue. I wouldn't consider having these stones replaced—assuming that someone *could* match the turquoise, of course; the discoloration makes it more valuable to me.

Perhaps if you have a huge cluster piece that has one stone that has turned dark green, you

An extremely fine example of inlay work, c. 1920s: a 3½-inch standup figure of the Zuni Fire God which can also be worn as a pin. The basic figure is in jet, inlaid with rounds of coral, turquoise, and white shell. The deer he is carrying is abalone and mother-of-pearl; his staffs, serpentine; and boots, spiny oyster. What makes this a remarkable piece is the precise fit of the individual inlay pieces (especially the tiny rounds, considering the tools of the time) and the overall feeling of life and action. *(FHFAC, HM, Al Abrams)*

might consider replacing it if it really is an eyesore.

What do I consider quality work in early Zuni inlay? Well, before it really became popular, most pieces were so individualized that someone who was familiar with Zuni jewelry could tell at least which family made any piece, if not the individual smith responsible. Design is important—the way the materials are combined—and especially the way the materials fit together. Abalone, for example, adds a depth in its shimmering when it is next to turquoise that you don't see when it is next to shell. And just in color sense, some colors don't look their best next to others. Most of the nicest inlay work seems to have been made during the 1920s. These pieces seem to be the ones with the stones flush to one another, really good silverwork, and fantastic designs.

Channelwork and overlay are more versatile than some of the other work. Channelwork is hard to outgrow—it stays pretty splendid. What makes a good piece of channelwork? First of all the design. You can get some real common design that doesn't work with this technique. That can glare at you and make the piece not as pleasing. In good pieces the design just flows together.

The second thing I look for is how well the craftsman fit the stones into the silver channels. The process of channelwork involves setting up a framework of silver to contain a number of small stones which are set in it and the whole ground down until it results in a smooth surface. In workmanship, the best channelwork has tightly fitting stones with a minimum of filler. Nothing bothers me more than seeing silver filled in where the stone was too small or having it filled in with something else—cement, but most often liquid solder. When everything is leveled down in the final technique of finishing, you get thin silver bars and thick silver bars and thick-appearing areas; it ruins the design.

Needlepoint and petit point both use small slivers of turquoise—and serrated bezels because that's the easiest way of working with very small pieces of turquoise. They probably both arise from the same historic background of finding a use for very fine chips of turquoise.

If you want to be nitpicking, needlepoint has the ends pointed and petit point has rounded ends. Both require a great deal of labor, but the designs and forms used are pretty much the same for either. In any case, when one buys a piece of it, most of what you are paying for is labor, not material.

I really don't care for needlepoint as much as other pieces because you don't see many pieces that can grab at you, that are powerful in design. In the needlepoint that I do like all the pieces of turquoise are very close together and you don't get any very wide expanses of silver. The pieces of turquoise are so small they can get lost. If enough turquoise is not put on, I consider that a design fault.

The uniformity of the turquoise and the size are important. It can vary with the needlework, so that you can get small pieces and large pieces in the same piece and they don't fit. I like best those pieces where all of the turquoise is of a uniform size and doesn't look like random sweepings from a workroom.

The standards by which fetish necklaces are judged are integrity of design for the unique pieces, pleasingness for the rest, I would say. There are only a few carvers who are readily recognizable either from their carvings or from the way they string a piece. Mary Tsekewa, for example, does exquisite miniature animals, mostly birds, nearly all identical in size, and strings them thirty-three to a strand, nicely spaced, that lay nice and flat in the bib. Andy Quain, Sr., frequently did one or more large birds in flight for the bottom. He does perched birds with their heads turned, nicely inlayed eyes, a lot of detail work, not just small lines to indicate where the wings are. Leekya also carved very detailed birds, but he really made his materials work for him. He would take a material such as shell, and by the way he carved, the ripples in the material would suggest feathers and other features. His pieces are also incredibly finished. There are no rough edges. But since he was not above buying fetishes from other carvers and selling them as his own, some necklaces which were sold by him aren't necessarily his work.

The way a fetish necklace is strung is very important. In the gallery we have one with forty-five really nice fetishes on it by seven different carvers, but they are all hung in a clump at the bottom so you can't really see them. You can say: this is a Leekya; that's a Mary Tsekewa; this one's an Andy Sr. and that's a David; but together—the way it's strung—it's a nothing.

There are a lot of considerations you have to take into account when you're thinking of purchasing a fetish necklace. A lot of people who buy fetishes probably know the carver. That, of course, is part of the mystique. A lot of others buy them because it's a fad. Some people come and say they really love the fetishes, but that they just couldn't wear them. So you have them try a

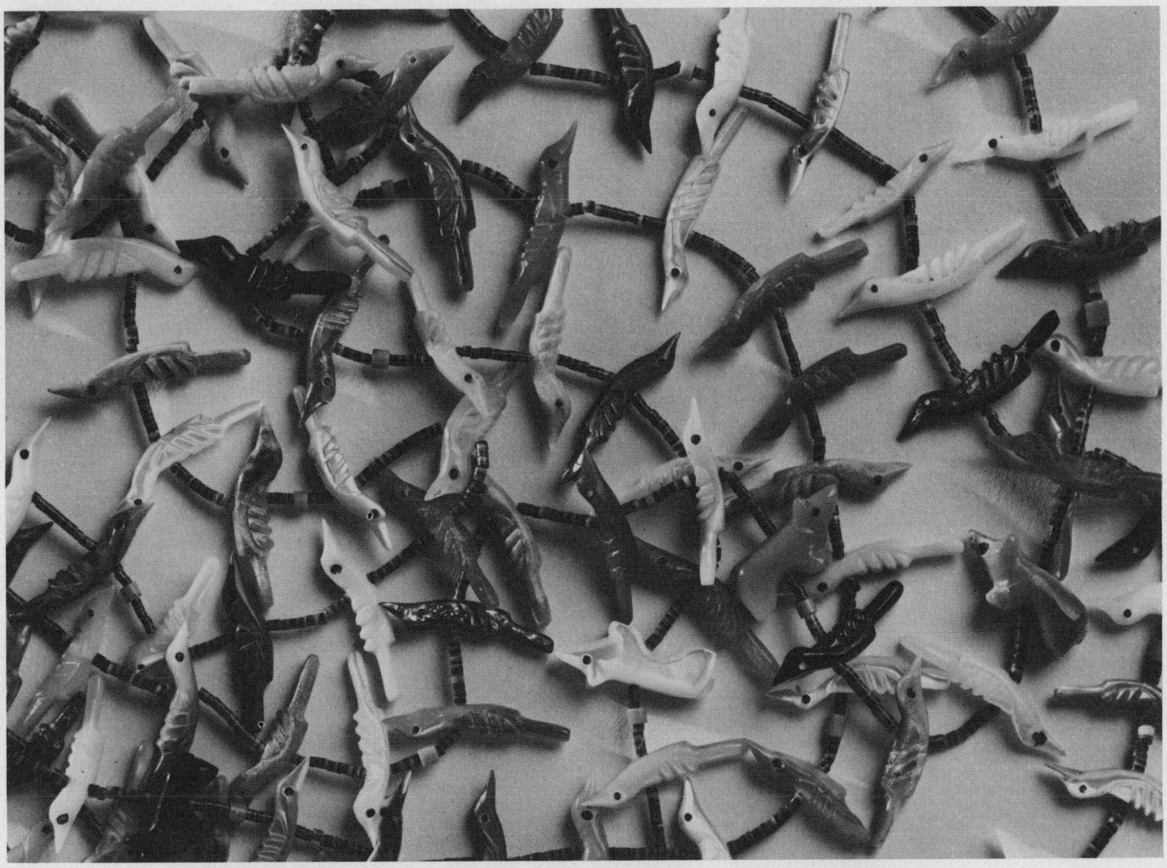

Detail of a five-strand fetish necklace by Lavina Tsikewa, daughter of David. The necklace is strung with very fine Santo Domingo heishi and contains 168 separate carvings in turquoise, coral, jet, serpentine, coconut shell, four colors of mother-of-pearl, and pipestone. Lavina's carved figures tend to be taller and slimmer than her father's. *(DNHC, Peter L. Bloomer)*

necklace on and show them in the mirror: yes, you can wear it—it takes a certain type of outfit to wear it with, but you can wear it. You must be careful, for most of them are very fragile. You break tails and beaks off very easily.

Some materials used in fetishes, like shell and mother-of-pearl, are not expensive at all; but many of them are. Some artists prefer to carve in one particular type of material. Diane Gaspar uses a lot of turquoise. (In the case of turquoise, you almost always have a treated turquoise, because if you're working with turquoise you're just going to lose part of it. Even with careful day-to-day wear.) The Rosetta family from Santo Domingo use coral a lot. I've seen them done in serpentine, shell, turquoise, coral, abalone, even jade. The quality of the fetish is the most important thing to consider—not really the material, except from the personal taste aspect.

In distinguishing imitation fetishes you just have to know what you are looking at. They use the same materials, the same animals, and they are strung the same way. Many of them don't have as much detail as Indian carved ones—they can look "squarely carved"—and don't have an integrity of their own. On the other hand, some Indian carvers like David Tsekewa do theirs very sketchily but very beautifully. The detail is about the same as the Taiwanese carvings. I know at least one carver buys the fetishes from Taiwan, adds a few of his own details, and sells them as his own. You really have to know the people you are dealing with and know they know where they got them from.

"Contemporary Indian jewelry has transcended tribal styles..."

DR. PATRICK T. HOULIHAN *is the director of the Heard Museum of Anthropology and Primitive Art in Phoenix. Previously with the Milwaukee Public Museum, Dr. Houlihan has been responsible for many new programs, exhibits, and research projects on the Indians of the Southwest.*

I'd say that my personal preference in Southwestern Indian jewelry is that early jewelry made by Indians *for* Indians, for Indian use—it has an ethnographic value in addition to its intrinsic value. It's heavier, has a heavier-quality silver, it's more "native" in design.

I also like some of the modern jewelry, by native craftsmen—there are a few really good ones today (and a multitude of inferior ones).

The older jewelry was *inherited* pieces, it was not just his, but his uncle's, his aunt's, his father's —it was related historically, kinshipwise, all of which made it much more important to the individual Indian.

It was less of a patron's art prior to 1900; after that the silver was lighter, it was produced for white use. You can see the same in Navajo rugs after 1900. The jewelry has to be lighter, it had to be bracelets, cufflinks, tieclasps, watch fobs, etc.

I would say that now 97 percent of Indian crafts are made for the white market.

Indians still do buy jewelry, but it doesn't mean what it used to. In the past, it was a storehouse of wealth. On the reservation you used to see women walking down the road wearing thousands of dollars' worth (by today's values) of jewelry. A lot of that has gone, and pawn has been banned from the Navajo Reservation. Today they don't need or use silver for buttons or hatbands.

Even though the bulk of the Indian jewelry is made today for the white market, do Indians still have a pride in their work? Very much so, they still enter competitions, compete, they want prizes, it enhances an individual smith's reputation, and this increases the marketability of his work.

The most important thing about contemporary Indian jewelry is that it has transcended tribal styles: so-and-so is a fine silversmith who happens to be a Zuni, so-and-so is a fine silversmith who happens to be a Navajo...Anyone with sense would buy on the basis of the name of the maker —that is, they would seek the work of fine craftsmen.

In the older work you can buy on a tribal basis; today you should know the maker and his or her reputation.

Bad work? You can see it very easily. In Zuni channelwork it is often the easiest to see. Look down the rows of the piece: if the corner of a stone is poorly cut, or if it is filled with silver solder, it means the maker can't cut stones, it means he didn't put the care into the piece that he should have. There are indeed objective measures. In a Navajo sandcast piece, if the edges are not smoothed off, or if it is poorly polished, it is an unfinished piece.

Then of course there is the quality of the turquoise. In jewelry that's been worn, salt and perfume will discolor turquoise. If part of a stone is yellowish green and the other half is blue, chances are it's been damaged.

Then there's the matching of stones: in a relatively new piece with fifty to sixty stones, if all the stones except three are matched, then you have a badly matched piece of jewelry.

On the other hand, in a real old piece the stones could well be unmatched; the Indians didn't care. But a new piece with unmatched stones is generally unacceptable, and an old piece with perfectly matched stones is possibly suspect.

"How much is this necklace worth?"

H. THOMAS CAIN *is curator of anthropology for the Heard Museum in Phoenix, which possesses an outstanding collection of Indian jewelry, acquired over many years. In addition to its superb collections, the museum annually sponsors fairs and displays of Indian handcrafted items. These not only serve as a market for smiths and other artisans, but also give the public an idea of what authentic Indian jewelry and other crafts look like. At such fairs the artisans themselves, and not the museum, set the prices for their goods.*

The expanding interest in American Indian jewelry is reflected in the increasing number of collectors who seek information from museums. The most frequent question is, "How much is this bracelet, squash-blossom necklace, or silver and turquoise belt worth?" The museum curator must patiently explain that museums are not in the business of making appraisals, even as to the value of items donated as tax-deductible gifts to the institution. The Internal Revenue Service feels there is less likelihood of hanky-panky if an unbiased professional appraiser makes this decision.

Most museum curators are glad to offer an opinion as to the age, quality, and provenience of an item (if they know, and if they don't they should always say so!) but they shy away from monetary evaluations.

Another question owners and potential collectors of Indian jewelry ask museums concerns the stability of the value in relation to the greatly inflated market prices of today. The simple and only honest answer is: "Who can say?" Any prediction as to the future values is sheer speculation. It seems unlikely a multimillion-dollar business is going to collapse overnight, and here in the Southwest the interest in things Indian is but one facet of the recent worldwide interest in "primitive" art.

There are relatively few certainties with regard to the Indian jewelry situation today. One is that old, quality pieces sell at spectacular prices —as witnessed by the 1975 auction of the C. G. Wallace collection, which grossed well over $1 million.

Despite the charm of old pawn jewelry, any honest appraisal of craftsmanship and quality of design will concede that the silversmiths of today are producing jewelry technically superior to the work of their grandfathers. The change in the market, which is now predominantly white, has also resulted in the mass production of cheap, tawdry, and spurious imitations that the gullible public continues to purchase. This commercialization is deplored by the connoisseur but it remains a fact of life. Museums and reputable dealers will certainly continue to show people the difference between junk and quality Indian craftsmanship. Anyone looking for bargains in this field of collecting is headed for disappointment. You will get exactly the quality that you pay for.

"Banks will lend money on Indian jewelry..."

BANKER M. (not his real initial) *is an officer of one of Santa Fe's largest banks. Like many bankers in the Southwest, he is knowledgeable on the subject of Indian jewelry, partly because he has a genuine personal appreciation of it and partly because a great many people, from time to time, involve him professionally in the subject. While the views he expresses are his own, he chose to remain anonymous because his remarks reflect, at least in part, the philosophy of his institution. There is no doubt that they are typical of the attitude of most banks in the Southwest toward Indian jewelry, as a wholesale/retail business and as a form of collateral or investment.*

Do banks lend money on Indian jewelry, and are they knowledgeable about it? Yes, they do lend money, but as far as being knowledgeable, a bank isn't necessarily an authority on the subject any more than it might be about any other commodity that is sold. What you are looking for is the credibility of your borrower and his financial responsibility and what are reasonable estimates of cash flow to satisfy the payments on borrowed money.

Banks will lend money to people who want to go into the Indian jewelry business, and it's considered a reasonably sound risk; but again, it depends upon the financial responsibility of the borrower in relation to the amount of money he wants to borrow.

You're dealing on the one hand with a product which has very high prices on a per-item per-sale basis and inherent high markups from the trader through the retail trade, and therefore you have a built-in risk factor which leans very heavily on the borrower.

Collections can serve as collateral for loans, but here again it depends upon the collection. The old pawn collector's quality jewelry has a much higher value intrinsically than some of the items sold on today's market. The newer items, while handmade, may lack the quality of workmanship and intrinsic value of the older pieces.

As a lender, I would lean toward jewelry that was handmade, of an older nature, and not mass-produced—even by hand—as it is today. I think the old-style jewelry will retain its value over the years, as opposed to some of the newer items. There's a proliferation of jewelry today which is not, generally speaking, as well made or intrinsically valuable as the earlier material. The newer items, being produced in quantity, are subject to the laws of supply and demand in the marketplace.

One of the things we're aware of today is the tremendous influx of new traders and dealers and manufacturers, plus the increased appearance of treated or machine-made products, which has to have an effect on the market: who sells it, who buys, and who doesn't buy it. We are constantly being asked to lend money to people who want to go into the Indian jewelry business, and who may be lacking not only in experience, but in personal net worth. Consequently, the risk is being more and more transferred from the investor to the lender. The investor has the greatest opportunity to profit, but the lender is assuming more of the risk in the venture.

The people who come to us for loans to start an Indian jewelry business are almost entirely non-Indians, and the results that we are beginning to see around the community are that, as these people buy in wholesale quantities, the profit margin on retail sales is shrinking. Another thing we notice is the increasing advertising of discounts—which indicates to us that these dealers are not turning the volume they expected in order to make a profit.

The discounting of jewelry made by Indians may be a cause for the prospective buyer to be sure what is being discounted, and why. But there has always been a tendency around here to discount jewelry—even old pawn—during the winter months when business is slow and to raise the prices again during the tourist season. We're now beginning to see discounts advertised during the summer months around here, when the influx of tourists is high. The appearance of plastics has got to have an influence on the market because, unless you're adept at determining the presence of such things, the buyer is going to be unsure of whether he's getting genuine stones or treated low-grade turquoise.

While the appearance on the market of treated or imitation or misrepresented material undoubtedly will cause some adverse effect on the business, once supply has caught up with demand these practices will diminish or disappear, since the profit incentive for this sort of thing will also disappear.

As for the best ways for a buyer to determine the reputability of dealers, I don't think I'm an authority on the subject, but as a *consumer* I would be inclined to rely on those dealers who have been in the business for a long time and who have a vast personal knowledge of it. Again, with the influx of so many dealers who are new to the business I think you have a problem in that they may not be entirely knowledgeable about their products and, too, may not be entirely *bothered* by that problem.

The rash of thefts of Indian jewelry probably has affected the market in more than one way. In the first place, the thefts imply that there is a high value to what is being stolen. Also, from the lender's standpoint, the problem of insurability comes up: the lender wants to be sure that the merchandise which is being financed by his loan is properly insured. This not only increases operating costs for the dealer to a significant degree, but it also should point up to the consumer that—insurance agents tell me—most homeowner policies only cover such things as jewelry up to a low—usually three-figure—amount. Therefore, the collector should realize that he has a valuable property on his hands and see to it that it is insured properly.

Another aspect of this business, to a banker, is the seasonal one: the borrower has got to see to it that he has a sufficient inventory on hand for his peak sales season, and this brings dealers to us in search of venture capital. Again, this places a risk factor with the lender. It poses the question of who's going into the business, the retailer or the bank?

We rely primarily on the credit risk of the borrower, but we also might, from time to time, review with the borrower his inventory, from the standpoint of how well it's moving and also if there might be changes he can make in his buying and selling patterns that would help him move his merchandise better.

It's not a bad idea for a prospective dealer in Indian jewelry to consult with a bank or similar lending institution before going into the business, because banks have an overall feeling for the pulse of the business community—the general situation, what's selling and what isn't. Bankers also would have a pretty good idea as to the amount of competition in a given field.

Banks don't work with museums or collectors in valuing items of jewelry because the figures *we* use would be strictly for internal control, and the release of any figures on our part might involve the question of liability. We wouldn't want to become involved in that, since our criteria would likely be entirely different from those that museums or collectors would use.

The Indian jewelry business has changed tremendously in the last ten or fifteen years. There is an enormous volume available now that wasn't there before. One last thing, from a lender's point of view, is that jewelry—if it isn't being bought for collections—is fashion, and fashion can be fickle.

"The whole thing is a Southwest phenomenon... the other area where it's taking off is Paris..."

HARMER JOHNSON *is a dealer and appraiser of tribal art, including American Indian art, based in New York City. He is also an auctioneer and a former member of the Sotheby Parke-Bernet firm. Mr. Johnson was an auctioneer in the historic C. G. Wallace auction in November 1975 in Phoenix.*

American Indian silverwork has a very regional interest. The best place to sell it at auction is in the Southwest. The few pieces that do sell in New York on the whole fetch quite disappointing prices. I remember one item after I left Parke-Bernet, a turn of the century squash-blossom with very good spiderweb turquoise which I bought for $200. About a year-and-a-half later the necklace was worth about $1,000.

The whole thing is a Southwest phenomenon. The other area where it's taking off is Paris. There are a lot of dealers in Paris setting up and the prices are astronomical. In some cases they are even higher than we are seeing in Phoenix. Paris is the world center for art, and the Paris market seems to be a little ahead of most other European centers, but the others are catching on. You also see interest in northern Italy in the industrial centers of Milan, Turin, and somewhat less in Florence. The Germans are less interested. I found surprisingly few Germans collecting jewelry. Everyone was asking for beadwork, quillwork, early pottery, early weaving, etc.—but not jewelry.

We've been seeing a rise in prices at auctions in Indian jewelry, but as with other areas of Indian art, when there is a rise in prices this results in a whole lot of things coming out of the woodwork from people going through their barns and attics. Then you get a flooded market and prices drop, polarizing the market.

We found in the Green auction in New York in 1971 that so much was being consigned that prices dropped tremendously. So now it's polarizing and the really great jewelry is taking off and fetching high prices and the mediocre material is depreciating. I think this is a very healthy sign—it shows that people are discriminating between the old and new material, but also between the good and the bad contemporary artists, in New York as elsewhere.

No one knew what was going to happen in the Wallace sale. We had presale estimates from about ten different sources that varied from $200,000 to $2 million. The difficulty with that sale was having over 1,100 lots, all of them jewelry, over a very concentrated period of three days. We had no idea whether people would fall asleep after the first 10 lots or even how many people would come to the sale. We were very pleased with the sale. There was nothing that really bombed. If everything did not bring the high prices, enough of the material did. It was the very elaborate squash-blossom necklaces which people seemed to grow tired of. Some of them were so heavy one could hardly wear them. They were almost like potlatch pieces, just status symbols. The very elaborate squash-blossom necklaces and some of the elaborate inlaid belts seemed to go for less. People were bidding on the smaller items, the good rings and the early bracelets and certainly the Leekya turquoise fetishes and the fetish necklaces.

I think the high prices on some items were a

reflection of what an auction is all about. There is an aura that is created around an auction by the auction gallery. The presale publicity, making sure everybody attends the parties before the sale, placing each of the items on a slide so that you see it as you are buying it—not just as a small item on a table in the background—are all important. It created the sort of auction atmosphere where you were going to create high prices. In one case there was a husband and wife bidding on one item—neither realizing that each was bidding against the other. It created an atmosphere where people probably paid more than they were planning on.

The Wallace sale must have been the biggest public auction of jewelry I've been involved with. In New York, all of the other sales I've been involved with have been ten pieces of this and twenty pieces of that—not really big sales. The sale really meant nothing at all except that the people who before the sale had been predicting that we were looking at the end of the American Indian jewelry movement were proven wrong. In an open sale, people were prepared to pay very high prices for good and very good material. That said more for the market than the high prices in galleries where the market is more controlled.

GLOSSARY

abalone
A gastropod mollusk of the genus ***Haliotus*** found in the waters off Southern California. Since prehistoric times its iridescent shell has been used for ornament by the Indians of the Pacific Coast and the inland Southwest. The shell can have a pink or reddish inner layer which is sometimes confused for coral. Abalone is still extensively used in Southwest Indian jewelry, particularly inlay work; its often patterned and ridged texture, and blue-green-pink-yellow-silvery highlights, producing dramatic effects.
almogen
A substance native to the Navajo Reservation which Washington Matthews described as being used for flux in the melting of silver coins by the early Navajo smiths. It has since been replaced by commercial products.
Anasazi *(ah-nah-SAH-zee)*
A Navajo word meaning The Ancient Ones or Those Who Are Gone and applied by modern archeologists to the prehistoric Pueblo Indians of the U.S. Southwest. Among the Anasazi after the 10th century A.D. worked turquoise became a major commodity for export and local use.
Angel Skin
Term applied to a very fine type of precious coral which is light pink in color.
anneal
To soften metal by heating until it reaches a dull red color, then allowing it to cool so that it can be wrought or worked without cracking. When cold metal is excessively worked, it becomes strain-hardened and brittle; it cracks because its molecular structure has undergone change. It may be necessary to anneal a metal a number of times in the course of working it. The annealing range of silver is 900-1200°F.
anvil
A hard piece of iron or steel (or even wood) upon which silver or other metal is beaten out or worked.
Apache
A group of tribes of Athapascan-speaking Indians of Arizona, New Mexico, Texas, and northern Mexico. The word is probably Zuni Indian in origin and originally included the Navajo, who were referred to by Spanish chroniclers as Apaches de Navaju. Unlike the Navajos, the Apaches had little friendly contact with Pueblo, Spanish, or Anglo peoples in the Southwest; they never evolved from a primitive hunting and gathering culture and did not take up silverworking, though they did wear some forms of metal jewelry, captured or purchased from other tribes.
Apache tears
See ***garnet***.
applique
A decoration, usually of silver or other metal, cut out and fastened by soldering or welding to the surface of a piece of (usually silver) jewelry.
argillite
See ***pipestone***.
Arizona ruby
See ***garnet***.
Athapascan
A language stock spoken by a number of Indian tribes in North America, including the Apaches and Navajos.
Atsidi Chon *(usu. AHT-see-dee chohn)*
Ugly Smith. An early Navajo silversmith known to have been the first, or among the first, of the Navajo smiths to set turquoise in silver. He also allegedly taught the first Zuni Indian to work silver.
Atsidi Sani *(AHT-see-dee SAH-nee)*
Old Smith. Traditionally the first Navajo to learn how to work iron and, later, silver; he apparently taught the latter art to his sons. Atsidi Sani also was known as Herrero (Spanish, ehr-EHR-o), meaning ironworker or blacksmith; also known as Herrero Delgadito (dehl-gah-DEE-toh) or Slim Little Blacksmith.
awl
A pointed tool used for punching holes or for marking surfaces as in engraving. Before they possessed dies, early Navajo and other Indian smiths used awls, along with files, to decorate the surfaces of their silver jewelry.

Aztec
A Nahuatl-speaking people whose empire was conquered by Cortez in 1519-1520. They were the last, not the first, of the great early civilizations of Central Mexico. Like the earlier Toltec cultures, they possessed gold- and silversmiths who had a high degree of proficiency in fashioning jewelry.

azurite
An attractive semiprecious stone, typically deep azure blue, derived from the mineral azurite, a blue basic carbonate of copper. A "turquoise look-alike" which won't fool an expert (azurite has a more "oily" appearance than turquoise—it might be said to resemble an obviously plasticized piece of turquoise).

backing
Material (such as epoxy, "plastic steel," or liquid metal) applied to the back of turquoise or other stones to provide cohesiveness and strength. The term ***backing*** is also used to refer to materials such as sawdust, cardboard, and tissue paper placed beneath a stone as cushioning, to help protect the stone from shocks and jolts. Backing, in some instances, performs the function of "padding out" a very thin or otherwise unusable stone.

bakelite
See ***"phonograph record."***

baroque
A free-form cut stone, also referred to as ***nugget***, having no exact symmetrical shape and conforming as nearly as possible to the original shape of the natural stone. Widely used today since it wastes little turquoise in the grinding and polishing. ***Baroque*** as applied to a style or trend in Indian jewelry can take the classical definition: "marked by elaborate and sometimes grotesque ornamentation."

Basketmakers
A prehistoric culture of the Southwest which predated and developed into the Pueblo culture.

bellows
An instrument that by contraction and expansion forces air through a nozzle; used by early silversmiths to control the temperature of charcoal fires in a forge. Early ones were handmade and resembled concertinas.

"bench"
As an adjective applied to Indian jewelry (as in bench made, bench work), means made by an Indian "under supervision," such as a situation in which the Indian comes to work in the morning, is issued silver and turquoise of known quantity and quality, and works the day "at a bench" (this as opposed to issuing jewelry materials to an Indian who makes the jewelry on his own at home). Bench work is supposed to yield the advantage of consistent and conveniently reorderable pieces.

bench bead, bench craft bead
A partly handmade, partly machine-made bead which is typically punched and rounded out of sheet silver by machine, then soldered and finished by hand.

bezel
A thin lip of silver or other metal, used to hold a stone against its mounting. The bezel is soldered to the mounting, the stone inserted when the metal is cool, often with padding beneath it, and the bezel is crimped or tamped against the stone.

blossom
See ***cluster medallion***.

blowpipe
A small metal tube used to add oxygen to a flame (such as a flame used in silverwork) by blowing through it, thus increasing its heat. Early Navajo blowpipes were often handmade of brass.

bola (or **bolo) tie**
A neckpiece worn under the collar, consisting of a thong or braided strip whose two ends pass through an ornamental device drawn tight against the throat. Each of the ends of the thong usually has a metal tip which also can be decorated or set with stones. A popular form of jewelry for men, it was adopted in the 1930s by the whites of the Southwest.

branch coral
See ***coral***.

butterfly
An ornament of butterfly shape, usually silver, sometimes set with turquoise, which spaces out the conchas on a belt, typically being alternated with the larger placques.

cabochon
An unfaceted, and sometimes uncut, but polished stone with a convex surface. Cut stones can be round or oval; uncut are baroque or free-form.

cameo shell
Pink shell of the "helmet" variety, native to East Africa, used in heishi and inlay.

cannel coal
A bituminous coal resembling jet, somewhat more brownish-black than black, less lustrous than jet, but occurring naturally in larger masses, thus yielding larger working pieces. Though workable varieties of bituminous coal are found on the Navajo and Hopi reservations, cannel coal has been imported from England for use in Indian jewelry, particularly inlay work.

cast
To shape metal by melting and pouring it into a mold. Also a piece of jewelry formed by such a process. (See sandcast, ***lost wax, centrifugal casting***).

centrifugal casting
The process of forming jewelry by pouring molten metal into a form on a machine which is then spun, casting the metal into an exact reproduction of the form by means of centrifugal force. *Not* a handmade (handcast or individually cast) process. Also called ***spin casting***.

chalchihuitl *(chahl-chee-WHEE-tuhl)*
An Aztec or Nahuatl word for jadeite or turquoise. In northern New Mexico, among descendants of early Spanish colonists, this word or variants of it are often used for turquoise rather than the Castilian ***turquesa***.

chalk
Soft or porous turquoise which cannot be used as gemstone unless oiled, stabilized, or otherwise treated. Sometimes referred to as ***oiling turquoise***.

channel inlay
See ***channelwork***

channelwork *(channel inlay)*
A compartmentalized form of silverwork whose interstices are filled with turquoise or other stones, shells, or coral. The inlaid materials should be hand-cut to fit their spaces exactly, and cemented in (originally, resin or pine pitch was used; pre World War II, common "airplane glue"; more recently, epoxies are used for this purpose). Usually the surface is then ground and polished flat, but this is not always the case. Often today the silver mountings are done by centrifugal casting, which is ethical only if the buyer is so informed. Channelwork originated in the 1940s; often channelwork is a "cooperative product" of Navajos (who make the silver framework) and Zunis (who cut and set the stones).

chasing
A method of engraving silver or other metals with an awl or other pointed instrument applied to the surface by hand, as opposed to punched or struck with a hammer.

chrysocolla
A copper-related mineral which is sometimes a look-alike for turquoise and not infrequently sold as such. Tests can reveal differences.

cire perdu
See ***lost wax***.

cloisonné
Decorations by pouring enamel into compartments formed by metal-design outlines secured to a metal ground. Some inlay work has on occasion been described as having a cloisonné effect.

cluster
A group of stones, each with its own bezel, arranged in a geometric pattern. This is typically a Zuni style, involving small stones of round, oval, or egg shape. However, when using multiple-stone sets, Navajos also use clusters. Often, clusters are grouped around a larger central stone.

cluster cut
Small turquoise stones cut to uniform size and shape for use in clusterwork.

cluster medallion
A largish ornament formed of clusterwork, usually a part or appendage (often the central motif) of a larger piece of jewelry. Oval or circular cluster medallions are often referred to as "blossoms"

cluster sidepiece
A matching, usually smaller clusterwork ornament accompanying a cluster medallion.

coin silver
Silver obtained from melting or hammering silver coins. Though its composition has varied in different times and countries, by contemporary U.S. definition coin silver is an alloy of approximately 90 percent silver and 10 percent copper. The Navajos and other Indian smiths used U.S. coins for silver for jewelry until 1890, and Mexican pesos (which usually had a slightly higher silver content) until 1930, when the respective governments actively enforced the laws against such practices. After that, Indian smiths used commercially made one-ounce silver slugs (and later, sheets) of the same fineness as coin silver, until around 1938 when the use of sterling silver (92.5 percent silver, 7.5 percent copper) became general, although it is rarely marked as such when used in Indian jewelry.

cold chisel
A steel or iron tool for cutting or incising cold metal such as silver.

color
When applied to turquoise, the hue of the stone which, along with luster, matrix, and hardness, determines its value as a gemstone. Turquoise ranges from white to green to deep blue in color.

concha or **concho**
Round or oval placque, usually silver, sometimes with scalloped edge, either unmarked, stamped with designs, and/or set with turquoise. Usually strung on leather for use as a belt. From the Spanish ***concha***: shell.

contemporary
As applied to Indian jewelry, a style of jewelrymaking, essentially free-form in nature, which departs from traditional materials and designs, favoring use of such materials as gold for metalwork and various stones (semiprecious and precious, most native to the United States but not necessarily to the Southwest) and other materials (including such things as wood and elephant ivory) for setting in metal. Another common meaning of ***contemporary***, as applied to Indian jewelry, is: made within an arbitrary time span of approximately the past twenty years; or made by someone who is still alive.

coral
Red or pink material used as decoration in Indian jewelry, often along with turquoise and other stones and materials. Coral is the skeletal deposit (calcium carbonate colored by manganese) of certain marine organisms. Historically, most gem coral comes from the Mediterranean, especially the coasts of Italy, but it occurs in other spots as well: much coral today is fished for commerce in the Japanese Sea and South Pacific. Prehistoric Southwest Indians worked reddish stones such as argillite; early Spaniards in the Southwest introduced coral trade beads; from the 1930s Indian traders such as C. G.Wallace were active in trying to import coral, especially in unfinished form, for use in Indian jewelry. Branch ***coral***—branching delicate twiglike natural coral pieces—was used as a design element especially by Zunis. Coral has the ability to take a polish, but it is most valued for its color, which ranges from pale pink (Angel Skin) to pale rose, cherry red, dark red, even white and black; the color traditionally favored by Southwest Indians was intense orange-red. Much coral was and is cut and drilled abroad and strung as bead necklaces by Southwest Indians. As natural high-quality precious coral becomes more difficult to obtain, due to the hazards of fishing it, depletion of coral beds by pollution, overfishing, etc., it has become more valuable, and imitation coral in Indian jewelry is not unknown.

country rock
Another term for the matrix or host rock in which turquoise is found.

crucible
A vessel for melting silver or other metal which is to be cast or otherwise shaped. Early Navajo smiths used prehistoric potsherds as crucibles or made their own from clay before they obtained commercially made vessels.

curio
In the sense of this book an imitation piece of Indian-style jewelry; the metal is usually not silver and the turquoise is not genuine in any sense of the word.

dead pawn
Jewelry that has been pawned by an Indian, usually with a trader, and then allowed to go unredeemed within the time specified. The trader then is free to dispose of the pawn as he sees fit, although he may keep it longer than he is legally required to. (see ***old pawn***)

Denver silver
Derogatory term used to denote machine-made imitation Indian silver jewelry which was first manufactured by a Denver firm in 1910. The practice spread through the Southwest.

depth
Another visual quality of turquoise, along with color, which influences its value; intensity or "Zat" might be roughly synonymous.
die
A metal tool bearing a design which is impressed into a piece of silver jewelry by hand hammering. Dies came into use in the 1870s, usually made by the Indians themselves from pieces of scrap iron or steel. It is thought that they originated from the stamps that were used by the early Spanish colonists to embellish leatherwork and adapted by ***plateros*** or silversmiths for use with that metal. Dies came into wider use when fine files (for filing the design into a die) became available in the 1890s. Later commercially made dies were used extensively.
die press
A machine, hand or power operated, which impresses a complete series of designs into a silver or other metal object. These are used in mass-producing Indian-style jewelry, even though the metal might be sterling silver. They usually do not leave as deep an impression in the metal as hand-stamping, and of course the design will be identical on every object—such as a concha—without the individual variations found in genuine handmade jewelry.
dragonfly
A Pueblo Indian design resembling the double-barred Christian cross later introduced by Spanish and Mexican colonists. A common design motif in jewelry of Isleta and Zuni pueblos.
drawn silver necklace
Ideally, a necklace made of sterling silber tubing, hand drawn through a drawplate to a very fine diameter, then cut into small elongated beads and strung, in the manner of a heishi necklace, in smooth single or multiple strands. Also called ***liquid silver***. Much "liquid silver" is not a handmade product.
drawplate
A sheet of hardened metal with a series of holes of decreasing diameter through which silver or other metal wire is drawn (usually with the aid of a pair of pliers) to the desired thickness. An old tool. Silver wire now comes commercially made in almost any diameter needed.
dye
A substance or compound used to color artificially low-grade turquoise; a great many things from prussian blue to black shoe polish to dye matrix have been used.
Eagle Dancer
A costumed dancer, heavily ornamented with eagle feathers, appearing in Pueblo and Plains Indians dance rituals, imitating the soaring of an eagle. A figure often depicted in Zuni and Hopi jewelry, particularly inlay (probably initiated by Anglo traders), it is usually depicted with outstretched arms. If masked, it represents an Eagle kachina.
epoxy
A very strong resin-based adhesive used widely in contemporary Indian jewelry for backing stones, such as turquoise, for cementing in the materials in inlay work, mending cracked or damaged turquoise stones, and even for solidly affixing stones (in newer jewelry designs) directly to the metal, without bezel or other holding device.
ferrule
Term used by some to describe the silver frames of Navajo channelwork, or the silver outlines in Zuni multicolor inlaid stonework.
fetish
An object, sometimes but not always of stone, with zoomorphic properties believed to possess preternatural powers. The fetish can be natural or deliberately shaped or carved. Stone fetishes are used in the kivas of various Pueblos of the Southwest, and replicas or adaptations of them are used in necklaces carved of turquoise or other materials and sold as jewelry. The Zunis are particularly well known for carved fetish jewelry.
filigree
Ornamental work of fine silver (or gold or copper) wire applied to silver (or other metal) jewelry surfaces; delicate lacy openwork. Much more a characteristic of Mexican jewelry, simpler forms of filigree—a relatively difficult form of silverwork—were incorporated and experimented with especially in Zuni and Navajo pieces of the 1930s and 1940s.
filler
In Indian jewelry, can refer to a wide variety of materials used to conceal or

disguise cracks or faults in a stone such as turquoise, for example, liquid aluminum, plastic resins dyed with India ink, silver dust mixed with epoxy resin. Often a filler is made to simulate a natural matrix color and appearance, or it can be used to "doctor" poorly done channelwork or inlay work. Filler is an inventive product and tool of modern lapidaries.

findings

The catches, swivels, clasps, and other small "utilitarian" parts used in the making of jewelry, including earscrews for earrings. Even in otherwise completely handmade Indian jewelry, the findings are usually commercially manufactured; this is not considered to affect the authenticity.

fineness

The degree of purity of a metal: 1.000 is pure or fine silver, without any alloys or other substances; in the United States, sterling is .925 fine and coin silver is .900 fine, since 1920. Fine silver has a brilliant luster but is too soft for general jewelry use. Fine gold also has very attractive visual qualities but is too soft for general jewelry use. The fineness of gold is expressed in carats, "24 carat" indicating pure or fine gold. (See ***melting point***.)

Fire God, Zuni Fire God

A traditional Zuni dancer often depicted in inlay work, usually a black figure with dots of coral and turquoise, with a deerskin slung over his shoulder. It is the Fire God who announces that the Shalakos are coming. In the C. G. Wallace auction of 1975, the highest price for a single item of jewelry was paid for an inlay figure of the Zuni Fire God.

firestain, fire scale

Grayish discoloration of the surface of sterling silver as a result of heating while working; this blemish is removed by the meticulous smith by polishing and other processes.

fluted bead

A flattened, conical, hollow bead, usually with ribbed or ridged decorative lines radiating from the center to the soldered edge of each half, often enhanced by oxidation. Buttons can also be fluted.

flux

A chemical which aids the soldering of metals such as silver by preventing the oxidation which usually takes place when metals are heated; oxidation will interfere with the "hold" or "fusing action" of a solder. The earliest Navajo flux (see ***almogen***) was mined on the reservation; later borax was purchased from commercial sources.

forge

A furnace, or a place with a furnace, where metal is heated and wrought, or melted and cast. The earliest Navajo silversmiths made their own forges, complete with built-in bellows; modern smiths use torches which use combinations of compressed air and gas, oxygen and gas, or acetylene and gas or butane, or Prestolite, which they use to anneal or melt silver.

fossil ivory

Ivory, such as from actual fossil animals such as the mastodon, that has been yellowed, darkened, or variegated by the passage of time.

fossil turquoise

Fossil bone or tooth colored blue with phospate of iron, thus not true turquoise, or even a true stone. Also called ***bone turquoise*** or ***odontolite***. Softer than true turquoise, and gray-appearing under artificial light.

foxtail

Strong braided steel wire used for the stringing of necklaces such as heishi.

garnet

Semiprecious gemstone (also known as Apache tears and Arizona ruby) native to certain areas of the Navajo Reservation and elsewhere in the Southwest, of translucent crystalline nature, usually deep red to brownish red in color. Well formed natural crystals of garnet are common, and garnet was one of the first, if not the first, stone to be set in silver by the early Navajo smiths.

gato

See ***ketoh***.

gem quality

When referring to turquoise, of the highest natural quality, in hardness, color, and luster; by implication, "directly from the mine," not adulterated or treated in any way, except being cut or shaped.

German silver

Alloy made of copper, zinc, and nickel in a 3:1:1 ratio. Used in trade goods in nineteenth-century commerce between European traders and the Indians.

Some early conchas traded to the Plains Indians were made of this alloy; it is used today in inexpensive imitations of Southwest Indian silver and turquoise jewelry. German silver jewelrymaking is still practiced to a limited extent by some Plains tribes.

Gilson turquoise
See ***synthetic turquoise***.

globule
See ***raindrops***.

graver
Burin or cutting tool used to incise silver or other metal.

hallmark
A mark stamped on metal to attest its purity or the identity of the maker of a piece of jewelry or article of precious metal. Although most Indian jewelry today is of sterling fineness, it is almost never so stamped; in fact such a stamp may indicate a machine-made item. Individual silversmiths' marks are sometimes used on pieces of jewelry, but these have been forged all too many times (and the same smith may change his hallmark stamp over a period of years).

hand cut
A stone, such as turquoise, cut and polished by hand, especially by the maker of a piece of jewelry.

handmade
Literally, a piece of jewelry that has been made entirely by hand, without the aid of machinery of any sort. Findings (which see) are excepted from this definition. However, power-driven grinders, buffers, and polishers usually are acceptable in making "handmade" jewelry—but from there it is a herculean task to get any two or three traders or smiths to agree on an exact definition of "handmade" work.

hand wrought
A redundancy, since "wrought" in metalsmithing specifically means worked by hand tools, thus by hand (see wrought). As applied to Indian jewelry, this term can denote that each of the individual components was made by hand—i.e., wire was hand drawn; silver, hand cast or hammered into the final form used.

Harvey Company, Fred Harvey Company
The first nationwide popularization and commercialization of Southwest Indian jewelry was initiated in 1898, when the Fred Harvey Company began ordering for resale Navajo silver that was lighter than that made for Indian use. Silver and turquoise were distributed to various traders, who in turn farmed them out to Indian smiths who made jewelry on a piecework consignment basis.

heishi, hesche, hishi, or **hieshi**
Thin or thick discoidal beads threaded together as in necklaces. Usually thought of as shell, but they can also be of turquoise, jet, or even silver. The Santo Domingo Indians of New Mexico are noted for their heishi necklaces. To make shell heishi, the shell is broken into pieces, pierced, and strung on a rod and rotated against a rough surface, by hand, until round. Machine-driven grinders and drills are used as well to make shell heishi. Even so, it can be imported from places like Taiwan and the Philippines cheaper than it can be bought from native American Indians.

historic
In the U.S. Southwest, historic times arbitrarily begin with the coming of the Coronado expedition in 1540; anything earlier is referred to as prehistoric—before written history, or more specifically, *European* written history.

hogan *(HOH-gahn)*
Navajo home. The earliest known is the three-forked-stick hogan; the later version is the octagonal dome-roof style.

Hohokam *(HO-ho-kahm)*
Prehistoric Indians of south-central Arizona. The first turquoise jewelry of the Southwest was found in Hohokam ruins predating the birth of Christ.

hollow beads
Silver beads made by stamping two hemispheres from sheet silver, soldering them together, grinding the weld flat, then polishing them. One of the earliest Indian handmade forms; nowadays many hollow beads are machine stamped, hand-welded, and buffed on machines.

Hopi style
See ***overlay***.

host rock
Matrix. (See also ***country rock***).
ingot
Metal cast in convenient form for later finishing, such as hammering, rolling, casting into jewelry.
ingot mold
Mold used for casting silver ingots. Early ones were often stone, or even depressions made in sand.
inlay
The use of stone, shell, and other materials in mosaic designs enclosed in a bezel, usually in zoomorphic or anthropomorphic images. If no bezels are used, the work is mosaic. Zunis are excellent at inlay work, and almost all of this is done by them.
intensity
Another subjective criterion for determining the quality of turquoise; the brilliance of its color, or its richness.
iron pyrite
See ***pyrite***
ironwork
Any of numerous hard-wooded trees and shrubs, including the ironwood tree of the Arizona desert or the manzanita bush of higher altitudes. Typically a light wood with dark streaks, ironwood has been set or inlaid in jewelry by modern smiths.
jacla
See ***jokla***.
jet
A compact, hard, velvet black mineral similar in appearance to coal. (Jet is in fact a form of fossil coal). It takes a good polish and is used in Indian jewelry in inlay work and beads.
jokla, jacla, jacklah
A short double loop of turquoise beads usually tied to the bottom of a turquoise or other bead necklace; originally worn as earrings, which were fastened to the necklace when not in use. Each loop of a jokla is usually ornamented at its pendant center, or elsewhere, with small groups of often tabular beads of contrasting color.
kachina
Denizen of the Hopi (or other Pueblo Indian) Pantheon. Representations of these varied colorful personages (more than 400 kachinas have been recorded) are carved from cottonwood root. Though the Hopis do not officially permit commercial representations of kachinas, kachinas have with increasing frequency in recent decades been depicted in jewelry (especially inlay) designs.
ketoh, keto, gato
Leather strap worn at the wrist to protect the skin from the snap of a bowstring. One of the earliest utilitarian objects to be decorated with silver and then silver and turquoise.
Knife Wing God
A Zuni animal spirit which is one of the most common decorative motifs in Zuni jewelry. Also called ***Knife Wing Monster*** and ***Knife Wing Bird***, it is usually represented as a humanlike form with knife-feathered wings and tail and a terraced cap.
lapidary
A worker of precious stones other than diamond.
lapis
Short for lapis lazuli, an opaque, typically deep blue semiprecious stone sometimes used in Indian jewelry, especially contemporary jewelry. Actually a mixture of several minerals (Lazurite, pyrite, and others) imbedded in a matrix of white calcite. A relatively soft gemstone, lapis in its paler varieties can be a turquoise look-alike, but it has an entirely different luster.
liquid gold
Fine tubular gold beads, hand drawn or machine-made, such as strung into a heishi-like necklace or choker; A contemporary form of jewelry. Also a term for a type of gemstone filler (see ***filler***).
liquid silver
Fine tubular silver beads, hand drawn or machine-made, strung usually into necklaces and chokers. Sometimes called silver heishi; a contemporary form of jewelry (see ***drawn silver***). Also a term for a type of silver solder.
liver of sulfur
Potassium sulphide, a common oxidizing agent used in silverwork.(See ***oxidize***.)

lost wax
A method of casting metal by making a wax model, coating it with clay to form a mold, and leaving small holes for the wax to escape when heated; molten metal is poured into the mold, filling the space left by the "lost wax." Also called ***cire perdu***.
Luroc
See ***synthetic turquoise***.
luster
The sheen or "light-reflecting quality" of the surface of a polished mineral or stone, such as turquoise.
malachite
A semiprecious stone, a carbonate of copper which is sometimes used in Indian jewelry, especially contemporary work. A relatively soft stone, malachite is typically a handsome bright green, or banded green and black, but in some of its varieties it can be a turquoise look-alike.
manta pin
A decorated silver pin originally used by Pueblo women to hold the manta in place. (The manta is a strip of usually cotton woven cloth wrapped about the body and secured over the right shoulder.)
matrix
The host, or country rock, in which turquoise is found. Often, as in the case of spiderweb, the matrix is considered highly desirable as part of the finished gemstone. Since turquoise is found in a variety of types of host rock, the matrix can vary greatly in color, texture, and effect.
melon seed bead
Term sometimes used for elongated hollow bead, pointed at each end (like a melon seed), which may be stamped or otherwise decorated.
melon shell
A shell, usually flesh-colored or light orange, used for inlay and heishi. Melon shells are large shells of the genus ***Melo***, native to the South Pacific.
melting point
The temperature at which solid metal turns to liquid. Pure silver melts at 1,761°F; sterling melts at 1,640°; coin silver's melting point is 1,615°.
mosaic
The process of producing patterns and designs with small pieces of turquoise, shell, or other stones and material set into or onto a piece of jewelry; differs from inlay in common Indian jewelry parlance in that there are no silver outlines or rules separating the pieces.
mother-in-law bell
Early form of silverwork; small silver bells whose original purpose was to warn a son-in-law of the approach of his mother-in-law (Navajo custom demanded that he not lay eyes on her). Typically worn on a sash or necklace.
mother-of-pearl
White pearly iridescent substance forming the inner layer of many shells; used extensively in inlay, mosaic work, necklaces, and other forms of Southwest Indian jewelry.
naja
The three-quarter-circle design pendant from hollow bead or other necklaces made by the Navajo and other Indian smiths. It is usually made of silver, sometimes set with turquoise or other stones. Design originally came to the area with the Spanish and Mexican settlers as an element on the headstall of a horse bridle; the Spanish in their turn obtained the design from the Moors. It is known even from Roman times as a charm against the Evil Eye, but it apparently never held such connotations for the early Navajo smiths.
Navajo
An Athapascan-speaking Indian tribe of the Southwest United States, close kin to the Apaches.
Navajo style
In making silver and turquoise jewelry the Navajos developed a simple, solid style of silverwork, decorated sparingly, first with engravings, later with die punch design elements. Later (by 1890) turquoise was set in the silver, again in large, eye-catching arrangements. Traditional Navajo style is still massive, with emphasis on silver set off by larger stones, usually turquoise.
needlepoint
A Zuni style of jewelry characterized by small, elongated stones, usually turquoise, that come to a point at either end; each is set in its own fine-toothed bezel, often with a dot of silver at the point, in multiple rows and delicate patterns, supported usually by thin frames of silver. In fine

needlepoint work, especially contemporary, the stones should be well matched and the settings perfectly aligned.

nugget

A natural mass of turquoise or other mineral. Also a style of finished stone (see ***baroque; Seafoam turquoise***).

old pawn

Indian jewelry which was pawned and allowed to go unredeemed by its Indian owner, then sold by the trader. Authorities differ on when pawn can be classified as "old." Some insist it must have gone dead in the 1930s; others will allow a 1940 or even 1950 time limit. There is an inference that old pawn is good, collector's quality jewelry, that since pawn was owned by an Indian it is made of genuine materials and is of esthetic value; but this is not necessarily so. Part of pawn's fabled desirability is its age, and the fact that it was worn by an Indian of earlier years. Most old pawn is now in museums or private collections.

olivella shell

Small shiny shells of the genus ***Oliva***, common in tropical waters, used in heishi and inlay work.

overlay

The classic Hopi design originated in the late 1930s by Fred Kabotie and Paul Saufkie working with the Museum of Northern Arizona, Flagstaff. A design is cut in one flat piece of metal, which is then welded to a solid piece of the same size and shape. The recessed areas are then blackened to form a striking design. Turquoise or coral is sometimes set in the hollow spaces, or on the raised surfaces, which are highly polished.

oxidize

To blacken silver, either naturally or artificially. Sterling silver, because of its copper content, will oxidize at the surface in the course of time and exposure to air, moisture, etc. Oxidation is often used as a design element; parts of a design (such as low places) are oxidized, often with liver of sulfur, to set them off from other parts (such as polished raised surfaces). The oxidation (dark coloration of parts) of Indian jewelry is usually considered part of a piece's "character" and should not be removed.

patina

The surface quality or luster of either silver or turquoise, which is the result of wear, of being worn, and of exposure to the elements; a natural polish which only time and use can give.

pawn

Jewelry that has been owned by an Indian and deposited with a trader as security against debts. The jewelry must be held by the trader for a specified time, after which it goes dead if not redeemed by its owner. Jewelry is not pawned for its full retail value; nor is the fact that it was owned by an Indian a guarantee of top quality. (See ***old pawn***.)

pectoral

An ornament worn on the breast, often suspended by a leather thong about the neck. Also, a medallion or disc made of turquoise, shell, wood, or bone, worn on the breast.

pendant

A hanging ornament, as from the bottom of a necklace or earring, made of silver, turquoise, or other stones and materials, or of a combination thereof.

pen shell

A dark or blackish-brown clamlike shell of the genus ***Pinna***, from tropical seas, used in heishi and inlay.

Persian

Turquoise from the Middle Eastern area now known as Iran, historically prized for its quality—although not all Persian turquoise is prime. It was first imported to the United States for use in Indian jewelry in the 1890s, and ranges from a light blue (usually used for setting in gold) to a deep intense blue, including matrix forms.

petit point

A form of Zuni work, much like needlepoint, employing small egg-shaped, round, or oval stones (as opposed to the narrow pointed stones used in needlepoint), in clusterwork or row-set designs. The validity of distinguishing petit point from needlepoint is disputed.

petrified wood

Wood from early geological ages which has been turned to stone (a form of agate) from the action of mineral-permeated waters. It is most commonly found at Petrified Forest National Monument and the Navajo Reservation east of Ganado, and its use in Indian jewelry was most prevalent (even a mild fad) during World War II, when turquoise was not readily available. Petrified wood occurs in reds to browns to beautiful multicolors; it takes a high polish and is very hard—its extreme hardness made it difficult to work with early tools. It is now illegal to use petrified wood from Petrified Forest National Monument.

"phonograph record"
Black bakelite, from the old 78 rpm phonograph records, especially the unridged central eye, though ridged portions were used also. It was used in the early twentieth century by Indian jewelrymakers, in place of such materials as jet in inlay work.

pipestone, argillite
Reddish stone used by Indians of the Plains and elsewhere for making the so-called peace pipes. It was traded extensively in pre-European times and used in the prehistoric Southwest for jewelrymaking. Pipestone is used by contemporary Indian jewelers as a stone for setting in silver and other metals, and for carving as beads, a use for which its relative softness makes it adaptable.

plasticize
To treat turquoise with plastic material to heighten its color and harden its surface so it can take a higher polish. The first efforts to plasticize turquoise consisted of placing stones in hot liquid plastic (which formed an easily discernible outer shell). Refinements of this technique now inject liquid plastics under high pressure and heat so that they infuse the entire stone, "stabilizing" it. The newer processes are so efficient as to make it difficult even for "experts" to spot a stabilized stone.

plastic steel
A form of backing used for turquoise stones.

platero
Spanish for silversmith. It is believed that the Navajos first observed, and later learned the art of silversmithing from Mexican plateros living in villages along the upper Rio Grande in New Mexico some time between 1850 and the late 1860s.

plug
An ornament of metal or stone inserted in the lower lip, the sides of the nostrils or septum of the nose, or in the earlobe.

pollen pistil
A form of squash blossom bead that includes silver representations of what would be the pistils of a flower, in the center of the "blossom petals" of each bead.

powder measure, powder charger
Small silver implement used to measure and hold the powder for a single charge of a breech-loading gun. An early Navajo silver form, now very rare (many were melted down and the silver reused).

prehistoric
In the U.S. Southwest that period of time which ended with the coming of the Coronado expedition in 1540 A.D. The prehistoric period began with the first coming of man to the Western Hemisphere, at least 15,000 years ago.

Pueblo
Spanish for village. In the Southwest this word refers to a number of Indian groups descended from the prehistoric Anasazi, who live in villages of stone- or adobe-constructed houses, often contiguous and sometimes containing two or more stories. Although languages differ, there is a basic homogeneity to Pueblo Indian culture.

pump drill
Ancient hand tool (much like a fire drill) with a sharp point, set in motion by the action of a twisted thong upon a crosspiece, used to drill holes in beads, particularly before the advent of power tools. Each bead is drilled halfway through from each side, resulting in an hourglass-shaped hole.

punch
A metal tool struck with a hammer to perforate or stamp designs in metal.

pure silver
Silver of 1.000 fineness which contains no impurities or alloys. It has a higher melting point than sterling or coin silver, and a high satiny luster, but is too soft for general use in jewelry, tending to wear down quickly.

pyrite
Crytallized isometric forms of metal, such as iron pyrite or fool's gold, sometimes found in association with turquoise, as a matrix; iron pyrite often appears as cubic bright brassy yellow forms or flecks.

Rainbow Man
A design often depicted in Zuni, and sometimes Navajo, jewelry: a

humanlike figure with a curving, rainbowlike body and a terraced cap; a protective spirit.

raindrops
Small rounded balls of melted silver often added to a piece for decoration.

reconstituted turquoise
Small or inferior pieces of turquoise ground and reconstituted with a binder to form a "manmade" turquoise stone. This is not considered a genuine turquoise.

repoussé
A design worked on a metal, such as silver, by pushing out the metal into relief from behind; sometimes the resulting raised design is further decorated, by modeling, chasing, embossing, or texturing on the front side. Repoussé has been employed in Indian jewelry from pre-twentieth-century times.

ropework
A design element of (usually thin) twisted or entwined silver wire, often used to encircle a bezel (see ***filigree***).

rough
A term, when applied to turquoise, that describes its uncut and unpolished state.

Saladoan
A distinctive Puebloan culture of southern Arizona (whose high point was 1350-1450) with definite ties to the prehistoric cultures of northern Mexico. Skilled producers of inlaid and applied mosaic, among other forms of jewelry.

sandcast
A piece of silver jewelry formed by pouring molten silver into a tufa-stone or other soft-stone mold in which the design has been carved on one flat piece of the stone, along with channels and air vents. A second piece is then secured to the carved stone, and the molten silver poured, allowed to cool, removed from the mold, and then filed, sawed, ground, and polished to its finished form. Sandcasts, like wrought or hammered jewelry, are often set with turquoise. Sandcast gets its name from the belief that the silver was poured into molded sand or sedimentary sandstone molds, but volcanic tufa is better able to take the high heat of the molten silver without cracking.

Santo Domingo
A pueblo on the Rio Grande between Albuquerque and Santa Fe, New Mexico, noted for its artisans who fashion hieshi and other stone beads and jewelry. There are now some excellent silversmiths at Santo Domingo, and residents of this pueblo are noted traders and purveyers of all types of Indian jewelry and crafts.

seafoam turquoise
Knobbly or "frothy" nuggets that can be polished, and set or strung, without cutting. The recessed areas may be artificially darkened to heighten the "drama" of this style. This type of turquoise comes from a number of mines, and only recently came into favor.

serpentine
A semiprecious stone native to the Southwest. A streaked dark green with a somewhat oily luster, it takes a good polish and is sometimes used in Indian jewelry (it is too hard to have been worked with the tools of early Indian jewelrymakers).

shadow box
A style of silver jewelry characterized by deep, blackened recesses in which turquoise and other stones are set. The raised portions of silver are usually undecorated and buffed or highly polished.

Shalako
A picturesque kachina with a tall, conelike body and a masked head, sometimes depicted in inlay work; a major dancer in the Zuni Winter Solstice ceremony (shalakos appear in the dances of other pueblos, but less frequently than at Zuni).

shank
The basic band of metal forming the part of a ring that fits around the finger. The shank is then incised or built up with further silver design elements and set with turquoise or other stones. Shank can also refer to the basic band of a bracelet.

silvermark
The mark of the craftsman who made a particular piece of jewelry (see ***hallmark***).

sing, sing tie
A small token (bead, coin, etc.), often of a contrasting color, attached to a

bead or nugget necklace as remembrance of a "sing" or dance in which an Indian has participated. Sing ties (authentic or otherwise) may be highlighted by dealers as "a cherished personalizing touch."

singer style
A form of mosaic inlay using chips of turquoise, coral, or other materials, bonded together with a material such as epoxy and inlaid in silver. It got its name, according to Neumann, from a Navajo family of smiths who originated it. The turquoise or coral may be real, treated, or artificial, and this is a difficult style in which to appraise the materials.

small stone
Term applied to jewelry styles such as needlepoint and clusterwork.

snake eyes
Small rounded cabochon-cut stones approximately 1 mm in diameter.

solder
To join two pieces of metal by fusing between them an alloy of the metal having a lower melting point.

Southwest
That portion of the United States which includes all of Arizona and New Mexico and—depending upon the source—adjoining portions of California, Utah, Colorado, Texas, and the Mexican states of Chihuahua and Sonora.

spiderweb
Thin, radiating lines of matrix found in some turquoise; turquoise containing spiderweb matrix. Delicate spiderweb tracery is especially prized in the turquoise used in Southwest Indian jewelry.

spin casting
See ***centrifugal casting***.

spiny oyster, spondylus shell
A red or white shell found in the Gulf of California, which since prehistoric times has been used with turquoise in Southwest Indian jewelry; in prehistoric times they were obtained over long-established trade routes. Used for beads and inlay. Also called ***thorny oyster***.

spondylus shell
See ***spiny oyster***.

squash
Trade "short form" for squash-blossom necklace.

squash-blossom
An adornment, usually trifoil, of silver petals soldered to hollow beads or shanks. There have over the years evolved many variations of the basic bead, especially as it appears in "squash-blossom necklaces". The design was introduced to the Southwest by the Spanish and Mexicans, who wore small metal "pomegranate bead" decorations on their clothing, etc., from which the Indian "squash-blossom" bead is believed to have derived; Anglo traders gave it the name squash-blossom, which it somewhat resembles. Squash-blossom is also the name given to a heavy silver necklace with hollow beads, squash-blossom beads, and a naja, and often heavily embellished with turquoise or other sets. There has in recent years been a tendency to call any large ornate necklace with a prominent central motif a squash-blossom.

stabilize
To treat turquoise with plastic or other substances to heighten its color and durability and increase its potential to take a polish. Stabilized turquoise is natural turquoise to begin with, but it has been artificially enhanced. The best stabilized stones are difficult to tell from high-grade turquoise, but they are not nearly as valuable and should not be sold as natural turquoise. An experienced, reputable dealer is your best bet against misrepresentation.

sterling
Silver of 92.5 fineness, with 7.5 copper alloy added. It is the most commonly used silver in contemporary Indian jewelry, though it is not marked as sterling when used in Indian jewelry. (Silver in its pure or fine state is too soft for general use in jewelry.)

Sun God, sun shield
Circular rayed sunburstlike design often seen in Zuni inlay, often with a rudimentary "face" in a central circle. A motif dating from prehistoric times in the Southwest.

sweating
Heat process whereby two pieces of silver are joined together. In Indian jewelry the term is applied almost exclusively to a process of Hopi overlay jewelry.

swedging
Method of producing a ridged surface on silver by pressing a sheet of silver against a ridged mold; the underside of a swedged piece is also ridged; an early technique.
symbols
Designs stamped into the silverwork of (or otherwise depicted on) Indian jewelry. While a few of them have traditional meanings for Indians, the vast majority of them do not; in fact, many "Indian symbols" were designed by non-Indians who deal in Indian jewelry. Basically they may have esthetic appeal, but no traditional or esoteric meaning.
synthetic turquoise
Artificial, manmade turquoise. Marketed under a number of trade names (Luroc, Gilson turquoise, Turquite are some examples), it can have the same composition, crystal structure, and other properties as mineral, or naturally formed turquoise. Though the better varieties are not necessarily inexpensive, synthetic turquoise is not considered to have the same value as natural gem-quality turquoise. Some synthetic turquoise is easy to spot, as it lacks the depth, luster, and "Zat" of real turquoise.
tab necklace
Necklace, usually turquoise, of large flattened beads of "corn grain" or more irregular tabular shape. One reason for the existence of tab necklaces is the fact that turquoise usually occurs in thin seams or vein deposits.
template
A precut pattern used to trace designs which are to be incised or cut from a metal such as silver.
thorny oyster
See ***spiny oyster***.
tobacco canteen
Small silver container shaped like an early water canteen used to hold tobacco by early Navajos, and usually carried in silver ornamented leather pouches the men wore by their side.
tortoise shell
The carapace of the desert tortoise has been used since prehistoric times in the Southwest for making rattles and is worn on ceremonial occasions. It has been used by the Indians for inlay work and for beads, along with the imported shell of the sea tortoise from the Gulf Coast. Federal law now prohibits the use of tortoise shell in jewelry since both animals are now endangered species.
trade beads
Beads of various shapes, usually made of glass, supplied by white traders and others to the Indians, from the time of earliest (sixteenth-century) Spanish contacts with them. Trade beads were made in a wide variety of colors; certain Phoenician blue glass beads, because of their resemblance to turquoise, were highly prized by early Navajo and other Southwest Indians. Authenticated early trade bead jewelry is valuable; authentication would require curatorial or other expert identification, and possibly laboratory analysis.
treat
To alter (usually low grade) turquoise to improve its color and hardness. Methods of treating include oiling, dyeing, waxing, plasticizing, applying liquid metals, and anything else the human mind is capable of conceiving. Treated turquoise, however attractive, durable, and useful, is not considered to be as valuable as good gem-quality natural turquoise.
Turquite
See ***synthetic turquoise***.
turquoise
A semiprecious gemstone found in the Southwest United States and other arid or semiarid areas of the world. It is a hydrated basic phosphate of copper and aluminum formed by surface waters percolating through altered rocks, which accounts for its usually being found at shallow depths. It ranges in color from white to green to deep blue, and often contains veins of the original matrix or host rock. It is opaque, has a hardness of from 5 to 6 on the Mohs' scale, and a waxy luster, which can be almost glassy when a hard stone is highly polished. It occurs in thin seams or veins or as nodules and grains. It has a conchoidal fracture and tends to be brittle. It has been used as an object of adornment by Indians of the Southwest since pre-Christian times and is regarded by them as possessing certain religious and magical properties. It is known as the Sky Stone and regarded as a symbol of the heavens, as well as a token of good luck, health and happiness.

variscite
A soft green or variegated gemstone, a hydrated phosphate of aluminum found in Utah in nodular masses. It sometimes resembles turquoise (and is sometimes sold as such).

wrought
Hand-worked, as in hammered, twisted, beaten, as opposed to cast (though even cast pieces are usually wrought to some extent).

Yei
Navajo holy person or god, depiction of such a person in Indian jewelry. The Yei (more properly Yeibichai) dance is a major Navajo ceremonial. Navajos do not officially sanction the representation of Yeis on crafts for sale.

Zat
An indefinable quality of turquoise relating to its seductive beauty and appeal: ". . .a good stone must possess. . .a property called the "Zat," which is something like the water of a diamond or the luster of a pearl. A fine-colored turquoise without the Zat is not worth much. . ." according to Joseph Pogue, from whom this term is usually adopted.

Zuni
An Indian pueblo some 30 miles south of Gallup in northwest New Mexico. A style of jewelry created by members of this tribe which includes mosaic, inlay, clusterwork, petit point, and needlepoint. Traditionally, Zuni style emphasizes the lapidary aspect of the jewelry, with silverwork serving mainly as an inobtrusive mounting for set stones.

INDEX